IMPLEMENTING NEGOTIATED AGREEMENTS

The Real Challenge to Intrastate Peace

KREDDHA

Implementing Negotiated Agreements
The Real Challenge to Intrastate Peace

Edited by

Miek Boltjes

T·M·C·Asser Press
The Hague

Published by T·M·C·ASSER PRESS
P.O. Box 16163, 2500 BD The Hague, The Netherlands
<www.asserpress.nl>

T·M·C·ASSER PRESS' English language books are distributed exclusively by:

Cambridge University Press, The Edinburgh Building, Shaftesbury Road,
Cambridge CB2 2RU, UK,
or
for customers in the USA, Canada and Mexico:
Cambridge University Press, 100 Brook Hill Drive, West Nyack, NY 10994-2133, USA
<www.cambridge.org>

ISBN 13: 978-90-6704-240-6
ISBN 10: 90-6704-240-4

All rights reserved.
© 2007, Kreddha International and T·M·C·ASSER PRESS, The Hague, The Netherlands

Lay-out: Oasis Productions
Cover design: Heijdens Karwei

No part of the material protected by this copyright notice may be reproduced or utilized in any form or by any means, electronic or mechanical, including photocopying, recording, or by any information storage and retrieval system, without written permission from the copyright owner.

PRINTED IN THE NETHERLANDS

Foreword

The importance of reaching sustainable political agreements to end armed conflicts between states and population groups that claim, often legitimately, the right to self-determination, or that demand a degree of autonomy or a share of natural resources, has become increasingly obvious to the international community. Since the end of the cold war many such conflicts have become visible or have flared up, making all of us aware of the many wars that continue to destroy the lives of large numbers of innocent people in all parts of the world.

It is shocking to realise that so many political agreements concluded to end intrastate wars and conflicts are not or not fully implemented, a situation that often leads to renewed tensions and fighting. This excellent book, written by an impressive and eminent group of people who have worked to resolve such conflicts and who have experienced the difficulties of ensuring proper implementation of agreements, could not come at a better time when the United Nations and a number of regional organisations are struggling to understand the needs, pitfalls and complexities of peacebuilding, especially in countries where internal conflicts have raged.

In Timor-Leste, we have struggled to rebuild a country ravaged by violence, and continue to have our share of challenges in this respect. Progress in implementing the Good Friday Agreement in Northern Ireland continues to be difficult, while in Indonesia the difficulties of implementing the agreement reached between the government and the Free Aceh Movement (GAM) are becoming evident as I write this foreword. In the Sudan, some parties to the peace agreements are yet to demonstrate their ability and commitment to fully implement the accords, while the people of Sri Lanka are again witnessing the consequences of a breakdown of agreements with respect to the ceasefire even before reaching a political agreement.

The authors of this book help us understand the difficulties of implementation. They also suggest ways in which implementation can be improved. There clearly is not one solution to the problem of inadequate implementation, but several ways of strengthening the agreements themselves and the mechanisms that help to insure their implementation. The newly established Peacebuilding Commission of the UN and those governments and non-governmental organisations and individuals who are professionally involved in peacebuilding will find the wealth of experience of people like Francesc Vendrell, Niek Biegman, Dennis Haughey and Devasish Roy, and many others who have contributed to this book indispensable to their work. The analysis provided by the editor, herself a mediator in intrastate conflicts, brings clarity and vision to an otherwise difficult field to penetrate.

Dili, Timor-Leste – 28 August 2006
Dr. José RAMOS-HORTA
Nobel Peace Laureate and
Prime Minister of Timor-Leste

Summary of Contents

Foreword by *José Ramos-Horta*	V
Acknowledgments	VIII
Preface	IX
Kreddha and the Centre UNESCO de Catalunya	XI
Table of Contents	XII
List of Abbreviations	XIX

I	The Implementation Challenge in Intrastate Peace Processes: an Analysis – *Miek Boltjes*	1
II	Recurrent Challenges to the Implementation of Intrastate Peace Agreements: the Resistance of State Authorities – *Fernand de Varennes*	49
III	Reflections on Implementation Mechanisms of Selected Autonomy, Self-Rule and Similar Arrangements – *John Packer*	69
IV	The Implementation of the Good Friday Agreement in Northern Ireland – *Denis Haughey*	87
V	The Discordant Accord: Challenges in the Implementation of the Chittagong Hill Tracts Accord of 1997 – *Devasish Roy*	115
VI	Challenges Faced by Tibetans in Reaching a Lasting Agreement with China – *Lodi G. Gyari*	147
VII	From Compromise to Process: the Implementation of the South Tyrolean Autonomy – *Jens Woelk*	157
VIII	Third Party Involvement in the Negotiation and Implementation of Intrastate Peace Agreements – *Geir Sjøberg*	177
IX	The Role of Third Parties in the Negotiation and Implementation of Intrastate Agreements: an Experience-Based Approach to UN Involvement in Intrastate Conflicts – *Francesc Vendrell*	193
X	Implementing the Framework Agreement in Macedonia: the Role of the International Community – *Niek Biegman*	205
XI	Adjudication of Intrastate Disputes: a Review of Possible Mechanisms – *Wendy Miles*	211
XII	The Settlement of Treaty of Waitangi Claims of Maori Groups in Aotearoa/New Zealand – *Morris Te Whiti Love*	229

Appendices	253
About the Authors and Other Contributors	323
Index	335

Acknowledgments

My thanks go first to Onno Seroo of the Centre UNESCO de Catalunya, who was instrumental in bringing the authors and other contributors together to extensively discuss the subject of this book. He created the conditions for a perfect meeting and for the book project to get well off the ground.

I am grateful to Niek Biegman, Lodi Gyari, Denis Haughey, Wendy Miles, John Packer, Devasish Roy, Geir Sjøberg, Fernand de Varennes, Francesc Vendrell, Morris Te Whiti Love and Jens Woelk for their thought-provoking and lucid preparatory papers, which allowed all contributors to immediately get to the core of the issues and to benefit from each others' experiences and insights. They worked tirelessly and patiently to create, refine and update their chapters and to include in them numerous experiences in response to the questions and requests I sent them. I wish to thank Robert Atsir, Mustafa Jemiloglu, Kuupik Kleist, Gert van Maanen, John Momis, Pau Puig I Scotoni and Marian Staszewski for their equally invaluable and insightful contributions which are reflected particularly in the first chapter of this book.

Many thanks go to Susan Kirincich, who helped get this book started, and to my colleagues at Kreddha, Cecilia Peláez Paladino and Inga Frengley, who painstakingly helped me prepare the manuscript and format it so we could make the finish line. For offering a place of refuge when I needed to write in solitude, I thank Alegra and Drew Michael and Maristella Vicini.

I owe my greatest debt of thanks to Michael van Walt. I could not have concluded the work without his continued encouragement, support and generous help.

The Hague, December 2006					Miek BOLTJES

Preface

The purpose of this publication is to better understand why intrastate peace agreements are being badly implemented or not implemented at all, to gain insight into what parties and other actors in intrastate peace processes currently do to prevent non-implementation, and to explore what more can be done to promote effective and satisfactory implementation of intrastate peace agreements in the future.

The chapters address these issues from different perspectives, corresponding to the background and specific experiences of their respective authors. The authors write from personal experience with intrastate peace processes and autonomy arrangements. Some were involved in the negotiation and implementation of agreements, while others played third party roles in these processes. These experiences are complemented by empirical and comparative analysis.

The information presented in the first chapter is based on the authors' experiences as well as those of other high level diplomats, leaders of parties in intrastate conflicts, international lawyers and representatives of international organisations, all of whom were personally involved in intrastate peace processes. Work on this book began with the engagement by Kreddha and the Centre UNESCO de Catalunya of these individuals in their personal capacity in a five day meeting in Sitges, Spain.[1] A wealth of experiences derived from knowledge of and experience with some fifty or more peace processes was shared at that meeting and is reflected here. Some situations are discussed in great detail in the book's chapters, such as those relating to the implementation of the Chittagong Hill Tracts Accord, the Northern Ireland process, Tibetan experiences, the settlement of Treaty of Waitangi claims of Maori groups in New Zealand, and the implementation of agreements in Macedonia and South Tyrol. But experiences gained in many other processes, including those in Sri Lanka, East Timor, Bougainville, the Crimea, Georgia, Catalonia, Nagaland, Moldova, Albania, Russia and the Balkans were equally instrumental in reaching an understanding of the problem and the development of ideas to face and overcome the tremendous challenge of implementation in intrastate peace processes.

It is hoped that the many experiences shared and discussed in this volume will contribute to the creation of a situation in which political negotiations become the preferred way to end intrastate conflicts and to bring about change.

---

[1] Short biographies of the authors and other contributors are found on page 323.

This would be possible if an international climate were created in which state governments as well as non-state parties would be expected and required to fully implement agreements just as they are required to comply with international treaties and other (enforceable and legally binding) commitments. Considering that most of the armed conflicts that rage in the world today are conflicts within states, governments, international organisations, appropriate international courts and tribunals as well as non-governmental entities and organisations should focus some of their energies and resources to contribute in a meaningful way to give intrastate peace processes and agreements a real chance.

Kreddha and the Centre UNESCO de Catalunya

Kreddha

Kreddha – the international peace council for states, peoples and minorities – is a non-profit organisation led by a council of eminent persons from all parts of the world. It is dedicated to the prevention and resolution of violent conflicts between population groups (autonomous regions, (indigenous) peoples and minorities) and governments of existing states. The organisation exists to facilitate and empower state governments and the leadership of population groups worldwide to create the conditions for diverse communities to live in peace in an environment that allows them to actively participate in the society, state and region to which they belong.

Kreddha facilitates dialogue and negotiations between parties and mediates when requested to do so. It monitors and assists in the implementation of peace agreements, and helps consolidate peace where it has been initiated. In support of the peace processes that it facilitates, Kreddha also undertakes thematic and comparative research and organises expert meetings on issues of particular importance.

Centre UNESCO de Catalunya

Centre UNESCO de Catalunya is a Barcelona-based non-governmental organisation founded in 1984 with the objective of creating a stable and permanent presence of Catalan culture in UNESCO and other international organisations. The Centre maintains official relations with UNESCO and has consultative status with the UN Economic and Social Council (ECOSOC). It organises high level international meetings in Catalonia in the fields of human rights and the prevention of conflicts, sustainable development, values education, interreligious and intercultural dialogue, cultural diversity and linguistic pluralism. It offers advisory services in these fields to the different levels of the Catalan public administration and to foreign governments. The Centre has also convened numerous international expert conferences jointly with UNESCO and the UN. Since 1993 the Centre has participated with its own voice (and without vote) in the works of the General Conference of UNESCO. It has also been active since 1998 in contributing to the work of the UN, in particular the Office of the UN High Commissioner for Human Rights and ECOSOC and its subsidiary bodies, in particular the UN Commission on Human Rights (now the Human Rights Council).

Table of Contents

Foreword by *José Ramos-Horta* — V

Summary of Contents — VII

Acknowledgments — VIII

Preface — IX

Kreddha and the Centre UNESCO de Catalunya — XI

List of Abbreviations — XIX

Chapter I
The Implementation Challenge in Intrastate Peace Processes: an Analysis — 1
MIEK BOLTJES

1.	Introduction and Conclusions	1
2.	Concepts Central to the Issue	2
2.1	Intrastate conflicts	2
2.2	Autonomy arrangements	3
2.3	Parties	6
2.3.1	First parties	6
2.3.2	Third parties	7
2.3.3	Fourth parties	7
2.3.4	Second – kindred or godfather – parties	8
3.	Understanding the Implementation Challenge	8
3.1	Walking the walk much more difficult than talking the talk	9
3.2	Shortcomings in the terms of the agreement	12
3.3	The political regime factor	14
4.	Facing the Challenge	16
4.1	Measures employed	17
4.1.1	Designing the peace process with a view to implementing agreements reached	17
4.1.2	Ensuring broad ownership of the process	17
4.1.3	Entrenching the agreement	22
4.1.4	Creating institutions and processes for effective power-sharing	25
4.1.5	Monitoring and verification	27
4.1.6	Implementing in phases	28
4.1.7	Incentives and sanctions	29
4.1.8	Engaging international organisations	30

4.1.9	Agreeing on ways to resolve disputes before they occur	31
4.2	Parties' and other actors' roles	34
4.2.1	First party roles	34
4.2.2	Roles of second – kindred and godfather – parties	34
4.2.3	Third party roles	36
4.2.4	Fourth party roles	40
4.2.5	Roles of 'friends of the peace process'	42
5.	Searching for Additional Ways to Secure Implementation	43
5.1	Broader use of UN mechanisms and agencies	44
5.2	Effective use of regional organisations	45
5.3	Including dispute resolution clauses in peace agreements	46

Chapter II
Recurrent Challenges to the Implementation of Intrastate Peace Agreements: the Resistance of State Authorities — 49
FERNAND DE VARENNES

1.	Introduction	49
2.	Intrastate Conflicts Setting, Root Causes and Characteristics	50
2.1	The setting of intrastate conflicts	52
2.2	Root causes of intrastate conflicts	53
2.3	Immediate events ('sparks') precipitating violence	59
3.	Intrastate Peace Agreements: Addressing the Root Causes of Intrastate Conflicts	61
4.	The Implementation Problem: State Authorities' Resistance to Implementing Intrastate Peace Agreements	63
5.	Concluding Remarks	66

Chapter III
Reflections on Implementation Mechanisms of Selected Autonomy, Self-Rule and Similar Arrangements — 69
JOHN PACKER

1.	Introduction	69
2.	Selected Autonomy Arrangements and Their Implementation Mechanisms	73
2.1	Crimea	73
2.2	Macedonia	76
2.3	Gagauzia	77
2.4	Northern Ireland	79
3.	Some Observations on Autonomy Arrangements and Implementation Mechanisms	80
4.	Concluding Remarks	82

Chapter IV
The Implementation of the Good Friday Agreement in Northern Ireland 87
DENIS HAUGHEY

1.	Origin and Development of the Conflict	87
1.1	British colonialism	87
1.2	The establishment of the Republic of Ireland and the State of Northern Ireland	89
1.3	The 'double minority' problem	90
1.4	Bloody Sunday	91
1.5	Towards agreement; the involvement of the government of the Republic of Ireland	92
2.	The Good Friday Agreement; a Multiparty Inter- and Intrastate Agreement	94
3.	Summary of Events since the Signing of the Good Friday Agreement	96
4.	Implementation of the Good Friday Agreement	98
4.1	Cross-border cooperation mechanisms and agencies	99
4.2	Implementation of provisions requiring decommissioning of arms	101
4.3	Additional implementation mechanisms and bodies created outside the agreement	103
4.4	Periodic review of the Good Friday Agreement	104
5.	Internal and External Influences on the Peace and Implementation Processes	105
5.1	Public opinion and changes in government attitudes in the United Kingdom and Ireland	105
5.2	The effects of EU membership	106
5.3	American public opinion	107
6.	Third Party Involvement	107
6.1	The United States presidential envoy	107
6.2	The European Union's role	108
7.	Obstacles and Spoilers in the Implementation of the Good Friday Agreement	109
7.1	The Unionist community	109
7.2	Paramilitary organisations	110
8.	Postscript	111
9.	Concluding Remarks	112

Chapter V
The Discordant Accord: Challenges in the Implementation of the Chittagong Hill Tracts Accord of 1997 115
DEVASISH ROY

1.	Introduction	115

2.	Historical Background	118
3.	The Chittagong Hill Tracts Accord of 1997	122
3.1	Reception of the 1997 Accord	123
3.2	The implementation of the 1997 Accord under review	125
3.2.1	Non-implementation and violations of written and unwritten provisions of the 1997 Accord	125
3.2.2	Implementation and change of government	129
3.2.3	The absence of constitutional safeguards	130
3.3	Expectations with regards to the implementation of the 1997 Accord and the post-Accord situation	133
4.	Possible Mechanisms to Ensure Implementation	134
5.	The Negotiation Process, the Ceasefire and Other Agreements Leading up to the 1997 Accord	137
6.	Reconstruction and Development in the Implementation Phase	139
7.	The Challenges Ahead	142
7.1	The intra-indigenous violence	142
7.2	Settler-indigenous conflict	143
7.3	Towards implementation of the 1997 Accord	144

Chapter VI
Challenges Faced by Tibetans in Reaching a Lasting Agreement with China 147
LODI G. GYARI

1.	Pragmatic Approach to Negotiations	148
2.	The Violation and Repudiation of the Seventeen Point Agreement	150
3.	Third Parties	151
4.	The Dalai Lama's Approach	152
5.	The Territorial Dimension of the Tibetan Issue	153
6.	Third Party Involvement and the Interest of the International Community	154
7.	The Time Factor	154
8.	The Dalai Lama is the Key to a Solution	155
9.	Hope for the Future	156

Chapter VII
From Compromise to Process: the Implementation of the South Tyrolean Autonomy 157
JENS WOELK

1.	Introduction	157
2.	From Conflict to Compromise	158
3.	Substance and Status of the Compromise	162
4.	The Powers of the Autonomous Province of South Tyrol	164

5.	Mechanisms for Implementing the South Tyrolean Autonomy	166
5.1	Negotiating and drafting legislative decrees in joint commissions	166
5.2	Safeguarding South Tyrol's autonomy; the status of the enactment decrees in the Italian legal system	169
5.3	Established 'equality' in implementation negotiations and institutions	171
5.4	Asymmetrical regionalism	171
6.	The Functioning of the South Tyrolean Autonomy After its Full Implementation; Evaluation and Future Perspectives	172
7.	Concluding Remarks on Austria's Role	174

Chapter VIII
Third Party Involvement in the Negotiation and Implementation of Intrastate Peace Agreements 177
GEIR SJØBERG

1.	Starting Points	177
2.	Different Facilitator Roles	178
2.1	Examples of lead roles	179
2.2	Examples of coalition roles	180
2.3	Examples of supporting roles	180
2.4	Examples of exploratory roles	180
3.	Generating Momentum	180
4.	Asymmetry	184
4.1	Negotiations	184
4.2	Legitimacy	184
4.3	Governance	185
4.4	International blacklisting	186
5.	Human Rights	187
6.	Monitoring Mechanisms	188
7.	Humanitarian Aid and Development Assistance	190
8.	Concluding Remark	191

Chapter IX
The Role of Third Parties in the Negotiation and Implementation of Intrastate Agreements: an Experience-Based Approach to UN Involvement in Intrastate Conflicts 193
FRANCESC VENDRELL

1.	Intrastate Conflicts	193
2.	Conflicting UN Charter Principles Conditioning UN Involvement in Intrastate Conflicts	194
3.	UN Intervention in Inter- or Intrastate Disputes of a Self-Determination Nature	196

4.	Government Acceptance of Third Party Involvement	197
5.	Mediation, Good Offices, Facilitation and Negotiation	199
6.	Carrots, Sticks and Group of Friends	200
7.	Implementation of Autonomy and Self-Determination Arrangements	201
8.	Verification and Arbitration	203

Chapter X
Implementing the Framework Agreement in Macedonia: the Role of the International Community 205
NIEK BIEGMAN

Chapter XI
Adjudication of Intrastate Disputes: a Review of Possible Mechanisms 211
WENDY MILES

1.	Dispute Resolution Agreements	211
2.	International Dispute Resolution Bodies	213
2.1	Use of international courts in intrastate disputes	213
2.1.1	International Court of Justice	214
2.1.2	Regional permanent international courts	215
2.2	Use of arbitration in intrastate disputes	217
2.2.1	UNCITRAL Model Arbitration Rules	218
2.2.2	Ad hoc arbitration	219
2.2.3	International arbitral institutions	219
3.	The Enforceability of Arbitration Agreements and Awards	226
4.	Conclusion	227

Chapter XII
The Settlement of Treaty of Waitangi Claims of Maori Groups in Aotearoa/New Zealand 229
MORRIS TE WHITI LOVE

1.	Origins of the Maori Claims	230
1.1	Events leading up to the Treaty of Waitangi	230
1.2	Alienation of Maori land	231
2.	The Treaty of Waitangi Act and the Establishment of the Waitangi Tribunal	233
3.	Social and Political Context of Tribunal Operations	234
4.	Composition of the Waitangi Tribunal	236
5.	The Parties	237
5.1	Representation of the Crown	237
5.2	Maori representation: customary representation, modern representation, and level of representation	237

6.	The Mandate and Powers of the Waitangi Tribunal	238
7.	Claims, Claims Management and Research	239
8.	The Two-Phase Claims Settlement Process	241
8.1	The Waitangi Tribunal inquiry and reporting process	242
8.1.1	Preparations for the hearing	242
8.1.2	The hearing	242
8.1.3	The Tribunal report with findings and recommendations	244
8.2	The bilateral negotiation process	244
8.2.1	Crown assessment of claims	244
8.2.2	Mandating	244
8.2.3	Deed of mandate	245
8.2.4	The Crown negotiation team	245
8.2.5	Funding	245
8.2.6	Terms of negotiation	245
8.2.7	'Agreement in principle' and 'heads of agreement'	246
8.2.8	Deed of settlement	246
8.2.9	Settlement legislation	247
8.2.10	Statutory acknowledgements and deeds of recognition	247
8.2.11	Protocols	247
9.	Substance of Settlements	247
10.	Implementation of Tribunal Recommendations and Settlements Resulting from Bilateral Negotiations	248
11.	Privy Council	249
12.	Conclusions	250

Appendices	253
About the Authors and Other Contributors	323
Index	335

List of Abbreviations

AAA	American Arbitration Association
ACHPR	African Court of Human and Peoples' Rights
BIH	Bosnia and Herzegovina
BNP	Bangladesh Nationalist Party
CACJ	Central American Court of Justice
CCJ	Caribbean Court of Justice
CEDAW	Convention on the Elimination of Discrimination against Women
CERD	Convention on the Elimination of Racial Discrimination
CHT	Chittagong Hill Tracts (Bangladesh)
CIETAC	China International Economic and Trade Arbitration Commission
CLO	Crown Law Office (New Zealand)
COMESA	Common Market for East and Southern Africa
DUP	Democratic Unionist Party (Northern Ireland)
EAIP	European Alliance with Indigenous People
ECHR	European Court of Human Rights
ECJ	European Court of Justice
ETA	*Euskadi Ta Askatasuna* (Basque Fatherland and Liberty)
EU	European Union
GA	United Nations General Assembly
GATT	General Agreement on Tariffs and Trade
HKIAC	Hong Kong International Arbitration Centre
IACHR	Inter-American Court of Human Rights
ICC	International Chamber of Commerce
ICJ	International Court of Justice
ILO	International Labour Organisation
IMF	International Monetary Fund
IRA	Irish Republican Army
ITLOS	International Tribunal on the Law of the Sea
IWGIA	International Work Group for Indigenous Affairs
JSS	PCJSS (*Parbatya Chattagram Jana Samhati Samiti* (Chittagong Hill Tracts People's Solidarity Organisation)) (Bangladesh)
LCIA	London Court of International Arbitration
LTTE	Liberation Tigers of Tamil Eelam
NATO	North Atlantic Treaty Organisation
NGO	Non-Governmental Organisation

NLA	National Liberation Army (Republic of Macedonia)
NSGT	Non-Self Governing Territories
ODA	Official development assistance
OECD	Organisation for Economic Cooperation and Development
OSCE	Organisation of Security and Cooperation in Europe
PCA	Permanent Court of Arbitration
PRC	People's Republic of China
SAARC	South Asian Association for Regional Cooperation
SDLP	Social Democratic and Labour Party (Northern Ireland)
SIAC	Singapore International Arbitration Centre
SLMM	Sri Lanka Monitoring Mission
TAR	Tibet Autonomous Region
TJAC	Court of Justice of the Andean Community
TUF	Tamil United Front (Sri Lanka)
TULF	Tamil United Liberation Front (Sri Lanka)
UDA	Ulster Defence Association (Northern Ireland)
UN	United Nations
UNCITRAL	United Nations Commission on International Trade Law
UNDP	United Nations Development Program
UNESCO	United Nations Educational, Scientific and Cultural Organisation
UNHCR	Office of the United Nations High Commissioner for Refugees
UNICEF	United Nations Children's Fund
UNITAR	United Nations Institute for Training and Research
UNMIK	United Nations Interim Administration Mission in Kosovo
UNOMB	United Nations Observer Mission on Bougainville
UNOMIG	United Nations Observer Mission in Georgia
UNRISD	United Nations Research Institute for Development
UPDF	United People's Democratic Front (Bangladesh)
UUP	Ulster Unionist Party (Northern Ireland)
UVF	Ulster Volunteer Force (Northern Ireland)
WGIP	Working Group on Indigenous Populations

Chapter I

THE IMPLEMENTATION CHALLENGE IN INTRASTATE PEACE PROCESSES: AN ANALYSIS

Miek Boltjes[*]

1. INTRODUCTION AND CONCLUSIONS

Intrastate peace agreements involving autonomy arrangements are badly implemented, if at all. This is a problem not only for the people on the ground, for whom the implementation may be vital and without which the conflict may flare up again. The problem extends to *all* intrastate peace processes that are inevitably affected by the poor record of implementation worldwide. Comparative research presented in this publication shows that governments often have great difficulty mustering or sustaining the political will to divest themselves of power. This makes it very difficult for population groups that strive for a greater degree of self-government to end armed struggle and enter into political negotiations with them, let alone make substantive concessions. To do that, they must have the confidence that the government they eventually conclude an agreement with has the true intent and the will to share power and responsibilities in accordance with the terms of that agreement.

This chapter starts with the discussion of a few concepts that are central to the issue: intrastate conflicts, autonomy arrangements and parties – first, second, third and fourth parties. It then explores the reasons for non-implementation of intrastate peace agreements, touching upon parties' political will to implement, shortcomings in the terms of agreements and the relevance of the nature of political regimes. It goes on to study a variety of measures employed by parties and other actors to promote implementation, including various forms of entrenchment; institutions and processes for effective power sharing; monitoring and verification; carrots and sticks; and dispute resolution mechanisms. The chapter concludes by looking at additional ways to secure implementation, both in terms of making broader use of existing international organisations and

---

[*] Director of Dialogue Facilitation, Kreddha

M. Boltjes (ed.), *Implementing Negotiated Agreements*
© 2007, Kreddha International and T·M·C·ASSER PRESS, The Hague, The Netherlands

their mechanisms and by developing new means, including recourse to adjudication.

A close look at the cases studied and the experiences shared in this publication reveals that the *implementation* of an intrastate peace agreement may actually be a much greater challenge for the parties than *negotiating* the agreement in the first place. Now it is becoming clear that, however difficult making concessions may be, it is not the greatest obstacle to bringing an intrastate peace process to a good end. The much greater obstacles and the most painful ones for parties to overcome are those that emerge in the implementation phase of such a process. In light of this realisation we develop a new appreciation for the importance of all possible measures that can serve to help parties fulfil their commitments, a large variety of which are discussed in detail throughout this publication. We conclude that it is not about finding *the* solution to cure all problems, nor that one formula fits all situations. Instead, we believe that 'more is better' and that success may lie in applying a variety of measures appropriate for the situation and political regime in question, and not only by the principal parties to the peace process, but by other relevant actors as well.

To be sure, the analysis, opinions and conclusions expressed in this chapter are those of the author only. But the analysis is drawn from the wealth of experience and knowledge of the authors who contributed to this book as well as of the other experts who participated in the Sitges meeting hosted by Kreddha and the Centre UNESCO de Catalunya.[1] They all took the time to delve into the subject in great depth at the meeting and again on their own as they prepared the chapters of this book. This chapter attempts to bring all this together, and to analyse the materials and discussions in the hope that this will stimulate thought and help parties and other practitioners involved in peace processes to develop and apply this knowledge to suit the situations they face.

2. CONCEPTS CENTRAL TO THE ISSUE

2.1 Intrastate conflicts

Most armed conflicts in the world today are intrastate conflicts, that is, conflicts that rage within sovereign states.[2] Vendrell estimates that since the creation of

---

[1] The meeting, entitled 'Expert meeting on ensuring full implementation of intrastate peace agreements involving self-rule arrangements as a contribution to peace consolidation and conflict prevention and the role of third parties therein', was held from 8-14 May 2003.

[2] In this publication the term 'state' is used to describe sovereign states. It is not used to describe component states of a federation (e.g., in the Nigerian, Mexican, Indian or US context).

the United Nations (UN), 90 percent of armed conflicts have tended to be intrastate, whereas only ten percent were truly international or inter-state in nature.[3] Some are new conflicts that have emerged in recent years, but almost all have existed for a long time, and many have deep roots in colonial history or in old conflicts that have remained unaddressed or have been badly addressed in the past.

Many intrastate conflicts pit a government against a particular population group within the boundaries of the state: an ethic or religious minority, a distinct and often indigenous people, or the population of a particular region of the state. Sometimes the dispute involves challenges to the claimed sovereignty of the state over the territory of a population group which does not consider itself to be an integral part of that state or wants to separate from it. But this is usually not the case, at least not initially.

In chapter II, De Varennes identifies some commonalities among the intrastate conflicts he studied in terms of their setting, root causes and characteristics. Most situations involve population groups that constitute a very substantial portion of the inhabitants of defined territories that are historically or traditionally 'theirs'. The conflicts generally centre on issues of linguistic, cultural or religious rights, rights affecting employment, land rights and resource allocation, issues of discrimination and political representation. Mostly, they involve combinations of these issues. De Varennes also finds that many intrastate conflicts involve the erosion or elimination of previously existing autonomy arrangements or the denial of claims to self-determination.[4]

In this publication we use the term intrastate conflict to describe conflicts between population groups (indigenous peoples and other distinct peoples, minorities, and the populations of non-self-governing territories and autonomous regions) on the one hand and governments of sovereign states that exercise jurisdiction over them on the other. The term intrastate conflict as used in this publication does not include disputes between a state and individual citizens or companies of that state, and these kinds of disputes are not the subject of this publication.

2.2 Autonomy arrangements

The focus on autonomy arrangements as a means of addressing intrastate conflicts can be explained, as De Varennes does in chapter II, by 'the direct relationship between the root sources of tension of most conflicts and the type of measures needed to address them.'[5] This is not to say that all intrastate conflicts

---

[3] Vendrell, chapter IX.
[4] De Varennes, chapter II, section 2.
[5] De Varennes, chapter II, section 3.

can be resolved by means of autonomy arrangements, however broadly these are defined. In some cases other solutions, such as the creation (or restoration) of full independence for a population group and territory, or the redrawing of boundaries to better accommodate the interests of parties and other stakeholders, may be more appropriate. Nevertheless, autonomy arrangements– broadly defined as we do below – can provide important ways to accommodate vital interests of the parties in many, if not most, intrastate conflicts.

By autonomy we mean any arrangement that provides for a measure of political, cultural, and economic self-government for a population group within the framework of a state, by means of a division of competencies and executive, legislative and judicial powers between the government of the state and the government of the autonomous entity.

The concept of autonomy is a politically loaded one for many governments as well as self-determination movements. Governments often fear and resist granting autonomy to a people, community or region due to the loss of control they believe it represents. They also tend to fear that granting such autonomy puts the state on the slippery slope to disintegration. Self-determination movements on their part are often apprehensive about autonomy for the exact opposite reason: they see their aspirations for independence thwarted and feel they will be left at the mercy of the very government and state they are struggling against.

In principle, autonomy can be whatever parties agree it should be. There is no one model or definition of autonomy that fits all situations. Autonomy is a practical mechanism for the distribution of power, which allows for a specific group to govern itself to a certain degree in one or more fields. The Organisation of Security and Cooperation in Europe (OSCE) describes the essence of autonomy as a mechanism to ensure 'the effective participation of minorities in public life.'[6] Others describe it in terms of self-government and stress that autonomy arrangements can, in some circumstances, amount to virtual independence for a population group. Indeed, both descriptions are correct, as virtually everything is possible in the context and negotiation process of autonomy. In all cases, however, autonomy arrangements are crafted within the framework of the state and do not disrupt the state's territorial integrity.[7]

Autonomy arrangements are mostly *territorial* but they can also involve *functional* forms of self-governance that are not tied to a specific territory within the state. They can be *symmetric* or *asymmetric* and tailored to the specific needs of the population groups involved. Symmetry and its antonym relate in this con-

---

[6] Packer, chapter III.
[7] See for a discussion Packer, chapter III.

text to the equality or inequality of the component parts of the state and of their political and economic participation in the state. Autonomy arrangements generally involve self-government in cultural, educational, religious and linguistic matters. But autonomous authority can also be more encompassing and include all aspects of the domestic affairs of the autonomous entity, and even some areas of international relations, trade, defence and monetary policy. Packer emphasises that whereas in the past the responsibility for defence and the conduct of foreign affairs, the power to print money and to determine citizenship were considered exclusive prerogatives of independent states, today virtually any division of powers and responsibilities and any institutional arrangements are possible in the context of autonomy.[8] Indeed, the precise content of the autonomy arrangement depends on the terms of the agreement establishing the autonomy agreed to by the parties.

Autonomy arrangements directly address the asymmetry of power which usually exists between the minority or non-dominant population group and the state (and its government), and/or between the minority population group and the majority or dominant population group in the state. Such arrangements provide a means for power sharing which gives the non-dominant/minority population group a degree of control over its affairs and enables it to protect itself against potential abuse and discrimination by the state or the dominant group/majority within that state.

Autonomy can be analysed in terms of the division of powers and responsibilities (competencies) for specific subject-matters (such as education, defence, environment, law and order) between a central and an autonomous government and in terms of the allocation of powers with respect to executive, legislative and judicial spheres of government. Critical to any analysis of autonomy are the specific institutions and processes that give it shape. Packer speaks of a matrix of possible kinds of autonomy arrangements in chapter III, emphasising the range and diversity of possibilities. In most discussions on autonomy the emphasis is on those areas and institutional arrangements that provide for *division of powers*; that is, on the degree of separateness of the autonomous entity. Equally important, however, are the areas of *joint authority*, the common interests of the entities in question and the institutions and processes which allow them to function together.

In this publication the term autonomy arrangement is used in its broadest sense to include all types of special-status arrangements that provide for a degree of self-government for a population group within the framework of the state. In this broad sense, autonomy arrangements are a preferred means to re-

---

[8] Packer, chapter III.

solve intrastate conflicts because they maintain the state's territorial integrity while providing the desired legal and political protection as well as decision-making power to the population group in question.

2.3 Parties

Intrastate conflicts, intrastate peace processes and the implementation of autonomy arrangements feature various actors and stakeholders, a number of them referred to as 'parties'. To distinguish between them, it has become common to refer to mediators and facilitators as third parties, to the principal parties that are in conflict or are negotiating with each other as the first parties, and to other parties that are playing a supporting role in peace processes as fourth parties. Below, we elaborate on the use of these terms, and add a fourth category, that of second – 'kindred' or 'godfather' – parties.

2.3.1 *First parties*

In this publication we use the term 'first parties' or simply 'parties' for the entities that are in conflict with each other. They are the principal owners of the conflict and its solutions and are responsible for the implementation of agreements. Having said that, first parties cannot act in a vacuum, and are dependent upon and must take into account the interests of other stakeholders, both domestic and foreign.

In intrastate conflicts the first parties are usually the government of the state, on the one hand, and the population group and its leadership with which the government is in conflict, on the other. The latter are referred to by many different terms in the literature and in the press; rebels, insurgents, freedom fighters, and guerrillas are some examples. In this chapter we use the term 'self-determination movements'. This term is used in its broadest sense to describe movements with a support base in a population group, with various political claims and objectives that can range anywhere from independence, autonomy or land rights, to cultural rights, economic betterment, control over natural resources and recognition of linguistic rights.

More concretely, the first parties are often made up of (but are not necessarily limited to) the political and military leaders of the government and those of the self-determination movement.

In this publication, the terms 'party' and 'parties' are used to mean first parties, unless expressly stated otherwise.

2.3.2 Third parties

The term 'third parties' is used to refer to governments, international governmental or non-governmental organisations, and other organisations, groups or individuals who promote or facilitate the resolution of a conflict. Third parties can, for example, be invited to mediate, arbitrate or provide good offices to help resolve a conflict, or to monitor the implementation of negotiated commitments. A third party is typically not involved or otherwise a stakeholder in the conflict or its outcome, although it may have or be perceived by others to have a stake in *the resolution* of the conflict. A third party engages itself to advance the *process* of conflict resolution, but ideally does not have an interest in a particular outcome.

An example of a third party discussed in this publication is the Norwegian government in relation to a number of peace processes that it has been involved in facilitating. Its involvement, as discussed in chapter VIII, includes support for negotiations as an official facilitator appointed by the parties; sponsorship and facilitation of secret back channel negotiations; provision of neutral venues for talks; assistance in enhancing the negotiation capacity of a party to bring parity to the negotiation process; monitoring the implementation of negotiated commitments; and engagement of the support of other actors (e.g., governments in the region and elsewhere) for a peace process.

2.3.3 Fourth parties

The term 'fourth parties' is used for governments, international governmental or non-governmental organisations and (although rarely) individuals that play a supporting role in peace processes other than that of the third party. Fourth parties may support a peace process financially and may encourage and support the implementation of peace agreements by providing peace dividends that benefit the people on the ground. Fourth parties can also provide diplomatic and political support to the peace process or to aspects of it, or to the third party in its efforts.

The assistance provided by international and regional organisations in the implementation of the Framework Agreement in Macedonia, discussed by Biegman in chapter X, such as the training of the police, financial assistance, and election process support, are examples of fourth party roles. The role of governments that participate as 'friends of the Secretary-General of the UN' in a specific peace process, discussed later in this chapter and by Vendrell in chapter IX, is an other example of a fourth party role, as are Norway's and other governments' efforts in organising donor conferences in support of peacebuilding and to provide peace dividends.

Fourth parties are often stakeholders. Neighbouring states, multinational investors and international organisations, such as the UN High Commissioner for Refugees (in relation to refugee flows linked to the conflict), can all be stakeholders in conflicts and their resolution and implementation and may choose to play fourth party roles for that reason. The Russian Federation for example plays an important fourth party role in the Georgia-Abkhaz peace process and clearly has a stake in the conflict and its outcome.[9]

2.3.4 Second – kindred or godfather – parties

Yet another type of actor and stakeholder that does not fit into any of the categories described above can play an important role in the implementation of agreements ending intrastate conflicts. In a number of cases, states with a historical, ethnic, strategic or other interest in the situation of the population group and its self-determination movement play a crucial role in peace processes leading to political agreements, the implementation of which may also depend on their continuing interest and engagement. We could call these states 'second parties' to highlight their closeness to the first parties, and think of them as kindred states and godfather states to indicate both the closeness and the nature of their relationship with the first parties. Austria's *schutzmacht* role in pursuing an agreement between the Italian government and the people of South Tyrol, discussed by Woelk in chapter VII, provides a good example of a kindred state role. So does Ireland's engagement in the Northern Ireland peace process, described by Haughey in chapter IV. Portugal's role in the UN facilitated negotiations with Indonesia to bring an end to the conflict in East Timor and its support for the implementation of the agreement that ensued could be considered an example of a godfather role.[10] Not all second parties are stakeholders in a conflict or its solution, although kindred states often are.

3. UNDERSTANDING THE IMPLEMENTATION CHALLENGE

Most intrastate peace agreements, including those involving autonomy arrangements, are not well implemented, a situation that often leads to renewed con-

---

[9] The Russian Federation's role is formally labelled 'facilitator', and that of the OSCE 'participant' (Staszewski, presentation at the Sitges expert meeting). However, it is the UN (through the Secretary-General's Special Envoy) that is the third party facilitator. The Russian Federation is not viewed by either party as the non-partisan third party.

[10] In a formal sense Portugal was a first party, since it was still considered by the UN to be the administrative power of its former colony.

flict. Understanding the root causes of specific conflicts, the reasons for the obstructive behaviour of parties and other factors contributing to non- or bad implementation of peace agreements is crucial in trying to improve their implementation. Below, we identify and discuss a number of recurrent reasons for and factors contributing to non- or bad implementation of intrastate peace agreements.

3.1 Walking the walk much more difficult than talking the talk

Both parties in an intrastate conflict may, for a variety of reasons, obstruct or discourage the full implementation of peace agreements.

De Varennes' empirical analysis of some thirty intrastate conflicts and peace agreements presented in chapter II suggests that implementation is most often jeopardised by the state authorities' failure to carry out the terms of the peace agreement. The governments of states are often unable or unwilling, for a variety of reasons, to properly implement intrastate peace agreements, especially if they involve autonomy arrangements. Government authorities, as well as individual civil servants that make up those authorities, are often unwilling to divest themselves of any measure of political power.[11] Political leaders, moreover, are afraid to be considered weak for making concessions, especially if these concessions involve self-government for the movement that their government has been at war with. This could be branded by the government's own political supporters, by the opposition or both as capitulation, rewarding unlawful violence, giving in to 'criminals' or 'terrorists', incompetence in solving an insurgency or protecting the country's sovereignty and territorial integrity or, even worse, as a 'betrayal of the nation'.[12] Popular perceptions, whether correct or not, can be vital especially to those who come to power or maintain it through elections.

De Varennes points out that '[a]t the end of the day, the fundamental compromises involved in most peace agreements rely on the willingness of state authorities to divest themselves of some of their political authority.'[13] This requires political will on the part of the government, the ruling parties, opposition parties and individual politicians, which is often susceptible to the pressures of electoral politics and bureaucratic entrenchment. The self-determination movement often feels hostage to these factors because of its inability to influence them effectively. Thus, all too often, the implementation of intrastate peace

---

[11] Roy also points to the difficulty but necessity of obtaining bureaucratic support for the implementation of agreements. See chapter V, section 5.
[12] De Varennes, chapter II.
[13] De Varennes, chapter II, section 4.

agreements becomes almost entirely dependent on the willingness or ability of governments to fulfil their promises.

Changes of government or of regime can disrupt peace processes and the implementation of peace agreements. Even the political manoeuvring leading up to elections can affect these processes negatively. In the worst case, the continuation or resumption of armed conflict may be seen as being beneficial to the political interests of one or more parties vying for power. The lesson from Bangladesh and the 1997 Chittagong Hill Tracts (CHT) Peace Accord, as Roy points out in chapter V, is that implementation of the agreement can run into severe difficulties when governments change over, especially if the party that was not involved in the negotiation of a peace agreement and opposes its terms comes into power.

In some cases, the government party may never have had the will to implement the agreement. It may have decided to enter into an agreement to gain important concessions from the self-determination movement (for example, surrender of arms) without ever seriously intending to implement its side of the bargain. Roy acknowledges that it is possible that the Bangladesh government which negotiated the peace agreement with the Jana Samhati Samiti (JSS) may itself never have intended to implement all the commitments it made. It may have decided 'to promise the earth to induce the guerrillas to lay their arms down'[14] and there was little the JSS could do to press the government to live up to its side of the deal once the movement had laid down its arms. Regardless of the true motivation of government leaders in this case, it is not uncommon for deceptive strategies to be advocated or implemented to end 'insurgencies.' Tibetans also question whether the Chinese government ever really intended to implement the Seventeen Point Agreement discussed in chapter VI, or whether it was just part of a strategy by that government to acquire control over the territory, after which it could discard much of the agreement.

Self-determination movements are also liable to obstruct the implementation of peace agreements and often face internal political problems similar to those faced by the government side. Within the movements and among possible competing factions, leaders may fear being perceived as selling out the cause by settling for autonomy instead of full independence or otherwise settling for less than they claimed they stood for. Leaders who compete for recognition or power may take the opportunity to increase their influence by taking a hard line against concluding or implementing an agreement involving autonomy. In the Chittagong Hill Tracts, to mention one example discussed in this publication, the United People's Democratic Front, which competed for leadership with the

---

[14] Roy, chapter V.

JSS, strongly opposed the peace agreement and violent confrontation ensued between these two indigenous movements. This situation has reinforced any misgivings that the government may have had about implementing the agreement and strengthened the position of those opposed to it on the government side.

Among all parties to a conflict there may be vested interests in its continuation. In some cases individuals within the armed forces or paramilitary groups have developed an economic interest in the conflict, such as arms trade, drug trafficking, mineral extraction or logging: activities that have funded their organisations (and enriched them personally) and that cannot be protected without the capacity to use force.

In many cases the perception, at least in political circles, of the armed forces' importance wanes when the latter are not immersed in a war to 'protect the nation' and its values, and their budget may also be affected when there is no longer an armed conflict. Self-determination movements may want to maintain the capacity to defend themselves against dissident groups that may well use force against them as well as to maintain the political leverage being armed provides. De Varennes has also pointed to the entanglement of the identity of some minorities with armed struggle and the perceived nobility of armed resistance as an obstacle to proper implementation.

In most cases there is a deep-rooted feeling of distrust between the two sides, which seriously hampers proper implementation.[15] This issue of trust is a recurrent one in this analysis and publication, and is central to the proper implementation of peace agreements. Trust is not built at the time of implementation however: this must start during the negotiation process. Sjøberg emphasises in chapter VIII that in terms of the building of trust the negotiation and implementation of intrastate peace agreements are intrinsically linked. Moreover, bad or incomplete implementation of peace agreements often leads to renewed tensions and armed conflict. Thus, for example, the Papua New Guinea government's failure to fully implement the 1976 Bougainville Agreement providing for the decentralisation of power to the province was an important cause of the renewed outbreak of conflict there in 1989, according to the Governor of Bougainville, John Momis.[16] The mistrust created by bad implementation made a second attempt at negotiating a peace agreement all the more difficult.

---

[15] De Varennes, chapter II, section 4.

[16] Momis, presentation at the Sitges expert meeting. The Papua New Guinea government showed great reluctance to empower the provincial governments in accordance with the expectations following the decentralisation of the country. This was especially true in Bougainville, where the provincial government wanted more authority to deal with grievances related to the copper mining activities on the island.

To sum up, lack of (political) will is one of the major causes of non- or bad implementation of intrastate agreements. The obstacles this creates, together with the other factors discussed below, are indeed formidable. Rarely is it realised that the implementation of an intrastate peace agreement, once concluded, is generally a much greater challenge than negotiating the agreement in the first place. The need for parties to make concessions is often seen as the greatest obstacle to achieving an end to a conflict. It is felt that once an agreement is reached the conflict is resolved. Now it is becoming clear that for parties to make concessions verbally or in writing is a relatively minor obstacle in bringing a process to a good end. The much greater obstacles and the most painful and difficult ones for the parties to overcome are those that emerge in the implementation phase of such processes. It is for this reason that so many peace processes collapse and fail *after* agreements have been signed by the conflicting parties. The conclusion of peace agreements does not necessarily end violent confrontation. It is only once an agreement has been satisfactorily implemented that one can evaluate the success of the process and establish whether it has ended the conflict.

3.2 Shortcomings in the terms of the agreement

Besides lack of (political) will, many other factors contribute to the lack of implementation of intrastate peace agreements. For example, if an agreement is arrived at under so much pressure that either or both of the parties are seriously dissatisfied with it; if it is badly drafted, rushed or (intentionally) incomplete; if, when it involves an autonomy arrangement, it is not entrenched or insufficiently so; or if its implementation is not verified or monitored, then the agreement is less likely to be well implemented.

Vendrell points out that a bad agreement is worse than no agreement and is unlikely to be implemented satisfactorily. An agreement is bad if it is considered deeply unsatisfactory by either or both parties. If, for example, one party experiences the agreement as perpetuating or rewarding and legitimising an unjust situation, that party will resist its implementation.

Similarly, an agreement forced on one or both of the parties is unlikely to be implemented adequately, because the party on whom it was forced will resist it. Even if the political leaders of the coerced party can agree to its terms, the population may oppose it. Such 'bad' agreements may serve to end violent conflict for some time while the aggrieved party is not strong enough to change the situation. But sooner or later the conflict will flare up again, possibly more brutal and more difficult to resolve for the added bitterness caused by the new sense of injustice and injury brought about by the agreement.

The Seventeen Point Agreement imposed on Tibetans in 1951 and discussed by Gyari in chapter VI is a good illustration of this, since it was flawed from the start. It did not come about consensually as the result of genuine negotiations between two parties on an equal footing, but was imposed by the Chinese government with the use and threat of overwhelming force. Besides imposing China's sovereignty on the Tibetans in exchange for promises of autonomy, a major defect in the terms of the agreement was that even this autonomy was only made applicable to less than half of the territory and population of Tibet, leaving the greater part of the country outside its scope. Gyari reveals that this was one of the important reasons why the agreement never worked and inevitably led to armed revolt in 1956 and the years that followed.

It should be noted that agreements are not always imposed by one of the parties on the other: they may be imposed by an outside power, and may even be considered wrong by both first parties. Unless the parties themselves are in control of their destiny, it is very difficult to obtain a peace agreement and political agreement that will be implemented and sustained. Settlements imposed by outside parties may be useful in the short-term, for example to end armed clashes, but are unlikely to provide long-term solutions to tensions, unless the first parties determine of their own accord that the solutions imposed are in their best interest.

Implementation can also be thwarted by deficiencies in the peace agreement itself. Where an agreement is vague or ambiguous on important points, even when this is intentional,[17] it can lead to renewed disputes. Leaving important issues outside the agreement can also be cause for continued tensions.

A common problem is caused by the failure of parties to include specific provisions for implementation mechanisms and institutions in the agreement. These can include monitoring bodies and procedures but also the institutions and the institutional relations that are necessary for the parties to exercise the responsibilities and powers provided for in the agreement, as well as the mechanisms to ensure the needed cooperation and coordination in the exercise of those responsibilities and powers. The success of political agreements involving autonomy arrangements is often dependent on the institutional arrangements provided for. These issues, as well as the need for entrenchment of agreements involving autonomy arrangements, will be discussed in more detail below.

The failure to entrench the CHT peace agreement and the lack of accepted third party monitoring of its implementation undoubtedly greatly contributed to the failure to implement it properly. The CHT peace agreement is not protected

---

[17] Haughey points to the problems that resulted from the intentional omission of a clarification of the relationship between Sinn Fein and the IRA in the Good Friday Agreement. See Haughey, chapter IV.

by any constitutional safeguards, so that any enacting legislation can be reversed by a simple majority in the Bangladesh parliament and can even be challenged in the High Court as unconstitutional. This creates ongoing insecurity and mistrust on the part of the Jumma people of the CHT concerning the commitment of the government to implement the autonomy and restore the land rights they were promised. As for the completely unentrenched oral commitment the government is said to have made with respect to the withdrawal of Bengali settlers, who were transferred to the CHT as part of the counter insurgency strategy, the Bangladesh government and the country's main political parties have made clear that they have no intention of carrying out this contentious promise.

Rushed negotiation processes also invariably lead to flawed agreements and consequently problematic implementation. Roy believes that the fact that the parties were in some sense 'racing against time', perhaps out of fear that the process would be derailed by spoilers, contributed to the lack of proper implementation mechanisms and time frames in the CHT Peace Accord. Clear timelines for the implementation of each phase and its subsequent verification could have helped to hold the Bangladesh government to its commitments.[18]

In the case of the Northern Ireland Good Friday Agreement, no independent mechanism or agency has been charged with *overall* monitoring of the agreement's implementation, although for certain aspects of the agreement such mechanisms have been created. In his discussion of this deficiency, Haughey notes in chapter IV that 'implementation of the Good Friday Agreement has been a serious bone of contention from the very beginning.' There has been 'constant bickering and allegations that this or that party to the Agreement has not fulfilled this or that aspect of their obligations.'[19]

Finally, lack of endorsement of peace agreements by important stakeholders (within the country and outside) can also affect their proper implementation. This is certainly the case if such stakeholders view the implementation of an agreement as harmful to their interests.

3.3 The political regime factor

In analysing and overcoming obstacles to implementation of intrastate peace agreements the type of government system and regime in place in the state concerned may be important. Some experts believe that democratic systems are more conducive to autonomies than authoritarian regimes.[20] It is not clear how-

---

[18] Roy, Chapter V, conclusion to section 6.
[19] Haughey, chapter IV.
[20] Packer, chapter III, section 4.

ever that intrastate peace agreements are more readily implemented by democratic than by non-democratic governments; possibly a topic for useful further research.

The notion of self-government for communities within a state corresponds more to the concept of democratic participatory governance than dictatorial governance. As we have shown above, an important way to ensure implementation of intrastate agreements involving autonomy arrangements is by entrenching the agreement or arrangement constitutionally. Respect for the constitution is essential if constitutional entrenchment is to be effective and this may be more likely to exist in democratic countries. Similarly, entrenchment in special or ordinary laws (such as the Greenland Home Rule Act for example) is only valuable in states where the rule of law is deeply rooted, where there is widespread respect for the rights of minority populations and where solemn agreements entered into by the government are respected.

Democratic systems may more readily allow for transparent mechanisms to be put in place to address problems relating to implementation. On the other hand, pressures of democratic power politics may encourage governments to drag their feet when it comes to implementing peace agreements that are unpopular with a section of the electorate. Taking a populist stand against aspects of an agreement that can be portrayed as hurting the interests of a section of the population or the state as a whole can be a useful tool for politicians to gain votes. This is precisely what has happened in Bangladesh with respect to the CHT peace agreement.

It may be worth investigating whether different types of democratic systems (for example, adversarial two-party systems or consensual multi-party systems) are more or less conducive to government implementation of peace agreements involving autonomy arrangements. It may also be that certain non-democratic systems are better suited to implementing autonomy than others.

Looking at one-party states we see that an important degree of autonomy was implemented by Tanzania in Zanzibar while the country was ruled by a single party; in communist Yugoslavia, implementing local autonomy in a federal context was less problematic than it has been in the post-communist states of former Yugoslavia; and – as Packer points out – a progressive autonomy arrangement was implemented for the Kurds of Iraq in the 1970s by the Baathist regime, although it was eventually withdrawn unilaterally.[21]

In conclusion, while the existence or development of democratic values and institutions are helpful in creating positive conditions for the implementation of agreements involving autonomy arrangements, and while respect for the con-

---

[21] Packer, comments at the Sitges expert meeting.

stitution and rule of law is an important factor, the existence of a democratic system alone is no guarantee for proper implementation by the government, nor by other parties. In some cases, the competition for votes and the often less than constructive role of opposition parties in democratic systems, especially in those where the winner takes all, can seriously jeopardise peace processes and the implementation of agreements.

4. FACING THE CHALLENGE

The conclusion of a *good* agreement is key to its satisfactory implementation. Although some experts feel that in some cases even a flawed agreement can be a useful starting point for a process that could eventually lead to a better agreement,[22] the golden rule seems to be that no agreement is better than a bad agreement. The chances that a bad agreement will be implemented well are slim. A good agreement is one that addresses the root causes of the conflict as well as the interests of the parties and other major stakeholders in line with the new realities on the ground. It provides the best chance that the parties will muster the political will to implement the agreement fully and to overcome the many obstacles to good implementation, some of which have been identified in section three of this chapter.

Having said that, much can go wrong in the implementation of a good agreement and many measures can be taken to help ensure that such agreements, as well as flawed ones, have the best chance of being adequately, if not fully, implemented. In light of the realisation that implementation of commitments is much more difficult for parties to do than making the concessions necessary to conclude an agreement, we develop a new appreciation for the importance of considering and employing all possible measures and activities that can serve to help the parties fulfil their commitments. Some of these will be discussed below. This discussion is by no means exhaustive and is intended only to indicate the range and variety of measures and mechanisms that can be considered when intrastate peace agreements are being negotiated and drafted. Many of these measures and mechanisms are presented in their context and addressed in more detail in the following chapters. Here we present an overview rather than an indepth analysis of them and hope that the way in which the various possible measures and mechanisms are grouped and approached – first by presenting the different *kinds* of measures and mechanisms and then by discussing the role of the various *actors* (i.e., the first, second, third and fourth parties) in the imple-

---

[22] Roy, comments at the Sitges expert meeting. See also Roy, chapter V, section 5.

mentation process – will stimulate thought and help practitioners to develop and apply those that are appropriate to the situations they face.

4.1 Measures employed

4.1.1 *Designing the peace process with a view to implementing agreements reached*

What happens during the negotiations largely determines the outcome of that process as well as the ability and willingness of parties to implement any agreement reached. The negotiation of an agreement, its conclusion and its implementation are all phases of one ongoing process and should not be seen as separate processes. Negotiations towards an agreement must be conducted with a view to the issues that might arise during implementation and the agreement itself should therefore include a plan for dealing with those issues and with any setbacks they might cause. If this is not done, to quote Sjøberg,[23] 'the negotiation is like dry swimming'.

It is also essential to deal satisfactorily with implementation issues early in the negotiations, as this may increase the level of trust that parties have in the negotiation process and their ability and willingness to make concessions as part of the package they are negotiating. If parties (especially non-state parties) do not have confidence that commitments made by the other side will be seriously implemented, they are not inclined to make concessions or even agree to phased implementation of measures. They will seek full vindication of their demands in such a way that upon signing of an agreement their dependence on the other side will be so minimised that the fulfilment of the agreement will not depend on implementation by the other side. Clearly, any agreement involving an autonomy arrangement requires ongoing relations of interdependence, cooperation and adjustment between the state and the non-state party. This of necessity requires a long, if not perpetual process of implementation of political agreements. Thus, for such agreements to be negotiated, it is essential that parties trust that the other side will honour its commitments in word and in spirit.

4.1.2 *Ensuring broad ownership of the process*

Participation of a broad section of the population in a peace process, for example through the involvement of civil society leaders and organisations, in such a way that the population feels a sense of ownership of the agreement that

---

[23] Sjøberg, comments at the Sitges expert meeting.

is concluded, can contribute greatly to the full implementation of that agreement.

Broad participation should be ensured both with respect to the negotiation and the implementation of agreements and should include (potential) spoilers. The sense of ownership will cause the population and its civil society organisations to put pressure on all parties to the agreement to fulfil their commitments and to prevent a recurrence of violent conflict. Sjøberg affirms in chapter VIII that all important interest groups should be represented in a negotiating process and that 'if negotiations are initiated without the participation of all key parties, it is important to have a strategy that includes the various groups and interests along the way.'[24] He goes on to discuss the kinds of groups that need to be involved in one way or another. These include interest groups, civil society broadly defined, women and local intermediaries.

It may seem obvious, although it is not always adequately recognised and addressed, that unless the leaders of both parties, at the highest political levels, are intimately involved in the negotiation process and feel ownership of the process as well as of the agreement that ensues, chances of an adequate implementation of the agreement are slim. Vendrell emphasises that such leaders should include the real (political and military) decision makers who can deliver, while Roy notes that the support of bureaucrats may also prove to be crucial.[25]

One example of the creation of broad ownership of a peace process is the way the Bougainvillians negotiated their peace agreement with Papua New Guinea. According to Momis, 'the Bougainville Peace Agreement was negotiated in a typically Melanesian way, reaching important decisions through an inclusive, consultative and consensual method.'[26] The process was costly and lengthy as a result, but it ensured that the people felt that they participated in determining the outcome of the process and in taking responsibility for their own destiny. The success of this process can be attributed to several factors, but most important among them is the way in which the negotiation process was conducted in accordance with Melanesian culture and practice. People were consulted at every level in Bougainville by their leaders. Decisions were taken by consensus, following lengthy deliberations, starting at the village level. Negotiation teams that took part in the talks with the Papua New Guinea government were very large and very representative. The leaders that took part in these talks could explain to their own people the process, the problems encountered and the positions taken from personal experience.

---

[24] Sjøberg, chapter VIII.
[25] Vendrell, chapter VIII and Roy, chapter V, section 5.
[26] Momis, presentation at the Sitges expert meeting. John Momis was governor of Bougainville at the time of the negotiations.

The sense of ownership and responsibility for the agreement concluded between the Bougainville leaders and the government of Papua New Guinea has been an important factor in its successful implementation so far. Atsir points out that the people of Bougainville did not feel that the peace agreement was forced upon them by outside parties. The predominant feeling is that 'peace was created by the Bougainvillians and therefore they own this peace'.[27] In 2002 and 2003 Bougainvillians successfully conducted a highly participatory process of constitution-making resulting in the adoption of the autonomous province's own constitution in 2004. Elections were held in mid 2005 for the Bougainville House of Representatives and for the presidency of the autonomous province. The decommissioning of weapons of the Bougainville Revolutionary Army occurred in stages and was verified by the UN, also in accordance with the terms of the agreement.[28]

It is important to actively involve women in the process. Experience shows that there are few women who participate in the negotiations themselves. As members of the negotiation team, individual women contribute their understanding, insights, capacities and skills which may be different from those of men. Issues of personal pride, ambition and power, all of which can complicate the achievement of peace and of political agreement, tend to be less prevalent among women in these situations. Women are often driven by the priority they place on the needs of the families on the ground and of non-combatants, including children and others they must care for, and consequently may provide a different perspective than that of the male leaders of armed movements.

As part of the broader population and the civil society organisations that represent them, the impact of women as a group is often crucial. Although the role and influence of women varies in different societies, their impact as a group on peace processes is always felt and can be pivotal in some cases. Sjøberg notes that '[w]ithout women's participation, there is less likelihood that a peace agreement will take adequate account of women's interests and needs. If a peace agreement is deficient in this respect, it will be more difficult to ensure that it has the broad support of civil society in the implementation phase, and the chances of the agreement breaking down will be greater.'[29]

In Bougainville, which is largely a matriarchal society, the women played a crucial role in the peace process. It was they who initiated the peace process by organising the people on the islands and calling upon Bougainvillians to resolve their own internal differences. They drew support from clan chiefs, politi-

---

[27] Atsir, presentation at the Sitges expert meeting.
[28] The UN declared stage III of the Weapons Disposal Process complete in May 2005.
[29] Sjøberg, chapter VIII.

cal leaders and church leaders, all of whom created the conditions necessary for a peace process to take root.[30]

- Ensuring parity between negotiating teams

Autonomy arrangements can uniquely address the asymmetry of power between various population groups within a state. Before such a situation is created, however, the issue of asymmetry of the parties engaged in a conflict and the effect thereof on the negotiations to end it must be addressed.

Generally state and non-state parties in conflict are unequal in terms of military, economic and international political power and in terms of the capacity to conduct political negotiations. They also often have unequal access to financial, legal and other expert assistance and to logistical support. For negotiation processes to be successful in terms of bringing parties to a mutually beneficial and sustainable solution, it is important to create parity between the negotiating teams of the two sides, regardless of the differences in the power of the parties outside the negotiating process. Thus a situation needs to be created where neither side dominates. Woelk points out in chapter VII that in negotiations between South Tyrol's autonomous government and the Italian government, the legal fiction of equal standing of both delegations is maintained 'favouring the joint search for compromise and agreement and excluding unilateral imposition of a solution.'[31] This he compares to the fiction of equal sovereignty of states in negotiations at the international diplomatic level, where the major differences of power, size, and so forth of states are set aside in favour of a formal equality of status.

Parity can be approached when both sides are equally well equipped to undertake the negotiations. This may be achieved by ensuring that each party is financially independent of the other in its ability to cover all of the expenses involved in the preparation and conduct of negotiations, including the consultations with civil society and others; each party has the capacity to analyse issues and proposals under consideration and to develop its own proposals; each party has access to professional high quality advisory services, including legal, technical, and political advisors when necessary; each party's team has well developed negotiation and conflict resolution skills; and each party is exposed to other situations, in the international arena, that can help to broaden insights and learn from the experience of others.

Population groups are often not well equipped to conduct negotiations. The effect can be that their negotiation teams feel uncomfortable and vulnerable and

---

[30] Atsir, presentation at the Sitges expert meeting.
[31] Woelk, chapter VII, section 5.

are excessively suspicious and cautious in their dealings with the other side. The 'weaker' side may be inclined to make decisions out of fear rather than from a position of confidence and full understanding. Fear of making decisions or indecisiveness can drag a process on and jeopardise it unnecessarily. A process will be most smooth and productive where both parties are well informed and confident.

In many cases the lack of (legal) expertise and support in the negotiation process, especially on the side of the non-state entity, can result in flawed agreements that will cause tensions in the implementation phase. The contrast between the Bougainville and the Chittagong Hill Tracts negotiations is telling. The Bougainville side had a team of international legal advisors who played a major role in drafting the peace agreement in accordance with the wishes of the Bougainville leaders, while the CHT negotiation team had no such support.

Lack of confidence does not only arise from military weakness or lack of capacity. Gyari remarks in chapter VI that the most significant change in China's attitude in talks with Tibetans since the 1980s is the self-confidence that Chinese leaders have developed in the past twenty years. Today, for the first time, the Chinese side is willing and appears able to listen to what the Tibetans have to say. Productive negotiations, he experienced, are only possible when parties are self-confident. Negotiations based on fear will not lead to sustainable agreements. If both parties feel that they are able to negotiate an agreement that is in their and their constituents' best interest, they can have confidence and trust in the process. Only then can an agreement emerge in the implementation of which both parties have a vested interest.

In intrastate peace processes where third parties have a facilitating role, they have an important and difficult role in ensuring parity between the parties with respect to the negotiations. Vendrell and Sjøberg recommend that third parties do so by strengthening the weaker party in terms of its ability to take part on an equal basis in negotiations, thus helping to reduce the asymmetry in the negotiation process.[32] Empowering the weaker party by means of skills training (including legal training and support) is an essential role of the third party. Third parties can also (help to) design the negotiation process in such a way as to ensure that the parties participate on an equal footing. This is not a partisan intervention nor is it a substantive one. It has nothing to do with the content of the conflict or the merits of the positions and substantive arguments of the parties. Instead, it is a way to ensure balance in the *process* and to prevent imposition of solutions by one party on the other, which only leads to more frustrations, tensions, unrest and conflict, because the population in question will not genu-

---

[32] Sjøberg, chapter VIII.

inely accept terms that have been imposed against its will. To accomplish this without losing the trust of the stronger of the parties, third party facilitators must act transparently and explain in all honesty what they are doing and how this will contribute to the peace process and benefit both parties.

4.1.3 Entrenching the agreement

A crucial measure to secure implementation of an agreement involving autonomy arrangements and to ensure that once the agreement is concluded it is honoured and cannot or not easily be changed unilaterally, is the entrenchment of the agreement, for example in the constitution or in special legislation. The stronger the entrenchment, the more confidence it will create among the parties that the agreement will hold. Such entrenchment can be negotiated and included in the agreement concluded between the parties.

Autonomy arrangements and other political aspects of peace agreements can be entrenched by incorporating the arrangements or their principal features in the constitution of the state in question. This is usually done by means of one or more constitutional amendments. Entrenchment in the constitution creates confidence because constitutions are the highest law of the land and generally cannot be changed easily; usually a qualified majority of the parliament or other legislative body is required. One can envision a similar entrenchment in a constitutional or special basic law of the autonomous entity.

A stronger form of entrenchment is referred to as *double* entrenchment. An autonomy arrangement is doubly entrenched if neither party can change it without the agreement and active cooperation of the other party. This is usually done by including a provision in the constitution, and possibly in the special law of the autonomous entity, that the arrangement may only be modified by one party with the consent of the other, usually expressed by means of a legislative act (sometimes requiring a qualified majority) or constitutional amendment by that other party.

A good example of double entrenchment of an agreement is contained in the Bougainville Peace Agreement of 30 August 2001 which provides for broad autonomy for Bougainville and for the holding of a referendum on the definitive status of Bougainville in ten to fifteen years after the establishment of the autonomous government. The principal elements of the Bougainville Peace Agreement are entrenched in the Papua New Guinea constitution and cannot be changed by the national government without the concurrence of the autonomous Bougainville government.[33] Thus, Article 326 of the agreement states:

---

[33] Momis, presentation at the Sitges expert meeting.

The constitutional arrangements implementing this agreement may be amended only in accordance with both requirements (a) and (b) below:
(a) After approval by the National Parliament in accordance with the amendment provisions contained in the National Constitution; and
(b) (i) In the case of the referendum provisions, after a vote in which a two-thirds absolute majority of the Bougainville legislature vote in support; or
   (ii) In case of the autonomy provisions, after a vote in which a simple majority of members of the Bougainville legislature vote in support.[34]

Importantly, the agreement also subjects 'constitutional provisions concerning the above entrenchment arrangements ... to the above procedures and requirements.'[35]

The provisions of the South Tyrolean autonomy (referred to in chapter VII as the Second Autonomy Statute) have a specially protected status in the Italian legal system because they were adopted as a constitutional law by the Italian parliament. Viewed in its context, the constitutional rank is a form of entrenchment even though the South Tyrolean autonomy is not anchored in the constitution itself. A constitutional law passed in 2001 further strengthened the guarantees in favour of the autonomous province by limiting the power of unilateral interference of the Italian state. This new provision comes close to creating a double entrenchment. The enactment decrees comprising the South Tyrol autonomy statute cannot be changed unilaterally by the state due to the nature of the process by which they were and are negotiated and the constitutional umbrella which the autonomy statute provides. The Italian parliament also cannot amend, overrule or abolish the enactment decrees by the passage of subsequent laws.[36]

In countries where the constitution can be easily modified (for example in the Russian Federation or the People's Republic of China), single entrenchment in the constitution may not provide enough security for the non-state party. Double entrenchment may be essential in these cases. Even in those countries where constitutions are not easily amended, however, it is conceivable that in case of serious disputes between the central government and an autonomous region sufficient unity in the national or federal legislature can be mustered to

---

[34] Bougainville Peace Agreement, Arawa, 30 August 2001. The agreement also contains a requirement for consultation about any proposed amendments in Article 328: 'The National Government and the autonomous Bougainville Government will inform each other of any proposed amendments; consult over them through the agreed consultation procedures or the agreed five-yearly reviews before they are formally moved (or, in the case of Private Members' Bills put to the vote for the first time); and resolve any differences through the agreed dispute resolution procedures.'
[35] Bougainville Peace Agreement, Article 329.
[36] Woelk, chapter VII, sections 3 and 4.

fulfil the requirements for passing a constitutional amendment to change aspects of the agreed autonomy, especially if sentiments of nationalism are evoked. Thus, even in these systems double entrenchment provides much more security to the autonomous entity and more stability in the country as a whole.

The Greenland Home Rule Act that forms the basis for Greenland's autonomy is not entrenched in the Danish constitution. Yet, according to Kleist, this has not impeded the ongoing process of implementation and, indeed, expansion of the autonomy of Greenland.[37] Thus, depending on the country in question and the extent to which the parties are convinced that it is in their mutual best interest to fully implement the agreement, entrenchment in a special law or even an ordinary law or laws may provide a sufficient level of confidence if parties are confident that those laws will be respected. Indeed, an agreement that satisfies the interests of both parties is the best security for implementation.

Although emphasis is put mainly on the need to entrench the gains acquired in the peace agreement by the non-state entity, attention should also be paid to entrenching the commitments and concessions made by the self-determination movement and future autonomous entity. These can also be entrenched in the country's constitution (for example, the competencies to be exercised jointly and the competencies to be exercised exclusively by the central government, as well as the institutions to be created for the exercise of joint responsibilities). In addition, the agreement or aspects of it can be entrenched or doubly entrenched in a constitutional or quasi-constitutional law adopted by the autonomous entity, as has been done in Bougainville.[38] This may satisfy the needs of the government of the state to ensure that the autonomous entity cannot make changes to the agreement unilaterally, while at the same time providing the autonomous entity with a nucleus for its constitutional and legal framework.

Packer cautions that political agreements including autonomy arrangements must be amendable to adapt to changes in circumstances. The autonomy of South Tyrol is set out in a constitutional law and is thus difficult to amend. At the same time, both parties (the German speaking population of South Tyrol and the government of Italy) recognise that autonomy is a *process* which requires ongoing negotiations to permit all stakeholders to adapt their mutual relations and the nature of the autonomy to changing realities. Thus provision is made for a continuous process of negotiations between the stakeholders within the framework of the principles of the autonomy statute and under its constitutional umbrella, which makes it possible to modify aspects of the autonomy status and of the relations between the autonomous entity and the central gov-

---

[37] Kleist, presentation at the Sitges expert meeting.
[38] Constitution of the Autonomous Region of Bougainville, Part XXII.

ernment as both parties feel this better responds to their changing needs. The nature and extent of Catalonia's autonomy also continues to be the subject of political debate and negotiation with the Spanish government.

Entrenchment of autonomy agreements may not be sufficient in all cases. A legal entrenchment is most effective in countries which have a strong tradition of respect for the rule of law. Where this is not so, entrenching provisions in a constitution or special legislation may not offer the parties the necessary guarantees. Staszewski, for example, points out that in trying to facilitate the conclusion of a comprehensive agreement to end the conflict between Georgia and the Abkhazians, the need for substantial guarantees has been raised repeatedly. In this case, where the parties 'do not believe in agreements "on paper" unless there is something else, in particular some material guarantees',[39] entrenchment is not enough, and some forms of international guarantees may need to be developed. This does not mean that if guarantees are provided 'the Abkhaz will immediately accept autonomy or federal arrangements',[40] Staszewski adds, but guarantees probably need to be found in order for the process to move forward.

4.1.4 Creating institutions and processes for effective power-sharing

The establishment of institutions and processes that enable the autonomous entity to exercise its newly allocated responsibilities and the two entities to exercise the joint responsibilities provided for in the peace agreement is crucial to successful implementation. The allocation of competencies does not in itself create a working autonomy arrangement. For this to occur, institutions and processes must be negotiated and put in place in a timely manner. In some cases the creation of institutions or the modification of existing ones requires a passage of laws, while in other cases this can be done by an executive or administrative decision at the appropriate level of government.

A good example of an agreement that focuses on the creation of institutions and processes to give shape to the implementation of an autonomy in a disputed region is the Good Friday Agreement discussed in chapter IV. Much of the Agreement is devoted to setting up institutions and processes to make it possible for the newly autonomous Northern Ireland government to function independently from the British government in some areas, together with it in others and together with the government of the Republic of Ireland in yet other areas. Prominent among these institutions are three cross-border bodies: the North/South Ministerial Council, the British-Irish Council and the British-Irish Inter-

---

[39] Staszewski, presentation at the Sitges expert meeting.
[40] Staszewski, presentation.

governmental Conference. The first of these, the North/South Ministerial Council, oversees the operation of six Implementation Bodies,[41] also established under the terms of the Agreement and charged with coordinating certain governmental functions on a cross-border basis between Northern Ireland and Ireland. This council is composed of ministerial level representatives of the government of Ireland and the local government of Northern Ireland. The British-Irish Council is made up of ministerial level representatives of the British and Irish governments, the devolved administrations of Wales, Scotland and Northern Ireland, and the governments of the Isle of Man and the Channel Islands. It is the mechanism for cooperation among all these administrations regarding issues of common interest, such as energy, transport, communications and drugs. The third cross-border institution, the British-Irish Intergovernmental Conference, comprises representatives of both named governments only, and deals primarily with matters of concern to these two governments regarding Northern Ireland that are not devolved to the government of Northern Ireland. These cross-border institutions function well, are very useful and relatively non-contentious.[42] They are particularly important because they provide mechanisms to satisfy the interests of the principal parties in conflict in Northern Ireland. The Unionists feel part of Britain and the Irish nationalists identify with Ireland. The various cross- border bodies, together with the devolved Northern Irish government, provide the institutional avenues for the expression of these differing affiliations and for autonomous governance, and are one of the primary mechanisms for the implementation of the Good Friday Agreement.

A noteworthy feature of the South Tyrolean autonomy discussed in chapter VII is the institutions and processes that were put in place and continue to exist for continuous dialogue and negotiations between the Italian government and the South Tyrolean provincial government. These constitute the mechanism for the two sides to find solutions to problems as they come up and to negotiate new areas of autonomy. 'Though designed to implement the autonomy statute, the mechanism of enactment by decree continues to function even today after the last enactment decree entered into force. As time goes by, enactment decrees need to be amended, for which the same negotiation procedure in the joint commission must be followed.'[43]

---

[41] Good Friday Agreement, Belfast, 10 April 1998, Strand 2, paragraph 9.

[42] Haughey, chapter IV.

[43] Woelk, chapter VII, sections 4 and 5. The first of the two joint commissions set-up under the terms of the South Tyrol autonomy agreement deals with the autonomy of the Trentino-South Tyrol autonomous region, while the second one (which is smaller and part of the former) deals with the autonomy of the province of South Tyrol. The joint commissions are composed of equal numbers of members nominated by the state government on the one hand and by the autonomous

4.1.5 *Monitoring and verification*

Independent monitoring of the implementation of intrastate peace agreements and verification of specific milestones in the implementation process is critical. This is amply illustrated in some of the chapters in this publication. The task of monitoring and verification is normally assigned to a third party trusted by the parties that have concluded the agreement. This is the case in relation to the Good Friday Agreement, the Bougainville Peace Agreement, and the Macedonian Framework Agreement, to mention but a few of the cases discussed later in this chapter and in other chapters of this publication. Because of the important role of third parties in this regard, we discuss monitoring and verification under the heading Third Party Roles below. It should be pointed out here, however, that monitoring and verification can also be carried out by the parties themselves according to mechanisms and processes created by them. For example, the cease-fire concluded between the Indian government and the National Socialist Council of Nagaland (NSCN) in 1997 has been monitored effectively by a monitoring cell established by the parties and comprising of representatives of both sides in accordance with ground rules negotiated and agreed to by them. On the other hand, experiences with the three-member implementation committee established under the 1997 CHT Peace Accord, discussed in chapter V, are negative and illustrate the limitations and dangers of relying only on the parties themselves to undertake the task of monitoring and possibly of verification.[44] The CHT Peace Accord does not contain provisions for the committee's mandate, powers and functioning. In fact the committee has never functioned well and ceased to meet after some time.

In some cases parties choose to create international mechanisms for monitoring and verification. This was done under the terms of the Good Friday Agreement on Northern Ireland, where an independent international commission (under the chairmanship of a Canadian general) was set-up to supervise and certify the disposal of weapons. Parties in the Sri Lanka conflict also set-up an international monitoring mission, the Sri Lanka Monitoring Mission (SLMM), which monitored the implementation of the cease-fire agreement between the two sides and continually followed the situation on the ground. The mission was led by

---

region and autonomous province, for the first and second commission respectively, on the other. The commissions are involved in the drafting of the decrees that form the legal framework of the autonomy by enacting the principles in the autonomy statutes. The second commission has gradually transformed itself into a more permanent body for bilateral negotiations between the Italian government and the provincial government to resolve any issues and disputes that come up regarding the autonomy of the province.

[44] Roy, chapter V, section 7.

Norway and consisted of Norwegian and other Scandinavian monitors. As discussed below, this mission was also given the responsibility for ongoing conflict resolution on the ground at the micro-level.

4.1.6 Implementing in phases

Some changes are difficult for parties to embrace and put into practice immediately. Some need time to implement, while others are dependent on the completion of other aspects of the peace agreement. There are many reasons that may lead parties to opt for a phased implementation of peace agreements involving autonomy arrangements. Agreeing on a clear timeline for the implementation of each phase and on verification of the proper implementation of each phase can be an effective way to make the transition from the existing situation at the time the agreement is concluded to the situation envisioned by that agreement. Thus, phased implementation can serve as a way for each party to verify the implementation of specific aspects of the agreement by the other before proceeding to the next stage.

A phased approach can be developed as a confidence building measure even before an agreement is concluded. If both sides carry out certain limited commitments according to predetermined mutually agreed timelines, this can have a very important trust building effect on all parties and can facilitate the negotiation process and form a basis for taking joint responsibility to create the new political reality. Parties can build on the trust they have established during this preliminary phase. Phased implementation can also help build or consolidate trust after the agreement is concluded.

Roy notes that the one aspect of the CHT Peace Accord that was well implemented was the repatriation in the CHT of Pahari refugees from India, which he attributes to the fact that it was done in phases.[45] Woelk also agrees that the operational calendar included in the 'Package' for implementation of the South Tyrolean autonomy served to ensure proper implementation as well as to build confidence.[46]

In a number of peace processes parties have chosen to agree on an autonomy arrangement for a limited period of time, followed by a referendum to determine the final political status of the autonomous region. An example is the Bougainville Peace Agreement, which provides for a very extensive autonomy for Bougainville within Papua New Guinea (PNG) and for a referendum to be held ten to fifteen years after the establishment of the autonomous government.

---

[45] Roy, chapter V, section 7.
[46] Woelk, chapter VII, section 5.

In the referendum the population of Bougainville will be asked to determine its final status *vis-à-vis* PNG. The provision was modelled on the Matignon and Noumea accords of 1988 and 1998 respectively between France and the indigenous population of New Caledonia.[47] A similar provision was proposed by the United Nations and the East Timorese resistance to the Indonesian government in 1997 to resolve that conflict, and is found in the 2005 peace agreement between northern and southern Sudan.[48] Momis believes, in relation to the Bougainville Peace Agreement, that 'the deferred referendum on the issue of political independence will remind the National Government [of PNG] that it does not pay to ignore the Agreement.'[49]

4.1.7 Incentives and sanctions

The provision of peace dividends and other incentives for proper implementation of agreements can be an effective means of encouraging satisfactory implementation. This is often done in conjunction with monitoring (and verification). Such incentives may be called 'carrots'. Sanctions for not implementing agreements (which may be called 'sticks') can serve the same purpose. Both should be used only if they are credible, and therefore applied by entities that have the capacity and political will to follow through on the positions they take in relation to the peace process. Roy suggests that in most cases it makes more sense to talk of positive and negative incentives for implementation – 'carrots, no carrots, or big carrots'[50] – but recognises that sometimes safeguards or penalties for non-compliance can also usefully be built into the peace agreement. The CHT Peace Accord contained no safeguards or sanctions. But even if it had, Roy believes, they may not have been enforceable without a strong third party capable and willing to enforce them.

The most effective incentive is created by engaging the genuine interests of the parties in the implementation of the agreement. This requires the construction of an agreement that truly responds to the interests of all parties. In the same vein, a stick could take the form of raising the cost of conflict to both parties. Carrots and sticks can be enhanced by external actors and are discussed in some detail below, in dealing with the role of third and fourth parties.

---

[47] The 1988 Matignon Accord was to lead to a referendum on independence after ten years. This was replaced by the 1998 Noumea Accord, which provided for considerable autonomy and a right to call for a referendum on independence after 2014.
[48] Comprehensive Peace Agreement 2005, available at <http://www.usip.org/library/pa/sudan/pa_sudan.html> (2 August 2006).
[49] Momis, presentation at the Sitges expert meeting.
[50] Roy, chapter V, section 7.

4.1.8 *Engaging international organisations*

There are a number of UN and regional organisations that can usefully be invited to assist parties in the process of implementation.

A good example of the assistance that such organisations can provide to parties in the implementation of intrastate peace agreements is the role played by a number of them in the implementation of the Framework Agreement in Macedonia. In that case, discussed in chapter X, the extensive use by the parties of NATO, the EU, the OSCE, the Council of Europe and also the UNHCR and other organisations to facilitate, monitor and assist in the implementation of the agreement has been successful.[51] Annex C to the Framework Agreement specifically invites organisations to perform tasks in relation to implementation. Thus, for example, the EU is invited to coordinate implementation; the Council of Europe and the European Commission are asked to supervise the conduct of the census provided for in the agreement; the OSCE is invited to observe elections, also provided for in the agreement; the UNHCR is invited to assist in the repatriation of refugees and displaced persons required to take place under the agreement; the European Commission and the World Bank are asked to assist in financing implementation, including measures to strengthen local self-government; and the EU, the OSCE and the United States are invited to help train the police and develop a plan to ensure equitable representation of ethnic communities in the police. The Framework Agreement invites the international community to assist in the process of strengthening local self-government by helping with the legal work involved and by training lawyers, judges and prosecutors of all ethnic communities. It is also asked to assist in the implementation of the agreement in the area of higher education and to support projects designed to improve inter-ethnic relations.

The positive experience with the extensive involvement of regional and international organisations at the invitation of the parties in Macedonia could serve as a precedent for parties in other conflicts. International organisations not only bring added capacity to assist in the implementation of agreements. Their involvement also raises the confidence among all concerned stakeholders that the agreements concluded will indeed be implemented.[52]

---

[51] Most of the organisations discussed also played an important role earlier in the process leading up to the agreement.

[52] In different circumstances, the government of East Timor invites the United Nations High Commissioner for Refugees (UNHCR) to determine whether political asylum seekers in East Timor should qualify for refugee status.

4.1.9 Agreeing on ways to resolve disputes before they occur

Implementation of intrastate peace agreements often leads to disputes between the first parties. Disputes may arise regarding the interpretation of the agreement (the language or the intent) or as to whether a party has properly implemented its provisions. That such disputes arise is normal and should not be cause for concern, provided that the parties have put in place effective ways of addressing such disputes ahead of time.

A minimum requirement for peaceful and effective resolution of disputes arising out of the implementation or non-implementation of an agreement is the inclusion in the agreement itself of a workable mechanism to deal with these disputes. The agreement may include a clause that provides for mediation by a third party acceptable to both sides; for a process of negotiation; for the submission of disputes to a constitutional or supreme judicial court for adjudication; for arbitration; or for a combination of these and other political and legal processes.

The Chittagong Hill Tracts Peace Accord does not contain provisions for dispute resolution. As a consequence, only a Bangladesh court can adjudicate disputes that arise between the parties. Since the Bangladesh courts are perceived by the indigenous peoples of the CHT to be an instrument of the state that was a party to the conflict, this option does not inspire the trust that an impartial mechanism might.

The Sri Lanka Monitoring Mission referred to earlier, which monitors the implementation of the cease-fire agreement between the two sides, was also given the mandate to resolve disputes since the agreement provided that the SLMM is 'the final authority to interpret the agreement'.[53] Of course this was not a final political settlement of the conflict but a cease-fire arrangement. Nevertheless, this kind of role for a third party, which needs to be carefully considered before taking it on, can provide a useful means to deal with disputes when they come up both for interim and final political agreements.

Not all disputes lend themselves to legal resolution by adjudication. Political disputes may best be dealt with by an agreed negotiation or mediation process.[54] The inclusion of possible appeal to judicial or arbitral bodies respected as independent by both sides can, however, contribute significantly to the level of confidence that parties, especially the weaker ones, have in the peace agreement and the process of implementation. These judicial or arbitral mechanisms can be domestic or international.

---

[53] Discussed in Sjøberg, chapter VIII.
[54] Van Maanen, comments at the Sitges expert meeting.

Although an obvious choice for adjudication of disputes arising out of intrastate agreements would appear to be the national courts of the state in question, such courts are often not perceived to be independent and impartial where the dispute involves the state as one of the parties.[55] In such cases a domestic solution could be sought in the creation of a special chamber of the constitutional or supreme court to deal with disputes arising out of the agreement and its implementation. Both parties would then have a say in the composition of such a chamber and perhaps its terms of reference. Parties may prefer to agree on adjudication by a special commission or arbitral tribunal. This has the advantage of treating the parties as equal in relation to any dispute, thus effectively offsetting the otherwise asymmetric relationship. Parties would have an equal say in the composition of the commission or arbitral tribunal and would have equal access to it.

It may be that one or both of the parties would have more confidence in an international rather than a domestic mechanism. It could also be that, given the political sensitivity of the issues involved, the parties would prefer for disputes to be dealt with by institutions and individuals not associated with the situation. Reference to an outside body can be a face-saving way for political authorities not to be implicated in the substance of the discussions and resolution of politically sensitive disputes, but only in the choice of mechanism and forum for their resolution. To respond to such needs, the commissions and arbitral tribunals mentioned in the previous paragraph can be domestic but they could also be international or hybrid in nature. Miles explores the possible use of existing international and regional courts and arbitral tribunals for resolving disputes concerning the implementation of intrastate peace agreements in chapter XI. Some of her conclusions are discussed in the last section of this chapter.

A very interesting, primarily domestic mechanism for the resolution of disputes arising out of an intrastate agreement, which uses negotiation, adjudication and, until recently, the possibility of appeal to an extranational body, was created in Aotearoa/New Zealand. The Treaty of Waitangi, concluded in 1840 between the British colonial administration and the indigenous Maori peoples of Aotearoa/New Zealand, recognised British sovereignty over the islands but also extensive Maori rights which could not be infringed upon by the colonial power. The terms of the treaty were not properly honoured by the British and later the New Zealand governments. In 1975, the Treaty of Waitangi Claims Tribunal was set-up and a bilateral negotiations process between the New Zealand government and Maori groups established to resolve the disputes which arose from the bad or non-implementation by these governments of the treaty.[56] The

---

[55] Miles, chapter XI, section 2.

[56] The Treaty of Waitangi Act of 1975, amended by the Treaty of Waitangi Amendment Act of 1985, giving the Tribunal powers to consider historic claims.

workings of both mechanisms are discussed in detail by Te Whiti Love in chapter XII.

The result of the still ongoing process is a series of settlements between Maori claimants and the government of New Zealand, enforceable at law. The settlements involve the transfer of land rights and water resources, economic components that establish sustainable economic bases for the tribes, and the establishment of tribal governance entities with a degree of autonomy and self-management. They also often involve an apology by the government for past wrongs.

The settlements are full and final, which is important both to the government and the tribes. Legislation is needed to give the settlements reached between the government and the claimant tribe binding force. This legislation is an act that binds the government, but is not entrenched beyond that.

The Privy Council in London has been used on sixteen occasions for appeals from New Zealand's Court of Appeal and Maori Appellate Court decisions regarding Maori claims arising out of the Waitangi Treaty. Even though seldom used and now abolished,[57] Maori thought highly of this mechanism; they perceived it to be close to the British Crown and considered it to be supranational because it provided appeal to a court outside the framework of the New Zealand state and therefore not involved in New Zealand's own political interests, moods and prejudices.

According to Te Whiti Love, 'with the establishment of the Waitangi Tribunal, which conducts its enquiries on the basis of the Treaty, and the negotiation process that leads to settlements between Maori groups and the Crown, the implementation of the treaty has become the basis of an important process of dispute resolution between the Crown and the Maori people today.'[58] The success of this process may be in the combination of the recommendatory process of the Tribunal, which is treaty based; the negotiations between the Maori and the government on the basis of the Tribunal's recommendations; and the conclusion of settlements which are made binding by the passage of legislation; the process thus comprises a mixture of adjudicative, political and legislative elements.

This implementation and compensation mechanism is a unique response to intrastate disputes rooted in the bad implementation and violation of a historical

---

[57] In October 2003 the New Zealand parliament passed an act establishing a new court of final appeal to replace the Privy Council for appeals originating in New Zealand. The Supreme Court of New Zealand was established to, inter alia, 'recognise that New Zealand is an independent nation with its own history and traditions; and to enable important legal matters, including legal matters relating to the Treaty of Waitangi, to be resolved with an understanding of New Zealand conditions, history, and traditions' (Supreme Court Act 2003, section 1(a)).

[58] Te Whiti Love, chapter XII, section 12.

agreement, and it may not be readily duplicated elsewhere. Many aspects of it, however, do provide valuable lessons that could be applied in other parts of the world.

4.2 Parties' and other actors' roles

Below we look at implementation of intrastate peace agreements from the perspective of what various actors involved in peace processes can do. We ask how they can help ensure that intrastate peace agreements, especially those involving autonomy arrangements, will be fully implemented.

4.2.1 *First party roles*

The proposal and adoption of the substantive and procedural measures that we have discussed thus far come about in large part through the efforts of the first parties. It is the first parties who negotiate the terms of an agreement, who design the manner of implementation, and who agree on specific implementation provisions that provide assurance to them that the agreement will be implemented properly. Thus primary responsibility for ensuring good implementation clearly rests on the first parties. Others can nevertheless play important roles in helping first parties to fulfil this responsibility, to prepare them for the difficulties that lie ahead, to help resolve the obstacles and disputes that may arise in the course of implementation, and to put mechanisms in place that help to ensure that the parties stay on the agreed course.

4.2.2 *Roles of second – kindred and godfather – parties*

In the process of implementation of the Northern Ireland Good Friday Agreement and the South Tyrol autonomy agreement, discussed in chapters IV and VII respectively, kindred states, i.e., the Republic of Ireland and Austria respectively played and continue to play a crucial role. These second parties were instrumental in bringing about negotiations and were in effect negotiators and signatories of agreements concerning the entities in conflict, even if they were not the principal subjects of those agreements. Once agreements were concluded that provided for a long-term solution to the conflict between the population group and the state in question, the second party remained engaged to ensure their proper implementation.

The process of implementation of the South Tyrolean autonomy was embedded in guarantees at the international level. The terms of the autonomy were set out in the De Gasperi-Gruber agreement, which was contained in an annex to the peace treaty between the Allies and Italy after World War II,[59] thereby creating an international obligation for Italy *vis-à-vis* Austria to implement the autonomy. Since Italy needed to implement the agreement in its domestic sphere, Austria's role was effectively to monitor that implementation. The UN also played a role by putting the issue on its agenda. The necessity of a formal 'declaration of conflict settlement' by Austria in order for the UN to remove the issue from its agenda, and for such declaration to be given *after* the implementation process had been concluded, was an important incentive for Italy to implement the agreement well.[60]

In the case of Northern Ireland, it was the participation of the Irish government in talks on the future of Northern Ireland, at the insistence of the Northern Irish nationalist parties, that eventually made the peace process possible. The first agreement involving the Irish government, the principal Northern Irish political parties and the British government was concluded in 1973, shortly after the Bloody Sunday tragedy caused the British government to drop its opposition to Irish government involvement. In 1985, an agreement was signed between the Irish and British governments, which gave the former the right to be consulted on all matters concerning the internal government of Northern Ireland and committed the British government to make all possible efforts to reach consensus with the Irish government on these matters.[61] After the signing of the Good Friday Agreement in April 1998, the role of the Irish government in relation to the implementation of the agreement and ongoing negotiations on Northern Ireland has only increased, as the discussion in chapter IV shows.

As the above examples show, kindred states can have a decisive impact both on the negotiation and the implementation of intrastate agreements. A study of the role of Hungary and Sweden with respect to ensuring the implementation of the Transylvania and Åland autonomies respectively would probably confirm this view.

Non-kindred states can play similar second party roles, as Portugal has shown in relation to East Timor in the latter's relations with Indonesia.[62] The United Kingdom, which was a party to the Joint Declaration establishing the autonomous status of Hong Kong within the People's Republic of China, can play a godfather role with respect to the implementation of that autonomy and Australia or New Zealand could conceivably take on such a role with respect to the implementation of Bougainville's autonomy agreement.

---

[59] Annex IV to the Treaty of Peace with Italy, Paris St–Germain, 10 February 1947.
[60] See Woelk, chapter VII, section 6.
[61] Haughey, chapter IV.

4.2.3 Third party roles

Third parties can potentially play very important roles because they can do things that neither first nor second parties can do. At the same time, their roles are delicate and some first parties may not wish to have them involved.

Viewing a peace process as a continuum, third parties can play a variety of roles during the various and interrelated phases of the process. Sjøberg gives an overview of the types of roles that third party facilitators can play in chapter VIII: *lead roles* such as those of the official facilitator appointed by the parties or the coordinator of active international support for a peace process, as well as confidential back channel roles; *coalition roles* as part of joint international efforts or of multilateral organisations involved in facilitating peace processes; *supporting roles* that can include financial and political support for other facilitators, humanitarian aid or support for reconciliation processes and human rights; and *exploratory roles* that involve contact building activities.

With respect to third party roles in monitoring, verification and guaranteeing the implementation of intrastate peace agreements, there are numerous experiences from which lessons can be drawn, some of which are discussed in this publication.

In Northern Ireland, an independent international commission (under the chairmanship of the Canadian general John de Chastelain) was set-up to 'monitor, review and verify progress on decommissioning of illegal arms.'[63] Although established before the signing of the Good Friday Agreement, in the context of a series of ceasefires, its current mandate and powers are set out in the Agreement. Haughey believes that the commission is not sufficiently effective because of its limited mandate, which does not permit it to adjudicate on the extent to which the paramilitary organisations are discharging their obligations under the Agreement, nor to impose sanctions on those that do not comply.[64] The result, in his opinion, has been that the commission has only sat and watched while the paramilitary organisations refused to dispose of their arms.

In Georgia, a UN Observer Mission (UNOMIG) is monitoring the implementation of the ceasefire in Abkhazia, which was concluded between the Geor-

---

[62] Vendrell addresses Portugal's role in relation to the process of resolving the conflict caused by Indonesia's occupation of East Timor. Portugal's considerable engagement in helping East Timor in the implementation of the agreement reached (between Portugal and Indonesia), and therefore in enabling East Timor to transition into and exercise its new independent status, can be considered a second party role.

[63] Good Friday Agreement, paragraph 4, 'Decommissioning' section. See chapter IV. The Independent International Commission on Decommissioning was first set-up in 1997.

[64] Haughey, chapter IV.

gian and the Abkhazian sides in late 1993. The parties have not reached a political agreements so far and 'the most important achievement of the mission as a whole is that the ceasefire has and is being held.'[65]

The role of third parties in the implementation of the Macedonian Framework Agreement discussed by Biegman in chapter X is particularly interesting. NATO, the EU, the OSCE and the United States have been monitoring and assisting in the implementation of the agreement at the express invitation of the parties. This invitation is contained in the terms of the Framework Agreement itself. The international actors are able to play their roles with respect to ensuring full and timely implementation effectively precisely because their involvement is set out clearly in the agreement.

The Macedonian government agreed to the involvement of NATO and the EU in large part because of its desire to become a member of these organisations.[66] This degree of leverage is not often at the disposal of third parties, but the skilful utilisation of any leverage that can facilitate the task of third parties in encouraging and even persuading parties to fully honour their commitments may be helpful.

Biegman points to the stabilising influence of the presence of a modest third party military force. In Macedonia this has helped to calm down and prevent incidents and provocations and has therefore had a positive impact on the implementation process. The experience in Bougainville with the presence of the multinational force known as the Peace Monitoring Group, which is unarmed, has been equally positive in diffusing tensions and ensuring proper implementation of commitments.[67]

In the Bougainville-Papua New Guinea conflict, third parties were not only critical in bringing the first parties to the negotiation table, but have also so far successfully monitored and verified the implementation of the ensuing peace agreement. These third parties, namely the governments of New Zealand, Australia, Solomon Islands, Fiji and Vanuatu (all members of the Pacific Forum) and the UN, set-up two missions to monitor the implementation of the commitments made by the parties in the course of the negotiations, including the 1997 cease-fire: the Peace Monitoring Group, set-up by the Pacific Forum governments, and the UN Observer Mission on Bougainville (UNOMB), set-up by the UN.[68]

Acting as the guarantor of the implementation of intrastate peace agreements is not an easy role to take on, as governments and others that do so must be

---

[65] Staszewski, presentation at the Sitges expert meeting.
[66] Biegman, chapter X.
[67] Atsir, comments at the Sitges expert meeting.
[68] Momis and Atsir, presentations at the Sitges expert meeting.

prepared to face the consequences of non-compliance with the agreement by one or both parties. Such third party guarantors must be willing and able to let the parties feel the consequences of violating or not implementing agreements reached. In Macedonia's case, the EU, NATO, the United States and the OSCE have, in practice, jointly taken on such a role. The Pacific Forum countries mentioned earlier, especially Australia and New Zealand, as well as the UN also to some extent took on a guarantor responsibility in relation to the Bougainville Peace Agreement.

Staszewski draws attention to the importance of guarantees in relation to the implementation of different aspects of peace agreements where there is a lack of trust between the parties. Georgians, for example, demand a guarantee for a 'sustainable return' for refugees to Abkhazia, while Abkhazians want security guarantees before letting all the refugees return.[69] The issue is of major importance and presents a challenge to the third party, in this case UNOMIG.

- Prerequisites for and obstacles to effective third party involvement

Third parties can only be truly accepted and effective when the first parties trust the person or persons in the third party team. This truth highlights the importance of individuals and individual relationships in the facilitation of peace processes. Existing relationships of individuals within third parties with key individuals of the first parties are important to the building of trust between the parties and the third party facilitator. In the Norwegian government's experience the manner in which third parties get involved can be very important. The Norwegian government has generally done so through pre-existing development cooperation relations and long-term personal relationships and bonds that developed within those frameworks or otherwise. One way of promoting trust that Vendrell has experienced is to ensure that both (all) first parties have a 'third party friend'. During the negotiations to resolve the conflict between Indonesia and East Timor, for example, each of the two UN Special Envoys was close to one of the parties: the first special envoy to the Indonesian government, and the second to the East Timorese resistance. Thus the two Special Envoys together contributed to creating trust in the third party (the UN) on both sides in the conflict.

The individuals involved may not be neutral, but the organisations or states that act as third party facilitators should ideally not be partisan. Small states such as Norway can be effective as a third party if they do not have their own agenda in the places where they play this role.[70] Having said that, it should be

---

[69] Staszewski, presentation at the Sitges expert meeting.

[70] Sjøberg, chapter VIII. Packer points out, however, that when it comes to third party states there are degrees of interest but states are never disinterested (comments at the Sitges expert

recognised that in practice governments that take on a third party role often *do* have a stake in the outcome of a peace process. Depending on the nature (for example, economic, strategic or humanitarian) and importance of their interests, this may hamper the effectiveness of their role.

A third party fails in its role when it becomes a first party: there are ample examples of third parties taking a frontline position and playing lead roles in peace processes in ways that makes one or all the principals feel that they are no longer in control of the process or its outcome. The temptation to take the limelight or to otherwise serve one's own interests poses a serious challenge to the difficult and important role that third parties can play. Reasons why third parties may usurp the process include the lack of professionalism and competence of some third party players at a time that conflict resolution is 'sexy' and fundable, ambition and desire for personal recognition.

The effective fulfilment of third party roles is difficult, if not impossible, when one of the parties does not want the third party's involvement. In the case of the Chittagong Hill Tracts conflict, the Bangladesh government did not want any third party involvement in the negotiations or in the implementation of the agreements, fearing that this would give undue importance to the conflict, the peace process and especially to the indigenous movement. The Chinese government has also consistently refused to have a third party or any other outside involvement in a dialogue or negotiations it might have with Tibetans.

Governments may resist third party involvement for a number of reasons, such as a fear of losing control over the process and the situation, of internationalising a conflict that they wish to regard as a purely domestic affair, and of giving the non-state party too much importance and strengthening its bargaining position.

A third party may be more likely to be acceptable to first parties for monitoring or guaranteeing the implementation of a particular intrastate peace agreement if that party was involved in facilitating the negotiation process that led to the conclusion of the agreement and fulfilled that task to the satisfaction of the conflicting parties. This was the case in Bougainville, Macedonia and, to some extent, in Northern Ireland. For this reason, third parties must ideally be able to

---

meeting). The United States rarely lacks an own interest and agenda in peace processes it gets involved in. In Northern Ireland, this has not hampered its ability to play a crucial role as third party in the peace process. Its involvement is effective in part because of the leverage the United States has due to the considerable moral, political and material support the Sinn Fein and even the IRA obtained from Americans on the one hand, and the US government's close relationship with the British government, on the other. The two US Presidential envoys played a crucial role in bringing these parties and other stakeholders (such as the government of the Republic of Ireland) to the negotiating table and assisting them to reach a mutually satisfactory agreement. Today the United States (including President George W. Bush's envoy) remains engaged to assist in the obstacle ridden process of implementation of the Good Friday Agreement.

make a long-term commitment that includes their participation in the implementation phase.[71]

4.2.4 Fourth party roles

Even without the active involvement of third parties, first parties can obtain some of the benefits of outside involvement by engaging the interest of fourth parties. Fourth parties can play important roles in persuading governments and population group leaders to pursue peace processes, and can make important contributions in ensuring or encouraging full implementation of agreements reached.

Often it is difficult to persuade a government to engage in negotiations with a population group or to engage members of the international community and public opinion to convince reluctant governments to accept talks (see chapters VI and IX). Fourth parties can play a role in this regard. Tibetan leaders, for example, have convinced numerous governments of the need for China to enter into negotiations with the Dalai Lama or his representatives to end the longstanding conflict in Tibet. Some of these governments play a very significant role by raising the issue in their own bilateral contacts with China.

Governments and international organisations can provide peace dividends as well as other incentives – carrots – for proper implementation of agreements. Fourth parties may also wield sticks with which they can (threaten to) punish violators of an agreement. As stated earlier in this chapter, they should be used only if they are credible, and therefore applied by actors that have the capacity and political will to follow through.

In Macedonia, both parties have a stake in Macedonia becoming a member of the EU and NATO and understand that unless the conflict is resolved along the lines provided for by the Framework Agreement, steps towards such integration with Western Europe cannot be taken. This incentive works because the agreement and the corresponding incentives respond to the genuine interests of the first parties. In contrast, big economic carrots offered to Abkhazia in relation to efforts to end its conflict with Georgia did not work because Abkhazians could not be persuaded to implement measures that they considered to be contrary to their principles and interests.[72]

Where a development cooperation relationship exists with a government that has entered into a peace agreement with a self-determination movement, the so-called donor country can contribute greatly to the implementation of that agreement by providing peace dividends to the parties on the ground that are tied to

---

[71] Sjøberg, chapter VIII.
[72] Staszewski, comments at the Sitges expert meeting

certain benchmarks in the implementation process. This kind of involvement, which falls far short of any form of guarantee, can be very helpful if it is well conceived and carried out consistently to provide rewards for implementation as well as withholding such rewards where a party fails to implement properly. Sjøberg aptly warns of the procedural constraints that governments and intergovernmental organisations may face related to the delivery of peace dividends (for example, aid) to the non-government party to the conflict. Creating expectations that cannot be met in this regard, he warns, 'will only damage the process in the long run. It is better to under-promise and over-deliver.'[73] He also emphasises that the aid must truly benefit the people on the ground: 'People must experience concretely that peace improves the conditions of their lives, in terms of security, social services, reconstruction and economic development. Real peace dividends can contribute importantly to generate popular support and momentum for a political process.'[74]

A number of donor governments exerted substantial pressure on the government of Bangladesh and the JSS to embark on a peace process and conclude a political agreement. They pledged considerable peace dividends before the agreement was concluded, but once the agreement was signed the pressure to implement it did not materialise and neither did the dividends. Many lessons can be learned from the missed opportunities of donor countries in this case. Donor countries could have had a very positive impact on the implementation of the Chittagong Hill Tracts Peace Accord if they had acted more forcefully in a coordinated and timely manner to provide economic incentives linked to the implementation of the accord and benefiting the people in the conflict area. Roy contends in chapter V that the donor countries and their intergovernmental organisations did not get much beyond ill conceived feasibility studies and discussions of controversial infrastructure projects wanted by one side in the conflict only and mistrusted by the other. They also required the presentation of projects for funding by the indigenous party in ways that were entirely unrealistic given the lack of capacity among indigenous organisations. An opportunity to influence positively the implementation of the peace agreement was lost due to bureaucratic requirements and lack of political will of donor countries to undertake what was evidently necessary. The lack of proper implementation and of concrete improvements to the conditions of the population on the ground has fuelled renewed violence. In fact, more people have been dying since the accord was signed than in the years before its conclusion.

It is evident that where more than one fourth party intends to provide peace dividends and other incentives for implementation of peace agreements and to

---

[73] Sjøberg, chapter VIII.
[74] Sjøberg, chapter VIII.

support the activities of third parties, these must be coordinated to be effective. Where such efforts are not coordinated they may not only lose effectiveness but can even be counterproductive. Attempting to achieve this coordination can be very difficult, given the various and often contradictory interests of all parties involved.[75]

Donor conferences can be an important tool to achieve a degree of coordination. In the case of Sri Lanka, such a conference served to identify what help was wanted and needed by the first parties and to coordinate approaches. Sjøberg emphasises the importance of including *all* the parties in these processes, as Norway did in the case of Sri Lanka and Sudan. The coordination of the activities of the international organisations invited to assist in the implementation of the Framework Agreement in Macedonia (both in the capacity of third and fourth parties) has been a crucial element in the success of that agreement's implementation thus far. Biegman concludes that this is perhaps the most important of the five factors he identifies as having contributed to making implementation of the agreement in Macedonia so much more successful than similar efforts elsewhere in the Balkans.[76] He describes in chapter X how NATO, the EU, the OSCE and other international organisations and the United States work together, each with their own particular task and niche and without competition for turf.

4.2.5 Roles of 'friends of the peace process'

In the Guatemalan peace process and the Georgia-Abkhazia negotiations, so-called groups of friends of the peace process were set-up to assist the UN Secretary-General where the UN was involved as a third party facilitator. Getting governments engaged and committed to support specific peace processes by means of these groups can be a very effective tool. Its effectiveness depends largely on the composition of these 'friends' in terms of the countries represented in the group and especially the individuals that are actively involved.

Groups of friends have not always been as helpful as they could have been because the exclusively government membership of such groups has tended to result in bias in favour of the government side in some intrastate conflicts. Van Walt, who was involved in the Abkhazia-Georgia peace process from 1993 to 1996, recalls that when the Group of Friends of the UN Secretary-General on Georgia (referred to mostly as the Friends of Georgia) was first formed in 1993 or 1994 to help the UN in its facilitation of those negotiations, the reference only to Georgia in the name immediately caused mistrust on the Abkhazian side

---

[75] Sjøberg, chapter VIII.
[76] Biegman, chapter X.

and made it impossible for the group to have any positive impact for quite some time. Some of the individuals in the group also created much hostility due to their obvious bias and damaged the trust which the UN Special Envoy had managed to instil among the Abkhazian leadership.[77] According to Staszewski, the later contribution to the peace process of that Group of Friends, consisting of the United States, Great Britain, Germany, France and the Russian Federation, was very significant. 'Formally it got observer status [at the negotiations], but its de facto role proved to be much more meaningful.'[78] Vendrell's experiences, discussed in chapter IX, serve to reinforce the need to act with caution in regard to the formation and use of these groups of friends.

Both the positive and negative experiences with groups of friends of peace processes raises interesting questions about the potential benefits of modifying the composition of these groups to include non-governmental actors, and the use of this kind of mechanism to support the efforts of third party facilitators other than the UN.

5. Searching for Additional Ways to Secure Implementation

The chapters in this publication and the other valuable contributions to the Sitges expert meeting remind us of the vital importance of implementing intrastate peace agreements and reveal the extreme difficulty for the parties of doing so. The international community has a clear interest to assist parties and otherwise make it possible for them to honour their commitments fully. Every time that an intrastate peace agreement is not implemented it makes it more difficult for the parties in other intrastate peace processes to develop the confidence that any agreements they may reach will not follow the same fate. Without confidence in the implementation of an agreement, it is hardly possible to persuade parties to make the concessions and take the risks that any peace agreement requires of them.

Governments may be aware of the ways in which international organisations and other governments can support their efforts to implement intrastate peace agreements. But population groups, the non-state actors, are often either not aware of or do not have access to the kind of assistance that could help them to ensure the best possible implementation of agreements to which they are a party.

In addition to making existing mechanisms available to the non-state entity as well as to the government side, new ways of promoting full implementation

---

[77] Van Walt, comment at the Sitges expert meeting.
[78] Staszewski, presentation at the Sitges expert meeting. Staszewski referred to the role of the Group of Friends from 1997.

should be sought and considered. Some ideas may involve the expanded use of existing mechanisms, while other ideas involve the creation of new mechanisms. Below we make a preliminary attempt at exploring what more could be done to help parties to ensure proper implementation of the intrastate peace agreements they enter into.

5.1   Broader use of UN mechanisms and agencies

Within the human rights field, the UN has numerous mechanisms for monitoring and reporting on situations that affect human rights. The UN High Commissioner for Human Rights can monitor, report on and draw international attention to situations involving human rights violations in any part of the world. This could include monitoring the implementation of particular intrastate peace agreements where these are likely to affect the enjoyment of human rights. The High Commissioner is already committed to playing an important role in the early warning and prevention of violent intrastate conflicts as part of her/his mandate and plays a crucial role in peace building in many post-armed conflict areas. Monitoring implementation of peace accords could be seen as an integral part of this activity, since it is an effective contribution to the prevention of a recurrence of violent conflict and is essential to peace building.

Special Rapporteurs report to the UN Commission on Human Rights on the respect for and violations of specific categories of human rights. Human rights treaty bodies also monitor human rights situations in all parts of the world. Using the same rationale as set out in the previous paragraph, and in cooperation with the High Commissioner on Human Rights, these Special Rapporteurs and treaty bodies could pay particular attention to relevant aspects of implementation. As De Varennes shows in chapter II, the root causes of intrastate conflicts often include discrimination against population groups and other violations of human rights. As a result, the peace agreements arrived at frequently involve commitments by the parties to respect existing or emerging international human rights standards. It would seem appropriate that monitoring the implementation of those aspects of intrastate peace agreements that affect the human rights situation in the concerned country be included in the mandate of the rapporteurs, the High Commissioner for Human Rights and the relevant human rights treaty bodies.

Specialised agencies of the UN, such as UNDP, the ILO, UNICEF and UNESCO can also monitor and report on aspects of implementation of peace agreements that are related to their area of work and expertise. The UNHCR already plays an active role in monitoring, reporting on and persuading parties to implement peace agreements where this affects the flow and situation of refugees and displaced persons. These agencies could also be invited by the parties to help them monitor and implement various aspects of the peace agreements they enter into, much as the parties to the Framework Agreement in Macedonia invited regional organisations to assist them.

The ILO has a special responsibility with respect to agreements involving the status and rights of indigenous peoples within states. This responsibility is based on ILO Convention 169 concerning Indigenous and Tribal Peoples in Independent Countries (1989). The convention provides, *inter alia,* for the protection of human rights and the integrity of indigenous peoples, for their participation in decision-making processes and for a degree of self-governance.

The Permanent Forum for Indigenous Issues of the UN does not have a conflict resolution mandate. Nothing prevents it and its members however from monitoring and drawing attention to issues related to the implementation of intrastate peace agreements involving or affecting indigenous peoples. Indeed, given the unique composition of the Permanent Forum (equal number of representatives of UN member states and of indigenous peoples from all parts of the world) this body would be very well placed to raise issues that other UN bodies and regional organisations may not be in a position to address in a non-partisan manner or in a manner that would inspire the trust of the non-state party to peace agreements. Kleist sees the Permanent Forum 'as a very important forum for these kinds of discussions and as a new forum that can facilitate a new way of dealing with problems that arise between states and non-states.'[79]

Finally, the role of the UN Secretary-General in monitoring and actively promoting the implementation of intrastate agreements could be enhanced. The desire of some states to exclude any involvement of the UN in what they consider to be their domestic affairs has been an obstacle in the past. The Secretary-General has the ability to bring potentially violent situations to the attention of the Security Council, although he has acknowledged that some reform may be needed in order for the UN to strengthen its capacity to prevent violent intrastate conflict.[80]

5.2   Effective use of regional organisations

Regional organisations also have mechanisms at their disposal that can be engaged effectively, as the implementation of the Framework Agreement in Macedonia shows. The OSCE's monitoring and democracy building mechanisms can greatly contribute to promoting good implementation, while the office of the High Commissioner on National Minorities' quiet diplomacy has

---

[79] Kleist, presentation at the Sitges expert meeting.
[80] Kofi Annan, *Renewing the United Nations: A Programme for Reform*, UN document A/51/950, 14 July 1997, para. 110.

already proved its effectiveness in preventing conflicts in a number of instances. Although the High Commissioner's mandate does not extend to situations of armed conflict, it does include situations in which peace has been achieved and autonomy agreements are being negotiated and need to be implemented.

5.3 Including dispute resolution clauses in peace agreements

As stated earlier, the importance of agreeing on effective means, including adjudication, for resolving disputes arising out of the (non-) implementation of intrastate peace agreements should not be underestimated. Non-state parties may not have confidence in domestic courts where these courts treat the state and non-state parties unequally. International courts and tribunals do not necessarily provide a better option. Unlike situations involving international disputes, parties in intrastate disputes typically do not have equal access to international mechanisms for the resolution of disputes such as the International Court of Justice. Miles analyses the possible use and relevance of existing international courts, arbitral tribunals and other mechanisms in chapter XI, and explores whether they could be relevant for intrastate dispute resolution. She finds that most permanent (as opposed to *ad hoc*) courts, tribunals and mechanisms of international organisations pose the same problem when it comes to the access and treatment of non-state entities. They are composed of or dominated by states and do not allow the participation of non-state actors such as self-determination movements or governments of autonomous entities. They are therefore often perceived by self-determination movements as being on the side of states and their governments.

Miles finds that arbitral tribunals could provide useful avenues for adjudication of intrastate disputes concerning the implementation of agreements, particularly because of their flexibility, informality and the possibility of keeping proceedings and outcome confidential. A particularly interesting arbitral institution to explore is the Permanent Court of Arbitration (PCA) in The Hague. As is the case with a number of other arbitral institutions, the PCA allows parties to decide on the composition of the arbitral tribunal, on confidentiality, on the venue of proceedings and other procedural matters, and allows non-state parties to bring disputes. While the PCA provides an international anchor which could be important for one or both parties, it can also accommodate the desire of parties for the mechanism to remain largely domestic in terms of the composition of the tribunal and, if need be, the venue for its meetings.

In 1993, the PCA adopted Optional Rules for Arbitrating Disputes between Two Parties of Which Only One is a State. These optional rules require the state party to agree to a waiver of its sovereign immunity. This aspect of the optional rules 'makes them particularly attractive for intrastate disputes [because] once a state has agreed to their application, it cannot then claim that it has immunity from prosecution and therefore refuse to be involved in the process or abide by any award.'[81] This addresses an essential problem in resolving disputes between states and non-state entities: the inequality of treatment between the parties. As long as population groups are denied access to courts and other dispute resolution mechanisms or are treated differently by them (for example by recognising the sovereign immunity of one of the parties) they are unlikely to have confidence in them. They may once again be tempted to seek independence as the only way to be fully recognised and heard. It should be noted that the PCA primarily deals with commercial disputes and that the rules may have to be adapted to some extent to deal with political ones. Miles concludes however that 'there is no clear political (or economic) reason why state parties, individuals or peoples should not consent to arbitration under the auspices of the PCA, provided that appropriate procedural rules could be agreed to deal with the particular nature of the disputes between the parties.'[82] This option deserves further study.

---

[81] Miles, chapter XI, section 2.
[82] Miles, chapter XI, section 2.

Chapter II

Recurrent Challenges to the Implementation of Intrastate Peace Agreements: the Resistance of State Authorities

Fernand de Varennes[*]

1. Introduction

> [T]he Imperial City has endeavoured to impose on subject nations not only her yoke, but her language, as a bond of peace ... but how many, great wars, how much slaughter and bloodshed have provided this unity.
>
> Saint Augustine, The City of God (circa 410 AD)

This chapter explores a recurrent challenge that has clearly been detrimental to the effective implementation of peace agreements involving autonomy arrangements. Research on thirty intrastate conflicts and peace agreements around the world shows that most of the cases that did not result in an ending to the violent conflict involved a refusal or unwillingness by state authorities to fully implement the terms of the peace agreement.[1]

Below, I examine some of the root causes of intrastate conflicts, based on thirty case studies which are briefly described in section 2.2. The common causes appear to centre around the violation of rights of minority groups by majority-controlled state authorities. The resolution of intrastate conflicts must clearly address these causes, and therefore necessarily involve the creation of mechanisms to protect minority groups from discrimination and oppression by the

---

[*] Associate Professor, Murdoch University School of Law, Australia.

[1] The research involved an examination of the origins and the claims made to buttress the use of violence against state authorities as well as the content of peace agreements that were concluded in relation to the thirty conflicts from Africa, Asia, Europe and Central America listed in section 2.2. Such a wide-ranging comparative study to determine what are some of the more recurrent causes of conflict, whether peace agreements address these causes, and why many conflicts are not resolved by the conclusion of such agreements has seldom – if indeed ever – been done before, not least because many of these peace agreements are not readily available.

M. Boltjes (ed.), *Implementing Negotiated Agreements*
© 2007, Kreddha International and T·M·C·ASSER PRESS, The Hague, The Netherlands

dominant group. Autonomy arrangements, which provide the minority groups a degree of self-government in the territory where they form a substantial portion (or the majority) of the population, are a preferred means to resolve intrastate conflicts because these arrangements maintain the state's territorial integrity while providing the necessary legal and political protection to the minority population.

Unfortunately, many peace agreements including autonomy arrangements are not or not fully implemented. In this chapter I show that this is mostly caused because the governments of the states in question are afraid or unwilling to give up substantial authority to the newly created autonomous regions.

2. INTRASTATE CONFLICTS SETTING, ROOT CAUSES AND CHARACTERISTICS

Most ethnic conflicts do not begin as a quest for territorial sovereignty or independence. The argument that intrastate conflicts always involve a separatist[2] threat to the unity of the state is a chimera. Of the thirty conflicts considered in the research, the vast majority[3] involved not innate antagonism, rejection of the state or an overt separatist threat in the initial stages, but demands by groups for improvements in the structures and institutions of the state. The movement towards separatism more often than not was a gradual process which began to appear after failed attempts by a minority or other group to maintain or obtain either autonomy, rights guarantees or legal protections in a state's constitution, or some form of equitable distribution of public and economic goods. The conflicts included in the study which did have a strong separatist dimension in the initial stages involved the denial of the international right of self-determination.[4]

---

[2] 'Separatism' here is used in the sense of a movement for the creation of a fully independent state.

[3] Chad; Democratic Republic of Congo (Banyamulenge); Cyprus; France (New Caledonia); India (Nagaland); Indonesia (Aceh); Indonesia (Kalimantan); Iraq (Kurds, Shi'a); Italy (South Tyrol); Lebanon (Muslims); Macedonia (Albanians); Mexico (Chiapas); Moldova (Transdniestr); Myanmar (Chin/Zomis, Kachins, Karens, Karenni, Mons, Wa); Niger (Tuaregs); Pakistan (East Pakistan/Bangladesh); Philippines (Moros); Rhodesia; South Africa (during apartheid regime); Spain (Basques); Sri Lanka (Tamils); Sudan (South); Turkey (Kurds); United Kingdom (Northern Ireland); and Yugoslavia (Kosovo).

[4] Eritrea, Palestine, West Papua, East Timor and the Western Sahara. The 1998 international conference of experts organised in Barcelona by UNESCO Division of Human Rights Democracy and Peace and the UNESCO Centre of Catalonia on the implementation of the right of self-determination as a contribution to conflict prevention proposed the following understanding of self-determination: '… an ongoing process of choice for the achievement of human security and

Empirical studies of conflicts involving minorities show links between the rights of minorities and autonomy arrangements on the one hand and the prevention of conflicts on the other. One example is the Minorities at Risk Project, which points out that the number of conflicts around the world has been increasing steadily since the 1960s although the intensity of these conflicts has in a general sense diminished in recent times, especially where minority rights are respected and some sort of autonomy arrangements has been negotiated.[5] To fully understand the links mentioned above one needs to appreciate the nature of the root causes of instability leading up to intrastate conflicts.

In most countries plagued with an intrastate conflict, what you have is not a 'minority problem' but a 'majority problem', or rather the refusal of state authorities to abide by basic principles of human rights and minority rights.[6]

---

fulfilment of human needs with a broad scope of possible outcomes and expressions suited to different specific situations. These can include, but are not limited to, guarantees of cultural security, forms of self-governance and autonomy, economic self-reliance, effective participation at the international level, land rights and the ability to care for the natural environment, spiritual freedom and the various forms that ensure the free expression and protection of collective identity in dignity.' Such an understanding is not however the same as the right of self-determination from a legal, international perspective, where it is much more limited in scope, and traditionally viewed as limited to the entire population (a people for the purposes of international law) of an existing state or non-self-governing territory. See for example Rosalyn Higgins, 'Post-modern Tribalism and the Right to Secession, comments', in C. Brölman, R. Lefeber, M. Zieck (eds.). *Peoples and Minorities in International Law* (Dordrecht, Martinus Nijhoff 1993), 29-33.

[5] Monty G. Marshall and Ted Robert Gurr, *Peace and Conflict 2003: A Global Survey of Armed Conflicts, Self-Determination Movements, and Democracy* (Center for International Development and Conflict Management, University of Maryland, 2003). Also available at <http://www.cidcm.umd.edu/peace_and_conflict.asp>.

[6] It should be pointed out that although it is normally members of an ethnic, religious or linguistic majority who control the state machinery and can therefore see their own language, religion or culture reflected or favoured in the operations of the state, there are in modern times well-known examples of a minority being politically dominant. The political exclusion of the non-white majority in apartheid South Africa is perhaps the most well-known. The subsequent preferences of the state for 'white languages' and the white 'race' had the effect of excluding or marginalising most non-white South Africans from a variety of employment opportunities and levels of power within an otherwise modern state structure. Not entitled to full citizenship, most South Africans were politically excluded in a state that was overtly non-neutral to an extreme degree. In fact, what occurred was the almost complete exclusion of the majority of the population from effective participation and representation in the public life of the state. It should nevertheless be added that there is nothing in international human rights to prevent a state from privileging the cultural, religious or linguistic preferences of the state (and its ethnic, religious or linguistic majority). In other words, human rights do not in themselves have the effect of automatically prohibiting such preferences, subject to one major proviso: no cultural, religious or linguistic preferences are permissible in international law if they amount to a violation of fundamental human rights such as freedom of religion, non-discrimination, etc.

Moreover, states controlled by a religious or ethnic minority – for example Iraq, South Africa during apartheid and Rhodesia – were almost always the scene of intrastate conflict.

This comparative study of intrastate conflicts indicates that such conflicts do not result from the mere presence of religious, linguistic or ethnic minorities. What is most remarkable when one considers human diversity in terms of its multitude of language, religious and cultural textures is that despite the perhaps tens of thousands minority or group combinations worldwide, there are in fact so few violent intrastate conflicts. For minorities – be they Catholics in Northern Ireland, Basques in Spain, Muslims in the Philippines, Albanians in Macedonia or Yugoslavia, or Kurds in Turkey – to rise up in arms against the state, there generally must be in place a relatively exceptional set of conditions given the actual absolute rarity of such conflicts in proportion to the number of minorities and other groups around the world.

When examining the thirty cases included in the study, some commonalities can be identified which explain where and why intrastate conflicts occur:

1. a similar type of setting;
2. a number of similar root causes underlying the tensions leading up to the eruption of violence; and
3. immediate events or 'sparks' which serve to ignite conflicts.

Understanding the setting, causes and characteristics of intrastate conflicts may help identify what needs to be kept in mind to ensure effective implementation of intrastate peace agreements.

2.1 The setting of intrastate conflicts

There is a particular setting which is common to most intrastate conflicts in Europe, Asia, Africa and other parts of the world. Intrastate conflicts almost always involve substantial minorities who are a majority in the part of the state in which they live or constitute at least a very high percentage of the population in a particular territory. The territory they occupy is also generally 'their' traditional or historical territory. These substantial minorities are almost never new arrivals in the state.[7]

---

[7] Among possible exceptions one can mention the Mohajirs in Pakistan and the Banyamulenge in the Democratic Republic of Congo, although one could argue that the presence of the Banyamulenge is actually quite long-standing. In both cases the minorities involved are very substantial.

Very small minorities or relatively recently established populations rarely revert to violence against the state in support of their demands. It is with larger, historically established minorities or other groups with some territorial identification that you find a setting with a potential for conflict under certain conditions. In all of the thirty intrastate conflicts studied, minorities constituted a substantial percentage of the population.

It seems clear that even in the setting just described, minorities generally will only revert to violence because of some additional long-standing sources of tension. The existence of a numerically substantial, traditional or territorially based minority is not in itself a cause of conflict, as demonstrated by the proportionally small number of actual intrastate conflicts worldwide.

2.2 Root causes of intrastate conflicts

[T]he state is more than a passive register of citizen preferences, and in policy deliberation state leadership and initiative are critical . . . Here we encounter another paradox: the state is the arbiter and broker of cultural difference, yet the state is unlikely to be wholly neutral in ethnic terms. In the distribution of power within their structures, states inevitably reflect the dominant groups within civil society (by class and interest, as well as ethnic derivation). As noted earlier, many states invest their national personality with the cultural attributes of the leading ethnic community. Even in countries with predominantly civic forms of nationalism, such as the United States, the argument that different communal segments (racial in this instance) were neutrally treated would be impossible to sustain historically. States are thus asked – figuratively speaking – to leap out of their own skins, to transcend their own cultural nature. Notwithstanding the intrinsic difficulties of this task, and the improbabilities of complete success, we contend that the larger requirements of statecraft – the imperative necessities of stability and comity within the polity – make partial realisation possible.[8]

Most of the thirty intrastate conflicts researched involved situations in which state authorities were involved for a long time in violations of the human rights of minorities, especially linguistic or religious rights, and rights affecting employment, resource allocation, land ownership or political rights.

The overview below shows the root causes of the various intrastate conflicts studied. They reflect grievances identified at the very preliminary stages, before conflicts erupted into violence:

---

[8] Crawford Young, 'Ethnic Diversity and Public Policy: An Overview', Occasional Paper No. 8, World Summit for Social Development, UNRISD, 1994.

State	Root causes of the intrastate conflicts
Chad (North-South)	Exclusion of and discrimination[9] against non-Muslim and southern ethnic groups in political institutions and army
DR of Congo (Banyamulenge)	Denial of citizenship, employment and associated rights which probably involve in many instances discrimination on the basis of ethnic origins
Cyprus	Move to weaken minority provisions, autonomy/power-sharing agreement favouring Turkish minority and attempted integration of the country with Greece
Ethiopia (Eritrea)	Denial of right to self-determination, discrimination in terms of language and ethnic preferences against Eritrean minority, abolition of federal/autonomy arrangements
France (New Caledonia)	Discrimination in use of indigenous languages by government authorities, extinguishment of traditional land and customary rights (constituting discrimination on the basis of language/ethnic origins)
India (Nagaland)	Unilateral Indian revocation of planned autonomy in 'Nine-Point Agreement', discrimination in government employment policies, loss of traditional land rights and resource use
Indonesia (Aceh)	Refusal to implement promised autonomy (federalism), discrimination in terms of use of Acehnese language in most public institutions, under-representation of Acehnese in public institutions in their region, transmigration[10] and land policies that discriminate against Acehnese

---

[9] What constitutes discrimination under international treaties should be explained briefly. Contrary to popular misconceptions, not all distinctions on the ground of religion, language, race and other characteristics are prohibited in international human rights treaties. While there is slightly different wording used in various decisional bodies such as the European Court of Human Rights or the United Nations Human Rights Committee, among others, the general approach is largely the same: for example, a state's religious, linguistic or racial preferences which have the effect of denying, excluding or disadvantaging individuals because of their religion, language or race would be deemed discriminatory only if it is pursued for an illegitimate purpose, or is in the circumstances unjustified or disproportionate to the objectives sought. Thus, the United Nations Human Rights Committee concluded that the exclusive use of English as the only language permitted under the Namibian constitution and legislation was discriminatory in not permitting the use of Afrikaans by local administrative authorities, and a breach of Article 26 of the International Covenant on Civil and Political Rights, in the absence of any reasonable justification for such an exclusive language preference (UN Human Rights Committee, Communication No. 760/1997, *Diergaardt v. Namibia*, views of 25 July 2000). For a more detailed look as to what constitutes discrimination in international law, see Fernand de Varennes, *Language, Minorities and Human Rights* (Dordrecht/Boston/London, Martinus Nijhoff 1996), Chapter 4.

[10] Indonesia and a number of other states where ethnic conflicts erupted had policies by which large numbers of individuals were transferred, usually, from more populous parts of the

State	Root causes of the intrastate conflicts
Indonesia (East Timor)	Denial of right to self-determination, discrimination in terms of use of local languages in most public institutions, under-representation of Timorese in public institutions in their region
Indonesia (Kalimantan)	Loss of traditional native land rights, without adequate compensation, discriminatory under-representation of Dayaks and Malay groups in public institutions, transmigration and resource policies[11] that discriminate against local groups
Indonesia (West Papua)	Denial of right to self-determination, discrimination in terms of use of local languages in most public institutions, under-representation of Papuans in public institutions in their region, transmigration and resource policies that discriminate against local Papuans
Iraq (Kurds, Shi'a)	Discrimination in language and government employment policies, denial of right to vote and participate in public life (democratic governance), discriminatory expropriation of land (mainly Kurds) and transmigration
Israel (Palestine)	Denial of right to self-determination, extreme discriminatory practices in terms of employment, access to public services, land ownership, transmigration programme (settlements in Occupied Territories)
Italy (South Tyrol)	Discrimination against German-speaking minority in terms of language use by public authorities during Mussolini regime, transmigration efforts via 'industrialisation' of South Tyrol, discrimination in most categories of state employment prior to autonomy arrangements

country to less densely inhabited areas. Sometimes presented as steps to assist the development of less advanced regions, these policies often had disastrous consequences, as they generally meant that members of the ethnic or religious majority, with government support, swamped areas to such an extent that local population, usually indigenous, would lose ownership and use of traditional lands, often without appropriate compensation if any. Additionally, the economic benefits associated with these 'transmigration' population movements within a state seldom flowed to the minority or indigenous populations which were gradually marginalised.

[11] Closely linked, though not always, to transmigration programmes are state policies which, in the name of development, nationalise or extinguish traditional resources uses or rights of minorities and indigenous populations. In Kalimantan, for example, the government of Indonesia effectively extinguished the traditional customary rights of the indigenous Dayaks and others in order to grant vast land-holdings to corporations involved in rice, oil palm and rubber plantations. This re-allocation of natural resources also had a clearly discriminatory impact on the basis of ethnic origins or even race, in the sense that the beneficiaries of these resource policies were almost always Javanese or others linked to them, whilst the Dayaks for their part usually lost any legal title or use of traditional resources and land.

State	Root causes of the intrastate conflicts
Lebanon (Muslims)	Discrimination in terms of access to certain categories of employment for Muslim group, ultimate political control guaranteed to Christians, despite Muslims becoming majority (discrimination on the basis of religion)
Macedonia (Albanians)	Exclusion of Albanian language from use in most national institutions (discrimination), huge under-representation of ethnic Albanians from a number of categories of employment in state institutions, refusal to set-up an Albanian language university (discrimination on the basis of language/ethnic origins)
Mexico (Chiapas)	Discriminatory language policies, extinguishment of traditional land rights, vast under-representation of Maya groups in public institutions
Moldova (Transnistria)	Initial replacement of Russian language by Romanian (Moldovan) in most areas of public administration (discrimination on the basis of language/ethnic origins), increasing exclusion of Russian speakers from various public employment opportunities
Morocco (Western Sahara)	Denial of right to self-determination; exclusion from main public service positions, lost of land rights and control over resources (discrimination on the basis of ethnic origins)
Myanmar (Karen and others)	Loss of promised federalism/autonomy arrangements, discrimination involving language policies and employment in state institutions, loss of traditional land rights
Niger (Tuaregs)	Non-recognition of right to use language of Tuaregs by public authorities, under-representation of Tuaregs in public service positions and loss of traditional land usage rights (discrimination on the basis of language/ethnic origins)
Pakistan	Discrimination as to use of language by state authorities
East Pakistan – Bangladesh	Denial of right to participate in public life
Philippines (Moros)	Historical land and transmigration programmes that discriminated in favour of Christian settlers, loss of traditional land rights and forms of autonomy, transmigration programme favouring Christians, under-representation of Muslims in most categories of public service (discrimination on the basis of language/religion/ethnic origins)
Rhodesia	Denial of right to vote and participate in public life (democratic governance), extreme discriminatory practices against Black majority, including denial of right to vote, land ownership, various categories of employment, etc.
South Africa (apartheid regime)	Denial of the right to vote and participate in public life (democratic governance), extreme discriminatory practices against Black majority, including denial of right to vote, land ownership, various categories of employment, etc.

State	Root causes of the intrastate conflicts
Spain (Basques)	Discrimination in terms of use of Basque language by government authorities and violations of freedom of expression in relation to use of Basque language during Franco era, abolition of previous autonomy arrangements
Sri Lanka (Tamils)	Discrimination in terms of use of Tamil language by government authorities, discriminatory quota system for admission to university, discriminatory employment policies against Tamil minority and transmigration programme which favoured Sinhalese majority
Sudan (South)	Forced Arabisation (discrimination) of southern minorities, violations of freedom of religion and discrimination on the basis of religion and language against southern populations in term of employment, use of language, religion, etc.
Turkey (Kurds)	Discriminatory language policies which discriminated against Kurds in areas of state services (public education, etc.), violations of freedom of expression in relation to private use of Kurdish, discriminatory land ownership and expropriation activities
United Kingdom (Northern Ireland)	Widespread exclusion of Catholic minority from state and private employment categories, discriminatory housing and voting rules
Yugoslavia (Kosovo)	Discrimination in terms of use of Albanian language by government authorities, discrimination in state employment (including public hospitals) and public housing, abolition of previous autonomy arrangements

The above overview illustrates that states that are the scene of intrastate conflicts tend to have a number of similar practices which persist over a long period of time. Among the most prevalent root causes of intrastate conflicts mentioned above are, in decreasing order:

1. Discrimination in access to various categories of employment and other opportunities, usually linked to language policies that unjustifiably disadvantage or exclude individuals from the linguistic minority;[12]
2. Discriminatory expropriation or extinguishment of traditional land ownership rights, often in combination with transmigration programmes that tend to disadvantage members of the minority in question;[13]

---

[12] Ethiopia, France, India, Indonesia, Iraq, Italy, Macedonia, Mexico, Moldova, Myanmar, Niger, Pakistan, Philippines, Rhodesia, South Africa, Spain, Sri Lanka, Sudan, Turkey, Yugoslavia.

[13] Chad, France, India, Indonesia, Iraq, Israel, Italy, Mexico, Morocco, Myanmar, Niger, Philippines, Rhodesia, South Africa, Sri Lanka, Sudan, Turkey.

3. Discrimination in terms of exercise of right to vote or right to participate in public life;[14]
4. Erosion or elimination of previously existing autonomy arrangement,[15] or denial of self-determination.[16]

These recurrent causes of tensions appear to constitute the initial deep-laid sources which eventually erupt into intrastate conflicts. Subsequent exploitation of tension by political entrepreneurs – individuals and parties which play the ethnic card in order to garner political support – and increasing levels of distrust and polarisation between those in control of the main state structure and substantial minorities that are excluded or severely disadvantaged by state authorities exacerbate these tensions.

From the thirty cases described above, it is also clear that once a conflict has started to slide down the path of violence, redress of the initial grievances in itself is seldom sufficient to stop the violence. This is illustrated in the case of Sri Lanka.

At independence in 1948, the Tamil minority leadership sought initially specific minority guarantees in the constitution, such as half the number of seats in the parliament or some other guarantees. By the early 1970s however, there was a segment of the Tamil population which became convinced that the Sri Lankan government considered them secondary citizens, as language and education policies in particular threatened the futures of many Tamil youths.

In May 1972, the first Tamil 'nationalist' movement, the Tamil United Front (TUF), arose in reaction to the discriminatory language policies of the government. The TUF's demands reflected the Tamil concern at the growing 'Sinhalisation' of the state, but they did not yet call for secession.

Insufficient changes in the language policies of the government led to a further radicalisation of some segments of the Tamil population with the establishment in May 1976 of the Tamil United Liberation Front (TULF). On 14 May 1976, the TULF declared that all attempts to cooperate with governments had failed and that only through a separate Tamil state could Tamil historical grievances be met.

The TULF won dramatic victories in the 1977 general election in northern and eastern constituencies. It continued to seek an accommodation with the government through parliamentary politics, but in the areas of language policies and minority protection it constantly encountered failure, with a subse-

---

[14] Chad, Congo, Indonesia, Iraq, Israel, Lebanon, Niger, Rhodesia, South Africa, Sudan, United Kingdom.

[15] Cyprus, Eritrea, India, Indonesia, Iraq, Myanmar, Philippines, Spain, Sudan, Yugoslavia.

[16] Eritrea, Indonesia, Israel, Morocco

quent and increased disillusionment. Small groups of more militant Tamil youth advocated increasingly armed force in order to achieve independence. The spiral into violence which had started with a first assassination in 1975 was followed in the 1980s by a dramatic intensification of armed conflict in Sri Lanka.

This timeline must be kept in mind when considering steps taken by the government to address the initial demands of the Tamils, mainly in the area of language. A new constitution in 1972 had further enraged – and radicalised – the Tamil minority since it made Sinhala the only official language. While these discriminatory measures were to be gradually withdrawn starting when the status of Tamil changed under the 1978 constitution and after the violence had in fact started, it was by then already too little too late. Nationalist and separatist movements had already emerged and gained strength before 1978 because of earlier government refusals to respect the rights of the Tamil minority in the area of language. Indeed, even today, according to some reports, Tamil speakers who are not fluent in Sinhalese are at a serious disadvantage in their dealings with the state in many parts of the country and one could argue that this is still discriminatory. Government language policies are not always implemented and many public institutions issue forms in Sinhala only or in Sinhala and English.

In light of the legacy of broken promises and untrustworthiness of political institutions in Sri Lanka, which tended to reflect the linguistic and other interests of the Sinhala-speaking Buddhist majority, it is widely recognised that there needs to be some form of autonomy for the Tamil minority with its concomitant control over political and legal mechanisms in order to achieve some sort of long-term peaceful solution to the conflict.

2.3 Immediate events ('sparks') precipitating violence

While there are root causes that in a sense provide the explosive environment which makes it likely a violent conflict will erupt, they are a backdrop against which more immediate events may serve as a catalyst, or spark, for the actual eruption of armed struggle or violence.

For example, on 17 March 2004, media reports in Mitrovicë/Mitrovica in Kosovo of the drowning of three Albanian boys in the Serb-majority municipality of Zubin Potok because they were chased into the river by Serbs who had unleashed a dog on them – reports that ended up being false – ignited pre-existing tensions in the province. Escalating confrontations between Albanians and Serbs led to gunfire battles, lobbing of grenades and seven dead, with subsequent clashes over a few days and the destruction of more than a hundred homes in Kosovo.

While the incorrect reporting of the drowning of the boys could be described as the immediate cause of this particular upsurge in conflict, it is necessary to properly contextualise the incident. The resort to armed fighting along an ethnic fault line was only possible due to the legal limbo in which Kosovo finds itself, where both the Serbian and Albanian populations can claim a number of their rights are being usurped or at least suspended until the final status of Kosovo is determined. With an Albanian majority in the province unable to assert political control over Kosovo because it is under the continued tutelage of the United Nations Interim Administration Mission in Kosovo (UNMIK) – which one could argue is in breach of their democratic rights if not the right of self-determination – and the Serbian minority being subjected to acts of intimation, violence and sensing it is extremely vulnerable to potential discrimination and exclusion if the Albanian majority were to rule unimpeded, there is an environment created by these breaches of rights which lends itself to further explosions of violence by unpredictable incidents such as the drowning as long as the root causes for the tensions are not remedied.

Similarly, the events of Bloody Sunday were not the underlying cause for the resurgence of the Irish Republican Army (IRA) in its campaign to eject the British authorities from Northern Ireland. While this incident, or spark, polarised the population along sectarian – essentially though not completely Catholic/Protestant – lines served as an impetus to the cause of the IRA, it did not of itself create the irredentist movement.

Bloody Sunday refers to the events that took place in Derry on the afternoon of Sunday 30 January 1972. A Northern Ireland Civil Rights Association march had been organised to protest against the continuation of internment without trial in Northern Ireland, in breach of the basic human rights of those interned, as well as other policies by public authorities which discriminated against members of the Catholic minority. As thousands of men, women and children took part in the march, it was prevented from entering the city centre by members of the British army. While there is still some controversy over the actual events during that day, the soldiers – insisting they had come under gun attack – shot dead thirteen unarmed men.

This spark led to an escalation which continues to this day, but the situation in Northern Ireland was already ripe for a violent conflict. This can be seen in the environment which existed prior to 1972. Up to 1971, the non-Catholic majority controlled the legal institutions of Northern Ireland: until recently, of the seven High Court judges, six were Protestant and one Catholic, a pattern repeated at all levels of the court down to Crown prosecutors, even sheriffs and clerks of the peace were it seems almost all Protestant. The security forces responsible for policing were also almost exclusively Protestant, as were the upper echelons of the administration of the state: senior administrative staff were usually 90-98 percent Protestant.

Even the right to vote was not permitted in a non-discriminatory way in Northern Ireland. In municipalities, which controlled important areas such as public housing and other career opportunities, some individuals could vote up to six times if they had businesses of a certain value – and most of these happened to be owned by Protestants. There was also until the end of the 1960s at the level of some municipal elections another restriction limiting to two or three the number of adults who could vote under the same household. As Catholics tended to be poorer and with more children, in practice this regulation tended to exclude more Catholics from the right to vote since it was more frequent to have young Catholic adults staying at home for longer periods of time. Through these and other techniques, it was possible for example to have a town with a Catholic majority like Londonderry/Derry – Northern Ireland's second largest municipality – controlled by a non-Catholic city council. The one person one vote rule for municipal elections was only approved in 1969.

These, with other examples of violations of basic human rights of the minority, were the underlying causes for the emergence of tension which ultimately exploded in uncontrollable violence. Indeed it was in reaction to these human rights violations that the civil rights movement emerged in the 1960s leading up to demonstrations and marches towards the late 1960s. Other violations of rights of the Catholic minority occurred when state authorities reacted to the civil rights movements after 1968 by adopting internment without trial and interrogation techniques, which would eventually be deemed as torture or inhumane and degrading treatment of Irish nationalists. Then followed the killing of demonstrators as the spark which ignited the conflict, followed by shootings by the IRA, and the spiral into war had begun in earnest. Yet the conflict needed the underlying root causes of decades of discrimination against the Catholic minority for more extremist elements to take benefit of the spark provided by the Bloody Sunday deaths.

3. INTRASTATE PEACE AGREEMENTS: ADDRESSING THE ROOT CAUSES OF INTRASTATE CONFLICTS

[It] is not difficult to establish that violations of the rights of free exercise [of religion] and non-discrimination intensify conflict in divided multi-ethnic societies, nor to project with reasonable confidence that the observance and implementation of those norms will serve to reduce conflict.[17]

---

[17] David Little, 'Belief, Ethnicity and Nationalism', U.S. Institute of Peace, 1996, available at <http://www.usip.org/religionpeace/rehr/belethnat.html> (2 August 2006).

Most of the thirty intrastate conflicts examined that have ended or dramatically abated involved peace agreements which provided for autonomy,[18] outright independence[19] or even de facto separation.[20] Most of the other peace agreements include provisions for protecting the rights of the (usually minority) group involved in the conflict. This normally takes the form of provisions enshrined in the constitution or specific rights legislation, mostly dealing with language use or religion and the prohibition of discrimination in specific areas of contention.

The focus on autonomy as one of the preferred means to resolve intrastate conflicts can be explained by the direct relationship between the root sources of tension of most conflicts and the type of measures needed to address them.

Autonomy arrangements directly address the asymmetry of power between the dominant group and a minority in a conflict, and the latter's usual underrepresentation and weakness in terms of political and public life involvement as well as vulnerability to discriminatory practices. Autonomy is often the preferred formula for conflict resolution in intrastate peace agreements because it constitutes a power-sharing formula which in effect gives a group the structural and political control with which it may protect itself against the often discriminatory practices of state authorities.

Where, as in most cases, autonomy takes a territorial form, it enables a group to form a de facto majority in a sub-unit of the state, thereby exercising effective control on the levels of government in the sub-unit, allowing it to occupy there a prominent, controlling position in political and public life, and thus ensuring that its interests are reflected in the linguistic, religious or cultural preferences of that level of government. If effectively put into place with adequate powers, autonomy subtracts from (usually) majority control the most contentious issues which state authorities were unable, or even unwilling, to address previously: transmigration programmes which favour the dominant group(s) and tend to discriminate against the minority by extinguishing or improperly compensating for their lost land rights; discrimination in terms of use of language by state authorities with resultant disadvantages for the minority in terms of access to employment, educational and other opportunities, etc. Autonomy can, in other words, permit the new local authorities to stop or limit the most damaging policies of central authorities. It permits the accommodation of the claims of minorities while maintaining the unity of the state.

---

[18] France (New Caledonia), India (Nagaland), Indonesia (Aceh), Italy (South Tyrol), Mexico (Chiapas), Philippines (Moros), Spain (Basques), Sudan (Southern minorities), United Kingdom (Northern Ireland).

[19] Eritrea, East Timor, East Pakistan (Bangladesh).

[20] Cyprus, Moldova, Yugoslavia.

Provisions in the constitution or in legislation to protect the rights of minorities serve a similar purpose, though in a more diluted form. For members of a minority, rights represent limits to what the majority, which overwhelmingly control state authorities, may impose. Freedom of religion, freedom of expression, non-discrimination based on language, religion, race or ethnic origin, the rights of minorities to use their own language among themselves and to practice their religion and enjoy their culture, are all protections against unjust or unfair ethnic preferences of the majority controlling the state. The protection of rights, either alone or in combination with autonomy arrangements, is often a prominent and almost indispensable feature in peace agreements.[21] These thus act in preventing state authorities from (1) imposing the characteristics of the majority on the minority against its will; (2) restricting the expression of linguistic, religious or cultural characteristics among members of a minority; or (3) using unreasonable or unjustified distinctions when laying down conditions for the accessibility to services, privileges and benefits provided or allowed by the state.

4. THE IMPLEMENTATION PROBLEM: STATE AUTHORITIES' RESISTANCE TO IMPLEMENTING INTRASTATE PEACE AGREEMENTS

Most of the peace agreements in the thirty cases examined were not (fully) implemented. The main obstacle to implementation has been the resistance or outright refusal of state authorities to proceed with political settlements which required autonomy arrangements or compliance with the international legal obligation of self-determination.[22]

The rebel or insurgent movements are usually required under peace agreements to cease their armed confrontation against the authority of the state and in some cases disarm or at least symbolically disarm and renounce violence. In return, state authorities must 'reward' them by granting autonomy over a territory or sharing power in a way which the group finds acceptable. In practice however, state authorities find it difficult to divest themselves of political power.

---

[21] See generally Christine Bell, *Peace Agreements and Human Rights* (Oxford, Oxford University Press 2001).

[22] This has occurred for example at various times in Ethiopia, India, Indonesia, Iraq, Israel, Morocco, Myanmar, Philippines, Rhodesia, South Africa, Spain, Sudan, and the United Kingdom. There is of course always the argument that 'it's the other side which failed first', as shown in the recent travails of the Belfast ('Good Friday') Peace Agreement. For the purposes of this chapter, I have considered whether there has been a breach of the actual commitments contained in an agreement, instead of the 'spirit' of a text or some other claimed misbehaviour.

In most cases, there is a deep-rooted feeling of distrust between the two sides: since most conflicts involve a complete failure of dialogue or compromise between state authorities and insurgents and violence is used in order to achieve a political and structural re-alignment of the state, such a distrust is quite understandable.

Usually, peace agreements tend to fail because state authorities balk at autonomy arrangements. Human rights provisions and other provisions dealing with the protection of minorities do not tend to be opposed to the same extent by governments, and have a greater record of full implementation.

In many cases, agreements have tended to fall apart when the time came to fully implement autonomy arrangements or the right to self-determination.[23] I do not wish to engage in any apportionment of 'blame': the research only serves to identify difficulties in the implementation of autonomy arrangements in intrastate conflicts because of the unique nature of such arrangements for state authorities.

In addition to the mutual lack of trust, state authorities must contend with the following:

- the perception of rewarding unlawful violence;
- having to negotiate and make concessions to so-called brigands or terrorists;
- incompetence or ineffectiveness in solving the insurgency;
- loss of political and in some cases legal control over part of the state;
- accusations of splitting the state or of being unable to defend its integrity or sovereignty;
- challenges by other segments of the political spectrum which may present members of the government that have negotiated the autonomy arrangement as 'traitors to the nation';
- fear of the government losing upcoming elections because of portrayal as weak and ineffective militarily in handling the conflict;
- election of new government determined to handle insurgency with 'stronger resolve' and to protect integrity of the state;
- the involvement of third parties to supervise the implementation of a peace agreement – while usually presented in conflict resolution circles as a desirable mechanism – can be portrayed as a needless and uninformed intervention in a state's internal affairs. Most rejections of third party involvement come from state authorities.

---

[23] Ethiopia, India, Indonesia, Iraq, Israel, Mexico, Morocco, Philippines, Sri Lanka, Sudan, the United Kingdom.

All or a combination of the above have played prominent roles in practically all of the autonomy arrangements which have failed to be fully implemented. In other words, while there was initially an agreed upon formula to end the conflict, the above factors subsequently contributed to derailing the accepted commitments which had been agreed upon by the parties as part of the solution to end the violence.

At the end of the day, the fundamental compromises involved in most peace agreements rely on the willingness of state authorities to divest themselves of some of their political authority. Due to their often complete dependence on the willingness or ability of governments to fulfil their promises, autonomy arrangements are likely hostage to the prevailing political climate and thus susceptible to its vagaries, such as might constitute upcoming elections where the unpopularity of the content of autonomy arrangements might become an electoral issue with members of the majority strongly opposed to it. It is often expected therefore that governments avoid full implementation of autonomy arrangements, arguing that insurgents have failed to disarm on time, been involved in criminal activities, have attacked government troops, etc.

Other conclusions from the examination of the thirty cases studied are:

1. The level of violence in an intrastate conflict usually falls soon after the conclusion of a peace agreement.[24]
2. Adoption of human rights and other provisions to protect minorities against dominant groups tends to ensure that violence does not subsequently re-escalate to the same level, especially if these provisions specifically address linguistic or religious grievances that were at the root of tensions leading to conflict.
3. Complete cessation of hostilities usually only occurs once full implementation of a peace agreement takes place, especially where this involves putting into place an autonomy arrangement.
4. Failure by state authorities to implement promised and effective autonomy often creates even greater mistrust and polarisation.
5. The worst case scenario involves a failure of state authorities to fully implement an autonomy arrangement coupled with a failure to adopt expected or promised human rights and other provisions to protect minorities. This combination tends to create conditions where the conflict will not only re-appear, but potentially become even more violent.

---

[24] Most peace agreements, at least in the immediate, dramatically lower the level of intensity in most of the cases observed, especially Ethiopia, India, Indonesia, Iraq, Israel, Morocco, Philippines, Rhodesia, South Africa, Spain, Sudan and the United Kingdom.

What is noticeable and deserves to be highlighted is that many of the 'concessions' made by state authorities in the peace agreements studied are not really concessions at all. In most cases studied, the groups opposing state authorities were victims of discriminatory policies and in the initial stages were demanding mainly non-discriminatory practices in areas of language use, job allocation, recognition of traditional land rights, etc. It was more often than not state ignorance of what are the rights of minorities in these areas that led to increased tensions and eventually to violence. Even today, it appears many governments are not fully aware of the rights to which persons belonging to minorities in particular are entitled under international human rights law, and thus mistakenly believe they are making concessions to insurgents when in fact they are only applying existing or emerging rights standards.[25]

5. Concluding Remarks

Intrastate conflicts do not exist in a vacuum. As shown above, one can identify some measures which help to stop violence by addressing the root causes of these conflicts. Most cases of successful peace agreements, at least in terms of bringing down the level of violence, include measures to guarantee the protection of the group involved in an intrastate conflict against state authorities. Such measures play a considerable role in addressing and responding to ethnic tensions. It is generally when minority members are subjected to discrimination or cannot obtain what might be considered 'fair' from public authorities to the degree appropriate to the strength of their relative numbers and their territorial concentration that a situation of ethnic conflict develops. Most intrastate conflicts are reactions to state policies of discrimination and political exclusion affecting substantial minorities. It is when the state is not neutral that many minorities and other groups seek the protection of 'autonomy', by which they can redress areas of grievances often described as 'minority rights', 'social and

---

[25] The human rights of minorities are fairly well elaborated in documents such as the UN Declaration on the Rights of Persons Belonging to National or Ethnic, Religious or Linguistic Minorities, the Framework Convention on the Protection of National Minorities; the Oslo Recommendations Regarding the Linguistic Rights of National Minorities, The Hague Recommendations regarding the Education Rights of National Minorities, and the Lund Recommendations on the Effective Participation of National Minorities in Public Life. They provide guidance as to the linguistic, religious and cultural elements in state practices that have to be understood and in some cases tempered in order to find that necessary balance to prevent ethnic conflicts. See also generally on the issue of the use of language by state authorities, Fernand de Varennes, *Language, Minorities and Human Rights* (The Hague, Martinus Nijhoff 1996).

economic justice', 'indigenous rights', 'nationalist aspirations' or 'self-determination'.

Often it appears that when a conflict has started down the path of violence, redressing the initial grievances may no longer be enough. Since there is usually before the eruption of conflict a period of attempts at finding some legal or political solutions to existing tensions, the path of armed struggle is usually only reverted to by radicalised segments of the minority population which have concluded that the initial demands will never be met by existing state structures and political mechanisms.

Autonomy arrangements thus appear as a preferred means for addressing these grievances in a general climate of distrust and animosity. They provide a form of political and legal control which gives substantial minority groups the tools to deal with the main matters of contention – including language and religious preferences, land and resource ownership, and employment – in a way which helps to avoid past discriminatory practices by state authorities.

One of the main lessons from the more successful peace agreements seems to be that policies of respect of the rights of minorities, of accommodation and autonomy are likely to contribute to peace. As UN Secretary-General Kofi Annan indicated in his Agenda for Peace presented on 17 June 1992 to the General Assembly, the threat of ethnic, religious, social, cultural or linguistic strife cannot be solved unless we address the 'deepest causes of conflict: economic despair, social injustice, and political oppression.'[26]

Where autonomy has been fully – and generously – implemented, intrastate conflicts have tended to disappear, and separatist sentiments along with them.

There appears to be one major difficulty which constitutes a daunting challenge for the success of peace agreements. The successful and full implementation of autonomy arrangements is dependent on the goodwill and willingness of state authorities to take the necessary steps. This is inherently difficult for many governments, as they fear to be seen by some as being weak, or accused of being unable to protect the integrity of the state, of bowing to so-called brigands or terrorists or of lack of political leadership. Changes in the political climate may also make it difficult for governments to implement promises they made in peace agreements.

---

[26] An Agenda for Peace: Preventative Diplomacy, Peacemaking and Peace-keeping, Report of the Secretary-General, UN Doc. A/47/277-S/2411 (1992).

Chapter III

REFLECTIONS ON IMPLEMENTATION MECHANISMS OF SELECTED AUTONOMY, SELF-RULE AND SIMILAR ARRANGEMENTS

John Packer[*]

1. INTRODUCTION

This chapter considers the implementation mechanisms in a selection of existing autonomy and self-rule agreements. Many exist, but this selection mainly draws from my own personal knowledge and experience. As such, this does not pretend to be broad or coherent. Rather, it aims merely to consider some cases and then to draw some lessons. No doubt a scientific approach would yield a better result.[1]

Before proceeding, some terminological matters require clarification. Some time ago when I was in Barcelona, I was asked to speak about implementation mechanisms of the right to self-determination. My short answer was that at the international level there are none.[2] I could say something similar about this exercise, because neither autonomy nor self-rule are stipulated as entitlements in international law and so there are no formal implementation mechanisms at the level of international law or more generally in international relations.

---

[*] Independent Consultant; Principal Investigator and Project Coordinator, Initiative on Conflict Prevention through Quiet Diplomacy, Human Rights Internet.

[1] One such current effort is the International Research Project on Regional Autonomy of Ethnic Minorities, which is being carried out jointly by the Center for International Conflict Resolution at Columbia University, the Department of Peace and Conflict Resolution at Uppsala University, Hong Kong University of Science and Technology, and the State Ethnic Affairs Commission of the People's Republic of China, in conjunction with the Office of the OSCE High Commissioner on National Minorities.

[2] For a written version of my more substantial and reasoned answer, see John Packer, 'Considerations on Procedures to Implement the Right to Self-Determination', in M.C. van Walt van Praag and O. Seroo (eds.), *The Implementation of the Right to Self-Determination in a Globalized World: A Contribution to Conflict Prevention and Resolution* (Barcelona, Centre UNESCO de Catalunya 1999), 149-165.

M. Boltjes (ed.), *Implementing Negotiated Agreements*
© 2007, Kreddha International and T·M·C·ASSER PRESS, The Hague, The Netherlands

To discuss implementation mechanisms raises the question of what one means. For the purposes of our discussion, I mean a general support for the inclusion (and follow-through) of autonomy arrangements within agreements, whether expressed or implied. I am interested in the instrumental use of certain arrangements in such agreements. In a broad sense, the way in which this is accomplished often includes actors and pressures outside the agreement itself – forms, influences and so forth that might be formal or informal, but which bear upon the implementation of the autonomy arrangements. Essentially, 'follow-through' is about doing what one says, or what one commits oneself to do, so applying agreed standards or otherwise acting according to one's undertaking. I also mean, especially for the purposes of the cases to which I will refer in a little more detail, those specific mechanisms expressly incorporated in an existing agreement. These should be analysed and understood as seeking not only the practical application of an arrangement, but also the generation of the confidence and trust necessary to make it work smoothly, endure and become 'normal'.

What does one mean by 'autonomy' and by 'self-rule'? That is more complex. Let me refer briefly to the views of one expert, Markku Suksi, a professor of international law at the Åbo Akademi University in Finland, who has defined autonomy roughly as 'mechanisms that promote organisational or institutional correspondence between the rulers and the ruled by facilitating the self-government in one way or another of those individuals that belong to a specific group.'[3] He observes that autonomy introduces the idea of asymmetry in government or governance in terms of institutional organisation and distinguishes this from federalism where states are predominantly organised in symmetrical ways. I follow a less formal and limiting understanding of autonomy arrangements. I think one can realise effective and substantial autonomy in a federal form, which is a distinction more about the nature of the constitution or the socio-political contract in the first place rather than about what power it distributes in effect. Professor Suksi also observes that autonomy and devolution[4] are not by definition disruptive of territorial integrity or national unity; indeed, to the contrary, they may contribute to stability and conflict resolution. Autonomy should be viewed as a practical solution to a practical problem that is available in certain situations where the more conventional rights construction (symmetrical, undifferentiated, and available to all) might not be sufficient to meet particular needs or demands. Finally, Professor Suksi goes on to speak about some other

---

[3] Markku Suksi, 'Concluding Remarks' in Markku Suksi (ed.), *Autonomy: Applications and Implications* (The Hague, Kluwer Law International 1998), 359.

[4] It is for me a different issue whether autonomy is achieved by means of power devolved 'down' from the centre or by means of a construction 'up' (e.g., a federacy) drawing the consent of constituent parts of the state. I will not here address this issue.

related ideas, which I just mention here, such as the links of governance, the idea of subsidiarity and notions of broader democracy. These are important contributors to the general politico-legal environment within which autonomies and self-governance arrangements may develop and function.

Autonomy, from my perspective, is just one construction for the division of jurisdiction within a state; it is primarily institutional and without prejudice to the subject-matter content of the jurisdictional division. What I mean is that we can set aside the subject-matter on which the power is to be focussed, for example education as a subject-matter domain or tourism as a subject-matter domain. How we divide up authority over education or tourism can be discussed in terms of the subject-matter. But autonomy is generally about the arrangements for the division of power. More precisely, it is usually about specific institutions and processes and less about specific subject-matters. It is often treated through the classic jurisdictional division between administrative, legislative and judicial spheres, and typically on a territorial basis. There are also autonomies of differing kinds and at different levels.[5] In other words, there is a matrix of possible kinds of autonomy within any state. How broad (i.e., which spheres or subject-matters are covered) and deep (i.e., single or multiple spheres and whether or not entrenched) are other variables which allow one to speak about conceptually 'thick' or 'thin' (or 'strong' or 'weak') autonomies.

How much the arrangement may be accepted and vigorously implemented does not in my experience turn on these variables. Rather, it is a matter of the specific design in the particular circumstances of a concrete situation its tailoring which determines its appropriateness and affects greatly its chance of success. As such, an apparently thin or weak autonomy may be appropriate if carefully tailored to a certain situation and thus work best. In this respect, I distinguish 'self-rule', which is by definition thicker and stronger insofar as it is less dependent; self-rule implies full legislative and executive authority, hardly (if at all) constrained. Self-rule may well be considered a form of autonomy, but it is the most far-reaching kind.

I first addressed autonomy in my own practical work in 1995 when I began to work with the then OSCE High Commissioner on National Minorities, Mr. Max van der Stoel.[6] He was involved in trying to avoid violent conflict erupt-

---

[5] For a review of these, see, e.g., Markku Suksi (ed.), *Autonomy: Applications and Implications* (The Hague, Kluwer Law International 1998), especially Hans-Joachim Heintz's chapter 'On the Legal Understanding of Autonomy' at 7-32.

[6] In fact, I first worked practically with the concept and claim of autonomy while at the United Nations where I worked on the situation in Iraq. The Kurds in Iraq had experienced first the granting and then the taking away of autonomy. This is a perfect example of failed implementation and inadequate security, which to this day inspires Kurdish mistrust of central Iraqi authorities and underlies current Kurdish demands for a new and specifically federal constitutional arrangement.

ing in Crimea because of disputes between various actors in the peninsula and central authorities as well as among actors within the peninsula itself: Crimean Tatars, other returned formerly deported peoples, the ethnic Ukrainian community (a minority in Crimea), and a substantial ethnic Russian population. The latter constitute a majority in Crimea but still a minority in Ukraine; some arrived only in the last two generations and others are indigenous to Crimea (or see it as their homeland).[7] There was the possibility of conflict not only between Crimea (the political entity territorially defined) and the state of Ukraine (which was reflected in Kiev), but also within Crimea itself, principally between Crimean Tatars and the rest of the population. This led to a dispute over whether to maintain, enlarge or curtail (even dissolve) autonomy within the constitutional framework of Ukraine. In this context, the High Commissioner asked me the seemingly simple question 'What is the content of autonomy in international law?' He gave me twenty-four hours to reply. My initial answer was short: autonomy has no determined content in international law, and so it may be almost anything and it may be almost nothing. Reflecting on some possible parameters, I then considered what might *exceed* autonomy. I looked at the minimum requirements for statehood on the assumption that autonomy must be less than a separate state, which I still believe is a good starting point. The minimum requirement of a state, if we think about it historically, is the power to raise an army, the power to print money, the determination of citizenship (which, at least in our contemporary world, fundamentally defines the population), and the determination of territorial borders. In other words, it is defence and security, monetary policy, the definition of the population, and maintenance of frontiers (bounding defined territory). In international relations, this almost amounts to the definition of the state – of any state.[8] So an autonomy arrangement within a state seems logically to have to be less than this.

In fact, there are all sorts of exceptions in real life. For example, in Montenegro today they use the Euro rather than the Dinar of the state of Serbia and

---

[7] For an account and modest analysis of the High Commissioner's engagement in Crimea and specifically the negotiation of the constitutional terms of the Autonomous Republic of Crimea, see John Packer, 'Autonomy Within the OSCE: The Case of Crimea' in Suksi, *Autonomy: Applications and Implications*, 295-316. For more general accounts of the situation of Crimean autonomy, see Gwendolyn Sasse, 'Conflict-Prevention in a Transition State: The Crimean Issue in Post-Soviet Ukraine', *Nationalism and Ethnic Politics*, Vol. 8, No. 2 (2002), 1-26; and Doris Wydra, 'The Crimean Conundrum: The Tug of War Between Russia and Ukraine on the Questions of Autonomy and Self-Determination', *International Journal of Minority and Group Rights*, Vol. 10, No. 2 (2003), 111-130.

[8] According to Article 1 of the 1933 Montevideo Convention on the Rights and Duties of States, 'The state as a person of international law should possess the following qualifications: (a) a permanent population; (b) a defined territory; (c) government; and (d) capacity to enter into relations with the other states.'

Montenegro and they used the Deutsche Mark before Germany switched to the Euro. There are certainly parts of constituted states that maintain entirely their own international relations, even determining frontiers. For example, the treaty determining maritime and land frontiers between Switzerland and France along Lac Leman is actually a set of treaties between the Republic of France and the Republic (i.e., the Canton) of Geneva, because it is not within the gambit of the Swiss Confederation to determine the frontiers of any Canton. The Cantons, however titled, are clearly sub-state entities in international law. I am therefore contradicting my starting point, because autonomous and self-rule entities, such as the Swiss Cantons, in fact exercise elements of statehood. In other words, virtually everything is possible in the context of autonomy and self-rule; it is all an open question for negotiation.

To use another real example, the Province of Québec in Canada participates in international events and represents itself in some international organisations. For example, there are three entities of Canada represented in la Francophonie: Canada, the province of Québec and the province of Nouveau-Brunswick. A few years ago the summit of la Francophonie was hosted in the City of Québec, with the prime minister of Québec and also the prime minister of Canada *jointly* presiding. Due to the subject-matter of the organisation and these events, it was appropriate and even sensible in terms of the Canadian constitution for there to be a joint hosting. In this case, the powers (regarding culture, sports, etc.) overlap and are in fact shared. Such possibilities are therefore not only theoretical, but already exist in practice.

The diversity of situations and the range of possibilities and practices of autonomy and self-rule arrangements makes it difficult to generalise other than to observe that much is possible.[9] To get a better sense of this, it seems useful to review briefly a number of situations, and then try to reflect upon them with a view to drawing some conclusions on the nature of these arrangements and their implementation.

2. Selected Autonomy Arrangements and Their Implementation Mechanisms

2.1 **Crimea**

The autonomy arrangement regarding Crimea is expressly foreseen and entrenched in chapter X of the Constitution of Ukraine,[10] while its content is

---

[9] For one compilation of such arrangements, see Hurst Hannum (ed.), *Documents on Autonomy and Minority Rights* (Dordrecht, Martinus Nijhoff 1993).

[10] For the full text of the Ukrainian Constitution, as adopted on 28 June 1996, see <http://www.rada.kiev.ua/const/conengl.htm#r10> (2 August 2006).

found in the Constitution of the Autonomous Republic of Crimea,[11] which is adopted by the parliament of Crimea and then subject to approval by the Parliament of Ukraine.[12] This is a two-step constitutional arrangement. In fact there is no independence on the part of the Republic of Crimea to determine freely its own autonomy as the autonomy is fundamentally granted by Ukraine. This partly follows from the fact that, according to Article 2(2) of the constitution, Ukraine is a unitary state. The autonomy was not negotiated in terms of federalism, as if there were two equal parties: there is one sub-state entity which exists essentially on the good will of the authorities of Ukraine to accept within its constitutional framework a specified asymmetrical devolution of power. One may complain that even this is not exactly a devolution of power since Ukraine retains the right to change this arrangement (i.e., to abolish the autonomy).[13] From this perspective one might argue that the Crimean autonomy is quite weak and has very limited procedural or institutional elements to protect it against an activist Ukrainian parliament, insofar as the autonomy (which is territorial) is also subject to respect the laws of Ukraine. If any law in Ukraine should change with some effect on the Crimean autonomy, there is the presumption that the conflicting aspect of the autonomy must yield. In terms of the subject-matter content of the autonomy, it is limited to those matters described in Article 137 of the Ukrainian constitution, e.g., the regulation of agriculture, fishing and public works. Many important areas of life do not fall within the competences of the autonomy, such as judicial regulation, safety and security, and so forth. Of course, the debate about the extent of Crimean autonomy, especially its competences, continues; it is an evolving process.

Aside from the main aspects of the arrangement, which arise largely from the fact that 70 percent of the population is ethnic Russian, the territorial autonomy of Crimea does not address the situation of the Crimean Tatars, who comprise 10 percent of the existing population in Crimea and claim the whole peninsula as their homeland. Crimean Tatars speak their own language, have their own traditions and customs, and are predominantly Muslim in contra-distinction to the Christian Ukrainians, Russians and others who inhabit the peninsula. Forcibly deported by Stalin during the Second World War, only about half of the community has been repatriated since Gorbachev permitted returns at the very end of the Soviet period. But even if all of Crimean Tatars would be repatriated, they would remain a numerical minority in the territory of the penin-

---

[11] An unofficial English translation is on hand with the author. For the official text in the Russian language, see < http://www.rada.crimea.ua/index_konstit.html> (2 August 2006).

[12] See Article 135 of the Constitution of Ukraine.

[13] See, e.g., Markku Suksi who hints at this in his chapter 'On the Entrenchment of Autonomy' in Suksi, *Autonomy: Applications and Implications,* 151-171 at 161.

sula. So the demands of the Crimean Tatars for public use of their language, schools, return of properties, guaranteed public representation, and so forth, raise another set of questions, which are partly territorial (the peninsula being their homeland, they invoke claims over all of it) but also largely non-territorial in nature.[14] This invites some further specification in constitutional and other terms. For example, there is the possibility for some solution in the context of non-territorial or cultural autonomy to be conferred upon the Crimean Tatar community through Article 11 of the constitution of Ukraine, which acknowledges the existence of 'indigenous peoples' within Ukraine.[15] This possibility has yet to be clarified (or exploited) in terms of relevant legislation. Such legislation would not be entrenched, as it would likely only be ordinary legislation, alterable by subsequent ordinary legislation.[16] Still, it remains one means by which the particular situation of a discrete group within a territorial unit (itself already differentiated in terms of powers) could be afforded a special autonomous arrangement with respect to those matters which concern that group especially or alone. A complicating factor which has yet to be satisfactorily addressed arises from the fact that a large part of the Crimean Tatar community is neither citizen of Ukraine nor even resident in Ukraine. While the group maintains both socio-cultural and political organisation as a 'nation', with its own international pan-Crimean Tatar Council (*Kurulthai*), there is no formal recognition or role for it within the Ukrainian political order. One possibility might be for the Ukraine to recognise and permit the Council to play some role within the context of such cultural autonomy as the Crimean Tatars may eventually obtain, of course subject to the laws of the state.

While some matters can reasonably be devolved territorially to the Autonomous Republic of Crimea and other matters can be addressed through conferral of powers to discrete groups like the Crimean Tatars (territorially limited or not), there remain matters which are of national (i.e., Ukraine-wide) nature and

---

[14] The Crimean Tatar demands remain pressing, not least with respect to the return of their lands and property. For example, in the absence of almost any movement in the actual return of lands in the rich Greater Yalta region, Crimean Tatar frustration resulted in September 2003 in acts of self-help as groups of Crimean Tatars simply seized a number of plots of land (see Interfax Ukraine news agency (Kyiv) of 10 and 11 September 2003).

[15] Article 11 of the Ukrainian Constitution provides as follow: 'The State promotes the consolidation and development of the Ukrainian nation, of its historical consciousness, traditions and culture, and also the development of the ethnic, cultural, linguistic and religious identity of all indigenous peoples and national minorities of Ukraine.'

[16] One well-informed commentator has doubted this opportunity will be exploited, as she recounts the overall situation and the on-going frustration of the Crimean Tatars; see Natalya Belitser, 'The Constitutional Process in the Autonomous Republic of Crimea in the Context of Interethnic Relations and Conflict Settlement', at <http://www.iccrimea.org/scholarly/nbelitser.html> (2 August 2006).

importance and that, at the same time, affect the citizens of the peninsula as well as Crimean Tatars as a group. This might apply to development of the continental shelf along the Black Sea, or to security, defence and maintenance of frontiers. These matters are issues of state, which reside with the authorities in Kiev, both legislatively and in terms of the executive. While there are ordinary Crimean members of parliament in the Ukrainian parliament, the Crimean Tatars have argued for reserved seats (i.e., exclusively representing the Crimean Tatar community) in Kiev in order to have at least some say over these matters that affect them, perhaps even more than other Ukrainians. So far this has not been accommodated directly. But indirectly alliances with political parties have worked to ensure the Crimean Tatars two representatives (from a total of 450 deputies) in the Ukrainian parliament.

2.2 Macedonia

A quite different situation exists in Macedonia. The Framework Agreement agreed in Ohrid on 13 August 2001[17] is a combination of constitutional arrangements and autonomies devolved through agreed reform of ordinary legislation. It is politically notable that there is no express reference to autonomy, but in effect autonomies would result through a significant process of constitutionally entrenched symmetrical decentralisation which empowers localities. In a deeply divided country where the main groups live compactly in geographically defined territories, such decentralisation accommodates existing diversity in practical terms by allowing each local self-government unit the power of choice. To be more precise, although paragraph 1.2 of the Framework Agreement appears to reject autonomy arrangements by emphasising the 'unitary character' of the state and emphatically declaring that '[t]here are no territorial solutions to ethnic issues', paragraph 3 then prescribes substantial decentralisation of government which in fact grants the same degree of practical choice sought by those who might have favoured autonomy. Such decentralisation of the unitary state called 'Macedonia' in effect allows the ethnic Albanian population (and some other concentrated communities) essentially the same powers of autonomy by means of a different constitutional technique. In terms of subject-matters, competences have been conferred to local self-government units over exactly the affairs which are relevant to the concerned communities and for which they wish to have effective control (not just a say). Not only do the subject-matters cover important issues within the communities where minori-

---

[17] For the text of the Agreement, see <http://www.coe.int/t/e/legal_affairs/legal_co-operation/police_and_internal_security/OHRID%20Agreement%2013august2001.asp> (2 August 2006). The text is also reproduced in Appendix E.

ties actually live, but there is also agreement at the state level regarding representation of minorities within central institutions, use of the Albanian language and some other concerns.

The Framework Agreement includes a set of implementation mechanisms comprising constitutional amendments as well as legislative modifications. It also incorporates the commitment of the international community, including donors, to assist in the implementation. Under annex C of the agreement, implementation and confidence-building measures begin with a section on international support, which is especially important for, *inter alia*, the conduct of a reliable and credible census, for the conduct of free and fair elections and for the return of refugees and internally displaced persons in conditions of safety and security.

2.3 Gagauzia

Another agreed autonomy arrangement is that of Gagauzia (Gagauz Yeri) in Moldova.[18] Gagauzia has achieved a very substantial autonomy at least in terms of competences conferred. On the other hand, it is not well entrenched. According to Article 111(2) of the Moldovan constitution,[19] pursuant to which 'Special Autonomy Statutes' are adopted, the autonomy may be substantially altered, suspended or even revoked should three-fifths of the parliament of Moldova so decide. This follows conceptually from Article 1(1) of the Law on the Special Legal Status of Gagauzia *(Gagauz Yeri)*, which states: 'Gagauzia (Gaguaz Yeri) is an autonomous territorial entity with a separate status as a form of the self-determination of the Gagauz, forming an integral part of the Republic of Moldova.'[20] Nonetheless, what has been granted institutionally and in subject-

---

[18] For the text of the arrangement, see 'Law on the Special Status of Gagauzia (Gagauz Yeri)', Law No. 334-XIII adopted by the parliament of the Republic of Moldova on 23 December 1994 and promulgated by the President of Moldova on 13 January 1995 by Decree No. 10-R, reproduced in English translation by the European Commission for Democracy through Law in Document CDL (95) 11, 14 February 1995. For a fascinating record of the OSCE HCNM's visit to Moldova in 1994 and his encounter with, among others, a variety of political actors then negotiating the Gagauz Autonomy arrangement, see Stefan Troebst, 'Gospodin Max' in 'Moldova: The Visit of the OSCE High Commissioner on National Minorities to Gagauzia and Transnistria in December 1994; A Documentary Account', *European Yearbook on Minority Issues*, Vol. 3 (2003-2004), 129-159.

[19] For an English translation of the text of the Constitution of the Republic of Moldova, adopted on 29 July 1994, see European Commission for Democracy through Law, Document CDL (99) 38, 6 August 1999.

[20] Remarkably, this is a contingent determination, as Article 1(4) provides: 'In the event of a change in the status of the Republic of Moldova as an independent State, the people of Gagauzia shall have the right to external self-determination.'

matter jurisdiction constitutes a far-reaching autonomy, almost to the point that the central authorities in Chisinau can foreswear many responsibilities, which is a possibly dangerous situation. The arrangement benefits from institutional guarantees in terms of a constitutional court which constrains the powers of the state, and it follows the rule of law both with regard to implementation of the arrangement and also to its extent.

While territorial in its circumscription, the basis of the autonomy is essentially ethnic in its motivation. In fact, the community residing in the territory to which the autonomy applies is ethnically mixed, even if predominantly Gagauz. According to Article 5 of the Law on the Special Legal Status of Gagauzia the territorial delimitation can change over time, because the territory of the autonomy consists of all the localities where the proportion of the Gagauz population exceeds 50 percent.[21] Thus, if and as the composition or the will of the population changes, so will the territorial autonomy. This is an interesting and uniquely dynamic element of such an arrangement.

Article 12 of the same law outlines the subject-matter jurisdiction of the autonomous entity. This covers many competences, including budgetary and judicial powers, powers of taxation and security, territorial administration, and so forth. It even extends to foreign policy and relations 'with regard to matters affecting the interests of Gagauzia'. Indeed, to this extent it approaches but does not attain independence, since the central authorities retain the power to reel in the autonomy should it threaten vital interests of the state.

Other key elements of the arrangement include the requirement in Article 3 of the law that 'the official languages of Gagauzia shall be Moldovan, Gagauz and Russian'; pursuant to Article 18, the budget of Gagauzia 'shall consist of such receipts as shall be determined by the legislation of the Republic of Moldova and by the [Gagauz] People's Assembly', i.e., it will be negotiated; and the administration of justice is, according to Articles 20-22, to be implemented according to a system of shared responsibility and cooperative formulae.

Notwithstanding the very substantial and legally sanctioned autonomy in Gagauzia, Moldova is still struggling with the de facto separation of Transnistria. In this case, the discussion is constrained by the central authorities' apparent unwillingness to discuss the extent of de facto independence which has been achieved through the use of force, with the help of Russian Federation troops stationed on Moldovan soil. In contrast to the Gagauz autonomy, the Transnistrian one has no legal basis. A large problem of corruption, criminality, gun-running and so forth has caused the central authorities to scrutinise carefully matters of

---

[21] In fact, Article 5 prescribes rules according to which localities may hold referenda on whether to join or withdraw from Gagauzia and thus form part of (or not) the autonomy arrangement. This is a highly democratic provision.

security, public administration, justice, education and other subject-matter domains. In view of the preoccupying situation in Transnistria and also the situations of other autonomous areas, such as Taraclia, the international community has advanced a proposal to settle the situation in Moldova by transforming it into a federal state,[22] perhaps along asymmetrical lines.

2.4 Northern Ireland

Finally, one may note the situation in Northern Ireland as foreseen in the Good Friday Agreement of 1998,[23] negotiated by the governments of the United Kingdom and Ireland and signed in Belfast on 10 April 2001 pursuant to multi-party talks in Northern Ireland. As a matter of law it is a devolution arrangement whereby powers from the central authorities are, by their authority alone, distributed to the regional authority. These powers may, and have several times been, suspended and can be withdrawn. Substantively the arrangement grants important autonomy to the regional Northern Ireland assembly and government.

What strikes one most in reading this arrangement is that there is little reference to specific competences or subject-matter jurisdictions aside from the obviously pre-occupying issues of security.[24] Rather, the Good Friday Agreement is almost entirely about institutions and processes. The principal subject-matter jurisdictional issues which are mentioned concern personal security, safety and national security, including weapons decommissioning, public security, policing and the administration of justice – essential aspects of the rule of law. But there is almost nothing about such matters as education and there is only a little bit about linguistic diversity, mentioned broadly in terms of human rights and identity.

Much of the Good Friday Agreement concerns matters of implementation, with a specific chapter addressing validation, implementation and review. It also extensively deals with institutional safeguards which are vested in the con-

---

[22] See especially the 'Proposals and Recommendations of the mediators from the OSCE, the Russian Federation and Ukraine with regards to the Transdniestrian settlement' distributed to OSCE participating states at the request of the Bulgarian Chairmanship (OSCE doc. CIO.GAL/11/04, 13 February 2004). See also the negative reactions of informed commentators, in particular Vladimir Socor ('Russia's Special for the CIS: Federalism Model Tested in Moldova', *IASPS Policy Briefings: Geostrategic Perspectives on Eurasia*, No. 59, 9 April 2004) and the earlier energetic exchange of letters published in *The Wall Street Journal Europe* (especially the editions of 16 June and 5, 12 and 19 August 2003).

[23] The text of the Agreement is reproduced in Appendix A.

[24] There is also a chapter on Rights, Safeguards and Equality of Opportunity which both includes substantive entitlements (notably regarding economic, social and cultural rights) and addresses matters of process and institutional arrangements.

struction of certain new institutions. This is interesting, and in fact where the Agreement has broken down the reaction has been to establish yet another mechanism, an independent monitoring and compliance body (the Independent Monitoring Commission) agreed between the British and Irish governments.[25] Such a concentration on institutions and process reflects the fundamental issue of a lack of trust and confidence; the underlying subjects would be less problematical to address and resolve once trust and confidence could be established. This, in turn, might be enhanced by some greater attention to some subjects and the development of some practical experience in addressing them.

The Good Friday Agreement presents a veritable web of institutional implementation arrangements. It stands out not only in terms of the constitutional framework of internationally recognised authorities in the United Kingdom, by which Northern Ireland is internationally recognised to exist; but also in terms of the bi-state cross border institutions and the institutions established within Northern Ireland itself.

3. SOME OBSERVATIONS ON AUTONOMY ARRANGEMENTS AND IMPLEMENTATION MECHANISMS

First, irrespective of the specific option or formula which one may choose or devise, it is vital to understand and appropriately value the *normative framework* within which a regime may be developed and applied. For a stable, deliberative, open and prosperous society which recognises and accommodates its existing and evolving diversity, there must be a participatory democracy operating under the rule of law with full respect for human rights including minority rights. This general formula is broad in scope and can accommodate a variety of forms and institutions.

With regard to *options and choices*, several further observations may be made. In the context of the OSCE we confronted this challenge in many places every day. In response, the High Commissioner on National Minorities found it useful to have elaborated a set of guidelines or general recommendations to which we could refer parties (and ourselves) to think about some of their problems, note the variety of options known in the world, and consider the choices they might make.

---

[25] For the text of this Agreement (published in draft on 4 September 2003 but only signed on 25 November 2003), see <http://www.nio.gov.uk/draft_agreement_between_uk_government_and_government_of_ireland_establishing_imc.pdf> (2 August 2006). For the text of the law establishing the Independent Monitoring Commission, see the Northern Ireland (Monitoring Commission, etc.) Act 2003, given Royal Assent already on 18 September 2003, at <http://www.legislation.hmso.gov.uk/acts/acts2003/20030025.htm#1> (2 August 2006).

Of particular relevance to autonomy arrangements and other governance arrangements, we convened a group of internationally recognised independent experts who produced a booklet called the Lund Recommendations on the Effective Participation of National Minorities in Public Life.[26] While one does not find the word 'autonomy' in the document, it is evidently about autonomy. This was partly a matter of political pragmatism: the political reality at the time, if not still so, was that if the term 'autonomy' had been mentioned then a number of governments and other parties would have dismissed the document. Our position was and remains that the terminology is less important than the substance of the matter: essentially, we were interested in getting parties to discuss ways of governing, including distributing or sharing power, in pluralist societies within a democratic context. We were interested in the answer to the question 'How can one create the politico-legal space in which differing groups of people with differing interests, needs and aspirations can live together?' If one takes a quick look at the Lund Recommendations, the answer to the question is revealed essentially through a simple division between territorial and non-territorial arrangements, applied according to some general principles. Each one of these principles and subsequent recommendations is supported by an explanatory note with references to the international standards which underpin them. In this sense, there is nothing new advanced; no new standards are established. Rather, all that has been previously agreed has been systematised and expressed in an easily and understandable language, with some further specification. The general principles seem beyond contest as they are fully rooted in basic standards of international law and fundamental commitments to democratic governance.

The second and third parts of the Lund Recommendations, on participation in decision-making and on self-governance respectively, reflect two vectors of institutional arrangements. The first is the idea of creating sufficient political space for groups to have a meaningful *say* over governance in their own lives. Participation is the minimum idea of any process-oriented decision-making. The second idea of self-governance means to enjoy a degree of *control*. So the different vectors offer modes of having a say and modes of having control. For some groups and some issues, a say is quite sufficient. But with regard to some other matters, perhaps ones more vital for the group, a say is not sufficient. The

---

[26] For the full text of the Lund Recommendations and Explanatory Note (which are available free of charge in a number of languages), see <http://www.osce.org/documents/hcnm/1999/09/2698_en.pdf> (2 August 2006). See also John Packer, 'The origin and nature of the Lund Recommendations on the Effective Participation of National Minorities in Public Life', *Helsinki Monitor*, Vol. 11 (2002), 29-61; and Kristian Myntti, *A Commentary to the Lund Recommendations on the Effective Participation of National Minorities in Public Life* (Turku/Åbo, Institite for Human Rights, Åbo Akademi University 2001).

international standards specifically foresee this insofar as they provide the right to effective participation in decisions and areas of public life *vis-à-vis* matters not only affecting those persons, but especially matters which affect them principally or alone. From the perspective of governance, it seems most reasonable that only those affected should have a (substantial) say, if not control, over something which only affects them. For example, with regard to a purely linguistic issue for the Crimean Tatars, one may ask what on earth any authority in Kiev (or elsewhere) would be doing regulating that matter. Surely it is only a matter for the Crimean Tatars. How such say or control will be facilitated could be subdivided in terms of territorial and non-territorial dimensions.

At the end of the Lund Recommendations, there is a chapter on 'guarantees' which includes legal safeguards and remedies also at constitutional level. Part of the idea includes subsequent review. This responds to the challenge of states in transition. Of course, every state is 'in transition' in some way and to some degree. Notably, the United Kingdom has in the last decade undergone the greatest devolution and constitutional changes in five-hundred years of its history. Other states are also in transition to differing degrees. So periodic review of arrangements is appropriate for any living democracy.

While the booklet was intentionally drafted from an OSCE (i.e., European) perspective, it was drafted by independent experts from around the world, because we simply sought to include the most competent persons. This has yielded a set of recommendations with universal validity and considerable international resonance (at least as a point of reference).

4. Concluding Remarks

In the light of the discussion presented above, and on the basis of accumulated experience, the following concluding remarks may be useful.

1. For the treatment of these matters, good and *democratic governance is important*, if not sine qua non. One can discuss autonomy regimes in less than fully democratic societies; the willingness of central authorities to carve out such political space depends in large measure on the interests of the powerful and may be agreeable even in authoritarian societies. A notable example was the previous Kurdish autonomy in Iraq, which granted considerable powers to the autonomous authorities. Notwithstanding the authoritarian nature of the Baathist regime in Baghdad, there was (briefly) meaningful Kurdish autonomy ... until it was withdrawn. So there may be a kind of paradox, but I would argue that, in general, one needs a demo-

cratic framework within which to fit autonomous regimes of the kind discussed here, and to entrench them to some degree.

2. *Structure and process are key.* Subject-matters for autonomy may vary; one may add to them, diminish them or modify them. For example, if we consider the autonomy regimes for Vojvodina and Kosovo in Serbia, the subject-matters in dispute essentially had to do with language use and representation: issues included the language of education, language of administration, and language use in the central authority. But what really proved the critical issue was the suspension of the powers and the absence of any process through which to reclaim them or otherwise to negotiate them, particularly in Kosovo. Fundamentally, and understandably, communities and their representatives want to have an effective say, if not control, over those things which affect them exclusively or substantially. So the subject-matter and forms can vary, but the structure and process are important especially to retain public confidence and trust.

3. *Both time and timing are critical.* Things evolve and opportunities come and go. In this regard, the situations in Crimea, Québec and Northern Ireland offer good examples. In terms of time per se, over time demographics, choices and attitudes change. In Northern Ireland, there have been and continue to be significant demographic changes while choices and their implications have altered significantly as, notably, the evolving European Union has drawn Ireland and the United Kingdom closer together (thus, for example, diminishing the significance of frontiers between them). Indeed, the situation in Northern Ireland has evolved substantially in the last generation or so, as the most recent census attests. The Catholic population continues to grow in relation to the majority Protestant population, while an increasing part of the population has identified themselves as neither Catholic nor Protestant.[27] Whether this reflects immigration or some other changes or both, it nonetheless demands a new and adequate response in terms of policy development to take into account this fact. Crimea is an example were the demographics changed even more substantially over the past generations, due first to a Stalinist internal deportation of Crimean Tatars and a subsequent Russian in-migration to the peninsula. Of course, it is never possible simply to roll back the clock; over time, lives become entangled. In this respect, it is perhaps wise to think in terms of evolving situations and not seek to fix them forever. Québec is a perfect example: what might have been both possible and ap-

---

[27] See the 'theme' tables (and the census results more generally) at <http://www.nisra.gov.uk/archive/census/2001/theme/theme_tables.pdf> (2 August 2006).

propriate thirty years ago may no longer be so today. At the same time, when opportunities present themselves, on the basis of political coincidences if not the hard work of enlightened leadership, they must be jumped upon.

4. *Perspective and paradigm are also important.* There is a myth about independence in the world today; it was probably always so, but it is especially so today. We are now so interdependent that the idea that one can separate and enjoy autonomy in the literal sense of auto-control is essentially a fiction. In fact, there are degrees of power. If that is true, we have then to rethink a paradigm in which we would invoke and negotiate 'autonomy', and I would suggest that in an era of complex interdependence we must understand, as a starting point, not the idea of independence but the idea of relative *interdependence*. Logically, this compels cooperation among responsible representatives and governments where various interests are managed collectively. In this context, in fact more space for political pluralism can be made as some matters are combined 'up' and others are devolved 'down'. Moreover, the common interest in social and economic development raises the value of stability and, thus, prizes cooperation, accommodation and compromise. Autonomy arrangements, of various kinds and degrees, fit well with such a paradigm.

5. Also *often of critical importance are the roles of third and fourth parties* – on occasion determinatively so. My own experience has been in the service of a third party (with a smallish office of some twenty staff) mandated by fifty-five states to act in the common interest, but rarely as an invited arbiter or mediator. We never had large sums of money nor other tangible goods to distribute or a similar basis of 'power', so we were pretty weak. But aside from the importance of ideas and opportunities to persuade authorities, there was the possibility to mobilise others. Specifically, we worked to mobilise fourth parties who had varying degrees of interest, which only reflects the above mentioned paradigm and its complexity. There are hosts of interests and many of them are absolutely legitimate ones. For example, security in Northern Ireland or security in Crimea are not only the interest of the people there, but there are evident regional and global interests in the age of terrorism, organised crime, the importation of contraband and so forth. There are also multifarious economic interests, both domestic and international, public and private. For example, it is difficult to discuss the situation in Northern Ireland and totally ignore the interests of the international commercial company Bombardier. Simply, there exist many interests in each situation and the roles of third and fourth parties are important among these.

It seems clear that the forms of autonomy (including self-rule and similar arrangements) and their effective implementation offer significant opportunities to accommodate existing and evolving diversity throughout the world. This is especially important from the perspective of preventing or resolving violent conflict and thereby contributing to social stability and economic prosperity. While there is already considerable experience with the forms and degrees of autonomy arrangements, there remains much to be learned from them. It is also true that the appropriateness of a specific form or degree of autonomy is largely a matter of context, such that each application will be at least somewhat unique. Still, some lessons can be drawn, not least that autonomy arrangements are important to consider. The Lund Recommendations offer a useful reference for alternatives in this regard. In an increasingly complex interdependent world the application of such arrangements is to be encouraged. To this end, especially independent, impartial and expert third parties can play significant roles. The challenge is to make this work to the benefit of all.

Chapter IV

THE IMPLEMENTATION OF THE GOOD FRIDAY AGREEMENT IN NORTHERN IRELAND

Denis Haughey[*]

Northern Ireland comprises six North Eastern counties of the thirty-two counties of Ireland, which is about 20 percent of the island of Ireland geographically speaking. It is sometimes referred to as Ulster, even though it comprises only two-thirds of the ancient Irish province of Ulster. Northern Ireland has a population of 1.7 million. Of that population, about 50 percent are of British nationality and they are variously referred to as Unionists (because they wish to preserve the union with Great Britain), Loyalists (because they are loyal to the British monarchy), or Protestants (because the overwhelming majority of them belong to the various Protestant churches). About 40 percent of the population is of Irish nationality, and they are generally referred to as Nationalists, though they are not of the skin-head and tattoo variety. Some of the Irish national population are referred to as Republicans, because they have tended to support the Irish Republican Army (IRA), an illegal paramilitary organisation dedicated to the use of force to advance the cause of a united Irish republic. The Irish national population in Northern Ireland is also sometimes referred to as the Catholics because the great majority of them belong to the Catholic church. About 10 percent of the population of Northern Ireland do not owe exclusive allegiance to either side.

1. ORIGIN AND DEVELOPMENT OF THE CONFLICT

1.1 British colonialism

The quarrel in Northern Ireland is not about religion, even though the British media constantly use the terms Catholic and Protestant as a kind of short-hand.

---

[*] Former Member of the Northern Ireland Assembly; former Minister of the Northern Ireland Executive.

M. Boltjes (ed.), Implementing Negotiated Agreements
© 2007, Kreddha International and T·M·C·ASSER PRESS, The Hague, The Netherlands

This practice has created the impression that the conflict in Northern Ireland is an obscure seventeenth century quarrel about trans-substantiation or about the power of the papacy, and British governments have not been unwilling to allow this impression to gain credence internationally. If the 'Irish problem' is depicted as an abstruse hangover from centuries-old religious wars, long forgotten everywhere else, then Britain's hand in creating the political slum that is Northern Ireland may escape the spotlight of reasonable inquiry by the international community. Religious bigotry does play a part in the thinking of a minority of people on either side, but it is not central to the problem. The problem rather derives from Ireland's experience with British colonialism.

During the long centuries of Britain's conquest and gradual absorption of Ireland into the British state, a significant population of settlers from Britain came to Ireland. Some were 'planted' by deliberate government policy through a process of confiscation of the lands of those most active in the resistance to invasion and conquest. As a result, the planted population of British settlers was mainly concentrated in the North of Ireland where resistance to British conquest was most prolonged and formidable. Some British settlers, however, came by natural migration, though in a colonial context. Today, the descendants of both these types of settlers make up about 15 percent of the population of the island of Ireland, and they are concentrated almost totally in the six North Eastern counties.

The vast majority of the people of Ireland never accepted absorption into the British state. A strong independence movement developed through the eighteenth and nineteenth centuries, regularly manifesting itself in armed uprising. Furthermore, as the British parliamentary franchise was extended from 1832 onwards, pro-independence politicians won more and more of the 108 Irish seats in the House of Commons. In the general election for the British parliament in 1885, the Irish National Party won 85 of the 108 Irish seats. By the end of the nineteenth century it appeared likely that the British parliament would shortly concede a measure of home rule to Ireland. This greatly alarmed the British population in the North-East, who foresaw themselves becoming a small minority in an Irish state, and they began to organise for armed resistance to any new devolved government in Dublin. In 1912 they set-up an illegal paramilitary organisation called the Ulster Volunteer Force (UVF). As a reaction, Irish nationalists all over Ireland set about the organisation of an unofficial Irish Volunteers army to defend any new Irish government.

In 1914 the British parliament finally passed an Irish Home Rule Act, giving Ireland a measure of internal autonomy. However, upon the declaration of war that same year, the Act was suspended for the duration of hostilities. Almost all of the UVF and the great majority of the Irish Volunteers enlisted in the British army. While the First World War was raging on mainland Europe, some of the more extreme elements among the Irish Volunteers, who had refused to enlist, determined to seize the opportunity of Britain's emergency and started an insurrection in Dublin at Easter, 1916. The insurrection was suppressed with excessive and unnecessary force by the British authorities, seriously alienating the great bulk of Irish nationalist opinion.

1.2 The establishment of the Republic of Ireland and the State of Northern Ireland

In the British general election of 1918, candidates committed to the establishment of an independent Irish republic took more than three-quarters of the parliamentary seats in Ireland. These elected representatives met in Dublin, set-up an Irish parliament with an executive government, and declared Ireland an independent republic. They then prudently went into hiding. Repression followed, leading to a protracted struggle between the British security forces in Ireland and Irish Volunteers loyal to the new and democratic, but unofficial Irish government. In 1920, in order to pre-empt any peace settlement, the British government partitioned Ireland. It set-up the state[1] of Northern Ireland in the North-East and drew the boundaries in such a way as to give Unionists the largest possible territory within which they would have a secure voting majority. However, fatefully, the new entity of Northern Ireland included large areas and many towns which were overwhelmingly Irish nationalist. Thus was the state of Northern Ireland established.

In 1921 a truce was called between the forces of the unofficial Irish Republic – by now calling themselves the Irish Republican Army (IRA) – and the British forces. Representatives of the unofficial Irish government came out of hiding to meet with representatives of the British government in London. One of the British government's non-negotiable terms for a treaty was acceptance of the partition of Ireland and the existence of the six-county state of Northern Ireland. With very great misgivings, the representatives of the unofficial Irish government agreed to sign the treaty, rather than force a renewal of the fighting upon a war-weary population. This Anglo-Irish Treaty established the Irish Free State, a self-governing dominion within the British Commonwealth constituting the remaining twenty-six counties of Ireland. Within weeks of the Treaty being signed fighting broke out again, this time between Pro-Treaty and Anti-Treaty elements of the Irish Republican Army. For the next eighteen months Southern

---

[1] Northern Ireland is commonly referred to as a 'state', even though it is not a sovereign state, or even a federated entity within the United Kingdom. This reflects the fact that it is a separate administrative region, which has a separate civil service, a separate judiciary, and has enjoyed a high degree of internal autonomy for much of its existence.

Ireland experienced civil war. The forces of the new Irish Free State government prevailed and Southern Ireland settled down into an uneasy peace. Tiny remnants of the Anti-Treaty IRA continued a shadowy existence North and South, going through many splits and metamorphoses and occasionally launching small-scale attacks upon security forces and public property in Northern Ireland and even in Great Britain. Gradually it lost all credibility and almost ceased to exist. The people of Southern Ireland reluctantly accommodated themselves to the new arrangements. They declared Southern Ireland a republic in 1949 and left the British Commonwealth. Today, the Republic of Ireland is a sovereign independent state, with a population of about 4.3 million. It is a member of the European Union (EU), a member of the common currency zone and the second wealthiest state in the EU in terms of GDP per head of population.

1.3   The 'double minority' problem

Northern Ireland had a very different experience. The large Irish National minority was, and continued to be resentful of partition and reluctant to accept the legitimacy of the new Northern Ireland state. The British/Unionist majority were insecure. They were fearful of the large sullen minority within the borders of 'their' state and fearful of the new Irish Free State to the South. This is an important characteristic of the Northern Ireland problem. It is a 'double minority' problem. British/Unionists are acutely aware that they are a small minority on the island of Ireland. Irish Nationals in Northern Ireland are acutely aware of being an artificially contrived minority within the borders of an artificially contrived state. Both Unionists and Irish Nationals within Northern Ireland display many of the characteristics of a beleaguered minority.

The new Unionist government was also acutely aware that the Irish National population, being Catholic, had much larger families and was expanding at a faster rate than the Unionist/Protestant population. This obviously constituted a threat to long-term Unionist electoral control of Northern Ireland. Consequently the Unionist government resorted to a variety of strategies to deprive the Irish National/Catholic population of jobs and public housing in order to accelerate the already high rate of emigration among the Irish National population. Other measures taken to reduce the Irish National/Catholic threat to the future of the state included discriminatory voting practices, the gerrymandering[2] of electoral boundaries, 'special' police powers, and the general abuse of government power to deprive the Irish National population wherever possible. These prac-

---

[2] Note from the editor: Gerrymandering is the intentional division of an area into voting districts differing widely in population in such a way that individual votes will count more in one district than in another, ultimately giving an unfair advantage to one party in elections.

tices continued down to the 1960s and although Northern Ireland remained a part of the United Kingdom and subject to the authority of the UK government, no British government ever intervened to restrain the excesses of Unionist governments in Belfast, in spite of regular and shrill protests by representatives of the Irish National community in the British parliament.

1.4 Bloody Sunday

Consequently, the Irish National population never settled down within the Northern Ireland state. Discontent and violence leading to state repression have disfigured every decade of the state's existence. In the late 1960s a powerful civil rights movement began among the Irish National minority. Peaceful marches and demonstrations in support of civil rights reforms were met with violent opposition from aggressive Unionist mobs and the police and state security agencies attempted to drive the civil rights demonstrators off the streets by force, often colluding with loyalist mobs to do so. Eventually, in 1969, the British army was deployed in the streets of Northern Ireland in an effort to contain the disorder. Simultaneously, the British government – for the first time – began to pressurise the Belfast Unionist government for reforms. The reforms which eventually came, with great reluctance and much resistance from the Belfast authorities, were inadequate and too late to prevent the descent into violence.

As violence and disorder grew in Northern Ireland, the minuscule remaining elements of the old Anti-Treaty IRA regrouped and began to debate how they should respond. The majority wanted to support the civil rights movement in a peaceful struggle for reform. This enraged a militant minority who withdrew in 1969 and formed the Provisional Council of the IRA. They claimed that the majority of their former colleagues had lost the right to call themselves the IRA because they had 'betrayed the Republic', which they claimed had been established in 1918, and which had never been legally disestablished. Thus was born the Provisional IRA. As the disorder in the streets continued and the Provisionals began to attack the police and the British army, the Belfast Unionist government could think only in terms of using force against any expression of opposition. The British government also dithered, without any clear policy other than to support this repression. It allowed the British army to be used by the Unionist government in Belfast in a series of ever more repressive measures, including a seriously mishandled policy of interning suspects without trial, which led to scores of innocent people being put in jail. By this time two major British/Unionist/Loyalist terrorist organisations – the reconstituted UVF and a new organisation calling itself the Ulster Defence Association (UDA) – had launched a more or less indiscriminate campaign of murder against any Irish/nationalist/Catholic they could find.

In February 1972 the British army shot dead fourteen unarmed civil rights demonstrators in the streets of Derry City, an incident which became known as Bloody Sunday. As a consequence, the ranks of the Provisional IRA began to swell with recruits. The Provisional IRA's violence intensified and became increasingly indiscriminate and brutal, killing and maiming hundreds of people, British/Unionist and Irish/Nationalist alike. In May 1972 the British government proposed taking direct control of security and the police. The Unionist government in Belfast resigned in protest and the British government suspended the institutions of the Northern Ireland state. For the next eighteen months, Northern Ireland was administered directly from London by 'direct rule', as it was called.

1.5 Towards agreement; the involvement of the government of the Republic of Ireland

During the eighteen months of direct rule efforts were made to generate an agreement on a new form of government, involving a partnership between the more moderate elements in the Ulster Unionist Party and the moderate anti-violence Social Democratic and Labour Party (SDLP) which represented the vast majority of Irish Nationals. The SDLP insisted that the Irish government must be involved in any new arrangement, in order to reflect and legitimise the different nationality and national allegiance of Irish Nationals within Northern Ireland. British governments and Unionist governments in Belfast had always stridently resisted any involvement on the part of the Irish government in the affairs of Northern Ireland.[3] However, the tragedy of Bloody Sunday had caused a radical rethink in British government circles in respect of Northern Ireland. In spite of Unionist protests, the Irish government was invited by the British government to participate in the ongoing talks about the future of Northern Ireland.

In December 1973 an agreement was signed between the British and Irish governments, the Ulster Unionists and the SDLP: the Sunningdale agreement. In May 1973 a new Northern Ireland assembly had been elected by proportional representation and in January 1974 a new power-sharing executive government was formed in Belfast. Accommodation of the sense of identity of Irish Nationals was to be through a North-South Council of Ireland, whose purpose would be to institutionalise joint action between the Irish government and the new government in the north on a wide range of matters affecting both parts of the island. The power-sharing executive held office for five months. It collapsed

---

[3] In 1970, for instance, the British prime minister, Edward Heath, had brusquely rebuffed the protest of the Irish prime minister at British army curfews in Belfast, declaring that this was an internal UK matter, and no business of the Irish government.

when the Ulster Unionist Party withdrew its ministers in protest at the failure of the British Labour government – who retained control of policing and security under the new arrangements – to protect and sustain the executive in the face of widespread violent protests by armed loyalist gangs, the blocking of roads by loyalist mobs, and the paralysing of every aspect of life in Northern Ireland when loyalist-controlled power-workers' unions closed down the power stations. As a consequence, direct rule was restored.

This incredible and shameful abdication of its responsibilities by the British Labour government reinforced the widespread belief among Irish Nationals that no British government would ever stand up to Unionist extremists, but would much rather suppress discontent among Irish Nationals, by force if necessary. It also led to the collapse of support for the pro power-sharing elements in the Unionist community and the strengthening of the belief among the Unionist population that they must, and could, recover exclusive power for themselves, by simply refusing to cooperate with, or even discuss, anything less.

From May 1974 onwards, since there was no longer any significant element in the Unionist community prepared to support power-sharing arrangements, the SDLP came increasingly to the view that the Northern Ireland problem could only be solved by a resolute partnership of the British and Irish governments. By the late 1970s the British government was reluctantly persuaded to explore this approach, and after several years of sporadic negotiation, the Anglo-Irish Agreement was signed in 1985. This agreement, which was registered with the United Nations, accorded to the Irish government the right to be consulted about all matters concerning the internal government of Northern Ireland and committed the British government to make every possible effort to reach consensus with the Irish government about such matters.

Significantly, the agreement also contained the proviso that in the event of the formation of a new power-sharing government on a basis which had widespread acceptance in both communities, the matters devolved to such a government would cease to come within the purview of the two governments under the terms of the agreement. This proviso was conceived as a means of encouraging the Unionist population to reach accommodation with the Irish national population. The Anglo-Irish agreement caused major trauma and anger in the Unionist community, who regarded it as a form of 'joint-sovereignty' and a shameful betrayal of their interests by the British government. But it also led to a growing acceptance among Unionists that some form of accommodation with the Irish National community was unavoidable if they were ever to regain any measure of power within Northern Ireland. In the late eighties and early nineties inter-party talks began to take shape, eventually evolving into formal sessions under the chairmanship of the British Secretary of State for Northern Ireland.

Simultaneous to these developments, the Provisionals were gradually coming to the conclusion that their campaign of violence was leading nowhere. Equally, they realised that if a new power-sharing administration were established in Belfast, no British government could afford to abandon it in the face of street violence after the shameful debacle of 1974. They knew they had to find a point of entry into the political negotiations about the future of Northern Ireland or risk being completely excluded for the foreseeable future. In the late eighties they began to put out feelers through their political alter ego, Sinn Fein, both to the British and Irish governments and to the leader of the SDLP, John Hume.

After protracted talks with the Provisional leadership, John Hume succeeded in negotiating a joint declaration by the British and Irish governments – the so-called Downing Street Declaration of December 1993. The key element in this declaration, as far as the IRA were concerned, was the statement that the future of Ireland was a matter to be determined by the people of Ireland alone, by means of concurrent majorities, North and South. This conceded the sovereign right of the people who live in Ireland to determine the future of Ireland without interference from Britain. The concession, by Britain, of sovereignty to the people of Ireland, was balanced by a declaration that Northern Ireland would remain part of the United Kingdom, until a majority of its people decided otherwise. The British and Irish governments undertook to enact the necessary legislation immediately in the event that the people of Northern Ireland should vote for Irish reunification. This led to an intensive debate within the Provisionals (Sinn Fein & the IRA), and culminated in an IRA ceasefire in the autumn of 1994. This was followed, one month later, by ceasefires on the part of the UVF and the UDA.

2. THE GOOD FRIDAY AGREEMENT; A MULTIPARTY INTER- AND INTRASTATE AGREEMENT

After lengthy prevarication by the British government,[4] which almost precipitated the collapse of the entire peace process, full round table talks were eventually put together in May 1996, involving the political parties representing the

---

[4] The reluctance of the British government of Prime Minister John Major to begin the talks was not due to any reluctance to devolve power to Northern Ireland. It derived from the fact that Major had lost his majority in the House of Commons and depended upon the votes of Ulster Unionist MPs to hold on to power. He was therefore reluctant to begin talks in Northern Ireland which could cause tension between his government and the Ulster Unionists, and the loss of their support in Parliament.

main armed groups, Sinn Fein (IRA), the Progressive Unionist Party (UVF), and the Ulster Democratic Party (UDA), along with the British and Irish governments, and the 'constitutional' parties in Northern Ireland.[5] These inclusive talks were chaired by the former United States senator, George Mitchell, with two deputy chairs – the former Finnish prime minister, Harry Holkerri, and the Canadian general, John de Chastelain.

The outcome was the Good Friday Agreement of April 1998,[6] which was quickly endorsed by huge majorities in concurrent referenda in Northern Ireland and the Republic of Ireland. The main terms of the Good Friday Agreement are:

- affirmation by both governments that the future of Ireland is for the people of Ireland alone to determine, by means of concurrent majorities in both parts of the island;
- that Northern Ireland will remain part of the United Kingdom until a majority of the people of Northern Ireland, in a referendum called for that purpose, shall decide otherwise;
- that if a majority of the people of Northern Ireland, in such a referendum, voted to become part of the Irish Republic, both governments would make immediate legislative provision for that;
- a commitment by all parties to the agreement, to the use of 'exclusively peaceful and democratic means' to further their political aims;
- a commitment by all parties to the agreement, to use every effort to secure an end to violence;
- the election of a new Northern Ireland assembly of 108 seats by proportional representation;
- the designation of each member, according to his/her choice, as Unionist, Nationalist or Other;

---

[5] The 'constitutional parties' who *supported* the Good Friday Agreement were: the Ulster Unionist Party, representing more than half of the Unionist community; the SDLP, representing more than half of the Nationalist community; Alliance, a small cross-community party with about 7 percent of the vote. The 'paramilitary'-related parties, all of whom *supported* the Agreement were: Sinn Fein, allied to the IRA, representing about 40 percent of the Nationalist community; the Popular Unionist Party, allied to the UVF, with about 2-4 percent of the vote; the Ulster Democratic Party, allied to the UDA, with about 1-2 percent of the vote. The 'constitutional parties' who *opposed* the Good Friday Agreement were: the Democratic Unionist Party, a Protestant fundamentalist party led by Ian Paisley, representing about one third of the Unionist community; the United Kingdom Unionist Party, a small Unionist party favouring total integration of Northern Ireland into the UK; a number of tiny Unionist splinter parties; and independents.

[6] The text of the Good Friday Agreement is reproduced in Appendix A.

- the requirement of 'cross-community consent' – overall majority of members, including at least 40 percent of both Unionists and Nationalists – for certain decisions;
- the requirement of 'parallel consent' – overall majority of members, including at least 50 percent of both Unionists and Nationalists for certain designated decisions, and in any case where thirty members call for it;
- the election by the assembly of a first minister and deputy first minister by parallel consent, the two to act jointly as heads of the executive;
- the formation by the assembly of an executive government by means of the D'Hondt formula;[7]
- the devolution of a wide range of powers to the new institutions;
- the normalisation of Northern Ireland society by reduction of security forces and military installations to peace time levels;
- the reform of the Northern Ireland police, following the report of a Commission of Inquiry (the Patten Commission);
- an extensive equality and human rights agenda;
- extensive entrenchment of cultural and linguistic rights;
- the release of all paramilitary prisoners within two years;
- the acceptance by all parties of an obligation to do everything possible to secure comprehensive decommissioning of all paramilitary weapons and explosives within two years;
- the establishment of an independent international commission on decommissioning, under the chairmanship of the Canadian general, John de Chastelain, to supervise and certify the disposal of weapons;
- The Agreement also includes a provision for periodic review of the working of the Good Friday Agreement.

3. Summary of Events since the Signing of the Good Friday Agreement

Elections for the new assembly were held in May 1998. The Ulster Unionist Party won twenty-nine seats, the SDLP twenty-four, the DUP (Paisley – anti-agreement Unionists) twenty, Sinn Fein eighteen, and a variety of smaller parties won the remaining seventeen seats. The assembly quickly elected David Trimble, the leader of the Ulster Unionist Party, as first minister and Mr Seamus Mallon of the SDLP as deputy first minister, by parallel consent. Both were to

---

[7] The D'Hondt Formula is the procedure used for the distribution of Committee Chairs in the European Parliament.

hold office in 'shadow mode' until the election of the executive. However, the Ulster Unionists refused to proceed to the election of an executive – which, on the above figures, would necessarily involve the election of two Sinn Fein ministers –, until the IRA began the process of decommissioning of weapons. The IRA refused on the grounds that they were not signatories to the Good Friday Agreement and were not bound by any of its provisions. Sinn Fein declared that they were not the IRA and could not be held accountable for anything the IRA might or might not do. The stalemate continued until December 1999, when the Ulster Unionist Party eventually agreed to form the executive in advance of decommissioning on a 'good faith' basis.

Subsequently, the IRA carried out two acts of decommissioning, certified by the Independent International Commission on Decommissioning, but it did not give a commitment to dispose of all of its arms. From that time the executive continued an uncertain existence, because of Ulster Unionist impatience with the prevarication of the IRA over the arms issue, and the accumulating evidence of the continuance by the IRA of unacceptable activities. It became increasingly clear that the IRA was continuing to import arms, continuing to train its 'volunteers', and continuing to engage in community control and enforcement activities on the ground. There was also abundant evidence of the continuation of illegal money raising rackets on the part of the IRA as well as the other paramilitary organisations. Then, a series of dramatic incidents plunged the peace process into crisis. Three members of the IRA were arrested in Colombia and charged with providing training and assistance to the FARC anti-government guerrillas, who control a major international drug-smuggling operation and exert fairly brutal control over a significant part of Colombia. The IRA has also been blamed for a raid on an important British army base on the Eastern outskirts of Belfast (Castlereagh) and the seizure of sensitive intelligence material from that base, though no hard and fast evidence has yet been made known. More recently, the IRA was found to be conducting a spying operation on Sinn Fein's government partners in the executive and on the Irish and British governments, even to the extent of taping private telephone conversations between Prime Minister Blair and President Bush!

In October 2002 the Ulster Unionist party withdrew from the executive over these issues, refusing to contemplate the restoration of the institutions until the governments secured explicit undertakings from the IRA. The executive and the assembly were then suspended by the British government. Elections for a new assembly were to be held on the 1st of May of 2003. They were initially postponed to 29 May, to give the IRA more time to consider a response. When the response came it was considered inadequate by both governments. Consequently, the British government dissolved the assembly and cancelled the elections, indicating a possible election in the autumn, but without setting a definite date.

As a consequence of mounting pressure from the two governments and the other political parties, the IRA announced a third act of decommissioning on 21 October 2003, which was confirmed by the Independent International Commission on Decommissioning. This was to have been part of a choreographed sequence of events, involving the Leader of the UUP, David Trimble, and the two governments, leading to the restoration of the institutions. However, in the event, the IRA failed to give the necessary undertakings about the final ending of all paramilitary activity and David Trimble aborted the exercise. Even so, the two governments agreed to hold fresh elections for the assembly on 26 November 2003. The outcome of the election was a setback for the centre or moderate parties (UUP and SDLP). Sinn Fein became the majority party in the Irish National community and the anti-agreement DUP became the majority party in the Unionist community. As a consequence, the stalemate deepened.

4. IMPLEMENTATION OF THE GOOD FRIDAY AGREEMENT

Implementation of the Good Friday Agreement has been a serious bone of contention from the very beginning. There has been no independent mechanism or agency charged with overall adjudication of how well, or to what extent, the various parties to the Agreement have fulfilled the obligations which they undertook in signing the Agreement. The period since the signing of the Good Friday Agreement in 1998 has, therefore, been disfigured by constant bickering and allegations that this or that party to the Agreement has not fulfilled this or that aspect of their obligations. However, a variety of mechanisms have been created or have developed in the broader context of the peace process for implementing various parts of the Agreement.

The British and Irish governments kept their word in relation to the release of paramilitary prisoners: all were released from jail within the two-year time span envisaged in the Agreement. The British government and parliament completed the incorporation into Northern Ireland law of the European Convention on Human Rights, as was agreed in Paragraph 2 on Rights, Safeguards and Equality of Opportunity. The Irish government took steps to remove Articles 2 and 3 from the Irish constitution, which claimed territorial sovereignty over the whole island. The British government has established the Northern Ireland Human Rights Commission and the Northern Ireland Equality Commission, as was agreed, to implement the equality and human rights provisions of the Agreement. There has also been a considerable reduction in military installations and troop levels since the signing of the Agreement. In fact, in May 2002 the British government handed over to the Northern Ireland executive a number of military bases and the site of the Maze Prison, to be used for the purposes of stimulating economic and social regeneration.[8]

The Equality Commission has functioned successfully, supervising the implementation of the equality requirements laid down in Section 75 of the Northern Ireland Act, the British legislation establishing the institutions agreed in the Good Friday Agreement, and dealing with the wide range of equality functions which are its remit. The Northern Ireland Human Rights Commission, which has the remit of advising the British government on the 'scope for a Bill of Rights for Northern Ireland', as well as a range of monitoring functions[9] has functioned less successfully. It was riven by internal disputes and disagreements, leading to the resignation of a number of its members. It has recently been reconstituted under the chairmanship of Professor Monica McWilliams, a former Assembly Member, and a leader of the Women's Coalition.

4.1 Cross-border cooperation mechanisms and agencies

During the negotiations leading to the Good Friday Agreement, Unionists successfully argued that they felt part of a British community embracing all of the islands in the British-Irish archipelago, and that this British community needed to be given institutional expression. Equally, representatives of the Irish National community in Northern Ireland argued that Irish Nationals in Northern Ireland had a particularly close relationship with the people of the Republic of Ireland, which must also be given expression. Additionally, as a consequence of the Anglo-Irish agreement of 1985, the two governments were committed by international treaty to consult closely about the affairs of Northern Ireland, with the proviso that any matters devolved to an agreed administration in Belfast would be removed from the purview of the two governments. The Good Friday Agreement has, consequently, made provision for three different levels of cross-border cooperation – a North/South Ministerial Council, a British-Irish Council and a British-Irish Intergovernmental Conference.

The two governments acted together in the immediate aftermath of the formation of the executive to implement these provisions, which are provided for in Strand 2 and Strand 3 of the Good Friday Agreement. The North/South Ministerial Council, comprising ministerial representatives from the two adminis-

---

[8] The various steps taken to implement the Good Friday Agreement are detailed by the two governments in a joint paper published on 14 July 2001, entitled 'Achievements in the Implementation of the Good Friday Agreement', which is available at <http://www.nio.gov.uk/achievements_in_implementation_of_the_good_friday_agreement.pdf> (2 August 2006).

[9] Good Friday Agreement, paragraph 5, *Rights, Safeguards and Equality of Opportunity.*

trations in Ireland, was established immediately upon the formation of the executive and had its first plenary session on 13 December 1999. On 17 December the inaugural session of the British-Irish Council, comprising ministerial-level representatives of (i) the British and Irish governments, (ii) the devolved administrations in Wales, Scotland and Northern Ireland, and (iii) the governments of the Isle of Man and the Channel Islands, took place in London. On the same day, the inaugural session of the British-Irish Intergovernmental Conference, comprising ministerial-level representatives of the British and Irish governments, was held, also in London.

During the lifetime of the assembly and the executive the *North/South Ministerial Council* met regularly and set in train a variety of measures for cooperation between the government of Ireland and the Northern Ireland administration. These have mainly focused on the operation of the six Implementation Bodies[10] established in December 1999 under the terms of the Agreement.[11] Although called implementation bodies, these are, rather, cross-border agencies charged with coordinating certain governmental functions on a cross-border basis within Ireland.[12]

The British-Irish Intergovernmental Conference has also met regularly and functioned successfully, dealing with a wide range of matters of concern to the two governments, and in particular, 'non-devolved Northern Ireland matters', i.e., matters which are not devolved to the Northern Ireland administration in Belfast.

The British-Irish Council has met much less frequently, but has initiated a number of useful projects involving cooperation between all of the administrations involved in the areas of drugs, transport cooperation, energy cooperation and the development of trans-European communications technology networks.

Whereas these institutions, conceived in the Good Friday Agreement, are important and necessary components of the Agreement to reflect the differing world-views of the British/Unionist and Irish/National communities, the cross-

---

[10] The six North/South 'Implementation Bodies' are:
(a) an implementation body for inland waterways, known as Waterways Ireland;
(b) an implementation body for food safety, known as The Food Safety Promotion Board;
(c) an implementation body for trade and business development, known as The Trade and Business Development Body;
(d) an implementation body for special EU programs, known as The Special EU Programs Body;
(e) an implementation body for language, known as The North/South Language Body;
(f) an implementation body for aquaculture and marine matters, known as The Foyle, Carlingford and Irish Lights Commission.

[11] Good Friday Agreement, paragraph 9, Strand 2.

[12] Since the establishment of the six 'Implementation Bodies' above, a further agency has been established to deal with tourism on an all-Ireland basis.

border institutions have actually proven extremely useful and relatively non-contentious.

The Commission on Policing for Northern Ireland, which the Agreement makes provision for, could be regarded as an implementation mechanism of a kind. It was established by the British government under the chairmanship of Mr. Chris Patten, a British Conservative Member of Parliament and until recently a European Commissioner. The report of Mr Patten's Commission, which made a wide range of recommendations about changes to policing in Northern Ireland, recommended the appointment of an independent 'oversight commissioner' to monitor the implementation of the report. This recommendation was accepted by the two governments. A high-ranking officer from the New York State Police Department[13] was appointed by the governments to this position. He visited Northern Ireland regularly and made a series of reports upon the implementation of the Patten reforms. His reports were constructive and supportive of the measures being taken to implement a wide range of changes in policing. They were not uncritical however, and his criticisms have been taken extremely seriously by the British government and by the Northern Ireland police authorities.[14]

4.2 Implementation of provisions requiring decommissioning of arms

In general, the implementation measures referred to above have proceeded without anything more serious than the ordinary partisan wrangling. Provisional Sinn Fein has quibbled about the record of the two governments in implementing the equality, human rights and cultural rights provisions of the Agreement, and in particular the record of the British government in respect of normalisation. However, the most serious area of disagreement has been the issue of implementing 'the decommissioning of illegally-held arms in the possession of paramilitary groups.'[15]

The Agreement commits all the signatory parties 'to use any influence they may have, to achieve the decommissioning of all paramilitary arms within two years following endorsement in referendums North and South of the Agreement, and in the context of the implementation of the overall settlement.'[16] This loose form of wording was part of the constructive ambiguity employed by

---

[13] Mr Tom Considine, who had been Director of the United States Drugs Enforcement Agency.

[14] Mr Considine has now been replaced as Oversight Commissioner by Mr Al Hutchinson, a high-ranking officer from the Royal Canadian Mounted Police, who had previously been Mr Considine's deputy.

[15] Good Friday Agreement, paragraph 2, 'Decommissioning' section.

[16] Good Friday Agreement, paragraph 3, 'Decommissioning' section.

the negotiators to throw a veil over the relationship between Sinn Fein and the IRA in order to facilitate the peace negotiations. It was commonly accepted and widely known that the most senior leaders of Sinn Fein are also members of the Provisional IRA's Army Council – the controlling body of the Provisional IRA. However, the Unionist parties and government ministers, both Irish and British, would have balked at meeting openly with the leadership of an illegal paramilitary organisation. It suited them to maintain the fiction that Sinn Fein and the IRA were two entirely separate and distinct entities. However it suited the Provisionals' leadership even more so, because it allowed them the luxury of insisting that the IRA had agreed to nothing, that Sinn Fein had merely agreed to 'use any influence they may have', and that Sinn Fein could not be held accountable for the actions or inactions of an 'entirely separate' organisation.

This constructive ambiguity about the relationship between Provisional Sinn Fein and the Provisional IRA has returned time after time to haunt the agreement and has disastrously undermined the peace process. In the event, the Provisionals made no move to implement the decommissioning of arms within the two-year time period envisaged in the Agreement. Incredibly, neither government made any move to impose any sanction upon Sinn Fein for this bad faith. Consequently, First Minister David Trimble of the Ulster Unionists at various times threatened to resign or actually did resign and removed his ministers from the executive, plunging the institutions established under the Agreement into a series of suspensions. Throughout its existence therefore, the executive had a very uncertain existence.

The Independent International Commission on Decommissioning preceded the Good Friday Agreement, having been established in 1997 in the context of the paramilitary ceasefires and the ongoing peace process. It was headed by the Canadian general, John de Chastelain, and included Ambassador Andrew Sens of the United States, and Brigadier Taunu Niemenen, a high-ranking officer in the armed forces of Finland. The Independent International Commission on Decommissioning's independence and integrity has never come into question, but it has not been able to play a proactive role in negotiating a solution to the decommissioning problem because its remit is too limited. Its powers are set out in Paragraph 4 of the Decommissioning section of the Good Friday Agreement: 'to monitor, review and verify progress on decommissioning of illegal arms…' It does not have the function of adjudicating on the extent to which the paramilitary organisations are discharging their obligations under the Agreement, or any capacity to impose sanctions on defaulting parties. Consequently, the Commission could only sit and watch while the paramilitary organisations refused to move to dispose of arms.

4.3 Additional implementation mechanisms and bodies created outside the agreement

Nonetheless, the impasse over the decommissioning issue gave rise to both informal and semiformal implementation mechanisms of a kind. The crisis which developed in the spring of 2000 over the failure of the IRA even to begin the process of decommissioning led to the suspension of the institutions. This prompted the Provisionals to offer a means of 'putting weapons beyond use', short of actually destroying them. The Provisionals' offer was to put quantities of their arms in dumps and to seal the dumps in such a way and under such supervision as to make it impossible for the arms to be used.[17] On this basis, the institutions were restored on 30th May 2000.

The two inspectors subsequently made a number of visits to Ireland, put themselves into the care of IRA personnel and conducted inspections of a number of arms dumps, verifying that the arms had been put beyond use in sealed dumps and that the seals had not been broken at any time. This implementation mechanism had not been provided for in the agreement, and the procedures which the inspectors were monitoring had not been envisaged in the Agreement. However, no process such as the Northern Ireland peace process can ever be expected to progress in an orderly fashion. Events, as they actually happen, are often untidy and unforeseen, and require creative and inventive address. This was such an occasion.

As a consequence of the continuing stalemate over the completion of decommissioning of weapons, the two governments were increasingly turning their minds to the much more fundamental problem of the links between political parties such as Provisional Sinn Fein and secret paramilitary armies such as the Provisional IRA, to dealing with the problem of ongoing paramilitary activity and the means of securing a final end to it. Since the signing of the Good Friday Agreement, there had been repeated evidence of continuing violent activity on the part of the IRA and the Loyalist paramilitaries. These activities included violent repression, including murder, of dissidents within their own organisations and members of rival organisations, unofficial community policing such as punishment beatings and even murder of criminal elements such as drug dealers and car thieves. They also included involvement by all the paramilitary organisations in criminal racketeering to raise money for their own organisations.

---

[17] Two international inspectors were invited to supervise this procedure. The inspectors were Mr Cyril Ramaphosa, the highly respected former senior negotiator for the African National Congress in the South African peace process, and Mr Martti Ahtisaari, the equally respected former Finnish prime minister.

In April 2003 the British and Irish governments issued a joint declaration calling for 'acts of completion' in relation to decommissioning and the ending of all paramilitary activity.[18] Furthermore, in September 2003, the two governments established an Independent Monitoring Commission[19] whose remit would be:

- (i) to monitor and report on the incidence of alleged paramilitary activity,
- (ii) to investigate allegations of the involvement in paramilitary activities of ministers or Parties in any future executive, and
- (iii) to report on the progress of any formal programme of security normalisation undertaken by the British government in the context of 'acts of completion' by paramilitaries.

The Independent Monitoring Commission has made a number of reports since its establishment, giving its assessment of current levels of paramilitary activity.

4.4 Periodic review of the Good Friday Agreement

The provision for periodic review of the Good Friday Agreement was only used once during the lifetime of the assembly elected in May 1998. One year after the signing of the Agreement, and in a context where the two governments had made considerable progress in fulfilling their obligations under the Agreement, the Provisionals had still made no move to deal with the question of weaponry. As a consequence, the Ulster Unionist Party refused to agree to the formation of an executive. In an effort to break the deadlock, the two governments invited Senator George Mitchell to return to conduct a formal review in the autumn of 1999. After holding talks with all the parties, he announced in mid November that he believed a basis did exist for the establishing the institutions and moving forward the issue of decommissioning. At the same time, the IRA issued a statement pledging their good intentions in relation to the disposal of arms. Consequently, David Trimble and his party decided to make an act of faith in the good

---

[18] These are dealt with in paragraphs 12-17 of the Joint Declaration. The full text of the Joint Declaration is available at <http://www.nio.gov.uk/joint_declaration_between_the_british_and_irish_governments.pdf> (2 August 2006).

[19] This Commission is composed of Lord John Alderdice, the former Speaker of the Northern Ireland Assembly and a member of the small Alliance Party; Mr John Grieve, a former senior officer of the London Metropolitan Police; Mr Joseph Brosnan, formerly Secretary-General of the Department of Justice in Ireland; and Mr Richard Kerr, a former deputy director of the United States Central Intelligence Agency.

intentions of the Provisionals and formed the executive on the 2nd December 1999, and devolution came into effect.

It is likely that the personal prestige and influence of Senator Mitchell was an important factor in pushing the Provisionals to pledge their good intentions on the issue of decommissioning. Even more important, however, was the fact that he was the personal representative of President Clinton. In the event, the Provisionals did not live up to their word. On 30 January 2000, the Independent International Commission on Decommissioning reported privately to the two governments that there had been no decommissioning by any major paramilitary group. The secretary of state for Northern Ireland therefore announced the British government's intention to suspend devolution unless circumstances regarding decommissioning changed. The IRA responded that they were prepared to consider 'how to put arms and explosives beyond use, in the context of the Good Friday Agreement *and in the context of the removal of the cause of conflict.*' The introduction of this piece of sophistry about the so-called causes of conflict convinced most people of the IRA's bad faith. The secretary of state suspended devolution from midnight on 11 February 2000.

The review mechanism was not used again, in spite of the series of crises which dogged the life of the executive and the assembly. However, in the wake of the assembly election of 26 November, 2003, and in the absence of any agreement on the re-formation of the executive, the British and Irish governments launched a second review.

5. INTERNAL AND EXTERNAL INFLUENCES ON THE PEACE AND IMPLEMENTATION PROCESSES

How did the Good Friday Agreement come to be signed by all of the participating parties after so many years of conflict? A major part of the reason lies in the changing attitudes among the population of Great Britain and of the Republic of Ireland. Another important factor is the gradual internationalisation of the Northern Ireland question as a result of the European Union membership of the United Kingdom and Ireland, and of the involvement of the United States.

5.1 Public opinion and changes in government attitudes in the United Kingdom and Ireland

Whereas in the past most British people had an aspiration to maintain the unity of the United Kingdom, Northern Ireland has been such a troublesome responsibility that most British people no longer regard it as a necessary or integral part of their mother country. Equally, the international embarrassment caused by abuses of civil rights and human rights in Northern Ireland, both by the old Unionist government and indeed by the British government itself, has become wearisome to the British. Whereas there is a small residual feeling of some obligation towards the Unionists in Northern Ireland because of their loyalty to the British state down the years, there is a growing acceptance that the British state has an equal responsibility to Irish nationals living in Northern Ireland, which it has not always fulfilled. Northern Ireland is an inherited responsibility to be borne with resignation and from a sense of duty rather than any commitment or affection. There is, therefore, a widespread willingness – even anxiety – in Great Britain to be rid of responsibility for this troublesome region, which has been so costly in financial, political and military terms.

Equally, in the Republic of Ireland there has been a decline of the ancient 'irredentist' feelings which predominated some decades ago. As the Republic of Ireland has become wealthier and stronger with the maturing experience of membership of the European Union, ancient resentments of British domination have faded. There is, in fact, a growing community of interest between Britain and Ireland in Europe and the wider world. There is also a revulsion at the ferocity and barbarity of the conflict in Northern Ireland, and a strong wish not to import such trouble into the Irish state.

There has been, and there is, a willingness on the part of the British and Irish governments to do everything required of them to settle the quarrel. They have a common interest in resolving the problems of Northern Ireland and have formed a strong partnership to do just that.

5.2 The effects of EU membership

The very fact that both the United Kingdom and Ireland have been member states of the European Union since 1973 has had a significant impact on the development of events in Northern Ireland and not least upon the peace process.

Firstly, EU membership has been a significant constraining factor upon British policy towards Northern Ireland; the receipt of so much help, financial and otherwise, in coping with the effect of the long years of conflict upon the Northern Ireland economy generates certain sensitivities in London which might not otherwise be there.

More generally, membership of an enormous international union, within which great powers like Britain, Germany, France and Italy pool their sovereignty and submit to collective decision-making on a wide range of vital issues, has softened the edges of the sovereignty argument in relation to Northern Ireland and has set the traditional territorial dispute in an entirely different context. Growing awareness of the importance of the European dimension has had a major impact upon the thinking of the IRA and Sinn Fein and was an important factor in persuading them to abandon the armed struggle. Indeed, the development and growth of the European Union has also had an impact upon the thinking of independence-minded people in Scotland, the Basque Country and, no doubt, in other European regions.

Lastly, European summits bring the government leaders of Britain and Ireland into constant contact and meetings between the two prime ministers in the wings of these summits to deal with the current state of affairs in Northern Ireland is an established routine.

5.3 American public opinion

There is considerable interest in and concern for the Irish problem throughout the United States and this has been an important factor in the conflict. In US censuses, about forty-five million Americans declare that their ethnic origin is Irish. Perhaps as many more have some known Irish element in their ethnic mix. The United States has proved to be a fertile fundraising ground for the IRA and this has concerned successive Irish and British governments, as well as all the constitutional parties in Northern Ireland.

American opinion has always had a major bearing upon events in Ireland and has always been a major consideration in London, where the 'special relationship' between the United Kingdom and the United States is a matter of considerable importance. British concern not to alienate American opinion has always been an important constraint upon the policies pursued by British governments in Northern Ireland. On the other hand, American sympathy for the Irish case has traditionally been a major lever in the hands of Irish governments in their struggle to influence British policy. Successive British and Irish governments, as well as most of the political parties in Northern Ireland, have devoted considerable time and efforts to informing and shaping opinion among Irish Americans and in American government circles.

6. THIRD PARTY INVOLVEMENT

6.1 The United States presidential envoy

Presidents Carter and Reagan made public statements and private representations to the British government at various times, but US governments did not become directly and openly involved in the problem until President Clinton appointed the former US Senate Majority Leader, Senator George Mitchell, as his personal envoy to Ireland. Senator Mitchell went on to chair the peace talks, established in the wake of the Downing Street Declaration of December 1993 and the subsequent paramilitary ceasefires, and played a key role in the negotiation of the Good Friday Agreement.

The administrations of President Clinton and President George W. Bush have continued a direct involvement in the efforts to fully implement the Good Friday Agreement. President Bush himself has made several important statements and interventions in the Northern Ireland situation since his election, confounding the pundits who predicted that a Republican administration would jettison the Northern Ireland peace process as a major foreign policy issue for the United States.

Moreover, President Bush, as one of the first measures of his administration, appointed Ambassador Richard Haas as his personal envoy to Ireland, and the ambassador became a central and crucially influential figure. In the first place Ambassador Haas quickly mastered the complexities and nuances of the Northern Ireland situation and established a rapport with all of the major players. He showed great skill in bringing the enormous influence of the US government to bear in a measured way in order to progress agreement. The government of the United States has a particularly close relationship with both the British and Irish governments, and good relations with Washington are, as already stated, a matter of prime importance in London and Dublin. Most importantly, since 9/11, the world has changed. For those like the IRA and Sinn Fein, who have resorted to terror in the past to pursue a political agenda, the world climate is now distinctly wintry. Those parties with relationships to terror organisations are acutely aware that combating terror is now the number one priority in the White House. The IRA in particular realise that running foul of the American administration would probably be their death knell. They have already stretched the patience of the United States through their involvement with narco-terrorists in Colombia and with ETA in the Basque Country, and they know that they are now at the limit of their credit in Washington.

6.2 The European Union's role

Although the European Union has never become politically involved in the Northern Ireland situation, it was helpful in that it provided funding to combat Northern Ireland's social and economic decline, which was exacerbated by the violence. When the European Structural Funds were doubled and concentrated in a smaller number of 'objectivised' regions in the late 1980s, Northern Ireland did not automatically qualify on economic criteria as an Objective 1 Region, because it had a GDP per head of population ratio greater than the '70 percent of the European average' threshold. Nevertheless, it was agreed by the EU Council of Ministers that Northern Ireland should have Objective 1 status as a means of helping to resolve the internal political problems of the region.

When the paramilitary ceasefires were declared in the autumn of 1993, the President of the European Commission, Jacques Delors, announced the establishment of a special programme for peace and reconciliation in Northern Ireland, which to date has contributed more than five hundred million euros to the Northern Ireland economy. The programme supports social and economic development projects undertaken by local partnerships involving both sections of the community.

In addition to all of this help, the European Commission is a major contributor to the International Fund for Ireland, a fund for the assistance of cross-community developmental projects in Northern Ireland and the border counties of the Republic, established at the initiative of the former Speaker of the US House of Representatives, Thomas P. 'Tip' O'Neill, in the wake of the Anglo-Irish agreement of 1985. The United States, Canada and New Zealand are the other major contributors. The International Fund has contributed several hundred million euro towards easing unemployment problems and generating new economic activity.

7. Obstacles and Spoilers in the Implementation of the Good Friday Agreement

There has been an unwillingness on the part of some of the players within Northern Ireland, most notably representatives of the Unionist community and the political representatives of the paramilitary organisations on both the Unionist and Nationalist sides, to take some of the steps necessary to resolve the conflict in Northern Ireland.

7.1 The Unionist community

Many Unionists are still fearful of being absorbed into an Irish state in which they would be a small minority. They are fearful of any development which might, in their view, weaken their position of being part of the United Kingdom. Hence they are extremely fearful of any cross-border cooperation within Ireland, which might blur the distinction between North and South or contribute to any growth of integration between the two parts of the island. They are extremely suspicious of and apprehensive about, for example, the work of the implementation bodies, the cross-border agencies developing North-South cooperation in a number of fields. Unionists have been notoriously reluctant to accommodate the need of Irish Nationals in Northern Ireland for a close relationship with fellow Irish Nationals in the Republic of Ireland.

Equally, many Unionists – and not only Unionists – have difficulty in accepting the bona fides of Sinn Fein and the IRA. The prevarication of the IRA in relation to the decommissioning of weapons and continuing evidence of covert IRA activity, has convinced many people in the Unionist community that the IRA's current ceasefire is tactical and not permanent. They fear that the political activities of Sinn Fein are designed to weaken and destabilise Northern Ireland politically, and that at the appropriate time the IRA will re-launch their campaign of terror.

Unionists are also constrained from risk-taking in pursuit of a political settlement by the knowledge that failure to find a permanent settlement will simply mean a continuation of the present situation, i.e., direct rule from London. This is by no means a bad outcome in the eyes of ordinary citizens in the Unionist community: it guarantees that they will remain part of the United Kingdom for the time being and will not be absorbed into a united Ireland in the immediate future. On the other hand, the events of recent years have raised suspicions in the Unionist community about the long-term intentions of the British establishment in relation to Northern Ireland, and there is also the fact that many Unionist politicians still yearn for political power in a devolved administration. The Unionist community is therefore torn between confused and conflicting fears, suspicions, aspirations and ambitions.

7.2 Paramilitary organisations

On the other hand, paramilitary groups – especially the Provisional IRA – have been unwilling to abandon a centuries-long tradition of recourse to arms to resolve political difficulties. There is abundant evidence that Provisional Sinn Fein and the Provisional IRA have been loathe to dispose of all of their weaponry because of a deeply ingrained suspicion of British governments and a lack of any real commitment to the democratic process. Moreover, possession of weapons gave them a uniquely powerful leverage with the two governments, and therefore a distinct advantage over the constitutional parties. Sadly, there are good grounds for believing that the two governments have been more concerned with preventing bombs going off in London and Dublin than they were with sustaining stable and workable institutions of government within Northern Ireland. Key to the governments' concerns is the placation of the Provisional IRA. If the latter are not exploding bombs in London or other British cities, then it is unlikely that the Loyalist Paramilitaries (UVF or UDA) will resort to setting off bombs in Dublin. During the period after the signing of the Good Friday Agreement, the two governments repeatedly shied away from confronting Provisional Sinn Fein and the Provisional IRA over the arms issue. The political outcome of this appeasement has been: (i) the growth of belief in the Irish National community that Provisional Sinn Fein may have the capacity to deliver something quite dramatic in terms of the reunification of Ireland; and (ii) a sharp decline in the Unionist community's belief in and support for the Good Friday Agreement.

It is also true that many of the armed groups have, in the last thirty years, developed illegal and very lucrative rackets to fund their organisations. Many individual members of the paramilitary leaderships have accumulated huge personal fortunes from criminal activity. The current joke among commentators is to refer to the Rafia (the IRA is often referred to as the Ra). The financial interests involved are now quite enormous and could not easily be protected without the capacity to use force. This consideration further inhibited the paramilitary organisations from disposing of their weaponry.

There is an additional factor in the case of the Provisional IRA. In the course of the last twenty years, a number of former Provisionals have broken with the organisation and formed new Republican terror groups such as the Real IRA and the Continuity IRA. Relations between the Provisional IRA and these dissident organisations are often very strained. These are not the kind of people who settle their differences by writing letters to the newspapers. The Provisionals have been reluctant to divest themselves of all weaponry, leaving themselves exposed to reprisals from the very dissident organisations which they have attempted to suppress in the past.

8. POSTSCRIPT

In the autumn and early winter of 2004 negotiations resumed between the British and Irish governments, the DUP and Sinn Fein, on the reformation of the institutions of the Good Friday Agreement. The Provisionals undertook to decommission all of their *materiel* in return for DUP agreement to reform the Executive under the leadership of Ian Paisley with a Sinn Fein deputy. The negotiations almost succeeded, and only fell apart at the last moment when the Provisionals refused to agree to any video or even photographic record being made of the decommissioning event.

However, the entire political climate changed radically only a few days later when, on 19 December 2004, Belfast's Northern Bank was robbed of forty million euros in Europe's largest ever bank raid. It was clear from the beginning that this was, and could only have been, the work of the provisional IRA. No other criminal or paramilitary organisation in Ireland has, or ever had, the resources or capacity to conduct such a complex and highly planned military-style operation. But quite the most disturbing and galling aspect of the robbery was that it was being planned, and was given the final clearance, by the very Provisional leadership which was at the same time negotiating in apparent good faith with both governments and the DUP to reform the institutions of the Good Friday Agreement.

This latest evidence of rank Provisional duplicity and cynical bad faith infuriated the two governments and all the other parties. The Irish Government was particularly angry, and openly accused the Provisionals' most prominent and visible political leaders of 'treating the entire Irish nation like fools'. The Provisionals denied, as they would, any involvement in the robbery. However they were acutely aware of the very significant change in the political climate in both islands and the fact that they had now finally exhausted their line of credit. Pressure upon the Provisionals increased accordingly and intensified when, in the spring and early summer of 2005, evidence began to emerge of a money-laundering operation among Provisional sympathisers in the far south of Ireland, involving banknotes which could be traced back to the Northern Bank robbery. Partly in order to distract public attention from investigations being carried on by police in both parts of Ireland into the Northern Bank heist and which were uncovering more and more evidence of the vastness of the Provisionals' financial empire (including their attempt to buy a bank in Bulgaria), the IRA finally offered to fulfil the obligations undertaken by them in 1998, and to complete decommissioning. The decommissioning event took place on 26 September 2005 and was witnessed by General de Chastelain and his commission as well as two very well-known clergymen – one Catholic and the other Protestant. The Unionists political leadership remains hugely unimpressed however, since there is no other video, photographic or written evidence of what was decommissioned. And Unionists are not alone in their scepticism about the completeness of IRA disarmament. For the time being, as we approach the end of 2005, the political situation in Northern Ireland remains stalemated, though it is rumoured that the two governments will renew efforts to recreate the institutions of the Good Friday Agreement in the spring of 2006.

9. Concluding Remarks

The Northern Ireland problem is the unresolved interface between the British and Irish nations. Northern Ireland is a part of the United Kingdom, yet part of the island of Ireland. Unionists perceive themselves to be British people, living in their own country. Irish Nationals in Northern Ireland perceive themselves to be Irish people, living in their own country. The problem is that they inhabit the same piece of earth. Each of the two major communities defines its identity by reference to a greater whole, extending beyond the borders of Northern Ireland itself, of which it believes itself to be a part. Resolution of this conflict of identities is impossible without the involvement of the two nations, Britain and Ireland, and the two sovereign governments of those countries.

Therefore, the Northern Ireland peace process is necessarily both intrastate and inter-state. The enormous Irish emigrant diaspora throughout the English-speaking world, and especially in the United States, generates in many countries an intense interest in the affairs of Ireland. Additionally, there is the European Union factor. The Northern Ireland problem cannot any longer be confined within the borders of Northern Ireland, or even within the borders of United Kingdom.

Even though the peace process is currently stalled and the institutions of the Good Friday Agreement in suspension, the outlook is not uniformly bleak. There is some evidence that the Irish government is now sufficiently concerned by the threat of organised crime to deal vigorously with the IRA and other paramilitary and criminal organisations. The British government may well feel encouraged to do the same. There is, moreover, no doubt that the world has become a distinctly chilly place for terrorist organisations, made even chillier by the recent tragedies in Madrid, London, Bali, Morocco and Amman. This may have an impact on the thinking of the Provisional IRA and the other paramilitary organisations, and convince them that there is no future for secret private armies. There is some recent evidence that Ian Paisley's DUP is trying to break out of its anti-agreement mindset and explore possibilities for the sharing of power with the Irish National community. No political situation ever remains entirely static. There is always the possibility of progress.

Chapter V

THE DISCORDANT ACCORD:
CHALLENGES IN THE IMPLEMENTATION OF THE
CHITTAGONG HILL TRACTS ACCORD OF 1997[*]

Devasish Roy[**]

1. INTRODUCTION[1]

The signing of the Chittagong Hill Tracts Accord (hereafter the 1997 Accord or the Accord) on 2 December 1997 heralded the consolidation of a much-publicised truce between the government of Bangladesh and the indigenous people's political party known as the Parbatya Chattagram Jana Samhati Samiti (Chittagong Hill Tracts People's Solidarity Organisation) or PCJSS (JSS in short). The JSS had until then sustained a protracted low intensity guerrilla war against successive regimes in Bangladesh for almost twenty-five years through its armed wing, the People's Liberation Army, better known as the Shanti Bahini or Peace Force. Decommissioning on the side of the guerrillas, without accounting for some minor armed deployments, had actually taken effect more than five years earlier, when the JSS had declared a unilateral cease-fire. This situation was formalised with the signing of the 1997 Accord, which also included a general amnesty for the erstwhile guerrilla fighters.

Today, many questions are being raised as to whether the 1997 Accord was a failure.[2] The resultant situation of 'peace', or rather, the absence or near-ab-

---

[*] The text of the Chittagong Hill Tracts Accord is reproduced in Appendix C.
[**] The Chakma Raja, Chittagong Hill Tracts, Bangladesh; Bangladesh Representative of Commonwealth Association of Indigenous Peoples (CAIP).
[1] This essay is based in part upon an earlier paper entitled 'The Chittagong Hill Tracts "Peace Accord": Whose Peace?', which was presented at the workshop on 'Dimensions, Dynamics and Transformation of Resource Conflicts between Indigenous Peoples and Settlers in Frontier Regions of South and Southeast Asia', organised by the University of Zürich and held in Mont-Soleil, Switzerland, on 25-29 September, 2002. Some sections of these texts are identical. However, the paper for Mont-Soleil had a strong focus on the question of peace consolidation, while this essay more specifically focuses on the political and implementation aspects of the Accord, its aftermath, and the negotiations preceding the signing of the Accord.
[2] See, for example, R. Samaddar, *Those Accords: A Bunch of Documents*, SAFHR Paper Series No. 4 (Kathmandu, South Asia Forum for Human Rights 1999) and C. Nunthera, 'Peace

M. Boltjes (ed.), Implementing Negotiated Agreements
© 2007, Kreddha International and T·M·C·ASSER PRESS, The Hague, The Netherlands

sence of organised conflict between the indigenous guerrillas and the government security forces still holds. The past half decade since the 1997 Accord has shown little or no violence against security forces or Bengali settlers by the indigenous people.[3] although the reverse is somewhat less true.[4] However, the post-accord situation has seen the rise of a new armed conflict that threatens peace, a conflict between erstwhile allies from among the indigenous autonomist activists. Many young indigenous men have met violent deaths in armed confrontations between the opposing sides that are usually known as the pro-Accordists and the anti-Accordists. The anti-Accordists – consisting largely of members of the United People's Democratic Front (UPDF) – had rejected the pre-1997 negotiation process as a sham. The pro-Accordists are led by the JSS. The commissions and omissions of the police and other government security forces regarding this conflict have led locals to believe that although these forces are ostensibly neutral, they are not really interested in applying the law when the victims of the violence are indigenous people, whoever the perpetrators of the violence might be. Perhaps this is at least partly due to the unwritten government policy to not interfere in such intra-indigenous fratricidal conflicts. The other reason may be the ethnicity of the security personnel: hardly any of them belong to the indigenous groups. Or at least that is what many indigenous people tend to believe. Whether or not this perception is based on fact or opinion is secondary to the need for the police force to be seen as neutral in inter-ethnic conflicts. There is much room for improvement here.

Accords as Instruments of Conflict Transformation: Arrangements that Work and Arrangements that Don't (Mizo Accord, 1986, Assam Accord, 1985, Bodo Accord, 1993)' (paper presented at workshop on 'Dimensions, Dynamics', Switzerland, 2002).

[3] The indigenous population of the CHT is not a homogenous entity. It is made up of communities of eleven distinct peoples with their own languages, culture and heritage. Although the hill district councils are to include representatives of all the peoples of the region, there have been complaints of discrimination against the indigenous groups with small populations, both by the majority Bengali people and by the indigenous groups with the larger populations (e.g., Chakma and Marma). The laws refer to the CHT peoples as indigenous, hillmen, or tribes in different instruments, but the latter expression is the most favoured by government leaders and functionaries. The JSS uses the generic term Jumma (from the common swidden or jum cultivation heritage of all the CHT peoples) to refer to the indigenous peoples and the indigenous population of the region.

[4] International Work Group on Indigenous Affairs (IWGIA), *The Indigenous World: 2000-2001* (Copenhagen, IWGIA 2002), 318. For a recent incident of organised violence and arson against indigenous people by Bengali settlers in the CHT, see *Prathom Alo* (Dhaka), 21 April 2003. See also Naeem Mohaiemen, 'PCJSS alleges gang rape of 9 ethnic women in Khagrachari', *Daily Star* (Dhaka), 31 August 2003 and Editorial, *Daily Star*, 9 September 2003. For a recent reassessment of the CHT peace process, see A. Mohsin, *The Chittagong Hill Tracts, Bangladesh: On the Difficult Road to Peace*, International Peace Academy Occasional Paper Series (Boulder, London, Lynne Rienner Publishers 2003).

The two main purposes of the 1997 Accord were to re-establish peace in the Chittagong Hill Tracts and to provide for a measure of autonomy to this southeastern border region that is topographically, demographically and culturally so different from the rest of Bangladesh.[5]

Many indigenous people of the CHT do regard the 1997 Accord as unsuccessful for having failed to bring total peace and for having brought about a devolved system of self-government that seems to have little or no teeth. Others have even questioned the contents and timing of the Accord itself and said that it had come 'too little, too late, too loud'.[6] A well-known writer on the CHT claimed, as early as 1998, that '[the] seeds of insecurity, discontent, inequality and further polarisation are inherent within the peace accord'.[7] Her sympathies are clearly on the side of those who feel that the 1997 Accord has compromised the interests of the indigenous people. Then again, some feel that five years is too short a period for such a judgment, especially where a party initially opposed to the Accord while in opposition is now holding the reigns of government. This is the stand of the JSS, who insist that it is not the contents of the 1997 Accord but its non-implementation that is responsible for the current political stalemate.

J. B. Larma, the president of the JSS, chairperson of the CHT Regional Council and member of the – now dormant – CHT Accord Implementation Committee, has time and again complained of non-implementation of the 1997 Accord in no unclear terms.[8] He is on record recently as having lamented thus:

> [Though] more than five years have passed after the signing of the Accord, most of the provisions, especially the main issues of the Accord, such as, formation of Land Commission for settling the land disputes, rehabilitation of returnee Jumma refugees and internally displaced Jumma families, withdrawal of temporary camps of security forces and military administration, preparing voter list only with the permanent residents of CHT, effective enforcement of the three [hill district coun-

---

[5] Although there is no doubt that the question of autonomy forms one of the most crucial parts of the 1997 Accord, the word itself has been studiously avoided in the document. This is due to the reluctance of the government negotiators to use the word, based perhaps on the absence of any formalized provisions on 'autonomy' in the national constitution and other laws.

[6] Samaddar, *Those Accords*, 8.

[7] A. Mohsin, 'Chittagong Hill Tracts Peace Accord: Looking Ahead', *Journal of Social Studies*, August-October 1998, 104-117 at 107.

[8] D. Talukdar, then MP and head of the CHT Task Force on Refugees, A.H. Abdulla, former Chief Whip and J. B. Larma together form the three-member CHT Accord Implementation Committee, which is no longer functional with the change in government in 2001. The present government has not reconstituted this committee.

cils] and the CHT Regional Council Act, rehabilitation of the Bengali settlers outside CHT etc. have either [been] left unimplemented or partially implemented.[9]

On the side of the government and the Bengali settlers, there have sometimes been some murmurs of suspicions that the JSS had not given up all its arms to the government. These suspicions have not however been voiced very forcefully, suggesting, I feel, that there is little or no truth in this allegation. I have heard of no other complaints of non-implementation against the JSS.

If we look at specific aspects of the 1997 Accord in a somewhat reductionist manner we can easily see both success and failure. This is relevant when we attempt to consider peace processes such as the CHT one within the context of a longer time frame. With such a view, we remind ourselves that the 1997 Accord is the third political accord on the CHT, preceded by the 1988 Agreement, signed by the 'moderate' indigenous leaders and the 1985 Agreement, signed by a faction of the Priti Group that broke away from the JSS in the early 1980s. But let us look further. I feel that in order to understand where the peace process is now heading towards, and even where it might ultimately lead to, it is necessary to also look into the political and administrative history of the region. Unless we understand the legacy of colonisation and the erosion of autonomy in the region, it is unlikely that we will understand what the indigenous people of the CHT – including the JSS and the UPDF – have in mind when they talk about a revival and revitalisation of autonomy. Perhaps this enquiry will also help us understand the dynamics of other similar peace processes, including challenges to the implementation of intrastate peace accords in different parts of the world.[10]

2. Historical Background

The contrast between the Chittagong Hill Tracts and the rest of the country, barring some minor pockets inhabited by indigenous peoples, could hardly be more striking. The CHT is hilly and mountainous while the rest of the country is largely composed of deltaic plains. The dominant language of the country is Bengali while in the CHT the indigenous groups have their own languages. Some of these are related to Bengali and other Indo-Aryan languages, whilst others are totally different and belong to the Tibeto-Burman group of languages.

---

[9] Jyotirindra Bodhipriyo Larma, 'The CHT and its Solution' (paper presented at the Regional Training Program to Enhance the Conflict Prevention and Peace-Building Capacities of Indigenous Peoples' Representatives of the Asia-Pacific, organised by the United Nations Institute for Training and Research (UNITAR), Chiang Mai, Thailand, 7-12 April 2003).

[10] The text of the Good Friday Agreement is reproduced in Appendix C

Most of the indigenous people are Buddhist, Hindu or Christian, sometimes in conjunction with their traditional indigenous faiths, while in the plains, the religion of the majority is Islam. Most of plains Bangladesh had formed part of empires, kingdoms or other formalised state and quasi-state polities for many centuries. The CHT was composed of decentralised and largely unformalised self-governing chiefdoms and chieftaincies that were independent of external political control until only after Bengal itself was colonised by the British between the eighteenth and nineteenth centuries.[11]

Like many other sub-Himalayan mountain areas on the tri-borders of India, Burma and Bangladesh, the CHT was first colonised, not by a kingdom or empire from the neighbouring plains, but by British imperialists.[12] In the case of the CHT, the British were motivated both by strategic and economic interests. They achieved their aims through military deployment and diplomatic subterfuge, leading to an exploitative trade treaty, and ultimately, direct colonisation.

By the 1780s, the British East India Company had converted the major chiefdoms and tribal confederacies of the region into British tributaries.[13] This, however, did not come about before a decade-long guerrilla war – one of the first known guerrilla wars of South Asia against a colonial power and led by the Chakma chief or *raja* – was brought to an end through an economic blockade that cut off the supply of salt, iron, clay and other necessities that were not available in the region.[14] In 1787, the Chakma Raja Jan Bux Khan signed a truce with the British Governor General, Lord Cornwallis, promising to pay an annual tribute of hill cotton to the British East India Company and to regard his chiefdom as a British tributary.[15]

Despite the British-Chakma treaty of 1787, the East India Company's successor, the British Indian government, did not formally annex the region into British Bengal until almost a century later, in 1860. The government renamed

---

[11] Bangladesh Groep Nederland, 'The Road to Repression' in *The Charge of Genocide: Human Rights in the Chittagong Hill Tracts*, Papers for Conference on the Chittagong Hill Tracts, Chittagong Hill Tracts Campaign, Amsterdam, 11 October 1986, 23; Claus Dieter Brauns and Lorenz G. Loffler, *Mru: Hill People on the Border of Bangladesh* (Basel/Boston/Berlin, Birkhauser Verlag 1990), 27; Ratan Lal Chakroborty, 'Chakma Resistance to early British Rule', *Bangladesh Historical Studies: Journal of the Bangladesh Itihaas Samiti* Vol. II (1977), 133-156; R.H.S. Hutchinson, *The Chittagong Hill Tract* (Delhi, Vivek Publishing House 1978), 8-9; A.M. Serajuddin, 'The Rajas of the Chittagong Hill Tracts and their Relations with the Mughals and the East India Company in the Eighteenth Century', *Journal of the Asiatic Society of Pakistan* Vol. XIII, No. 2 (1968).

[12] Bangladesh Groep Nederland, 'Repression', 23; Brauns and Loffler, *Hill People*, 27.

[13] Chakroborty, 'Chakma Resistance'; Hutchinson, *Chittagong Hill Tract*, 8-9.

[14] Serajuddin, 'Rajas'; Chakroborty, 'Chakma Resistance'.

[15] Serajuddin; Chakroborty; Raja Tridiv Roy, *The Departed Melody: Memoirs* (Islamabad, PPA Publications 2003), 30.

the region as the *Chittagong hill tracts*, due to its proximity to and its control by the plains region known as Chittagong, which is now a separate district. Until then, the Company was content with its revenue earnings from this territory, known in revenue records as Jum Bangoo or as the Kapas Mahal (or Cotton Department). The cotton tributes were gradually converted to cash payments. Between 1860 and 1947, the indigenous polities and alliances were gradually realigned, leading to political centralisation among some of its peoples and their chiefs, and to decentralisation in others. This ultimately led many chieftaincies and tribal confederacies to disappear into political and social oblivion.[16] However, throughout the period of British rule, which ended in 1947, the primacy of the indigenous peoples as against non-indigenous settlers was emphasised, and a quantum of administrative autonomy was retained in the reorganised quasi-traditional and partly formalised self-government system.

The period after British rule saw the erosion of autonomy in the CHT despite the introduction of franchise rights in the 1950s. The new Pakistani state, born out of a notion of nationhood for the Muslims of India, had little political space for the non-Muslim population of the region, especially as many of them had sought to merge the CHT with India, rather than Pakistan. It was not that those in favour of India during the partition were firm believers in Indian nationalism as such. What they sought to avoid was to become religious minorities and be subjected to discrimination by the new Islam-oriented, if not theocratic, state. Until the 1950s most senior government officials who were posted to the CHT were from the then West Pakistan or were Muslim refugees from India and they remained largely neutral in resource and other conflicts between indigenous people and Bengali settlers. Although mostly Muslim by faith, perhaps they did not feel any closer to the Bengalis than to the indigenous people. Things began to change as more and more Bengali-speaking East Pakistani bureaucrats started to be posted in the CHT, especially from the mid-1950s onwards. Many of these officials acted as fairly as they could under the circumstances. Others, however, were less than fair, and occasionally unscrupulous. This resulted in increased immigration of ethnic Bengalis, and a growing Bengali domination in service, commerce and other spheres of politics and economy in the hill region. The CHT leaders were unable to prevent the indigenous peoples' political and economic marginalisation with the phenomenal rise of settler population in the region and with successive government policies that discriminated for the Bengalis and against the indigenous people, overtly or covertly.[17]

---

[16] Hutchinson, *Chittagong Hill Tract*, 12; Brauns and Loffler, *Hill People*, 30; Willem van Schendel, Wolfgang Mey and Aditya Kumar Dewan, *The Chittagong Hill Tracts: Living in a Borderland* (Bangkok, While Lotus Press 2000), 25-32.

[17] See Subir Bhaumik, Meghna Guhathakurta and Sabyasachi Basu Ray Chaudhury (eds.), *Living on the Edge: Essays from the Chittagong Hill Tracts* (Kathmandu, South Asia Forum for

Bengali in-migration into the CHT had started during the nineteenth century, but even after the departure of the British in 1947, the settlers made up less than 10 percent of the population. This was to rise to almost 50 percent in 1991, making the indigenous people a near-minority in their ancestral homeland. The internal immigration policies of the different governments were not the same. The British government had allowed limited immigration into the CHT in order to facilitate trade and irrigation-oriented intensive agriculture, both of which were relatively new to the indigenous peoples. It was careful not to allow large scale immigration, fearing the growth of anti-British sentiments, which were more common in the plains of Bengal. The Pakistani government's role (1947-1971) regarding immigration was more ambivalent, while the role of successive Bangladeshi administrations on this issue has varied from covert encouragement (early 1970s) to a directly sponsored population transfer programme (1979 to 1984). The transmigration of the largely Muslim peasants from various lowland districts led to the displacement of tens of thousands of indigenous people, thereby partly civilianising the ongoing conflict and adding ethnic and religious overtones to a conflict that was hitherto largely restricted to the non-Muslim indigenous guerrillas and predominantly Muslim Bengali government security forces. Of course, that does not mean that innocent civilians, whether Bengali or indigenous, were not victimised earlier, but at least their number until then was not so visibly large. This part-civil part-military conflict continued up to the 1990s and it was not until the signing of the 1997 Accord that the organised internal war formally ended. In the meantime, thousands of lives had been lost, tens of thousands of people rendered homeless, and an untold number had to suffer the indignities of rape, torture and imprisonment. Although there were casualties on both sides of the ethnic divide, the indigenous people suffered the most because the balance of force was not on their side, among other things.[18] Moreover, the security forces had, on the whole,

---

Human Rights 1997); and Philip Gain (ed.), *Chittagong Hill Tracts: Life and Nature at Risk* (Dhaka, SEHD 2000) for a number of articles by CHT people and others on the pre-Accord and post-Accord situation respectively and of human rights, development and cultural issues. For land issues, see Rajkumari Chandra Roy, *Land Rights of the Indigenous Peoples of the Chittagong Hill Tracts, Bangladesh* (Copenhagen, International Work Group for Indigenous Affairs, Document No. 99, 2000); Raja Devasish Roy, 'The Population Transfer Programme of the 1980s and the Land Rights of the Indigenous peoples of the Chittagong Hill Tracts' in Bhaumik et al., *Living on the Edge*, 167-208; and Raja Devasish Roy, 'The Land Question and the Chittagong Hill Tracts Accord' in *The Chittagong Hill Tracts: The Road to a Lasting Peace*, Victoria Tauli Corpuz et al. (eds.) (Baguio City, Philippines, Tebtebba Foundation 2000). For the nature of the pro-Accord and anti-Accord conflict, see Chittagong Hill Tracts Commission, *Life Is Not Ours: Land and Human Rights in the Chittagong Hill Tracts, Bangladesh* (Copenhagen, International Work Group for Indigenous Affairs 1991), Update 4 (2000).

[18] Chittagong Hill Tracts Commission, *Life Is Not Ours*.

paid little heed towards the human rights of the indigenous people in their quest to contain the insurgency.

3. THE CHITTAGONG HILL TRACTS ACCORD OF 1997

The Chittagong Hill Tracts Accord contains four main sections. The text of the Accord is reproduced in Appendix B. Part A, under the heading 'General', recognises the Chittagong Hill Tracts as a 'tribal inhabited area' and deals with commitments to the passage of legislation as well as details of the composition of the committee that was to oversee the implementation of the accord. No time frame for implementation was agreed upon.

Part B is entitled 'Hill District Local Government Councils/Hill District Councils'. It contains detailed provisions on proposed amendments to the District Council laws to strengthen the councils' existing powers and to add more subjects under their jurisdiction.

Part C, entitled 'Chittagong Hill Tracts Regional Council', lays down the composition of a new unit of regional authority to be constituted styled as a 'regional' council incorporating the three hill provinces or 'districts'. In the case of both the regional and the district councils, the chairpersonship and two-thirds of the seats are to be reserved for indigenous or 'tribal' people.

Part D is entitled 'Rehabilitation, General Amnesty and other matters'. It provides for quite a wide range of issues besides the rehabilitation of the international refugees, the internally displaced people and indigenous fighters, and the granting of amnesty to the guerrillas and other indigenous people who were involved in the armed struggle. A specially constituted task force was to expedite the work of rehabilitation. The vexing and seemingly irresolvable issue of land is mentioned both in this part and in the district councils' laws. It includes provisions for land grants to landless indigenous families, for the cancellation of land leases to non-residents where such lessees had illegally left the land utilised, and for the formation of a Commission on Land to provide expeditious justice in land-related disputes, especially between indigenous people and settlers. Other important matters include the manner and timing of handing over of arms by the guerrillas and their return to normal life, affirmative action through quotas for reservation of jobs for local residents with priority to indigenous ('tribal') candidates, special allocation of development funds, the dismantling of non-permanent military camps, and the return of soldiers to peacetime permanent garrisons or cantonments (without any time frame).

An important crosscutting matter of the Accord is indigenous culture. This was treated as a fundamental issue by the recognition of the CHT as a 'tribal inhabited area' in part A, and reiterated, directly and indirectly, in parts B, C and D. The measures included the reservation of a specified number of seats for particular ethnic groups in the regional and the district councils, the proposed introduction of primary education in the mother tongues of the indigenous peoples, granting jurisdiction to the CHT councils over customary law, the recognition of customary land rights through the Land Commission law, and the reinforcement of the traditional chiefs' advisory, judicial and residential certificate-granting prerogatives.

3.1 Reception of the 1997 Accord

The signing of the 1997 Accord brought mixed receptions. The government led by the Awami League was quick to hail it as an historic agreement, time and again invoking it as one of its major success stories.[19] Not long after the event, the UN agency UNESCO even awarded then Prime Minister Sheikh Hasina with a peace prize. As for the indigenous people, there was cautious relief and a sense of anticipation on the conclusion of the Accord. But at the signing ceremony jubilation and celebrations on the part of the JSS were patently absent. The former underground party was welcoming the Accord very cautiously, reflecting in a way the general mood of the indigenous people.

A breakaway faction of indigenous student and youth groups hitherto allied to the JSS – now known as the United People's Democratic Front (UPDF) – unequivocally condemned the Accord as a sell-out to reactionaries as soon as it was signed. They vowed to continue the struggle for greater autonomy and constitutional safeguards. Other sections of the indigenous population were more cautious in their comments about the Accord itself and adopted a wait-and-see attitude.[20] Today, however, it would be difficult to find very many indigenous people in the Chittagong Hill Tracts who are happy with the way the 1997 Accord was and is being implemented.

The non-indigenous Bengali-speaking inhabitants, who now constitute almost half the population of the region, may be divided, for our purpose, into at least three distinct groups: (1) the settlers of the nineteenth century (the old

---

[19] The Awami League – now ideologically somewhat centrist – was the party that led the country to independence from Pakistan through a war of independence in 1971. The party believes in 'Bengali nationalism', which by definition excludes the non-Bengali-speaking indigenous people of the country. It framed the first national constitution that rejected the demands of the CHT people for a more multicultural concept of nationality, for administrative autonomy for the region, and for constitutional safeguards for their autonomy and culture. The more right-of-centre BNP was ostensibly more liberal towards non-Bengalis, but its orientation towards the Islamic heritage of Bangladesh was and is not acceptable to a large section of the non-Muslim people of the Chittagong Hill Tracts.

[20] Mohsin, 'Chittagong Hill Tracts', 107.

Bengalis), (2) the spontaneous migrants of the twentieth century (the natural migrants); and (3) the Bengali population transferees or transmigrants (government-sponsored settlers) of the 1980s. Initially they all condemned the 1997 Accord, which they felt had compromised their interests and turned them into second-class citizens.[21] Many of them even saw the role of big brother India behind the Accord, as it was widely believed that the guerrillas had used Indian territory, training, arms and other logistics at different periods of the war.[22] They alleged a sell-out to Indian hegemonic interests.

Some of the old Bengalis are now allied with the JSS against the government-sponsored settlers but not necessarily against the government of the day. Few of them openly speak against the Accord now.

The situation of the natural migrants (largely traders, manual labourers, etc.) has perhaps changed the least in the post-Accord period, because peace, and more importantly, unhindered mobility and transportation, both prerequisites for trade and commerce, are still threatened by the intra-indigenous conflict, like it was earlier threatened by the guerrilla-army conflict. Leaders from this group are among the least vocal Bengalis regarding the Accord, which is not surprising as business people the world over are seldom openly for or against any political grouping.

The government-sponsored settlers constitute one of the strongest political groups within the Bengali population. They now have more physical security than before because they are no longer threatened by an active guerrilla force and still continue to receive food grain support from the government, a system that was introduced since their advent into the region almost twenty-five years ago.[23] Moreover, they now have a member of parliament who has also been appointed chairperson of the CHT Development Board, that has access to reasonably large sums of development funds. Despite this, they are not content with the status quo. Many of them had expected the present right-of-centre BNP-led coalition government to give them a bigger say in the administration of the region. Two-thirds of the seats in the regional and district councils, as well as

---

[21] Ibid.

[22] Conversely, Indian sources have accused the Bangladesh government of sheltering and aiding anti-Indian separatist guerrillas from Northeast India. See, for example, Subir Bhaumik, *Insurgent Crossfire: Northeast India* (New Delhi, Lancer Publishers 1996) and Sanjoy Hazarika, *Strangers of the Mist: Tales of War and Peace from India's Northeast* (New Delhi, Penguin Books 1995).

[23] For details of the food grain support to the Bengali population transferees, see Naeem Mohaiemen, 'Rights of Ethnic Minorities and Indigenous People', in *Human Rights in Bangladesh 2003* (Dhaka, ASK (Ain O Salish Kendra) 2004), 155. See also R. Dewan, 'The CHT Accord and its Process of Implementation', *Daily Star* (Dhaka), 2 December 2003.

the chairpersonships of these councils are reserved exclusively for hill people.[24] The government-sponsored settlers have been among the most vocal critics of the 1997 Accord, saying that it has discriminated against them. Many of them rallied around the banner of the right-of-centre BNP and the right-wing Jamaat-e-Islami Bangladesh – when both of these parties were in opposition – and were prompt to castigate the 1997 Accord as having compromised the unitary character of the republic through what they saw was the establishment of a quasi-federal administrative set-up in the hill region.[25] The aforesaid parties are now partners in a coalition government. Informally, some members of the government have assured indigenous leaders that they have agreed to put aside their former reservations about the 1997 Accord, but then again, a number of public statements by some other senior members of the government purporting to draw attention to the alleged unconstitutionality of the 1997 Accord suggests that many within the government are against the implementation of the Accord.[26]

Until today, these differing, opposed and equivocal views on the 1997 Accord remain as stumbling blocks towards sustainable peace between the indigenous people and the Bengalis, as well as towards fuller implementation of the many important unimplemented provisions of the 1997 Accord, including those on land, demilitarisation, policing and other aspects of devolution to the regional and the district councils.

3.2 The implementation of the 1997 Accord under review

3.2.1 *Non-implementation and violations of written and unwritten provisions of the 1997 Accord*

According to the JSS, major provisions of the 1997 Accord have *not* been implemented by the government. These are the following:[27] (i) the withdrawal of (all

---

[24] The UPDF claims that the JSS, by signing the accord and failing to remove the Bengali settlers from the region has effectively legalized the permanent residence of the settlers. Conversely, the JSS has claimed that the UPDF has legitimized the settlers by participating in an election that includes the 'non-permanent-resident' settlers as voters.

[25] Willem van Schendel, 'Bengalis, Bangladeshis and Others: Chakma Visions of a Pluralist Bangladesh', in Rounaq Jahan (ed.),*Bangladesh: Promise and Performance* (Dhaka, University Press Limited 2000), 65-105 at 66.

[26] At least two senior members of the present cabinet have expressed reservations about the CHT Accord because of its alleged discrimination against Bengali people. On 11 March 2003, in an address in parliament, Prime Minister Khaleda Zia condemned the previous Awami League government for having signed an unconstitutional accord. For opposition criticisms of her speech, see *Prathom Alo* (Dhaka), 13 April 2003, 13.

[27] See, for example, Peace Campaign Group, *A Report on the Demonstration against the Government of Bangladesh at Paris Consortium 2002* (West Sagarpur, New Delhi, 2002). Re-

except a few) non-permanent military camps;[28] (ii) the transfer of land and law and order matters to the district councils; and (iii) the commencement of the work of the Land Commission. In violation of the provisions in the Accord, the government has appointed non-indigenous persons to the posts of the (cabinet-rank) minister for Chittagong Hill Tracts affairs and the chairperson of the CHT Development Board.[29] It also passed the CHT Land Commission Act of 2001 in violation of provisions of the Accord, reducing the geographical jurisdiction of the commission and providing too much power to its non-indigenous chairperson. These matters are relatively straightforward and the government is not in a position to deny the above. Two other allegations of the JSS are less unequivocal, but not necessarily without foundation or logic. According to the JSS, the government has included non-permanent residents of the region as voters in the recent parliamentary elections[30] and it has also included non-indigenous people within the list of the 'internally displaced'.[31]

---

cently more new camps have reportedly been established in the CHT. See International Work Group on Indigenous Affairs (IWGIA), *The Indigenous World 2005* (Copenhagen, IWGIA 2005), 379.

[28] As of March 2002 only thirty-five out of the estimated 520 (temporary) military camps are reported to have been dismantled. See IWGIA, *The Indigenous World: 2000-2001*, 318. However, writing in April 2003, Larma ('The CHT Issue and its Solution') has referred to the removal of only thirty-one camps.

[29] During the rule of the Awami League, both the posts of the CHT Affairs minister and the chairperson of the CHT Development Board were held by indigenous MPs. Now these posts are held, respectively by the Prime Minister herself (while an indigenous MP holds the *deputy* ministership) and a Bengali MP from the northern hill district. This suggests a concession to Bengali lobbies that had continually protested against the indigenous primacy in holding high political positions within the CHT self-government system.

[30] These elections were formally boycotted by the JSS.

[31] The JSS claims that 'non-tribal permanent residents' (those who 'permanently reside at a specified address, and legally own land, within a hill district') are not eligible to vote in parliamentary elections. The government says that this clause applies for elections to the regional and district councils, but not to parliamentary elections. In the case of the internally displaced people (IDPs), the JSS claims that only indigenous people fall within this category within the meaning of the Accord, while the previous head of the Task Force on Refugees and Displaced People clearly thought otherwise when he compiled a list of 90,208 'tribal' and 38,156 'non-tribal' IDP families (See International Work Group on Indigenous Affairs (IWGIA), *The Indigenous World 1999-2000* (Copenhagen, IWGIA, 2000), 290-291 and IWGIA, *The Indigenous World: 2000-2001*, 292-293.) Representatives of the JSS and the refugees had boycotted the meetings of this Task Force. The previous chair of the Task Force resigned from the post before contesting parliamentary polls of 2001 (which he lost), and the present government recently filled up the vacancy by appointing an indigenous person to the post. But it appears that the new chairman has not been provided with sufficient authority to change the status quo. Since there are no provisions for arbitration of disputes between the parties to the Accord, only a court ruling could clarify the above dispute.

Among the issues mentioned above, I would suggest that it is the stalemate on the land related matters that needs the most immediate attention because many believe that the success or failure of the CHT peace process is dependent very largely upon the resolution of the land-related issues.[32] Among them, the most intricate matter will perhaps be the work of the Land Commission, which is to deal with the complex issue of land titles and customary rights. The presence of a majority of indigenous people in the commission, as provided by law, suggests that customary law will be given due regard, but practical and legal complications may mean that it will take many years before the disputes are resolved.[33] The experiences of the Waitangi Tribunal in New Zealand, which deals with land claims of indigenous Maori people on what are now regarded as 'crown lands', may be potentially helpful towards the work of this commission.[34] However, it is important to remember that, despite their nomenclature, the functions of the Tribunal and the CHT Land Commission may have some basic differences. The work of the Waitangi Tribunal is largely to pro-actively inquire into the validity of Maori land claims, whilst the CHT Land Commission is to be more adversarial and reactive in its work to resolve disputes between litigants. However, the actual nature and scope of the commission's work will perhaps depend upon the way its work procedures are settled, as the law seems to leave it to the members of the commission to devise their work methods.

Although the commission finally met in 2005, as a body it is still far away from actually adjudicating disputes before it. This is primarily because many, if not all, of the indigenous members are unwilling to formally sit as a commission until after the concerned law is amended to bring it in conformity with the provisions of the 1997 Accord. The current law provides that in the event of disagreement among members of the commission, the decision of the commission's chairperson – a retired High Court judge – would prevail. Indigenous members – particularly the chairperson of the CHT Regional Council – have declared that this is tantamount to giving a veto power to the chairperson, which is against the norms of democratic decision-making.[35]

---

[32] Mohsin, 'Chittagong Hill Tracts', 114; Chittagong Hill Tracts Commission, *Life Is Not Ours*, 58.
[33] Roy, 'The Land Question', 40-41.
[34] See, for example, the chapter on the Treaty of Waitangi by Morris Te Whiti Love in this publication.
[35] The author, in his capacity as the Chakma Raja and ex-officio member of the commission, attended this meeting held at the Circuit House, Khagrachari, on 8 June 2005. The commission is headed by a retired High Court judge, and includes the chairperson of the CHT Regional Council, the chairpersons of the three hill district councils, the other two Rajas or chiefs, and the commissioner of the Chittagong Division, a civil servant. See *Prathom Alo* (Dhaka), 9 June 2005. For a

Apart from non-implementation of the express provisions of the agreement, the JSS has also claimed that the government has violated the *unwritten* part of the agreement. This allegedly contains provisions to dismantle cluster villages, stop government rations to the settlers and subsequently rehabilitate the government-sponsored Bengali settlers outside the CHT.[36] The government has denied the existence of any such understanding and it has not taken any measures to either rehabilitate the settlers outside the CHT or stop their rations. It is worth mentioning here that the European Parliament offered to provide grants to the government of Bangladesh to help it rehabilitate the settlers outside the CHT, but the government categorically rejected the proposal.[37] The government-sponsored Bengali settlers make up the only section of the CHT population that has uninterruptedly and regularly received food rations from the government since the 1980s, when they were first resettled here. This clearly suggests that their economic existence in the CHT is artificially subsidised by the government, implying that their situation would otherwise be very marginalised. Indigenous people have demanded that such discriminatory acts be stopped,[38] but successive governments have thought otherwise. Among the indigenous people, only the repatriated refugees from India (but not the internally displaced people) and ex-members of the Shanti Bahini guerrillas receive some food grain support from the government and this too was rumoured to be at risk of discontinuance by the present BNP-led government.[39, 40]

---

detailed discussion on the CHT land issues, including the likely impact of the commission's work, see Roy, 'Population Transfer' and Roy, 'The Land Question'.

[36] Peace Campaign Group Report (New Delhi, 2000) at 6-7 paraphrases the alleged explanation of the government representatives to the JSS representatives on the justification behind the government's non-inclusion of the settler repatriation matter as a written provision in the 1997 Accord with the following words: 'The domestic constituency does not allow the simple majority Awami League government to openly address the issue in the agreement ... because once the issue is addressed in the agreement, the opposition parties, particularly the Bangladesh Nationalist Party (BNP), [which is] opposing the Government's deal with the [JSS], will come out in the streets with mass agitation that can even raise the question of survival of the government in power. In that situation, the possibility of an agreement between the two sides will be jeopardised. Of course, the Government understands and supports the concern of the [JSS] over the issue and can include some provisions in the agreement for the gradual removal of the settlers from the CHT.'

[37] 'Budget Line B7-3010' of the European Parliament earmarked certain funds for the 'repatriation of Bengali settlers in the Chittagong Hill Tracts back to the plains'. See European Alliance with Indigenous Peoples (EAIP) Newsletter, Issue 3, December 1996, 3.

[38] For example, the Rangamati Land Declaration, adopted at a seminar on 'Land Laws, Land Management and the Land Commission in the Chittagong Hill Tracts', organised by the Committee for the Protection of Forest and Land Rights in the CHT in Rangamati, CHT on 7 June 2002 demanded that similar rations be provided to all inhabitants of the CHT.

[39] Interview by the author with government official who wishes to remain anonymous, September 2002.

[40] Mohaiemen, 'Rights of Ethnic Minorities', 155.

3.2.2 Implementation and change of government

The aforesaid situation of non-implementation and violations of the 1997 Accord include developments both before and after the change over of government in Bangladesh in 2001. The elections brought the BNP, the party that was opposed to the 1997 Accord, into power in alliance with the right-wing Jamaat-e-Islami Bangladesh.[41] Regarding some matters, such as the general pattern of providing development grants to CHT institutions, there seems to be no perceptible change in policy. At a much-awaited meeting between the prime minister, the chairperson of the CHT Regional Council (the JSS leader) and the CHT affairs deputy minister in April 2002, an uneasy agreement seemed to have been reached to maintain the *status quo* in the CHT.[42]

One of the few positive developments under the current BNP-led regime is the passage of the CHT Regulation (Amendment) Act of 2003 and the adoption of the National Poverty Reduction Strategy Paper (PRSP) in 2005. The former law seeks to transfer powers over administration of civil and criminal justice, currently vested upon district and divisional administration functionaries, to judges under the Ministry of Justice. This would not affect the partially autonomous justice administration system of the chiefs and headmen. Most provisions of this law were proposed by the CHT Regional Council and it is generally believed that the law has the broad support of different sections of the people of the region, particularly from among the indigenous peoples.[43] The other relatively positive development was the adoption of the PRSP including unqualified references to indigenous people and *adivasi*, the Bengalsi equivalent of indigenous people, and the need to address their political, social, cultural and economic rights and needs. The document does not have the status of a legal instrument but may be regarded in the nature of a policy document with potentially high political and legal value to the country's indigenous peoples, whose cultural identity and status has seldom been respectfully and accurately reflected in recent official documents. Nevertheless, the aforesaid developments continue to be overshadowed by other acts and omissions of a political nature, coupled with a deterioration of the human rights situation in the region. For example, the appointments of non-indigenous persons to some senior offices –

---

[41] It is important to note, however, that the BNP itself had conducted peace negotiations with the JSS during their earlier tenure in government.

[42] *Prathom Alo* (Dhaka), 21 April 2002. However, the Prime Minister's Khaleda Zia's March 2003 address in parliament suggests a dilution of her previous expression of cooperation (see n. 17 above).

[43] Raja Devasish Roy, 'Challenges for Juridical Pluralism and Customary Laws of Indigenous Peoples: The Case of the Chittagong Hill Tracts, Bangladesh', *Arizona Journal of International and Comparative Law*, Vol. 21, No. 1 (Spring 2004): 113-182 at 132-134.

cabinet-level post of the CHT Affairs Ministry and the chairpersonship of the CHT Development Board – do suggest a shift toward the accommodation of demands of the Bengali settlers. There are rumours that the present government has expressed to its bilateral development partner governments its unwillingness to devolve further powers to the hill district councils, including on land administration.[44] Moreover, a number of anti-Accord statements by senior members of the cabinet and rumours of non-continuation of food grain support to ex-fighters and refugees (but not to the government-sponsored Bengali settlers) hint at serious trouble for the Chittagong Hill Tracts peace process.[45]

The human rights situation in Bangladesh, both in the country as a whole, and in the CHT region, has undergone a sharp decline in recent years. Major incidents include arson attacks on an estimated four hundred houses in nine villages in the northern Mahalchari sub-district of the CHT in August 2003 allegedly by Bengali settlers and military personnel.[46] Until today, only investigations by journalists and civil society groups have taken place, whilst no independent and impartial enquiry has been conducted under government auspices. Coupled with the growing tension between settlers and indigenous people over land, fuelled by allegations of instigation of settlers by security personnel, the overall climate in the CHT is one of tension, which has the potential to explode into medium to large-scale violence, especially if locally-stationed security personnel refuse or fail to maintain their neutrality.

Therefore, an important lesson of the CHT peace process is that implementation of an accord may run into severe difficulties with changeover of governments, especially if those politically opposed to the accord come into power.

3.2.3 *The absence of constitutional safeguards*

The 1997 Accord is not protected by constitutional safeguards. This has three major implications. One implication is that the legislation resulting from the Accord enacted, in effect, only ordinary laws that may be amended with a simple majority in parliament. The CHT has only three representatives in parliament (one being a non-indigenous person) out of a total of thirty seats. At least theoretically, this could mean that this government or a future government that dis-

---

[44] Author's interview with representatives of a few Western European governments in Dhaka (who wish to remain anonymous) in June-September 2002.

[45] See *Prathom Alo* (Dhaka), 10 September 2002.

[46] See, e.g., International Work Group on Indigenous Affairs (IWGIA), *The Indigenous World 2004* (Copenhagen, IWGIA 2004), 293; Naeem Mohaiemen, 'PCJSS alleges gang rape of 9 ethnic women in Khagrachari', *Daily Star* (Dhaka), 31 August 2003 and the *Daily Star* editorial of 9 September 2003. For a recent re-assessment of the CHT peace process, see also, Mohsin, *The Chittagong Hill Tracts, Bangladesh*.

agreed with substantial devolution of powers could initiate legislation that has the effect of revoking the 1997 Accord or at least of diluting its provisions.[47]

Secondly, the absence of constitutional recognition of the special administrative status of the CHT and the cultural identities of the CHT peoples may and usually does mean the absence of long-term and fuller commitments to the rights and needs of the peoples of the CHT. In India, for example, specific legislative and administrative measures are periodically undertaken by invoking the constitutional provisions on positive discrimination favouring the women, lower castes ('scheduled castes') and indigenous peoples ('scheduled tribes'). The comparable provisions in the Bangladeshi constitution refer to women and the 'backward section of citizens'. The scarcity of legal provisions that address matters of interest to the indigenous peoples of the country is clearly noticeable, and it is ironic that the only reference to the indigenous peoples in the national constitution is equivocal, indirect, inaccurate and disrespectful. The vague expression of 'backward section of citizens' in the constitution may well refer to any disadvantaged section of the citizenry.

Thirdly, the absence of direct constitutional backing for the CHT self-government system with its primacy to indigenous peoples makes it susceptible to legal challenges in the High Court as a potentially unconstitutional arrangement.[48] In fact, two writ petitions in the Supreme Court of Bangladesh have challenged the constitutionality of the 1997 Accord the CHT Regional Council Act of 1998 and the three Hill District Council (Amendment) Acts of 1998 alleging a violation of the unitary character of the Bangladeshi state and discrimination against Bengali people.[49] The hearing of the aforesaid cases is yet to be completed.

In comparison, the relatively successful Mizoram Accord of 1986 has a strong entrenchment clause that safeguards arbitrary changes to some of the basic rights of the Mizo people. Their land rights and customary laws, for example, are now

---

[47] On the side of the indigenous people, the situation is fraught with many uncertainties, especially in the light of the fact that one of three members of parliament from the CHT is a non-indigenous person, and the non-indigenous electorate is growing faster than the indigenous voters are.

[48] Raja Devasish Roy, 'Administration,' in Philip Gain (ed.),*Chittagong Hill Tracts: Life and Nature at Risk* (Dhaka, SEHD 2000), 43-57. For a CHT law that was struck down as 'unconstitutional' after the region lost its special constitutional status in 1964, see *Mustafa Ansari v. Deputy Commissioner, Chittagong Hill Tracts and Another*, 17 DLR, 1965, 553. See also Amena Mohsin, *The Politics of Nationalism: The Case of the Chittagong Hill Tracts, Bangladesh* (Dhaka, University Press Limited 1997), 57-66.

[49] Writ Petition No. 4113 of 1999 *(Shamsuddin Ahmed v. Government of Bangladesh and Others)* and Writ Petition No. 2669 of 2000 *(Mohammed Badiuzzaman v. Government of Bangladesh and Others)* in the Supreme Court of Bangladesh (High Court Division).

part of the national constitution, and doubly protected by the mandatory requirement of consent of the Mizoram legislature prior to any amendments to it and the special legislative majority required for any amendments to the constitution.[50]

It is equally true that despite its avowed commitment to rescind the 1997 Accord, the BNP-led coalition government has signalled its de facto and de jure acceptance of the Accord as a political and administrative reality by continuing to deal with the legal and institutional arrangements that resulted from the Accord. This suggests that it may be very difficult for a successor government to repudiate an accord signed by its predecessor government, even though such accords do not have the sanction of international law like international treaties and are not entrenched through constitutional safeguards. The reasons may include the international reputation of a government and the practical difficulties of unbirthing institutionalised creations of accords.[51] Nevertheless, the relative successes of certain peace and autonomy agreements that are strongly entrenched, such as in Mizoram, India and South Tyrol, Italy suggest that the presence of entrenchment clauses may provide more sustainability to peace processes.[52]

---

[50] See paragraph 4(3) of Mizoram Accord 1986, and Article 371G of the Constitution of India. The relevant entrenchment clause reads: '[Notwithstanding] anything contained in the Constitution, no Act of parliament in respect of (i) religious or social practices of the Mizos; (ii) Mizo customary law or procedure; (iii) administration of civil and criminal justice, involving decisions according to Mizo customary law, (iv) ownership and transfer of land, shall apply to the State of Mizoram unless the Legislative Assembly of Mizoram by a resolution so decides'. See also Raja Devasish Roy, *Traditional Customary Laws and Indigenous Peoples in Asia* (London, Minority Rights Group International, March 2005).

[51] This phrase is borrowed from Imtiaz Ahmed, Amena Mohsin and Bhumitra Chakma, 'Administrative Reforms in the CHT: A Diagnostic Study of the Ministry of CHT Affairs' (paper presented at a 'Regional Workshop on Administrative Reforms in the CHT: A Diagnostic Study of the Ministry of CHT Affairs', Dhaka, 11 May 2002).

[52] The Mizoram Accord is constitutionally protected by a 'double entrenchment' clause, which safeguards against changes other than through an amendment to the Indian Constitution (requiring a specific majority in parliament) and without the consent of the Mizoram State Assembly (See C. Nunthera, 'Peace Accords as Instruments of Conflict Transformation: Arrangements that Work and Arrangements that Don't (Mizo Accord 1986, Assam Accord 1985, Bodo Accord 1993)' (paper presented at workshop on 'Dimensions, Dynamics and Transformation of Resource Conflicts between Indigenous Peoples and Settlers in Frontier Regions of South and Southeast Asia', Mont-Soleil, Canton of Berne, Switzerland, 25-29 September 2002)). The South Tyrolean autonomy is protected by a bilateral treaty between Italy and Austria (see Jens Woelk, 'From Compromise to Process: The Implementation of the South Tyrolean Autonomy Arrangement' (paper presented at Sitges meeting, 8-14 May 2003)).

3.3 Expectations with regards to the implementation of the 1997 Accord and the post-Accord situation

In this section I would like to pose the question of the wishes, aspirations and expectations of the parties to the 1997 Accord and consider whether the Accord has (so far) achieved what one or both of the parties intended it to achieve. I feel that this is one of the most difficult areas in the politics of accords and perhaps that to which the available literature has given the least attention. The major parties to a political agreement like the 1997 Accord may be ostensibly representing a position that is itself the result of many subsidiary agreements, compromises and temporary fusions of a vast and pluralistic array of thought, belief, ideology, interest and expediency. I shall also try to explore here whether there were any hidden agendas behind the formal positions taken by the parties to the Accord.

Did the JSS and the government of Bangladesh actually have a shared vision of a post peace-accord Chittagong Hill Tracts? I do not think so. The dispute between the JSS and the previous Awami League-led government over the unwritten part of the agreement forces us to conclude that the JSS and the then government almost certainly had different conceptions about such vital matters as the presence of the settlers and the temporary military camps, and also most likely about the question of policing and law and order, and the equally important question of land.

I would venture to guess that with an optimistic view the JSS may have expected the following scenario in the post-Accord situation: (i) settlers and army depart; (ii) an authoritative regional council overseeing the CHT administration; (iii) resolution of land disputes by annulment of settlers' land titles; and (iv) land and multi-ethnic police administration in the hands of the hill district councils. Actually, none of the above developments has occurred.

It is unlikely that all members of the JSS were so trusting that they actually expected the government to carry out all its undertakings, at least over a short period of time. Therefore, I would suppose that many within the JSS might have had serious misgivings about the process of implementation and the goodwill of the government of the day. What did they think? And what was their fallback position if the government reneged upon its promise, or at least if it did not implement key provisions of the agreement? The contingency plans of the JSS, if any, have not been made known to the public. However, there is little doubt that in the climate of a violence-weary CHT, with an omnipresence of security forces in the region, approaches other than pressure through civil means are hardly viable. Such pressures are monumental efforts in a majoritarian polity that has traditionally been unsympathetic to minorities.

Some have suggested that the persuasive leverage of major donors and lenders to the partially aid-dependent economy of Bangladesh could have a bearing on the nature and pace of implementation of the Accord.[53] Given that the 1997 Accord contains no clauses for third party monitoring of its implementation, this may be one of the few avenues left to the non-state party, in this case the people of the CHT, to pressure the government. Like the JSS, the UPDF has not made public its policy or strategy on making the government keep its promises, but it is unlikely that its choices are any greater than that of the JSS.[54]

Now what about the government negotiators? Did they expect to implement all that they had expressly agreed to in the 1997 Accord, not to mention their unwritten pledges, which I personally believe they did make? One possible answer could be that the government side never really believed in implementing all its commitments but was ready to promise the earth to induce the guerrillas to lay their arms down and come back to normal life. Once the guerrillas gave up their arms, there was little they could do. The fact that the peace process seemed to have the support of the government of India was crucial because of India's long, mountainous and forested border with the Hill Tracts, which served as the most strategic bases for the guerrilla camps.

In this case, the lesson to students of ethnic peace processes is that in order to ensure that the parties comply with their obligations, mechanisms should be in place to either make quid pro quo arrangements and carry out the mutual obligations on a parallel basis in phases, or to ensure the effective mediation of a third party to enforce the accord.

4. Possible Mechanisms to Ensure Implementation

As regards quid pro quo arrangements and carrying out mutual obligations on a parallel basis in phases, a writer on the CHT did suggest before the conclusion of the CHT negotiations that the repatriation of the international Pahari refu-

---

[53] Prior to the recent meeting of the Bangladesh Development Forum (informally known as the 'Aid Club') in Dhaka that met to decide on annual allocations of loans and aid to Bangladesh, the Bangladesh Adivasi Forum, led by JSS leader J. B. Larma, drew attention in the press to the non-implementation of the Accord. Last year, when the Forum met in Paris, Bangladeshi demonstrators petitioned the donors and lenders to speak in favour of implementation, but did not campaign against aid to Bangladesh.

[54] Although the UPDF is known to have serious misgivings about the process of negotiations as undemocratic and non-inclusive, and the contents of the 1997 Accord as being too weak on autonomy, it has recently expressed support towards the implementation of those provisions of the Accord that seek to safeguard the indigenous peoples' rights. This does not, however, imply any change in their rejection of the 1997 Accord in its totality.

gees from India to Bangladesh should be linked with a parallel rehabilitation of Bengali settlers outside the CHT.[55] The repatriation of the Pahari refugees to Bangladesh was done in phases. I am firmly of the opinion that this phased repatriation helped ensure that the refugees received most, if not all, of what they were promised by way of return of dispossessed lands, grants of money and food grain rations, etc. Taking for a moment the side of the autonomist underdogs, one could say with proverbial hindsight that decommissioning and arms hand-over by the guerrillas could have been linked to the dismantling of military camps and/or the rehabilitation of the government sponsored settlers outside the CHT. Of course, these were the theoretical options that were open to the JSS. Political exigencies may of course have suggested otherwise, both in the case of the CHT and in other comparable peace processes.

Yet another alternative to ensure the implementation of agreements is a suggestion by Darby and MacGinty to build safeguards or penalties for non-compliance into the agreement.[56] This was not done in the case of the CHT Accord of 1997 for reasons not known. Although it is easy to conceive, retrospectively, that such provisions may have deterred non-implementation on the part of the government, ultimately the question would perhaps have depended upon both the nature of the sanctions to be imposed, and the presence of an independent and strong mediator or other third party that was charged with implementing the sanctions.

Some of the available literature on peace processes, such as Richardson and Wang, 1993 and Darby and MacGinty, 2000 seem to strongly recommend third party mediation in an unqualified manner as necessarily benevolent and positive. However, it is well to remember that there may be situations in which a strong third party may well impose a 'solution' that is contrary to the interest of a party, especially the usually weaker non-state party, or one that benefits not the parties to the conflict or accord, but the mediating third party itself.[57] In the case of the Chittagong Hill Tracts, SAARC[58] could have been a possible third-party mediator, but the peace process had no distinguishable third party, as any third party involvement other than as a liaison agent was categorically rejected by the government.[59] This feature of the absence of third parties seems to have

---

[55] Rajkumari Chandra Roy, *Land Rights*, 158-159.

[56] John Darby and Roger MacGinty (eds.), *The Management of Peace Processes* (Hampshire, UK, Macmillan Press Ltd 2000), 259.

[57] This was an opinion mentioned in the aforesaid Sitges meeting that went unchallenged.

[58] The South Asian Association for Regional Cooperation (SAARC) was established when its Charter was formally adopted on 8 December 1985 by the heads of state or governments of Bangladesh, Bhutan, India, Maldives, Nepal, Pakistan and Sri Lanka.

[59] Formal meetings between the JSS and the government of Bangladesh were facilitated by one or more members of a 'liaison committee' consisting of people trusted by the JSS (one Bengali

also been carried forward into the implementation phase, as no independent third parties were identified to mediate, arbitrate or otherwise resolve disputes or disagreements between the parties in case of disagreement over the process of implementation. The 1997 Accord merely mentioned that there would be a three-member implementation committee led by the head of the government's Chittagong Hill Tracts Committee and including the president of the JSS and the chairperson of the CHT Task Force on Refugees and Displaced People.[60]

The authors mentioned above also seem to stress the usefulness of sanctions in deterring non-compliance with responsibilities under an accord. It is well not to overlook or underestimate the potential value of positive inducements or 'carrots', as opposed to negative sanctions or 'sticks'. In many situations where a party is guilty of non-implementation, especially where it concerns the state-party, it may make much more sense to talk of positive and negative inducements of carrots, no carrots or big carrots – providing or withholding aid, loans or other trade, political office or financial benefits and opportunities – rather than about sanctions and sticks.[61] Such an approach may also have the advantage of not unduly embarrassing the guilty party, especially if it is a state, as states are almost always concerned about their reputation and sovereignty.

In fact, Darby and MacGinty believe that:

> To make sure that agreements are fully implemented a sustained post-agreement political activity is required. The danger is that parties may wish to disregard or re-negotiate some provisions in an agreement that they find unpalatable. Some peace accords attempt to anticipate such problems by building safeguards or penalties for non-compliance into the agreement. The bottom line, however, is a strong political will to implement an agreement.[62]

The ironical twist however is: how does one foster such a will. To help bring forth such a will may well call for involvement in a political arena that is situ-

---

and the rest indigenous). However, these mediators' role started and ended with getting the two sides to the negotiating table. The signing of the 1997 Accord without external third-party mediation was boisterously capitalized upon as a 'unique Bangladeshi achievement' by the previous Awami League Government of Bangladesh.

[60] The committee consisted of Abul Hasnat Abdulla, MP, Chief Whip of the Government (convenor), J. B. Larma, President of JSS (member) and Dipankar Talukdar, MP and Chairman of the CHT Task Force on Refugees and Displaced People (member).

[61] Summary of the discussions of the first three days, as prepared by Michael van Walt, of the 'Expert meeting on ensuring full implementation of intrastate peace agreements involving self-rule arrangements as a contribution to peace consolidation and conflict prevention and the role of third parties therein', organised by Kreddha and the Centre UNESCO de Catalunya, held in Sitges/Barcelona on 8-14 May 2003. The summary was a draft only, given to this writer and other participants at the meeting.

[62] Darby and MacGinty, *Management of Peace Processes*, 259.

ated far from the marginalised ethnic minority's peripheral region, and where the rules are made by those who have little sympathy, and even less knowledge, about the indigenous people, but share a vague idea that the country requires these peoples' common resources.

At the Sitges meeting, the participants felt that it was vitally important to expressly include clauses on implementation mechanisms into the accord and to ensure the presence of other factors as mentioned below, to ensure that the peace process is sustained, the accord implemented and potential parties to an accord confident about reaching an accord. These included the following:

- The inclusiveness of the peace/negotiation process;
- quid pro-quo arrangements in phased implementation;
- building implementation safeguards into the agreements;
- inclusion of arbitration, facilitation or mediation arrangements for certain aspects, components of peace and autonomy agreements.[63]

In retrospect, it could be said that the safeguards such as those referred to above may well have benefited the CHT process and avoided the current impasse had they been incorporated into the 1997 Accord. That is of course a matter of conjecture. In any case, let us now look at the process of negotiations, leading up to the 1997 Accord. It might throw more light upon the problems in the implementation stage and even explain the reasons why safeguard arrangements, such as those referred to in the Sitges meeting, were not included in the text of the CHT Accord of 1997.

5. THE NEGOTIATION PROCESS, THE CEASEFIRE AND OTHER AGREEMENTS LEADING UP TO THE 1997 ACCORD

An important but largely unexplored dimension of the negotiation process leading up to the 1997 Accord is the little known pre-formal exchange of messages between the parties that has led some to believe that they had 'agreed to agree', whatever the contents of the future accord might be. Whether this is completely true will perhaps never be known, but there are clear indications that a strong political will at the highest levels of JSS and the Bangladesh government was favouring an agreement. This could suggest that the parties were able to develop trust based upon the idea of a win-win situation for both, which required their mutual cooperation. Conversely, one could say that the two parties needed the accord to get out of a situation that may be described as a 'mutually hurting

---

[63] See n. 55 above.

stalemate'.[64] Another possibility is that there were strong but discreetly communicated inducements from external sources, like encouragement from persuasive lobbies like India, Western donor agencies, or oil and gas lobbies.[65] Given the complexities of the matter, it may yet take awhile to uncover the exact nature and extent of such inducements, if any. However, in the case of a hurting stalemate, I am inclined to think that it applied much more in the case of the JSS, than the government of Bangladesh. In the case of the latter, it was probably the desire and/or the need for a political achievement to placate its supporters and to score against its political opponents, rather than any exceptionally hurtful stalemate that induced it to enter into peace talks and negotiate a peace agreement. In addition, I would also not rule out altruistic feelings on the part of some of the senior government leaders. Be that as it may, the nature of the negotiations does suggest that the parties were in some ways racing against time, perhaps out of a fear of subversion by spoilers. This may perhaps at least partly explain why the 1997 Accord provisions on implementation, including on specific time frames, are few and rather vague.

Among other lessons that the CHT negotiations process offers us are the impacts of the ceasefire and earlier accords on the negotiations leading up to the 1997 Accord. The 1997 Accord was preceded by two other political agreements on the CHT: the Priti Group Accord of 1985 and the so-called Moderate Leaders' Agreement of 1988, that had bypassed the then underground JSS. The Priti Group Accord of 1985 was signed between a breakaway faction of the JSS and the army commander of the CHT region. Besides ensuring the surrender of the renegade guerrillas, little of substance resulted from it, including the only substantive issues covered in the accord: (i) the return of dispossessed lands to the indigenous people; and (ii) a halt to further population transfer. We can perhaps draw two lessons from this: first, that viewed from a long-term perspective, the negotiation and the implementation stage can be viewed as one process rather than mutually exclusive phases and implicitly then, the boundary between peace and conflict/war cannot also be drawn so very easily.[66] Second, that to achieve results, you have to have an agreement that involves the political arm of the government at the highest possible levels, and not a mere bureaucrat. Conversely

---

[64] John M. Richardson and Jianxin Wang, 'Peace Accords: Seeking Conflict Resolution in Deeply Divided Societies' in Kingsley M. de Silva and S.W.R. de A. Samarasinghe (eds.), *Peace Accords and Ethnic Conflict* (London, Francis Pinter 1993), 171.

[65] Although it is not confirmed, the CHT is believed to have some of the largest gas reserves in the country. The same could be true for oil.

[66] The number of people killed in recent years due to the pro and anti-Accord violence is estimated to have exceeded the number of violent deaths at certain periods prior to the ceasefire of 1992. Can we then say that the CHT is now less peaceful than during the period of the guerrilla-security forces conflict?

however, the post-1997 situation can also suggest that implementation may be difficult even with broad political support, if the bureaucracy does not support it. But then again, even if the 1988 agreement was signed only with political lightweights on the side of the indigenous people, it did lay down the basis for the district council system, which was strengthened through the 1997 Accord. Thus it seems that the legacy of a seemingly weak political agreement may in fact have disproportionately high and long-lasting legal and administrative implications.

The ceasefire process in the CHT also had some very interesting features. During the ceasefire, the army complained that the JSS was using it to reorganise, rest, gather intelligence, and strengthen itself, since the army was no longer at liberty to apprehend or confront suspected guerrillas.[67] On the other hand, the guerrilla leaders feared that too long a cease-fire might make it difficult for their battle-weary fighters to go back to war should the negotiations fail. Therefore, it seems that a long ceasefire can create a great deal of pressure upon an underground guerrilla force to forsake war and settle for peace. This is because a ceasefire may be the only wartime opportunity for an underground fighter to freely meet his (and less occasionally, her) family and friends without fear of arrest or death and to enter into a free dialogue with civil society and feel the pulse of the people's wishes and aspirations, besides seeing for herself or himself the havoc caused by the war upon non-combatants.

6. RECONSTRUCTION AND DEVELOPMENT IN THE IMPLEMENTATION PHASE

The period immediately following the signing of the 1997 Accord saw a frenzied rush by government development planners, bilateral development partners of the government and representatives of multilateral development agencies – notably the Asian Development Bank and the UNDP – to mount needs assessment missions, socio-economic surveys, grassroots opinion-seeking dialogues and the like to set the base for medium to large scale development projects in the region. The government invited reconstruction experts from post-conflict regions worldwide to advise it. Promises were made to restart development interventions with a bottom-up approach.

However, given the long history of so-called development projects that created dams that swallowed up people's ancestral homes, concentration camps

---

[67] Similar allegations on the alleged 'abuse' of ceasefires by guerilla fighters have been made by state security forces in Sri Lanka and in Northeast India.

disguised as model villages, and collective farms and forest reserves that excluded indigenous people, development projects in the region came to be synonymous with 'dislocation, disruption and destruction'.[68] Some said that they would rather stay like the inhabitants of the remoter areas – who remained without formally structured 'development' for the entire duration of the internal war – than risk being victimised by inappropriate externally-oriented and imposed development projects.[69]

Large corporate-style NGOs oriented around the internationally-acclaimed micro credit schemes were not to be left behind. However, very few of the larger government managed projects could be implemented due to bureaucratic red-tape and later due to declining security conditions triggered by the abduction of a number of Western European development personnel in 2000. Moreover, the sectoral priorities in many of the donor agencies' policies – favouring health, education, sanitation or whatever the case might be – sometimes led to either extremely reductionist interventions that overlooked the need for a more integral approach to the post-Accord situation or was too insensitive to work on culture and identity, which would have made it easier for ordinary people to 'feel, sense and smell the good effects of the Accord'.[70] Thus the impact of such post-war reconstructionist interventions upon the CHT peace process remain to be tested further. On the other hand, the credit-oriented corporate NGOs and an affiliate of the internationally acclaimed Grameen Bank have indeed done a great deal of banking. They have helped to further monetise the CHT economy, but without providing the borrowers with ways and means to achieve sustainable livelihoods, leading to increased consumerism and liquidability of lands and other assets rather than a higher quality of living. Recently, a number of donors and lenders have started, very cautiously, and sometimes at a pilot level, some socio-economic development work, including quick impact projects. We have to wait and see what their impact is on the peace process. Since the process includes both top-down and relatively inclusive development packages, I would tend to think that the results will be mixed.

Let us turn now to consider the links between peace building, development and economic matters. One would think that given the relative poverty of the

---

[68] Prashanta Tripura, 'Culture, Identity and Development', in Gain, *Chittagong Hill Tracts*, 98.

[69] Tripura, 'Culture, Identity', 98.

[70] In interviews with this author from 1998 to 2002, many CHT people (who wish to remain anonymous) have said that the thrust of the development programmes were too long-term and hence did not produce quick impact results. Especially ignored were needs on language, literature, music, etc., which are felt to be threatened and are central to the cultural identity and integrity of the people concerned.

CHT region in classical economic terms, development and economic matters would be important factors in rebuilding peace. In fact, in the late 1970s and early 80s, the government had sought to reductionistically look at the CHT problem as an economic problem and one that could be solved through developmental interventions. That did not actually succeed in either bringing the guerrillas to peace talks with the government or to reduce political support towards the autonomy movement. However, that was perhaps not so much because economic development was unimportant to the CHT people, but because the concerned programmes did not bring real benefits to them or were too small in scale. It is therefore surprising that when asked about it, many CHT people did not regard economic matters as highly relevant for the success or failure of the CHT peace process as the presence or absence of violence and the nature of ethnic relations.[71]

Thus it may appear, on the face of it, that the CHT situation reinforces the conclusion from *Coming Out of Violence*, a study of five conflict-ridden societies (South Africa, Northern Ireland, Israel-Palestine, the Basque country and Sri Lanka), that 'economic factors appear to have the lowest influence on the success or failure of a peace process'.[72] However, that is perhaps a somewhat over-simplistic approach because considering violence and ethnic relations as more important factors than economic matters towards peace building does not necessarily mean that economic factors *in fact* had less impact on peace processes. After all, it is difficult to imagine that developments such as the appropriation of the indigenous peoples' forest commons by the government, the inundation and displacement caused by the Kaptai Dam, the land dispossession caused by transmigrants, and economic exploitation by unscrupulous traders and money-lenders were merely minor factors in fuelling feelings of deprivation, injustice and neglect in the formative years of the unrest. Therefore, economic issues may appear to be relatively unimportant to many, but there should nevertheless be little doubt that they do matter towards the success or failure of the CHT peace process, no matter what respondents say when asked about the matter. Nonetheless, although economic factors are important towards the success or failure of peace processes, mainstream development interventions may be insufficient by themselves to usher in lasting peace, or peace that is fair and just.

---

[71] This is the common opinion of many people in the CHT as expressed in various public meetings, development and human rights related workshops.

[72] Darby and MacGinty, *Management of Peace Processes*, 251. Apart from Darby and MacGinty (who edited the research finding publication 'The Management of Peace Processes'), the other researchers were Pierre du Toit, Tamar Hermann, David Newman, Ludger Mees and Paikiasothy Saravanamuttu. The other factors besides the economy were violence, progress towards a political settlement, external actors, public opinion and symbols.

7. THE CHALLENGES AHEAD

Of the major challenges that lie ahead for the CHT peace process, I would identity the following five: (i) to bring about a peaceful and negotiated end to the intra-indigenous violence; (ii) to seek to reduce the chances of settler-indigenous violence; (iii) to continue efforts to otherwise implement the unimplemented provisions of CHT Accord; (iv) to strengthen and humanise the CHT self-government institutions; and (v) to protect and promote basic human rights, whether or not they are specifically mentioned in the 1997 Accord. Here I will limit myself to briefly discuss the first three challenges.

7.1 The intra-indigenous violence

The current intra-indigenous violence is perhaps keeping the pressure off the indigenous-settler conflict over political rights and natural resources for the time being, but it is weakening the indigenous people in various ways. The conflict is largely concentrated in the Chakma-inhabited areas and it is mostly the Chakma who are the direct victims of violence, but members of the other ethnic groups are also affected by the conflict in various ways due to restrictions on travel, pressure on business people and even ordinary people to pay 'contributions' and so forth. Indigenous society in the CHT, therefore, is getting more and more divided, its economy is dwindling and its social and human development through healthcare, education and training, among others, is about to stagnate. Bengali-speaking people too are suffering in the CHT, as victims of violence or of extortion. A number of attempts to broker a truce have failed. Perhaps the only thing that may force the warring parties to stop fighting is for them to realise that such warfare does amount to what Richardson and Wang call a 'mutually hurting stalemate', and that the only way out is peace. That, however, is not the mutual perception at the moment. If the parties do not find a way to stop the violence, the implementation of the 1997 Accord will almost certainly be further delayed. This may also lead more and more indigenous people away from politics in general or encourage them to seek alternative political affiliations. There is little doubt that the CHT people have had enough of violence and that they want peace.[73] This is perhaps the most important challenge facing the indigenous people. Only if they can stop the violence and conflict can they unitedly pool their resources to put pressure on the government of

---

[73] Such a desire for peace on the part of rural indigenous people in the CHT was poignantly brought forth in a recent documentary film on the CHT called 'Demanding Justice', directed by Mette Sejsbo and produced by Anders Dencker Christensen, Dansk AV Produktion Rentemestervej 2, 2400 Copenhagen NV, Denmark (+45 35829016, adc@davp.dk).

Bangladesh to implement the CHT Accord, provide constitutional safeguards to the CHT self-government package, resolve the land disputes, and bring forth social and economic development in the region.

It is known that a number of CHT citizens have met leaders of the opposing pro-Accord and anti-Accord political groups to seek a gradual reduction, and ultimately total cessation of hostilities. Although violence between the two groups is certainly not over, there has been marked reduction in the level of violence in 2004 and 2005 compared to previous years. It has been said that the opposing groups have been urged to initiate *unilateral peace initiatives* with a view to encouraging, or morally pressurising the other group to reciprocate. Whether and if such moves will be successful is still too early to tell. Support from various sections of the general public, however, has been overwhelming. In this context, it is worth noting that in the 1990s the peace process was in a way kick-started with a unilateral 'ceasefire' by the JSS which was later reciprocated by the government security forces.

7.2 Settler-indigenous conflict

The fragile peace process in the CHT is threatened from different fronts. Besides showing no signs of any abatement of violence between the pro and anti-Accordists, some of the old wounds of the internal war are now showing signs of opening up; the indigenous people and the Bengali settlers are again finding themselves in near-conflict situations. Seemingly mundane disputes over newly surfaced riverbed rice fields, over common pool resources like forests, pastures and water bodies, and over buying and selling of farm produce and other commodities are commonplace.[74] They usually do not involve violence, but that is not always the case. The CHT has numerous examples where a single act of violence by a member of an indigenous group against a Bengali person, or vice versa, for whatever reason, can spark of an ethnic riot of large proportions.

However, there are some differences in the manner of reactions. When indigenous people are the victims, the reaction is usually limited to peaceful demonstrations or petitioning of the authorities. Unfortunately, in the several instances of organised violence against the indigenous people over the past few years, very little seems to be been done by the police or other state authorities to bring the perpetrators of violence to justice.[75] This may not be surprising to some

---

[74] Indigenous people still do not visit the largest marketplace in the hill region – the *Reserve Bazar* – on market day as a sign of protest against (alleged) oppression by Bengali shopkeepers and day labourers. This has continued for more than two years now.

[75] On 19 April, a number of indigenous people's houses in Khagrachari town in the CHT were razed to the ground by Bengali settlers. Those guilty are not known to have been apprehended or prosecuted (see *Prathom Alo* (Dhaka), 21 April 2003).

since the law enforcing agencies in the CHT are almost exclusively composed of ethnic Bengalis. In the circumstances, the presence of discriminatory practices against the indigenous people cannot be ruled out. CHT leaders, including the traditional chiefs or *rajas,* have therefore sought to have law and order transferred as a subject to the district councils and have also asked for the deployment of a multi-ethnic police force in the region.[76] Although a small number of indigenous policemen from the CHT have been posted in the hill region at district headquarters and less frequently at sub-district headquarters, their numbers are quite insignificant. The government has consistently chosen to ignore the provisions of the Hill District Council laws that authorise the councils to recruit local police. In this regard there would seem to be no perceptible difference of views between the erstwhile ruling party, Awami League, and the present coalition led by the BNP.

In cases where the victim is a Bengali, if the authorities do not take prompt action against the guilty indigenous person or persons, Bengali mobs have been seen to take strong punitive action, not necessarily against the guilty person(s), but against any indigenous people who happen to pass through the nearest Bengali-controlled highway or waterway. Thus the recent history of the CHT shows that ethnic conflicts can indeed be quite 'intractable'[77] and that it is quite difficult to bring about a genuinely symbiotic relationship between peoples who have shared a long history of conflict over scarce resources and exploitation of one by the other.[78] However, the indigenous people and the Bengali-speaking people of the CHT have no other sound alternative but to seek to peacefully coexist. Perhaps they need to explore more innovative ways and means of giving each other space, in the political, physical and geographical sense at a micro level, and by trying to enhance mutual tolerance and respect through increased interaction in social and cultural spheres, amongst others.

7.3   Towards implementation of the 1997 Accord

We have seen from the above the various difficulties with regard to the implementation of the 1997 Accord. In accordance with the Accord, it should be the responsibility of the Accord Implementation Committee to deal with this problem. However, at present, there is no such committee. The present government does not seem to be interested in reconstituting this committee. The JSS on its

---

[76] 'Tribal leaders seek PM intervention in protecting livelihood', *New Age* (Dhaka), 31 August 2003.

[77] Richardson and Wang, 'Peace Accords'.

[78] Wolfgang Mey (ed.), *Genocide in the Chittagong Hill Tracts, Bangladesh* (Copenhagen, International Work Group for Indigenous Affairs 1984), IWGIA Document 51, 88.

part has not made any strong demands for its reconstitution either, perhaps because its memories of the earlier committee and its inaction are not very positive. During the rule of the previous government, this committee had actually met only a few times, despite requests from the JSS to have more frequent meetings. The committee had a 2-1 majority in favour of the government and was therefore potentially weighted against the JSS, although it did include the president of the party as one of its three members. In the present circumstances, it is difficult to gauge the potential value of this committee in helping implement the 1997 Accord.

Intrastate accords are made, broken, abused or implemented. In the case of the CHT, the biggest challenge is the non-implementation of many of its crucial provisions, including on self-government, land, demilitarisation, law and order and rehabilitation. The leader of the JSS has appealed for third party mediation. The government of Bangladesh must first agree to that. Only then can we start thinking of identifying the third party. However, the government may not easily agree to any overt mediation, given past trends. Perhaps one of the few ways to bring about a fuller and more faithful implementation of the 1997 Accord is through the persuasive leverage of the government of Bangladesh's development partners.[79] Money talks the loudest. Some of the donors and lenders have previously spoken out in favour of implementation, but not very consistently, nor very loudly, nor in concert. It is unlikely that they will act in concert. But since they have a strong say in the development process of the country, they need to be lobbied very hard, as do the national politicians and civil servants.

The second way is to promote advocacy measures within the broad ambit of human rights. Human rights in its contemporary understanding encompass civil, political, economic, social and cultural rights. The Government of Bangladesh is party to several international human rights treaties that it has ratified. These include the International Covenant on Civil and Political Rights, the International Covenant on Economic, Social and Cultural Rights, the Convention on the Elimination of Racial Discrimination (CERD), the Convention on the Elimination of Discrimination against Women (CEDAW) and on the Convention on the Rights of the Child, and last but not the least, the ILO Convention on Indigenous and Tribal Populations (No. 107 of 1957). A large part of the provisions of CHT Accord of 1997 – by coincidence perhaps rather than by design – coincide or conform with, the provisions of one or more of the aforesaid multilateral

---

[79] These include the World Bank, IMF, Asian Development Bank, Japan, United States, the Nordic countries and other OECD nations including Australia, Canada, the United Kingdom, the Netherlands, France, Germany and Switzerland. Since a large part of Bangladesh's annual budget is supported or subsidized by these lenders and donors, the latter, as a whole, have considerable influence on Bangladeshi affairs.

human rights treaties. A government – like that of Bangladesh – may not be legally compelled – in a domestic court of law – to carry out its political obligations, but it cannot deny its moral and legal responsibilities of upholding human rights, in a non-discriminatory manner, and of providing justice to the most disadvantaged section of its citizens. This is all the more so when many of those same rights are recognised as justiciable fundamental rights Bangladesh's national constitution.

Political and human rights activists of the CHT, along with their friends, will need to employ imaginative ways to lobby for change through politics development, and formal as well as informal human rights processes. It is no mean job for a war-ravaged society that has little access to education, healthcare, markets, and state welfare services that are taken for granted in other parts of the country. The CHT people, however, have no choice. They have a centuries-old tradition of resisting colonialism, racism and discrimination to draw inspiration from, but they must learn to be united again, and to struggle for their rights in new ways, alongside friends, both new and old. And in this work, they may draw encouragement from the provisions of the United Nations Draft Declaration on the Rights of Indigenous Peoples, which will hopefully be adopted by the United Nations General Assembly, after consideration of the current draft at the forthcoming session of the UN Commission on Human Rights. There are several provisions therein that are of particular relevance to peace processes and implementation of treaties and other agreements concerning indigenous peoples, which may serve as vital tools for advocacy on human rights, including those based upon political agreements like the CHT Accord. The most relevant one reads as follows:

> Indigenous Peoples have the right to the recognition, observance and enforcement of Treaties, Agreements and Other Constructive Arrangements concluded with States or their successors and to have States honour and respect such Treaties, Agreements and other Constructive Arrangements.[80]

---

[80] Article 36, Proposals of Chairman, Working Group on Draft Declaration, 11th Session, February 2006.

Chapter VI

CHALLENGES FACED BY TIBETANS IN REACHING A LASTING AGREEMENT WITH CHINA

Lodi G. Gyari[*]

Every struggle has its uniqueness. In the case of the Tibetan struggle, it has to do with the nature of the Tibetan people, our culture and religion, and above all the role of our leader, His Holiness the Dalai Lama. The non-violent nature of our struggle is the result of the personality of the Dalai Lama and his outlook on the world. His world view, his special bond with the Tibetan people and the respect he enjoys in the international community all make the person of the Dalai Lama key both to achieving a negotiated solution to the Sino-Tibetan conflict and to implementing any agreement that is reached. In this chapter, I will share some of the Tibetan experiences and challenges, as well as my own experiences as the official entrusted by His Holiness with the responsibility of reaching out to the Chinese government.

It is not the first time we have to negotiate with the Chinese authorities. As neighbours we have interacted with each other at various times in history. The situation we find ourselves in today is the result of the armed invasion of Tibet by Chinese communist forces in 1949/50 and the subsequent imposition on us of an agreement for the so-called 'peaceful liberation of Tibet'. Under the terms of that Seventeen Point Agreement[1] Tibet retained a considerable degree of political and cultural autonomy. Indeed, many of the terms of the Agreement, although imposed on us, were not unacceptable. Tibetans suffered immensely however in the more than five decades that followed the signing of that document. What went so wrong?

To begin with the Seventeen Point Agreement concerned only the area subsequently known as Tibet Autonomous Region (TAR) and its terms did not

---

[*] Special Envoy of His Holiness the Dalai Lama and former Minister of Information and International Relations of the Tibetan government in exile.

[1] The Seventeen Point Agreement for the Peaceful Liberation of Tibet, May 1951, hereinafter 'the Seventeen Point Agreement' or simply 'the Agreement'. The text is included in Appendix B.

cover the other Tibetan areas which have been incorporated into Qinghai, Yunnan, Gansu and Sichuan provinces. More than half of Tibet and the majority of its population were in these areas and so whatever rights provided for Tibetans in the Seventeen Point Agreement did not apply to Tibetans outside of TAR.

In the second place, even in the Tibet Autonomous Region, the Chinese authorities failed to properly implement the Agreement and repeatedly infringed upon the autonomy Tibetans were meant to enjoy. This, despite assurances given by the highest of the Chinese leaders, including Mao Tse-tung and Chou Enlai.

These two factors led to the national uprising of Tibetans against Chinese rule in 1959 the flight to India of Tibet's Head of State and spiritual leader, His Holiness the Dalai Lama. Once in freedom in India, His Holiness repudiated the Seventeen Point Agreement and established his government in exile to continue the struggle for freedom and to look after the welfare of the thousands of refugees who were escaping from Tibet.

1. PRAGMATIC APPROACH TO NEGOTIATIONS

Despite our sad experiences, the Dalai Lama has been very pragmatic and flexible in wanting to negotiate with the Chinese on the kind of political status Tibet should enjoy in the future and has held steadfast to his commitment to nonviolence as the only permissible means of achieving a negotiated solution. His Holiness has expressed his thinking in a number of public statements. In a message to the Nonviolence International, the Dalai Lama expanded on his thoughts. He said, 'Despite recent developments inside Tibet, which have seen an increase in repression, I am still committed to a nonviolent middle-way approach. Many younger people, and some older ones inside Tibet are losing patience and I can understand their feelings. But I feel strongly that non-violence is the only way and that it is the right way. And until my death there will be no change in my own commitment to non-violence.'[2]

His Holiness talked about the objectives of his non-violent struggle in an address to the European Parliament in October 2001, he said:

> I have led the Tibetan freedom struggle on a path of non-violence and have consistently sought a mutually agreeable solution to the Tibetan issue through negotiations in the spirit of reconciliation and compromise with China...my proposal envisages that Tibet enjoy genuine autonomy within the framework of the

---

[2] Foreword dated 8 May 2000 to Katherine Kramer and Yeshua Moser Puangsuwan, *Truth is Our Only Weapon: The Tibetan Nonviolent Struggle* (Bangkok, Nonviolence International, August 2000).

People's Republic of China. However, not the autonomy on paper imposed on us 50 years ago in the 17-Point Agreement, but a true self-governing, genuinely autonomous Tibet, with Tibetans fully responsible for their own domestic affairs, including the education of their children, religious matters, cultural affairs, the care of their delicate and precious environment, and the local economy. Beijing would continue to be responsible for the conduct of foreign and defense affairs. This solution would greatly enhance the international image of China and contribute to her stability and unity – the two topmost priorities of Beijing – while at the same time the Tibetans would be ensured of the basic rights and freedoms to preserve their own civilization and to protect the delicate environment of the Tibetan Plateau.[3]

It is our belief that ultimately our non-violent approach will succeed in bringing the Chinese leadership to the negotiation table to work out a mutually satisfactory solution. After many years of efforts on our part, the Chinese Government finally invited me to come to Beijing in September 2002 for discussions. I led a delegation to open a dialogue with the Chinese leaders. It was for the first time after almost a decade that we were able to have direct and high level contact with the Chinese government. The significance of that visit was not in the outcome but in the fact that it actually happened and that it was followed by a second visit in May-June 2003.

It was important for both the Tibetan and the Chinese side to re-establish contact and to undertake confidence-building measures. We have had lack of trust on both sides and with good reasons. So our effort was focused on building a little bit of confidence. I say a little bit because it will take some major moves of psychological importance and a long period of continued dialogue for us to develop genuine trust in each other.

These two delegations to Beijing were not the first I had been on. I visited Beijing in 1982 and 1984 as a member of the high level exploratory delegations and had the opportunity to meet with some of the top leaders of that period. The attitude of the Chinese leaders then was very different from that of today's leaders. In 1982 I found the Chinese leaders still suffering from the shock of the Cultural Revolution, of which they themselves were victims. They had a kind of victim-mentality, which we also had. So we often ended up trying to criticise the past together. There was an elderly communist leader from Inner Mongolia, Ulan Fu, for example, who was a member of the Standing Committee of the Politburo and the formal head of the Chinese delegation meeting us. In response to our complaint about his government's treatment of the Tibetan people, he

---

[3] Address of H.H. the Dalai Lama to the European Parliament, Strasbourg, 24 October 2001, Office of H.H. the Dalai Lama, Dharamsala.

spoke about his personal sufferings and those of the Mongol people during what he called the Ten Years of Madness. That was the sort of situation prevailing in 1982.

In 1984 the attitude of the Chinese leaders had changed. By then they appeared to have gotten over the Cultural Revolution and had overcome their victim mentality. I found them to be very arrogant and chauvinistic but without self-confidence. They saw conspiracy in everything that happened and were totally unwilling to have a dialogue. In fact they hardly gave us any opportunity to state our views.

During our two most recent visits the situation was very different. I found the Chinese leaders self-confident. I was pleased with this because it is always easier and more beneficial to deal with people who are self-confident than with people who are paranoid. This time the Chinese leaders gave us ample opportunity to state our views and listened to what we had to say.

There is an expectation that the new President of the PRC, Hu Jintao, will take some steps to bring about a change in Chinese attitude towards Tibet and the Tibetan people. Hu is the first President of PRC to have served as the head of the Communist Party in the Tibet Autonomous Region (from 1988 to 1992) and so has first hand knowledge of the Tibetan situation.

Experts discuss the good and bad sides of President Hu's policies during his tenure in Lhasa. Some people feel that he was ruthless and he might therefore be more difficult to deal with. Others believe that his first hand experience may make him more inclined to take positive steps on the issue of Tibet. I believe that anyone who has actual knowledge is in a better position to deal with a situation, no matter what his/her attitude is. Knowledge is always an important, whatever one's prejudices may be.

2. THE VIOLATION AND REPUDIATION OF THE SEVENTEEN POINT AGREEMENT

The Tibetan national uprising against the Chinese presence in Tibet in 1959 was the inevitable result of increased oppression and policies imposed by China in violation of the Seventeen Point Agreement. In spite of the Dalai Lama's efforts to cooperate with the Chinese authorities to implement the Agreement, the Chinese leadership initiated a series of policies that divided Tibetans and effectively replaced Tibetan political authority with Chinese rule. The people revolted and attempted to reaffirm their independence. China's own documents affirm that during the 1959 uprising and its aftermath eighty-seven thousand Tibetans died.[4]

---

[4] *Xizang Xingshi he Renwu Jiaoyu de Jiben Jiaocai*, PLA Military District's Political Report, 1960.

Tibetans had been unable to ensure the implementation by the Chinese authorities of the Seventeen Point Agreement. Although the Agreement was forced on Tibetans with the use and threat of force, it was vital for the survival of Tibet's identity and autonomy that the Agreement be fully implemented. Beyond the language of the Agreement, there was no guarantee that the PRC would live by its terms. In retrospect, the PRC appears to have considered the Agreement only as a step towards the full integration of Tibet into China.

3. Third Parties

There were no third parties involved in guaranteeing or monitoring the implementation of the Agreement. The United Nations had not responded to the Tibetan government appeals at the time of the invasion of Tibet and neither the General Assembly nor the Security Council formally considered the matter until it was much too late, in 1959 and in the early sixties. Even then, its involvement was limited to the passage of three General Assembly resolutions condemning the PRC for its actions in Tibet and calling for respect of human rights, including the right to self-determination of Tibetans. His Holiness the Dalai Lama turned to India's first prime minister, Jawaharlal Nehru, for help in 1956. Nehru sought and obtained assurances from China's prime minister Chou Enlai that the Seventeen Point Agreement would be faithfully honoured.

The flight of His Holiness from Lhasa in 1959 was the beginning of a new chapter in the history of Tibet. As the Seventeen Point Agreement was trampled on, it was repudiated by the Dalai Lama and out of practical necessity the Tibetan issue took on an international dimension. The Dalai Lama's presence in exile allowed the struggle for Tibetan freedom to continue, intensify and earn international respect, especially for its non-violent nature. The award to His Holiness in 1989 of the Nobel Peace Prize attests to this. This has created a new dynamic, in which the diplomatic engagement of the international community has become a reality.

The situation Tibet is in today is the result of China's invasion of Tibet, and the violation by the PRC of the agreement it imposed on us. China's failure to live up to its commitment made through its own imposed Seventeen Point Agreement resulted in a new political situation and today the Tibetan political struggle is aimed at re-negotiating the relationship of Tibet and China in a way that will satisfy the interests of both parties.

4. The Dalai Lama's Approach

In His Holiness the Dalai Lama we have a leader who is firm in his belief that we have to be honest and forthright in our political dealings. In 1988, he presented what came to be known as the Strasbourg Proposal,[5] in which he set out a framework for a future self-governing Tibet within the People's Republic of China. The Dalai Lama proposed that Tibet exercise self-rule in all its aspects, except foreign affairs and some aspects of defence.

Some of us were given the task of drafting the proposal after which I was sent to consult former President Jimmy Carter. His Holiness has a tremendous respect for Carter for his honesty, his religious conviction and his experience. I was pleased with the attention that President Carter paid to our document and the time he spent studying it. It was about nine pages long and he read every line. He even reread certain sections before turning towards me and asking, 'What is your bottom line?' I responded, 'Mr. President, that is our bottom-line!' pointing to what would become the Strasbourg Proposal. He then said that if this was our bottom-line, this was not the way to present it. He said we should take a tougher position and then negotiate down to this bottom line. I responded, 'Mr. President, that is also what I feel and many of us have tried to convince His Holiness of this.' His Holiness' answer to us on this was very revealing of his personality. He said, 'I am a monk. I am not a politician. I want to put everything on the table for the Chinese to consider.' In other words His Holiness was not willing to play political games by putting forward a higher demand and reducing it to a desired level in the process of negotiations.

His Holiness also does not wish to play with words. He wants things to be said exactly the way he means them. We Tibetans have a very strong aversion to the term 'autonomy' because of the experience we have of the so-called autonomy Chinese authorities have put in place in Tibet. The word autonomy is not found in the Strasbourg Proposal. Since autonomy is totally meaningless in the context of the situation in Tibet, we never wanted to use it in reference to the future of Tibet. His Holiness raised this issue during one of our meetings with him. 'Why are you not talking about autonomy, since that is what I am calling for', he asked. We argued that he should consider using another word. He said: 'Well all right, if you people want to call it something different you do so, but as far as I am concerned, if the media ask me, I am going to say very clearly that I am asking for autonomy.'

The above incidents illustrate the uniqueness of the Tibetan struggle and, in particular, its leader for whom I have the greatest respect and the great honour of working.

---

[5] Address of H.H. the Dalai Lama to the European Parliament, Strasbourg, 15 June 1988, Office of H.H. the Dalai Lama, Dharamsala.

5. THE TERRITORIAL DIMENSION OF THE TIBETAN ISSUE

Besides the issue of the degree and nature of autonomy of Tibet a major issue concerns the territorial dimensions of that autonomy: stated differently, to what areas and what sections of the population will any agreement on autonomy apply? Today, when the Chinese authorities refer to Tibet they mean the Tibet Autonomous Region and therefore exclude all the Tibetan areas and population currently in Qinghai, Gansu, Sichuan and Yunnan provinces. In terms of population, this leaves out more than half of the estimated six million Tibetans. Both from the point of view of territory and population, the majority are outside the TAR.

His Holiness the Dalai Lama has made it very clear that he is seeking a solution for the Tibetan people within the framework of the People's Republic of China. What we are striving for is the right of a distinct people, with a distinct culture, religion and language to be able to live together, to preserve that very distinctiveness through a common system that governs and that provides whatever facilities are needed. We will not survive as a people if we are dismembered or divided. If this happens we will, in the long run, be weakened as a people and as a culture.

The Chinese government needs to realise that leaving the Tibetan people divided will create instability. We need to learn the lesson from history. A major reason why the Seventeen Point Agreement failed was that it was made applicable to less than half the Tibetan territory and people. In fact, the Tibetan resistance started in those Tibetan areas that were not covered by the Agreement, where people felt their interests had not been considered. The fact that the Chinese authorities also failed to properly implement the Agreement in the TAR itself resulted in the spread of the revolt to all parts of Tibet by 1959. So I always tell the Chinese that from past experiences it is very clear that dividing the Tibetans does not work and is short sighted. I tell them that in order to have peace and stability they must address the whole problem. If they keep us divided, it will be devastating for us, but in the long run it will again create instability in our part of the world, which will harm China's own interests.

The Chinese side contests our estimated Tibetan population of six million. That can easily be resolved. Our real concern is that each and every individual who lives in the People's Republic of China and considers him/herself a Tibetan be taken into consideration and included in any solution the Tibetan and Chinese sides work out. The actual numerical figure is secondary to this and the Chinese authorities cannot have any objection to this.

6. THIRD PARTY INVOLVEMENT AND THE INTEREST OF THE INTERNATIONAL COMMUNITY

The Chinese authorities make it very clear that there cannot be any third party involvement on the Tibet issue. For the Tibetans, given our earlier experience with the Seventeen Point Agreement as well as the fact that the Tibetans are the weaker side in this equation and have renounced violence, international support in persuading China to accept an equitable negotiated solution is essential. As a policy we Tibetans do not advocate third party involvement and we believe the problem has to be resolved between the Chinese and Tibetan sides. However, we have learned that there are ways in which the international community can play a role in encouraging both the parties to resolve the Tibetan issue through non-violence and negotiations.

Resolving the Tibet issue is clearly of vital importance to us. But it is also important to the international community, particularly to our region of the world. The geopolitical importance of Tibet is something that has not received enough attention. After the disintegration of the former Soviet Union, Central Asia has re-emerged as a thriving and active region. The Central Asian region has been volatile in different periods of history. It was effectively frozen for the past several decades under Soviet and communist Chinese rule. But with the fall of the Soviet Union, parts of Central Asia have revived, so that the region has regained its importance. At the same time, the region could again become an area of conflict and we already see problems in some Central Asian countries. Tibet is an integral part of Central Asia politically, culturally, spiritually and economically. What happens in Tibet can have an important impact in the region, as history has shown. This is important to China, but also to Russia and India, only to mention the regional superpowers.

Any normalisation of India-China relations will have an impact on the resolution of the Tibetan issue. Conversely, it would be foolish for anyone to think that there can really be normal relations between India and China as long as the Tibet issue remains unresolved. The correct approach is not to put the Tibet issue under the rug, pretending that it does not exist, but to accept the reality of its existence and tackle it in order to allow for better Sino-Indian relations to develop. Delhi and Beijing, I think, are very much aware of that.

7. THE TIME FACTOR

One reason why the resolution of the Tibetan issue is so urgent and time-sensitive is the demographic transformation that is taking place in Tibet. The increasing settlement of non-Tibetans into Tibetan areas is posing the risk of Tibetans becoming an insignificant minority in our own land. Already today, the population transfer, combined with China's lopsided developmental programmes, results in the economic marginalisation of the Tibetans and the strengthening of the position of the Chinese settlers.

If the Tibetan and Chinese leaders do reach agreement on the establishment of genuine autonomy for Tibet, the implementation of such an agreement may well become impossible or meaningless for the Tibetan people once Tibetans are greatly outnumbered by Chinese settlers and marginalised by them economically.

8. THE DALAI LAMA IS THE KEY TO A SOLUTION

The Tibetan people's complete trust in the Dalai Lama is the key to reaching a negotiated solution with the PRC. The Dalai Lama's role will also be the key to the implementation of any agreement that is reached. His moral authority will ensure that Tibetans not only accept but implement the agreement, and his international stature will go a long way to encourage China to honour its commitments also.

Some Chinese leaders seem to believe that the problem is the Dalai Lama, and that they should wait until his passing away. They believe that the issue of Tibet will fizzle out once he no longer leads the movement. This is a most dangerous approach. Certainly, the absence of the Dalai Lama would be devastating for the Tibetan people and our movement. But his absence would also mean that China might be left to handle the problem without the presence of a leader who enjoys the loyalty of the entire community. This could eventually lead to violence. Right now there is no violence because of the moral authority of the Dalai Lama. Therefore, the earlier these Chinese leaders see the fallacy in their thinking and enter into a serious dialogue with the Dalai Lama, the better it is for both the Chinese and the Tibetan people and the world as a whole.

If the Tibetan issue remains unresolved and it happens that the Dalai Lama passes away, that will have serious implications for the legitimacy of China's presence in Tibet. Whatever the Chinese side or the people who support the Chinese position say, the Chinese presence in Tibet today is the result of an armed invasion. This presence has no legitimacy and only the Dalai Lama can bring legitimacy to the inclusion of Tibet as part of the PRC it if he chooses to do so as part of a negotiated solution.

There will be setbacks in the Tibetan struggle after the Dalai Lama passes away, as the Chinese side believes. But then, the Dalai Lama himself has said that although the institution of the Dalai Lamas is less than four hundred years old, Tibet had existed for a far longer period. There will be a big setback to the Tibetan people when the Dalai Lama passes away. However, this will not make the resentment and the bitterness among the Tibetan people go away. There may be a leadership crisis because of the desire of some to solidify their role and due to factionalism. However, one can be certain that the Tibetan position will harden in such a situation. Also, if the Dalai Lama, who the Tibetans deeply revere, passes away in exile, it will create a wound in the hearts of the Tibetan people which will not be healed for generations to come.

While the Dalai Lama has been the main foundation for the peaceful nature of the Tibetan struggle, we also need to appreciate the tenacity and patience of the Tibetan people, including the Tibetan leadership in exile. Despite the unimaginable suffering that they have endured, the Tibetans, the majority of whom continue to reside in Tibet, have been steadfast in adhering to non-violence. More than forty years have passed since the Dalai Lama and a sizeable number of Tibetans came into exile. Today, the second and third generations of Tibetans are shouldering the responsibility of our freedom struggle with the same determination and spirit. The Tibetan issue is very much alive and the essential Tibetan culture continues to flourish among the Tibetan refugee community.

Today, the Tibetans in exile have established a democratic structure for themselves with ordinary Tibetans having a direct say in the election of the highest officials of the Tibetan government in exile. Both the elected Tibetan parliament in exile and the executive have extended their full support to the Dalai Lama's efforts, signifying that all levels of the Tibetan political leadership have a united position.

9. HOPE FOR THE FUTURE

The Tibetan struggle has remained non-violent because of the influence of the Dalai Lama and because the international reaction to his message of non-violence has conveyed a sense of hope to the Tibetan people. While the Dalai Lama's hold over the hearts of the Tibet people will not diminish, in the absence of progress, hope cannot last forever. Just as agitation in the Baltic countries was the catalyst for the demise of the Soviet Union, so could loss of hope among the Tibetans lead to drastic measures that destabilise the entire region. As it is, already today sporadic incidents of bomb blasts occur in Tibetan areas. Similarly, for the first time a Tibetan in exile, who was participating in a hunger strike in New Delhi in 1998, immolated himself, in a desperate attempt to draw more attention to the Tibetan issue.

To date, Beijing has chosen to deal with the potential for unrest in Tibet by applying harsh policies through its armed police and security forces. His Holiness the Dalai Lama offers the Chinese leadership another alternative – a negotiated political solution based on mutual interests. He has offered his moral authority to ensure that a fair agreement which would ensure genuine self-rule for all Tibetans within the PRC would be faithfully implemented. If China would be guided by its best interest, it would wisely choose a negotiated settlement, guaranteed by the Dalai Lama.

Chapter VII

FROM COMPROMISE TO PROCESS:
THE IMPLEMENTATION OF THE SOUTH TYROLEAN AUTONOMY

Jens Woelk[*]

1. INTRODUCTION

Federalism is commonly understood as a dynamic process[1] rather than a static agreement between centre and periphery. This process-oriented view should also be applied to agreements on autonomy and peace. Such agreements are after all the result of a negotiated balance reflecting a wide range of case-specific factors and subject to continuous evolution due to technological, social and political change. Full implementation of an autonomy agreement does not occur overnight; often implementation is foreseen in stages from the very beginning. Furthermore, after autonomy arrangements are fully implemented, the need exists for adapting to new developments. Indeed, autonomy is a permanent process aimed at maintaining a balance between various rights and actors.[2]

The South Tyrolean autonomy is such a dynamic process. Thirteen years have passed since the formal declaration of conflict settlement and thirty-two years since the entry into force of the Second Autonomy Statute, the 'basic law' of the South Tyrolean autonomy. Because only few autonomy arrangements have been functioning in practice for so long, valuable lessons can be drawn

---

[*] Researcher and Lecturer in Comparative Constitutional Law, University of Trento; Senior Researcher, Institute for Studies on Federalism and Regionalism, European Academy of Bozen/Bolzano (South Tyrol).

[1] See for example C.J. Friedrich, *Trends of Federalism in Theory and Practice* (London, Praeger, 1968) and D.J. Elazar, *Exploring Federalism* (Tuscaloosa, University of Alabama Press, 1987). The same is true for regional systems.

[2] For a discussion on the dynamic concept of territorial autonomy, see J. Woelk, 'Minderheitenschutz durch territoriale Autonomie: 'Reservate' oder nachhaltige Integrationsprozesse?,' in *Jahrbuch des Föderalismus 2002*, (ed.) Europäisches Zentrum für Föderalismus-Forschung (Baden-Baden, Nomos Verlagsgesellschaft, 2002), 117 (in part. p. 125 ff.).

M. Boltjes (ed.), Implementing Negotiated Agreements
© 2007, Kreddha International and T·M·C·ASSER PRESS, The Hague, The Netherlands

from South Tyrol's experiences. The manner in which the province of South Tyrol gained autonomy – by means of a predominantly domestic agreement, arrived at through third party involvement and based on a previous international bilateral accord – and the process of negotiated and gradual implementation of the autonomy are of particular interest in this regard.

This chapter will first briefly examine the process that led to today's system of autonomy and the various stages it went through: from conflict to compromise and agreement, followed by implementation of the agreement until the final and formal declaration of conflict-settlement a decade ago. The implementation procedures with special decrees and joint commissions played a central role in this. These and the relations between the autonomous province and the state will be described and analysed in the second and main part of this chapter. Lastly, the role of the third party, Austria, will be looked at. Although the implementation process has been predominantly domestic, it was Austria's continuous and constructive role in the background that kept the interest of the Italian government in progress towards full implementation of the autonomy effectively alive.

2. From Conflict to Compromise

Today two neighbouring autonomous provinces, South Tyrol[3] (Südtirol in German and Alto Adige in Italian) and Trentino form an autonomous region in Italy called Trentino-Alto Adige/Südtirol. Until 1919 both provinces were integral parts of the Austrian-Hungarian empire's region of Tyrol. Even under Austrian rule the Southern province Trentino was completely Italian-speaking, while at that time South Tyrol was nearly completely German-speaking (still today the term 'South Tyrolese' is mostly used for referring to the local German speakers). After World War I, Trentino and South Tyrol were incorporated into the

---

[3] South Tyrol is situated in the very north of Italy on the border with Austria and covers only 2.4 percent of the Italian territory (7,400 square kilometres). Its major valleys form passageways through an overall mountainous terrain; the route across the Brenner Pass is the most important European north-south connection through the Alps. The population of ca. 460,000 inhabitants (corresponding to 0.5 percent of Italy's population) consists of approximately two-thirds German speakers, less than one-third Italian speakers (26 percent) and some 20,000 Ladin speakers. The majority of the German speakers live in the valleys and rural areas and the Ladin population is concentrated in two valleys in the Dolomite mountains in the south-eastern portion of the province. Due to the immigration policies of the past and the attempted industrialization, the Italian group is concentrated in the three major cities (the capital Bozen/Bolzano, where it is the 2/3 majority, Meran/Merano and Brixen/Bressanone) and in the southern parts of the province, bordering on the province of Trento (Trentino) which is almost entirely Italian.

Italian state by the 1919 Peace Treaty of Saint Germain[4] despite the overwhelming majority of German-speaking inhabitants in South Tyrol and the declaration made by President Wilson regarding the principle of self-determination.

In the following decades the Italian government under Mussolini passed executive decrees and legislation that subjected the inhabitants of South Tyrol to forced Italianisation, that repressed the presence and influence of German-speakers in all spheres of cultural, economic and political life, and that forbade schools, trade unions, political parties and names in the German language. This policy of forced assimilation not only created a deep-rooted historical trauma and distrust for all future Italian policies and motives, but also increased German nationalism.

After Austria was annexed by the German Reich in 1938, Hitler and Mussolini came to an agreement which offered the German-speakers of South Tyrol the options of German citizenship with the obligation to emigrate and resettle in the German Reich or to accept the Italian policy of assimilation. Eighty-five percent chose to resettle in Germany but only about one third actually left during the war and many of those returned after 1945.[5]

At the peace conference held in Paris after World War II, the Allies insisted on autonomy for South Tyrol, to be negotiated between Italy and Austria. The Austrian government was invited to the conference to submit its views on the peace treaty about to be negotiated with Italy. In turn the Austrian government asked the South Tyrolean People's Party (*Südtiroler Volkspartei* (SVP)) – until today the overall representation of the German-speakers in South Tyrol – to send three representatives as advisers. The aim was to have international guarantees for any agreement reached. The outcome of the bilateral negotiations was the 1946 De Gasperi-Gruber agreement.[6] This agreement between Austria and Italy, bearing the names of the two foreign ministers, Alcide De Gasperi and Karl Gruber, was signed in Paris on 5 September 1946 (and is also known as The Paris Treaty), and subsequently became Annex IV to the Treaty of Peace with Italy, signed in Paris-St. Germain on 10 February 1947.[7] It guarantees:

1. German-speaking inhabitants [...] will be assured complete equality of rights with the Italian-speaking inhabitants within the framework of special provi-

---

[4] H. Hannum, *Autonomy, Sovereignty and Self-Determination* (Pennsylvania, University of Pennsylvania Press 1996), 432-441.

[5] For an excellent description see A.E. Alcock, *The History of the South Tyrol Question* (London, Michael Joseph 1970).

[6] See Appendix D for the full text of the De Gasperi-Gruber Agreement (Paris Treaty), 5 September 1946.

[7] Annex IV to the Treaty of Peace with Italy, signed in Paris-St. Germain 10 February 1947 (49 *UNTS* 3.).

sions to safeguard the ethnical [*sic*] character and the cultural and economic development of the German-speaking element. [...]
2. The populations [...] will be granted the exercise of an autonomous legislative and executive *regional* power. The frame within the said provisions of autonomy will apply, will be drafted *in consultation also with local representative German-speaking elements*. (Emphasis added)

This bilateral agreement, later included in the multilateral peace treaty with Italy, constituted the internationally established legal basis for the negotiations on autonomy and justified kin state Austria's interest to monitor the fulfilment of the agreement[8] and to intervene as the minority's 'protecting power' (*schutzmacht*). However, there were two main problems. Due to the vague wording in many key areas, much would depend upon whether the Italian government would adopt a generous or a restrictive attitude. Secondly, the agreement

> did not contain the one thing that Italians wanted from it, namely Austrian renunciation of South Tyrol. [...] The shock and anger in Austria and Tyrol, north and south, at the failure for the second time in less than thirty years to obtain self-determination for the South Tyrolese led the Austrian government to take the line that the agreement was the best possible under the circumstances, but that did not mean Austria had renounced South Tyrol. The implication was that the agreement was only a temporary one, and for the Italians this meant that the territorial stability of an area where their kin was in the minority would be continually in question. The result was an Autonomy Statute restrictively interpretive of the Paris-Agreement, and restrictively applied.[9]

Italy violated the spirit of the agreement almost immediately by granting autonomous powers not to South Tyrol alone, but to the larger autonomous region of Trentino-South Tyrol, which included also South Tyrol's southern neighbour, the Italian-speaking province of Trentino. As a consequence, the German-speakers in South Tyrol were outnumbered by Italian-speakers in the regional government, which controlled regional political and economic matters. Moreover, the Italian government did not stop the policies of industrialisation of South Tyrol, which resulted in a continuous influx of Italian workers. The autonomy measures were considered to be inadequate by the South Tyrolese (i.e., the German-speaking inhabitants) and protests and public rallies began under the slogan 'Los von Trient': liberation from Trento, i.e., from the capital of the region

---

[8] Article 3: 'in consultation with the Austrian Government'.
[9] A.E. Alcock, *The South Tyrol Autonomy – A Short Introduction* (Londonderry, Bolzen/Bolzano, University of Ulster, May 2001), 6 (available at <http://www.provincia.bz.it/service/publ/publ_getreso.asp?PRES_ID=1899> (2 August 2006)).

that symbolised the disputed political entity. In 1959 the South Tyrolean People's Party left the regional government. The South Tyrolean political struggle for a satisfactory autonomous arrangement reached its height in the sixties with several bombings on power lines.

In 1955, the Allied occupation of Austria ended and Austria regained its sovereignty.[10] The country subsequently started playing a significant role in aiding the German-speakers in South Tyrol to obtain greater autonomy. However, Austria's attempts in 1959 to support the South Tyrolese, pressing for implementation of the principles laid out in the De Gasperi-Gruber agreement – autonomy for the province of South Tyrol alone, equality between the German and Italian languages and ethnic quotas in all public offices – were rebuffed by Italy on the grounds that implementation of the agreement was a domestic matter.

Following several years of fruitless talks, Austria filed unsuccessful legal proceedings against Italy under the European Convention on Human Rights and brought the dispute regarding the implementation of the South Tyrolean autonomy to the attention of the United Nations General Assembly. The General Assembly adopted two resolutions in the early 1960s,[11] encouraging the parties to resume negotiations to resolve all differences regarding the implementation of the agreement, thereby establishing this was not solely an internal Italian affair.

There were several terrorist bombings in South Tyrol during the 1960s and pressure to reach a solution for the province of South Tyrol intensified. In 1961, the Italian government established a mixed commission of nineteen members (eleven Italians, seven South Tyrolese and one Ladin speaker) in order to conduct an inquiry and draw up proposals for a solution on the basis of the De Gasperi-Gruber agreement. The commission's report, released in 1964, was considered insufficient, but it became the basis for subsequent negotiations on various levels: between the governments of Austria and Italy, within the Italian government, between the Italian government and representatives from the region and the province, etc. These negotiations, benefiting from the more tolerant political climate in Italy with centre-left governments (in particular under Aldo Moro), ultimately resulted in the adoption of a compromise in 1969.

---

[10] In May 1955 the occupation of Austria ended and with the State Treaty concluded with the Allied Powers it became fully independent within the frontiers of 1 January 1938, which were guaranteed by the Allied Powers. This guarantee removed any doubt that South Tyrol would remain with Italy.

[11] VII Resolution 1497 (XV), 31 October 1960 and Resolution 1661 (XVI), 28 November 1961.

3. SUBSTANCE AND STATUS OF THE COMPROMISE

The compromise arrived at is known as 'the Package of measures in favour of the population of South Tyrol' (hereafter 'the Package'). It consists of 137 administrative and legislative measures the Italian government offered to adopt in order to reform and to expand South Tyrolean autonomy. Ninety-seven of these measures concerned amendments to the Autonomy Statute of 1948, which resulted in the adoption of the so-called Second Autonomy Statute. The compromise also includes an eighteen-stage operational calendar for implementation, setting expiry dates.[12] The intention of this operational calendar was that once the Package would be implemented, Austria would formally declare before the UN that the dispute over the fulfilment of the De Gasperi-Gruber agreement was resolved and this matter therefore closed.

Both the Package and operational calendar were approved by the parliaments of Italy (4 December 1969) and Austria (16 December 1969). Already before that a narrow 53.4 percent majority within the South Tyrolean People's Party, representing close to all German-speakers in South Tyrol, had supported the compromise during an extraordinary congress in Meran/Merano. The strength of the unified South Tyrolean ethnic party together with Austria's involvement made reaching a compromise possible even without a referendum, which would probably have split the population, created dividing lines within the groups and reminded in some way of the 'option' thirty years earlier.[13]

The basic principles of the Package are:

- the creation of two autonomous provinces (South Tyrol and Trentino) within the autonomous region of Trentino-South Tyrol, to which broad legislative and administrative powers will be granted that were previously reserved for the state or the region;
- the application of the principles of ethnic proportionality and linguistic parity to employment in all state and semi-state bodies in the autonomous province of South Tyrol, with the exception of the jurisdiction of the ministry of defence and the national police forces.

The legal nature of the Package is difficult to define and controversial since it is not an international treaty under international law. Italy was very anxious to

---

[12] See for the text of the operational calendar: F. Ermacora, *Über den Stand der Südtirolfrage im Jahre 1981*, Österreichisches Jahrbuch für Politik 1981 (Andreas Khol/Alfred Stirnemann, 1982) 325.

[13] It is often a major weakness in similar situations that the representation of interests is either dispersed or not clearly or not broadly legitimated so that the state does not have a legitimate partner for negotiations. However, until today, the SVP regularly obtains some 85 percent of the German speakers' and over 60 percent of the Ladin vote and thus represents the political views of the German speakers of all shades of opinion.

underline that its international obligations regarding the South Tyrolean autonomy had already been fulfilled with its (unsatisfying) implementation of the De Gasperi-Gruber agreement, and insisted that further concessions be strictly within its domestic legal sphere. This excluded any intervention from the Austrian side, even in case of future amendments. Understandably, Austria did not agree with this view, but nevertheless participated in the adoption of this – political – compromise. Even though the agreement did not have the force of a treaty, it should be pointed out that it was much more than a mere gentlemen's agreement and that Italy was indeed bound under international law to abide by its commitments. Italy expected Austria to trust that the measures laid down in the Package and operational calendar would be fulfilled and Austria was to suspend all its activities with regard to the question at the international level (including at the United Nations) as it waited for the agreement to be implemented. On its part, Italy was bound to implement the Package under the estoppel principle of international law, which requires that a party which has gained advantages from a trust-based behaviour of another party cannot justify its own lack of compliance on the grounds that the agreement was merely political and not legally binding.[14] Austria's compliance with its commitments therefore bound Italy to its side of the bargain, as it were.

Disputes regarding the implementation of the Package between Italy and Austria could be submitted to the jurisdiction of the International Court of Justice in The Hague on the basis of UN Resolution 1497 of 1960, which expressly recommends such a submission in case of unsatisfactory results of negotiations.[15] In fact, not a single case was brought before the ICJ, despite the long time it took for full implementation (until 1992).

The Package of 1969 forms the basis of today's autonomy arrangement. Successful implementation of it led to the formal end to the dispute between Austria and Italy over the implementation of South Tyrolean autonomy as outlined in the De Gasperi-Gruber agreement of 1946. The sections below deal with the actual implementation of the Package and thus with the implementation of the South Tyrolean autonomy. They will touch upon the Second Autonomy Statute, the 'basic law' of the South Tyrolean autonomy; the joint commissions, established for the negotiations on the implementation of the autonomy statute; and the products of these negotiations: enactment decrees which, framing the concrete details of the provisions in the autonomy statute, form the essence of the South Tyrolean autonomy.

---

[14] P. Hilpold, 'Der Südtiroler Weg völkerrechtlicher Stufenlösung im europäischen Vergleich,' in S. Clementi and J. Woelk (eds.), *1992: Ende eines Streits. Zehn Jahre Streitbeilegung im Südtirolkonflikt zwischen Italien und Österreich* (Baden-Baden, Nomos 2003) 109-117 (at 110 ff.).

[15] VII Resolution 1497 (XV), 31 October 1960 (point 2).

4. THE POWERS OF THE AUTONOMOUS PROVINCE OF SOUTH TYROL

One of the first implementation measures was the amendment of the former statute through approval of a new statute, which came about with the adoption of constitutional law n. 1 of 10 November 1971 (in effect from 20 January 1972), followed by the publication of a unified text in 1972.[16] This unified text contains the measures of the former statute that are still in force as well as those of the new autonomy statute, hereafter called the Second Autonomy Statute. This 'basic law' contains the most important principles of the autonomy system and is protected as a constitutional law due to its special status within the Italian legal system. The constitutional rank serves as a double guarantee: interference by lower ranking ordinary national legislation is excluded and it is not easy to make amendments to the autonomy statute itself.[17]

The Second Autonomy Statute, although formally adopted for the region Trentino-South Tyrol, elevated its provinces, South Tyrol and Trentino, to the rank of autonomous provinces, transferring nearly all important legislative and administrative powers to them and leaving the region as a mere 'roof structure'. As a result, South Tyrol's autonomous powers are quite outstanding, not only when compared to other minority-situations, but even with regard to its northern neighbour Tyrol, a member state of federal Austria.

Generally, the provincial powers relate to economic, cultural, and social matters. They include: regulation for provincial offices and their personnel; toponyms (geographical naming), respecting the obligation of bilingualism in the province; preservation and safeguarding of historic sites and local customs and usage; town and country planning; environmental and natural resource issues; handicrafts; fairs and markets; local transport; local communications; local economy (e.g., agriculture, forestry, hunting and fishing, alpine pasturage, tourism); public works; water works; public welfare; kindergartens, professional education and vocational training. These exclusive competences can be freely

---

[16] Presidential Decree, d.p.r. 31.8.1972, No. 670. See Autonomy Statute Trentino-South Tyrol, available at <http://www.landtag-bz.org/downloads/Statuto_E.pdf> (2 August 2006); Hurst Hannum (ed.), *Documents on Autonomy and Minority Rights* (Dordrecht, Martinus Nijhoff, 1993) 460-495; M. Magliana, *The Autonomous Province of Bolzano-Südtirol*, Quaderno/Arbeitsheft No. 20, European Academy Bozen/Bolzano 2000-Appendix, 167-195.

[17] The autonomy statute has actually never been amended. After thirty years, in 2001 a constitutional law (No. 2/2001) further strengthened the guarantee provided against unilateral change in favour if the autonomous province by limiting the power of the Italian state to interfere, providing for the legislative assembly of the province to be involved in any amendment and granting it also the right to initiate amendments. In addition, the new version of Article 103 of the autonomy statute abolishes the possibility of a nation-wide referendum common for constitutional amendments in Italy under Article 138 of the Italian constitution.

exercised as long as the constitution, international obligations, the basic principles of the Italian legal system and the fundamental principles of socio-economic reforms are respected. The exercise of these competencies needs to be in agreement with the 'national interest', but it is expressly stated in the autonomy statute that the national interest 'includes the protection of local linguistic minorities'.[18]

Provincial legislation in the matters of secondary legislative powers has to respect the ordinary laws of Italy as well. These powers include local police issues, elementary and secondary education, roads, electricity, commerce, apprenticeships and vocational training, employment issues, public performances concerning public order and concessions for establishments open to the public, industrial protection, water supplies, hygiene and public health (including hospital services) as well as sport and recreation. After the full implementation of the Second Autonomy Statute and the declaration of conflict-settlement before the UN in 1992, the autonomous province in negotiations with the Italian centre-left governments obtained the devolution of a large number of additional competences not foreseen and guaranteed in the autonomy statute.

The provisions mentioned above regarding legislative and executive powers apply to both autonomous provinces in the same way. In addition, special provisions regarding the relations between the linguistic groups resident in the province apply to South Tyrol alone. These provisions establish a system of consociational democracy in accordance with the principles of cultural autonomy, linguistic parity and ethnic proportionality.[19]

The principle of cultural autonomy is established for the three linguistic groups in South Tyrol.[20] The provisions for the protection and promotion of cultural characteristics, including the proportional allocation of financial resources, the system of separate schools as well as separate cultural offices, are typical expressions of group-protection. Legislation ensures teaching in the mother tongue, equal status of the German and Italian languages in public offices, official documents and topographical naming, and equality of rights between the two linguistic groups.[21]

---

[18] Autonomy Statute, Article 4; see for an extensive analysis of the autonomy statute and its implementation – in Italian and German language – J. Marko, S. Ortino and F. Palermo (eds.), *L'ordinamento speciale della Provincia autonoma di Bolzano (*Padova, 2001), and J. Marko, S. Ortino, F. Palermo, L. Voltmer and J. Woelk (eds.), *Die Südtiroler Verfassung. Die Sonderrechtsordnung der autonomen Provinz Bozen/Südtirol* (Baden-Baden: 2005).

[19] See J. Woelk, 'The Case of South Tyrol: Lessons for Conflict Resolution?' (paper presented at conference entitled 'Voice or Exit', Berlin, June 2001), available at <http://www.eurac.edu/summeracademy/progr/Woelk.pdf> (2 August 2006).

[20] Autonomy Statute, Article 2, which states that the parity of rights of citizens of all language groups is recognized, and 'their ethnic and cultural characteristics are protected'.

[21] Treaty of Peace with Italy (1947), Article 1.

For representation in the public service, the autonomy statute provides for proportional representation of the language groups in public offices, a principle which has been consistently upheld by the Italian constitutional court. At the time of the census, every resident must make a formal declaration, based on the free choice of the individual, as to his or her language group: this declaration is the basis for the right to stand for public office, to be employed in the public administration or as a teacher, and to be given social housing. The principle of ethnic proportions, which has to be applied to all state and semi-state bodies operating in the province[22] as well as to the provincial and municipal administrations, was introduced to gradually reverse the Italian dominance in the public service. The representation of language groups in their respective proportions in all these areas must be achieved within thirty years of the implementation of the Second Autonomy Statute.[23]

5. MECHANISMS FOR IMPLEMENTING THE SOUTH TYROLEAN AUTONOMY

5.1 Negotiating and drafting legislative decrees in joint commissions

A remarkable feature of the South Tyrolean autonomy as laid down in the Second Autonomy Statute is the framework of institutions and procedures for continuous dialogue and negotiations between the Italian government and the South Tyrolean provincial government, created to enable both sides to jointly develop solutions for the issues that come up. The most important functional elements for implementation are two joint commissions. Although similar joint commissions exist in all five autonomous regions of Italy, only in Trentino-South Tyrol have they become the pivotal institutions of the whole autonomy system.[24]

The joint commissions were formed specifically for negotiating the details of implementation.[25] The Second Autonomy Statute provides for the imple-

---

[22] Autonomy Statute, Article 89.

[23] At the end of this period, in 2001, this objective has been achieved in most fields. Positions which are vacant because of a lack of qualified applicants from an ethnic group can only be filled by members of the other ethnic group for a non-renewable twelve-month period. There are recently some cases, especially in the Public Health service, of a more flexible interpretation and application.

[24] Cf., Articles 43 ASt (Autonomy Statute) Sicily, 56 ASt Sardinia, 65 ASt Friuli-Venezia Giulia, and 48 bis ASt Aosta-Valley. Whereas in the XIII legislature the Italian government has adopted twenty-three enactment-decrees for the Autonomous Region Trentino-South Tyrol and the autonomous province of Bolzano/South Tyrol, respectively, it has adopted only six for Friuli-Venezia Giulia, four for Sardinia and three for Sicily.

[25] Autonomy Statute, Article 107: the so-called Commission of Six and (where powers of the Region are involved) Commission of Twelve.

mentation of the statute by legislative decree and establishes two consultative bodies – the joint commissions – to be involved in the process of drafting these decrees.[26] The first, the Commission of Twelve, deals with issues regarding the entire region of Trentino-South Tyrol and is composed of an equal number of representatives of the state on the one hand, and of the region and both provinces (two members each), on the other. All members have equal standing. The second, the Commission of Six, is part of the former and deals with issues regarding the autonomous province of South Tyrol.

The Commission of Six is composed of three members nominated by the state and three members nominated by the province, two of the latter are nominated by the Provincial Council and one by the Regional Council (in practice, by half of its members, i.e., those elected in South Tyrol).[27] Three of the members belong to the German and three to the Italian language group.[28] It is important to note that besides the commission acting as a joint organ of state and province, it is also mixed in terms of the representation of the two major linguistic groups in the province: the state has to nominate one member of the German language group, while one member of the Italian language group is nominated by the province. This provision can only be considered as recognition of the ethnically plural character of both state and province,[29] and has been copied in other regions with minorities.

Although formally established as a consultative body of the Italian government and designed to be of a technical nature, the South Tyrolean Commission of Six – unlike similar bodies in the other autonomous regions – gradually transformed into an autonomous political body for bilateral negotiations between

---

[26] Article 107: '1. The executive measures implementing the present Statute shall be issued by legislative decree, following consultation of a joint Commission of twelve members of which six shall represent the state, two the Regional parliament, two the Provincial parliament of Trento and two that of Bolzano/Bozen. Three of its members must belong to the German linguistic group. 2. Within the Commission referred to in the previous paragraph a special Commission for the executive measures assigned to the competence of the province of Bozen/Bolzano shall be appointed, made up of six members, of whom three shall represent the state and three the province. One of the representatives of the state must belong to the German-speaking group; one of the representatives of the province must belong to the Italian-speaking group.' Translation by Vivienne Frankell, published by the Council of the Autonomous province of Bolzano/Bozen (text updated on 31 January 2001).

[27] According to Articles 25 and 48 of the second autonomy statute, the Regional Council is the assembly, the legislative body of the region. Its seventy members are elected in both autonomous provinces, thirty-five members each. The latter form, for issues and competencies regarding the autonomous provinces of Trentino and of South Tyrol, the two Provincial Councils.

[28] Article 107 para. 2.

[29] Cf., in this sense, S. Bartole, 'La presidenza della Commissione paritetica: implicazioni complesse di una decisione apparentemente semplice', Le Regioni 1995, 1163.

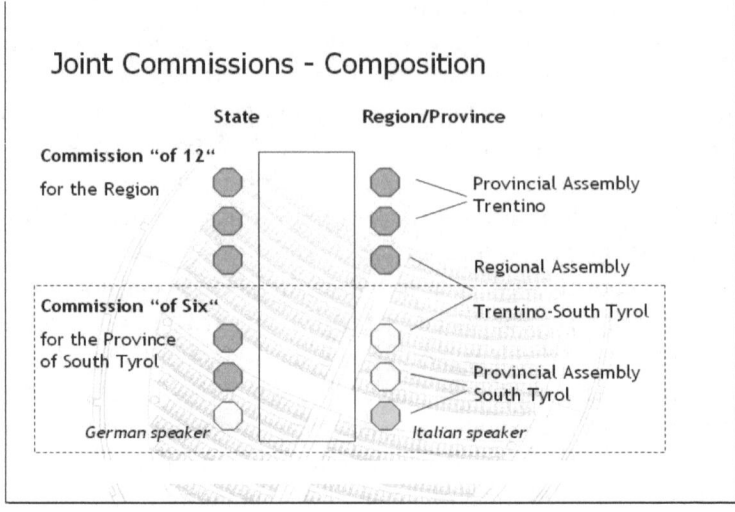

state and province. The members representing the province are nominated by the Provincial Assembly, in which the South Tyrolean People's Party occupies more than a simple majority of the seats. Its members include lawyers, prominent local politicians and more recently even members of the Italian parliament. This strengthened the commission's political legitimacy in negotiations and thus its political role and weight as the central institution for coordination and negotiation between state and province. Moreover, the active involvement of its representatives made it increasingly difficult for the Italian government to treat the outcome of negotiations as mere non-binding opinions. In practice, the Commission of Six has gradually taken on the role of drafting the enactment decrees, which are subsequently adopted by the government in the form of presidential and/or legislative decrees.

This important development has been confirmed by the Italian constitutional court.[30] A first substantial step towards a quasi-binding character of the Commission of Six' opinions was made in 1989, when the court handed down a judgment which declared a unilateral change by the Italian government of some details in a text elaborated by the Commission of Six illegitimate, because the government had not asked for the commission's opinion on such changes.[31] This renewed obligation to seek the commission's opinion comes close to recognising the binding character of commission opinions.

---

[30] In particular, Judgment 212/1984, commented on by U. Allegretti, 'La Corte ribadisce l'estraneità del parlamento all'attuazione degli statuti speciali', Le Regioni 1984, 1310.

[31] Judgment 37/1989, Le Regioni 1990, 897.

Some years later, the court went further and stated explicitly that the Commission of Six is a fundamental organ of cooperation between the state and the special (i.e., distinct) legal system established in the autonomous province on the basis of the autonomy statute rather than a mere advisory body of the government. In the same case the court decided that the president of the Commission of Six cannot be appointed unilaterally by the government (as is common for advisory bodies) but must be nominated by the commission itself.[32]

5.2 Safeguarding South Tyrol's autonomy; the status of the enactment decrees in the Italian legal system

The outcome of negotiations between the state and the province within the joint commissions is adopted in the atypical form of enactment decrees: according to Article 107 of the Second Autonomy Statute, they are to be adopted as legislative decrees, i.e., as legislative acts adopted by the government through delegation by the parliament.[33] Until recent years a number of them have been issued in the form of presidential decrees, but this did neither affect the procedure leading to their adoption nor did it change their nature as governmental norms with legislative rank (*atti del governo aventi forza di legge*).

Consequently, these enactment decrees constitute legislative acts which are part of ordinary law, but they do not need to be debated in or adopted by the national parliament. Therefore their deliberation can be kept separate from normal political process, and experts from both sides instead of politicians are involved in the elaboration of the decrees.

Moreover, the enactment decrees cannot be changed unilaterally by the state due to the nature of the process by which they are negotiated. Although formally of the same rank in the hierarchy of legal sources, subsequent ordinary laws adopted by the Italian parliament cannot abolish, amend or overrule enactment decrees. According to the Italian constitutional court, the enactment decrees are a 'legal source of atypical nature' because of the difference between their form (legislative or presidential decree) and their substance (implementation of the principles and provisions in the autonomy statute, which is a constitutional law). As a consequence, the simple application of the *lex posterior* rule cannot be admitted, if not by another, subsequent enactment decree.[34] The justification for this exceptional protection of the enactment decrees can be found

---

[32] Judgment 109/1995, Le Regioni 1995, 1159.
[33] Article 76 Italian Constitution.
[34] Italian Constitutional Court Judgments 20/1956, 22/1961, 151/1972, 180/1980, 237/1983, 212/1984 and 160/1985. See also U. Allegretti, 'La Corte ribadisce l'estraneità del Parlamento all'attuazione degli statuti speciali', Le Regioni 1984, 1310.

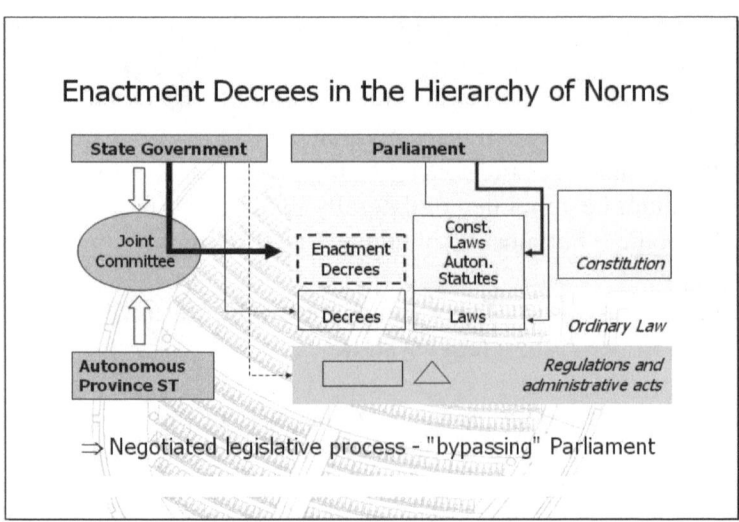

in the constitutional umbrella provided by the autonomy statute, which is the expression of a historical political compromise.[35] This constitutes an important guarantee of South Tyrol's autonomy.[36]

Disputes between the Italian government and the provincial or regional governments regarding the enactment decrees can be brought to the Italian constitutional court. So far, in the few cases decided, an attitude of judicial self-restraint by the court and a presumption of constitutionality of the enactment decrees can be observed, excluding its direct intervention into matters regulated by these enactment decrees, at least as long as no potential violation of other fundamental constitutional principles are involved. In an *obiter dictum* the court declared that the enactment decrees, as the 'historically valid [and binding] realisation of all abstract possibilities of implementing the regional special autonomy', constitute a 'limit', which has to be respected, otherwise 'uncontrollable consequences for the overall balance of the legal system established by means of the enactment decrees might be the result'.[37]

---

[35] The Italian constitutional court has considered the enactment decrees an expression of a 'separate and reserved power', different from the ordinary laws of the state: Judgment 237/1983, Le Regioni 1983, 1275. For the position of the enactment decrees in the hierarchy of legal sources see, e.g., F. Gabriele, *Decreti legislativi di attuazione degli statuti speciali*, in Enc. Giur., Vol. X, Roma 1988, 14.

[36] See F. Palermo, 'Ruolo e natura delle commissioni paritetiche e delle norme di attuazione', in J. Marko, S. Ortino, F. Palermo (eds.), *L'ordinamento speciale della Provincia autonoma di Bolzano* (Padova,:Cedam 2001), 826.

[37] Constitutional Court, Judgment 213/1998 (sub 4.2.), in *Giurisprudenza costituzionale 1998*, 1667, with a comment by F. Palermo, 'Non expedit della Corte al controllo di costituzionalità delle norme di attuazione degli statute speciali'.

5.3 Established 'equality' in implementation negotiations and institutions

The basic idea underlying the implementation process is to create situations and institutions in which the representatives of the state and the province as well as the major linguistic groups have equal number and standing in order to avoid dominance by one side or one group. In practice, this procedure is very similar to international diplomatic negotiations where, despite all differences, states are formally put on the same level. Of course, differences in position, power, resources and economic strength do exist between the parties and this will influence the negotiations. However, during the negotiations the legal fiction of equal standing of both delegations is maintained, favouring the joint search for compromise and agreement and excluding unilateral imposition of a solution.

5.4 Asymmetrical regionalism

In regional and federal systems a collective representation of the regions or federated entities is often institutionally established in order to allow this level of government to exercise its influence for safeguarding its interests. This is usually done by means of a special body or a parliamentary second chamber. Collective representation is useful in order to strengthen the political position of the regions as a whole. However, it does not often satisfy the specific interests of a single region. It leads to the necessity of compromise between the regions or federated entities, as a consequence of decision by majority vote, justified by the fact that all entities are vested with the same powers and functions. The result is a tendency toward homogeneity.

In the case of Italy's asymmetrical regionalism there are not only two 'classes' of regions – the special autonomous regions and the ordinary regions, there is also differentiation between the special regions. For this reason only bilateral relations of the regions with the state can fully guarantee respect for the specific needs of the former. These bilateral relations constitute the very nature of the special autonomy granted to the five special regions.[38] In the Italian constitutional experience, South Tyrol is the only case where the full potential offered by this special relationship has been used.

---

[38] Cf., S. Bartole, 'Art. 116', in *Commentario alla costituzione*, G. Branca (ed.), (Bologna-Roma, 1985), 85, and G. Pitruzzella, 'Modifiche delle norme di attuazione dello statuto siciliano: verso un «principio contrattualista» nei rapporti tra Stato e Regioni speciali?', Le Regioni 1988, 1608.

6. THE FUNCTIONING OF THE SOUTH TYROLEAN AUTONOMY AFTER ITS FULL IMPLEMENTATION; EVALUATION AND FUTURE PERSPECTIVES

Even though the detailed time-frame for enactment of the Second Autonomy Statute and the operational calendar could only be realised with considerable delay, the adoption of each implementation-decree had the effect of a trust and confidence-building measure. The unrealistic goal of full implementation of the autonomy statute within two years from its entry into force, as required under Article 108 of the Second Autonomy Statute, could not be achieved but the constitutional court of Italy did not consider the two-year period a peremptory period as the Second Autonomy Statute did not contain sanctions for not observing it.[39] Eventually, the process took ten times as long to complete. Only after twenty years, in 1992, was the implementation of the Package considered to be successfully and satisfactory concluded by all parties.

The Second Autonomy Statute governing the constitutional relationship between South Tyrol and Italy has remained unchanged for nearly thirty years. It has been reformed for the first time in 2001, in the general context of Italy's reform-process towards federalism. A first constitutional law concerning amendments to the statutes of the five autonomous regions reformed the institutional structure of the autonomy statute of Trentino-South Tyrol, mainly confirming and strengthening the separate and different features of both autonomous provinces while further weakening the position of the region.[40] Also the subsequent reform of the Italian constitution, introducing major changes to the relationship between state and regions (strengthening the position of the latter), has effects on the autonomous regions, which remain protected by a clause declaring only 'more favourable provisions' applicable to their autonomy systems.[41] However, the reform process is not yet concluded.

Overall, the implementation mechanisms based on bilateral negotiations between the state and the province as well as between the two major linguistic groups can be regarded as a success. The most important issues of the South

---

[39] Constitutional Court, Judgment 160/1985, in Le Regoni 6/1985, 1140, with a comment by S. Bartole, 'Le norme di attuazione degli statuti speciali come fonte permanente'.

[40] Constitutional Law of 31 January 2001, No. 2.

[41] Constitutional Law of 18 October 2001, No. 3. The 'salvatory clause' regarding preferential treatment for the autonomous regions (and provinces) is contained in the transitional provision, Article 11 of this constitutional law. See for further information on the constitutional reforms and their effects on South Tyrol's distinct legal system, F. Palermo, 'Südtirol und die italienische Föderalismusreform', in S. Clementi and J. Woelk (eds.), *1992. Ende eines Streits. Zehn Jahre Streitbeilegung im Südtirolkonflikt zwischen Italien und Österreich* (Baden-Baden, 2003), 119-134.

Tyrolean autonomy system – the census, the proportional quota system and the use of language – are regulated by enactment decrees.[42] Though designed to implement the autonomy statute, the mechanism of enactment by decree continues to function even today after the last enactment decree entered into force. As time goes by, enactment decrees need to be amended, for which the same negotiation procedure in the joint commission needs to be followed. The principle of negotiation and the special character of the autonomy thus continue to prevail over the principle of democracy and the participation of parliament, the latter remaining permanently excluded.[43]

After full implementation of the autonomy and the formal settlement of the conflict between Austria and Italy in 1992, the negotiated enactment-decrees even started to cover new areas like schools, roads, energy and the transfer of new powers to the province. These were not foreseen in the autonomy statute and contribute to a dynamic understanding and evolution of the South Tyrolean autonomy. Again, cooperation with the state is facilitated by the use of an instrument based on bilateral negotiations on – legally – equal footing, which at the same time constitutes a privileged channel for the direct representation of specific interests. Finally, there are even sectors regulated by legal sources of a different nature. The province's finances for example are guaranteed by the Second Autonomy Statute, but details are regulated in ordinary laws, which are developed through the same negotiation process (although finally approved by the Italian parliament due to their budget-relevant character).

Whereas in the past negotiations behind closed doors have produced positive results, in the future the lack of transparency (public access to proceedings of the meetings does not exist), of democratic influence and of accountability in the work of the joint commission could be seen as more problematic. Permanent bilateral negotiations regarding the technical details of a previously agreed framework agreement (i.e., Package and autonomy statute) as well as the official consultative character and function of these bodies were able to justify secrecy in the past, giving the consultations quasi-diplomatic character. However, since the joint commissions have become de facto law-making bodies, public interest in the way certain decisions are reached and in their underlying motivation increases. This is particularly true for decisions which change and

---

[42] D.P.R. 752/1976 regarding the census and the proportional quota system implementing Article 89 of the second autonomy statute, and D.P.R. 574/1988 regarding the use of language in public administration and judiciary implementing Articles 99 and 100 of the second autonomy statute.

[43] This has been confirmed by the Supreme Administrative Court of Italy, *Consiglio di Stato*, Opinion 3302/1995 as well as by the Constitutional Court, Judgments 160/1985 and 37/1989.

amend enactment decrees in force and even more so for those which are not covered by the original Package but concern new areas of competence.

Without the risk of damaging a successful key element of the South Tyrolean autonomy system, it seems possible to introduce some obligations of transparency in the work of the commission, at least in today's more tolerant political climate and after full implementation of the autonomy. Additionally, the powers of the legislative body of the autonomous province could be strengthened. The Provincial Council nominates half of the members of the joint Commission of Six, but these are not accountable to it (in particular, they do not have to report back on their activity), in line with the original concept of a consultative expert-body to the Italian government. From today's perspective, the Provincial Council, representing all linguistic groups, including the Ladins (who are not represented in the joint commissions), could be involved in the consultative process leading to the adoption or change of an enactment decree through the expression of a mandatory opinion.

7. Concluding Remarks on Austria's Role

The process of implementation of the South Tyrolean autonomy has been embedded in guarantees at an international level, mostly of a bilateral character.[44] It was the bilateral De Gasperi-Gruber agreement that was subsequently included in an annex to the multilateral peace treaty with Italy that created a real obligation for Italy *vis-à-vis* Austria. On the whole, the implementation of the autonomy agreement was an Italian obligation regarding its domestic sphere, which left Austria with a monitoring role. In the course of events, formal insistence on the international character of the autonomy did more harm than good: only when both Italy and Austria became more flexible and pragmatic in their respective positions did success – i.e., a well working autonomy in South Tyrol – become possible.

Success depended much on other factors. A compromise in the South Tyrol issue was not actively sought during the 1950s and 1960s due to the Cold War and because of Italian domestic politics. It is by no means a coincidence that the reform of the autonomy statute for South Tyrol took place in 1972, in the context of general decentralisation and regionalisation of Italy. At that time, the

---

[44] See for the international character and the bilateralisation of the conflict the contributions by M. Gehler, 'Vollendung der Bilateralisierung als diplomatisch-juristisches Kunststück', and P. Hilpold, 'Der Südtiroler Weg völkerrechtlicher Stufenlösung im europäischen Vergleich', in S. Clementi and J. Woelk (eds.), *1992. Ende eines Streits. Zehn Jahre Streitbeilegung im Südtirolkonflikt zwischen Italien und Österreich* (Baden-Baden, 2003), 17 and 109 respectively.

fifteen ordinary regions were effectively established, thus completing the regional system as designed in Italy's constitution of 1948. Once the negotiations had begun, the 'soft' pressure from the 'protecting power' Austria certainly contributed to keeping Italy's interests in the fulfilment of its obligations alive. Another positive influence was the progress in European integration: the democratisation of Central and Eastern Europe gave a new and final momentum to the solution of the conflict by completely changing its security dimension. The prospect of Austria's EU-membership at the beginning of the 1990s accelerated the final conclusion of the implementation of the Package.

The necessity of a formal declaration of conflict settlement by Austria – which would only act respecting the opinion of the South Tyrolese –, to be given after the implementation process had been concluded, was an important incentive for Italy to realise the principles laid down in the Package. The procedure for the approval of the final declaration mirrors the adoption of the Package more than twenty years ago: after the last of 137 implementation measures had been adopted on 22 April 1992, Italy notified this result to the Austrian government. By making express reference to the De Gasperi-Gruber agreement, to the Package, the operational calendar and the Second Autonomy Statute, it – quite surprisingly – confirmed the international anchoring of the Package (until then the most disputed issue between Austria and Italy!). At its extraordinary congress on 30 May 1992, the South Tyrolean People's Party voted in favour of declaring the dispute regarding the satisfactory fulfilment of implementation obligations ended (82,86 percent). On 5 June 1992, the Austrian parliament approved the declaration on conflict-settlement, underlining Austria's continuous monitoring role as well as the possibility of submitting future disputes to the International Court of Justice in case of gross violations. Finally, the declaration of conflict-settlement was presented to the UN Secretary-General on 19 June 1992, thus ending the dispute which had been pending there since 1960.

It can be concluded that the involvement of the kin-state Austria as a constructively acting outside party was of great value in securing full implementation of autonomy as provided for in the Package for South Tyrol.

Particularly relevant for other situations is the successful process of internationalised conflict de-escalation and the joint transformation of a conflict whose course was by and large negative, into a positive process with peace and stability as direct and sustainable results. The implementation mechanisms for the South Tyrol autonomy also offer interesting lessons for other conflicts: the operational calendar with its detailed, pre-established time-frame; the institutionalised negotiations between state and province in joint commissions; and the resulting enactment decrees, which cannot be changed unilaterally by the state. These procedures involving various actors – representatives of the minority, the majority (represented by the Italian government) and of Austria, a foreign state – ensured that the autonomy process based upon compromise, consensus and collaboration and its long-term orientation were not destroyed in its concrete implementation.

Chapter VIII

THIRD PARTY INVOLVEMENT IN THE NEGOTIATION AND IMPLEMENTATION OF INTRASTATE PEACE AGREEMENTS

Geir Sjøberg[*]

This chapter is based on observations of various peace and reconciliation processes, including some specific Norwegian experiences. The nature of Norway's involvement in these processes varies according to the needs of the parties, the interests of major powers, the roles played by other international actors and the Norwegian capacity to make a contribution. It focuses on three key areas: support for talks between the involved parties, support for monitoring of negotiated commitments, and support for peace dividends that benefit the people on the ground. The main purpose of this chapter is to share insights and lessons learned with regard to third party facilitation and the many factors that impact its effectiveness.

1. STARTING POINTS

At the outset, it may be useful to identify some of the starting points underlying Norwegian efforts for peace and reconciliation.

As a small country, Norway is not in a position to impose solutions on parties in conflict. Norwegian involvement as impartial facilitator of a peace process is contingent on the parties' genuine will to peace and full acceptance of Norway's role.

The role as impartial facilitator may be particularly suitable for a small country without vested interests. At the same time, the Norwegian approach is based on a certain capacity to make available financial means and to apply the required discretion.

---

[*] Advisor, Section for Peace and Reconciliation, Norwegian Ministry of Foreign Affairs. This chapter is based on the presentation given at the expert meeting in Sitges/Barcelona. It is the responsibility of the author and does not necessarily represent the views of the Norwegian Ministry of Foreign Affairs.

M. Boltjes (ed.), *Implementing Negotiated Agreements*
© 2007, Kreddha International and T·M·C·ASSER PRESS, The Hague, The Netherlands

In most cases, the Norwegian involvement for peace and reconciliation comes in the form of support for the efforts of a lead facilitator, such as the UN, regional organisations or other countries. Building good relations with all parties is crucial. So is patience and readiness for enduring involvement. Conflict resolution requires a long-term perspective and sustained and adequate coordination.

Broad and sustained international attention and follow-up is critical to help move any peace process forward (by ensuring that all efforts are mutually reinforcing and that they draw on past experiences). We must avoid competition between different countries, organisations and initiatives. Concerted support by the international community can help convince the parties that a negotiated solution is possible while also encourage their leaders to take the necessary steps in the cause of peace.

Norwegian involvement in peace and reconciliation processes has often started through the long-term commitment of non-governmental organisations or through collaboration involving academic institutions. Norwegian NGOs have during several decades gained wide international experience. In some cases, we have also cooperated with NGOs from other countries. As a result, invaluable contact points have been developed with a range of actors in many countries.

The nature of the Norwegian involvement in various peace processes differs. Broadly speaking, the contributions to most processes focus on three key features: Support for talks between the involved parties; support for monitoring of negotiated commitments; and support for peace dividends that benefit the people on the ground.

Experience underlines the importance of readily available and flexible financial resources in support of a process. Such resources must not be subject to extensive bureaucratic procedures. Decision-making needs to be rapid in order for initiatives to be put into action at important junctures. Confidence building measures do not necessarily require huge transfers, but timing will always be a key factor.

Experience has also pointed to the important premise that negotiations and implementation of intrastate peace agreements are intrinsically linked. Lack of proper implementation along the way will lead to reduced trust between the parties and complicate any process towards functioning settlements. Negotiations must thus be approached with implementation issues at the forefront.

2. Different Facilitator Roles

Norway is currently contributing in different ways to peace processes in Africa, Asia, Europe and Latin America. Facilitator roles differ greatly and can also change over time as a process unfolds. Norway's involvement as facilitator varies considerably depending on the nature of the concrete process and the aspirations of the parties, the interests of major powers, the roles played by other international actors, and the Norwegian capacity to make a specific contribution.

The parties' will to peace and acceptance of the facilitator are essential for a process to succeed. Careful political assessments are needed to prevent a facilitator from being used as a 'peace alibi', while the parties continue with armed conflict.

The degree to which major powers have interests in a conflict usually affects the kind of role a smaller actor can play. In many instances smaller actors can contribute most effectively by seeking to bring about broad support and persuade larger actors such as the United States and the EU to play constructive roles and, insofar as possible, to employ a multilateral approach, such as through the UN. In cases where a smaller actor is to take on a lead role, support from the relevant major powers will be helpful and usually also necessary.

Experience shows that there can be significant competition between various countries and actors for different types of facilitator roles. This poses an important challenge. Peace diplomacy has become increasingly widespread and is associated with a certain prestige. It is imperative that the various actors have well-defined roles that complement each other and that all efforts are closely coordinated in order for the international community to come across with a unified and effective message.

Even in cases where the parties have taken a strategic decision to pursue peace, setbacks must to some extent usually be expected along the way. It is important for a facilitator to have a clear perception of her role in the process. The basic conditions for taking on a commitment should always be clear for the facilitator and the parties. Generally speaking, a facilitator must show perseverance in difficult phases. However, if the fundamental approach of the parties change and the opportunity for making constructive contributions diminish, the facilitator must relate to such development by re-assessing the situation and her role.

The following is an overview of some different types of roles that can be played by an impartial facilitator:

2.1 Examples of lead roles

- Official facilitator of peace negotiations, officially appointed by the parties;
- Sponsor of a back channel, asked confidentially by the parties to facilitate secret negotiations;

- Promoter and coordinator of active international support for a peace process;
- Facilitator of dialogue aimed at promoting reconciliation and preventing armed conflict, based on early warning by involved parties.

2.2 Examples of coalition roles

- Member of a Group of Friends that actively supports a peace process;
- Member of a multilateral body that deals with a specific conflict/peace process.

2.3 Examples of supporting roles

- Providing financial and political support to other facilitator(s) in a negotiating process;
- Providing financial support and, in some cases, personnel for the implementation and monitoring of cease-fire/peace agreements;
- Delivering humanitarian aid, transitional aid and long-term assistance as a means of supporting a peace/reconciliation process;
- Promoting internationally recognised human rights as a means of advancing peace and reconciliation in the long-term.

2.4 Examples of exploratory roles

- Informal contact-building activities and identifying the respective parties' room for manoeuvre;
- Informal contact-building activities and confidence building projects using non-governmental actors;
- Supporting roles and exploratory roles can lay the groundwork for more substantive contributions at a subsequent stage, depending on how the process develops;
- In most cases, Norway does not play a lead role, but contributes in the form of support to the process and its lead facilitator.

3. GENERATING MOMENTUM

In order for a peace process to succeed the parties themselves must show real political will to find a negotiated and lasting resolution. At the same time, there are a number of elements a facilitator can focus on with the view to contribute to added momentum for a process. As highlighted above, leveraging broad and united international support is one critical element in such efforts.

Beyond the international efforts, a facilitator will also need to pay attention to certain internal dynamics of a process.

First, the degree of *inclusiveness* of affected parties in a peace process is a decisive factor. A facilitator cannot dictate who is to take part in a process, but the aim should always be to make it as inclusive as possible. Most conflicts involve more than two parties. When asked by two conflicting parties to act as facilitator in a process, the prospective facilitator should help them agree on how any other groups can be included in the process and on what conditions. This ought to be based on the prospective facilitator's own analysis of the conflict and the fundamental interests of the respective parties. The degree of inclusiveness in the process and the various parties' will to participate are factors that should be considered when deciding whether or not to take on the task of facilitator.

In principle, all important interest groups should be represented in a negotiating process. In cases where this is not possible, a realistic assessment should be made of the possibilities of implementing an agreement between the parties that do participate, and the degree to which such an agreement would constitute a viable basis for peace and reconciliation in the long-term. If negotiations are initiated without the participation of all key parties, it is important to have a strategy that includes the various groups and interests along the way. Sometimes it may be necessary and appropriate to restrict the negotiations to selected parties, but in such cases it is important to assess carefully any negative consequences it might have that certain parties do not take part. Such parties may feel excluded, which may make them oppose the process more strongly than would otherwise have been the case. In cases where a party is merely a spoiler whose only aim is to destroy the prospects of peace and reconciliation, it is important to analyse how the negative impact can most effectively be reduced.

The greatest possible degree of inclusiveness should also be sought in processes that require secrecy in certain stages. In cases where it is not possible to include all the parties in the introductory stages, the aim should be to do so as soon as politically possible.

Second, a framework that provides guidance as to how the most difficult issues are to be dealt with, thus prescribing a *holistic approach* from the moment real negotiations begin, can be an expedient approach. This also reduces the risk of the facilitator being used as a 'peace alibi' if and when the parties at the outset make certain concessions. In any event, a facilitator must watch out to not help to promote weak agreements that will not advance the peace process in the long-term.

Negotiating parties will instinctively position themselves for final talks on the most important issues. At the same time, it is usually not realistic to seek package solutions that encompass all issues at the same time. Such dilemmas have been reflected, *inter alia*, in the question whether the parties should begin a process by discussing a cease-fire agreement or by getting right down to negotiations on a peace agreement, on the presumption that the absence of a cease-fire and the constant threat of violence this entails will force the parties to advance more quickly than would otherwise have been the case.

In some cases, such as Sudan, the concept of 'humanitarian cease-fire' has been employed. The establishment of such a cease-fire for a specified period of time can be expedient, both in terms of getting aid to the victims of a conflict and in terms of creating political room for manoeuvre for the negotiations. The parties can earn a certain amount of political credit by agreeing themselves to a time-limited cease-fire. This also makes it possible for the international community and other actors to become more closely involved in the process.

In Sri Lanka the parties have followed a two-step approach. First they negotiated a cease-fire agreement that provided for an independent monitoring mechanism. Then they began the actual negotiations, where the parties have committed themselves to a solution based on federalism. Without such a mutual concession, it would have been extremely difficult to structure the negotiations in a way that was both targeted and inspired confidence.

Third, it is important to encourage the parties to *assume and demonstrate ownership* of the process and the results achieved along the way, and to help build mutual trust and respect. This can be done, for example, by seeking to ensure that the parties do not agree to something they cannot comply with and by not negotiating via deputies who have limited authority.

Fourth, in the implementation of negotiated commitments, it is essential to ensure *broad participation of civil society* as the process moves forward. One of the causes of internal armed conflicts is the lack of institutions to deal with various differences in society. A facilitator should insofar as possible seek to help the parties in a peace process establish democratic institutions, including through financial and technical contributions. This can be a critical means of ensuring that future conflicts can be resolved peacefully.

In some cases it may be appropriate to consider the establishment of a truth commission, in others a criminal court may advance a process. Judicial decisions can give a process the added dimension of justice, which can pave the way for further reconciliation efforts. There are, however, many ways of implementing such mechanisms, and it is important that they are properly targeted.

Peace and reconciliation processes generally attract wide attention in mass media. The parties have an obligation to as well as an interest in informing the public in order to help people to understand, assume ownership of and support negotiated results. Information communicated to the media by a facilitator should be closely coordinated with the parties, and be based on considerations of procedural efficacy. It may be particularly important that a facilitator has straightforward relations with the media in order to prevent any misunderstandings. False information in the press can create severe problems for a process, and must be minimised to ensure that the parties can focus their efforts on achieving functional compromises.

Fifth, it may be expedient to engage *local intermediaries* in a process, e.g., religious leaders, trade union leaders, NGO representatives and representatives of women's movements, to channel information on the situation and needs of the people to political leaders. In this way, all levels of society can be engaged in the process, including within the different groupings, in order to foster a common understanding of what is required for a peaceful solution. Norwegian mediators emphasised this in the Guatemala process, where the aim was reconciliation both horizontally (between those sitting around the negotiating table) and vertically (including between the upper classes and less affluent people). By linking these axes together, e.g., by using religious leaders who both understood grass-roots needs and had access to the top leaders, dialogue was facilitated across classes and structures. As the case of Guatemala shows, intermediaries can play an important part in solving practical problems as the process unfolds, and thus help to garner support for the results achieved at the negotiating table along the way. When the people are rally behind a process, opposition and extremist groups tend to become marginalised.

Sixth, experience shows that there are generally few *women* who participate in peace negotiations or are otherwise involved in drafting agreements that form the basis for the future development in their countries. Without women's participation, there is less likelihood that a peace agreement will take adequate account of women's interests and needs. If a peace agreement is deficient in this respect, it will be more difficult to ensure that it has the broad support of civil society in the implementation phase, and the chances of the agreement breaking down will be greater. It is important for a facilitator to encourage the participation of women in negotiating delegations, with a view to ensuring that the negotiating results safeguard the interests of the whole population.

Generating momentum also requires a number of other considerations. Some of these are addressed in more detail in the remaining sections of this chapter. They relate to asymmetry, human rights, monitoring mechanisms, humanitarian aid and development assistance.

4. ASYMMETRY

An internal conflict usually entails various degrees of asymmetry between a state party and a non-state party or parties. Such asymmetry poses a number of challenges that a facilitator must be ready to handle, including in relation to negotiations, legitimacy, governance, and international blacklisting.

4.1 Negotiations

Non-state parties tend to have less capacity than state parties to conduct diplomatic relations, influence public opinion, finance travel and participation in negotiations, including carrying out analyses of issues and proposals under consideration. Norway has on many occasions provided support to non-state parties in such respects in order to facilitate negotiations. A process will not get far if a party lacks the capacity or skill to negotiate, or is unable to assess proposals that are put on the table. Ideally, the parties must be able to empathise with the other party's situation. In some incidents, training in negotiating techniques has been offered, and efforts have been made to forge a common understanding of the key challenges.

4.2 Legitimacy

The legitimate exercise of government is increasingly contingent on a state's ability and will to protect its own citizens. For a state, or non-state party for that matter, to gain international legitimacy today, more is required than merely having control over territory. Parties in conflict are expected to follow generally accepted rules of governance. The provisions of international humanitarian law relating to internal conflicts are, however, much less comprehensive than those relating to international conflicts. Nonetheless, during the past ten years internal conflicts have been increasingly perceived as being the concern of the international community. For example, it has become increasingly more difficult for states to invoke internal affairs when they are criticised for human rights violations. The final document adopted at the UN World Conference on Human Rights in 1993 reads: 'the promotion and protection of all human rights is a legitimate concern of the international community.'

Non-state parties are usually not elected to represent their constituencies. They may or may not be fully representative *vis-à-vis* their constituencies. The same may hold true for state parties. In a democratic country, the state party usually has an electoral basis behind it. Hence, the participation in a peace process by the government side may in some cases be particularly influenced by domestic political considerations. It will always be important that a facilitator actively encourages the parties to bring on board all interest groups in the areas they control in support of a peace process.

Parties in internal conflict may or may not be recognised internationally as the legitimate representative of their constituencies. If only one side is recognised internationally, this may be a challenging factor for a facilitator. This can be illustrated by the Israeli-Palestinian conflict, where Norway had to decide whether – unlike the United States and under warnings from the United States – to deal with the PLO, and in so doing recognise the organisation as the legitimate representative of the Palestinians. A lesson is that a facilitator may, in certain cases, have to accept some degree of criticism from some corners for its efforts to bring the parties to the negotiating table.

4.3 Governance

In peace processes between a government side and non-state party(ies) involving negotiations of autonomy arrangements, the latter will be the *demander* needing constitutional amendments. Without entrenchment in the national constitution a peace agreement in itself may not provide any guarantees that future governments will honour and respect the provisions of the agreement.

As part of the process towards proper governance, non-state parties will need to transform from armed groups to civil organisations that can take part in democratic elections and assume political responsibilities within the framework of a peace agreement. Such transformation and the giving up of military capacity is more likely to take place if and when a peace agreement has been entrenched in the national constitution, making the process as irreversible as possible.

In conflicts where territory is an object, war-torn areas and areas controlled by non-state parties may have less developed public sector and state institutions. Such asymmetry will have implications in terms of needs related to reconstruction.

International assistance, from bilateral donors and intergovernmental organisations, is in many cases channelled largely through governments. Delivery of peace dividends in areas controlled by non-state parties will in such cases be contingent on effective cooperation and procedures on the government side. Bureaucratic systems, both on the part of donors and the recipient governments, may delay the delivery of assistance to war-torn areas. Such delays, or even eventual lack of disbursement altogether, may contribute to reduce a party's trust in the process. It is important that a facilitator pay attention to any possible procedural constraints related to the provision of aid. In particular, the parties need not be given expectations that cannot be met. This will only damage the process in the long run. It is better to under-promise and over-deliver.

A helpful approach may be to establish a committee of the parties to the peace process to discuss and agree on priorities for assistance and for its means of delivery to war-torn areas. Such approach may also serve a purpose in creating contact and dialogue between the parties and understanding for each other's needs. Moreover, such approach may prove helpful in leveraging support from international donors, through donor conferences, etc.

Assistance channelled directly through NGOs will usually not be subject to government procedures.

4.4 International blacklisting

International terrorism represents a paramount challenge for the international community. The struggle against international terrorism is an overriding aim of Norwegian foreign policy. Even before 11 September 2001, many individuals and organisations responsible for terrorist activities were subject to UN sanctions and as such blacklisted internationally. After the terrorist attacks in New York and Washington in 2001, the Security Council expanded the list of terrorist organisations and individuals subject to UN sanctions. The Council adopted Resolution 1373, setting out a number of concrete measures for combating terrorism. However, no annex was adopted that clearly specified the organisations/individuals to be covered by the resolution. There are no specific international criteria for blacklisting. Terrorism is primarily defined in a political context, not in a scientific or legal one.

When discussing blacklisting, it is important to distinguish between international (UN) and national blacklisting. In addition to the core of terrorist organisations that are subject to internationally binding UN sanctions, there are a number of organisations that are defined as terrorist organisations on a national basis by some countries, but not by others. The United States in particular, and to some degree the United Kingdom and others, have blacklisted some organisations that are not covered by the UN lists. For example, the United States, the United Kingdom, Australia, etc., have blacklisted the Liberation Tigers of Tamil Eelam (LTTE), whereas Norway, the EU and Japan have not done so.

Norway has not played a central facilitator role in processes involving terrorist organisations that are subject to internationally binding sanctions. Compliance with international obligations and fully supporting the fight against international terrorism are fundamental Norwegian policy aims. At the same time Norway has been, and is today, involved in peace processes involving non-state parties that have used means in their struggle to achieve political aims that they themselves define as military means, but which are perceived in international circles as terrorism.

The role of facilitator in a peace process involving parties that are blacklisted is a demanding one in terms of treating both parties equally. In conflicts where one party is using, or has used, methods that are perceived as terrorist methods in international circles, Norway may have an advantage as a facilitator through previous experience in the area. Dialogue with armed groups can help them enter into a peace process.

Blacklisting by some countries can create complications for a peace process, but in some cases it can also help resolve a conflict. For example, extensive blacklisting can make it clear to non-state parties that military/terrorist means will not be accepted. This may severely undermine the prospects of winning international support, if the approach for which they were blacklisted is pursued.

Experience from Sri Lanka shows that difficult issues can be solved through close dialogue with the countries concerned. Despite divergent political needs and aims, it is important that all countries pull in the same direction. Several countries that had banned the LTTE took part in the Sri Lanka Donors' Conference in Oslo in November 2002. These countries realised that unless the LTTE were involved, there would be no end to the conflict.

5. HUMAN RIGHTS

Human rights issues have a central place in most peace and reconciliation processes. Violations of human rights are normally part of armed conflict, both as a *cause* and a *consequence*. The correlation between peace and reconciliation efforts and human rights depends on the nature of the conflict.

If a peace agreement is to be sustainable over time, it generally has to include elements that provide a basis for the development of a state governed by the rule of law in which human rights are respected. It is important that a facilitator advises the parties as to how human rights violations can be avoided in the future, and what national human rights mechanisms should be established, including monitoring mechanisms and constitutional/statutory safeguards. Concrete efforts behind the scenes can often produce good results.

The role as facilitator provides a good opportunity to work closely with the parties to prevent human rights violations. For example, the facilitator may be well placed to give concrete advice and to assist in establishing monitoring mechanisms and making necessary amendments to legislation. By supporting educational programmes and training, a facilitator can also help enhance knowledge and understanding of human rights as they are defined in the Geneva conventions. Raising questions related to human rights can have a positive effect because it is a way of focusing on fundamental, overriding international ethical and legal norms that the parties must take into account in their efforts to find durable solutions. A facilitator can also help to engage other countries and actors in efforts to promote human rights.

It will always be important for Norway, which generally keeps a high profile in the human rights area, to have a holistic policy in the fields of peace, reconciliation, democracy and human rights.

6. Monitoring Mechanisms

Monitoring mechanisms are increasingly being viewed as appropriate tools in a peace and reconciliation context. Since the UN was founded, it has been in charge of a number of operations where the monitoring of cease-fire agreements and various forms of implementation of peace agreements has been a central ingredient. Considerable experience in this area has been built up within the UN system. Norway has contributed to UN peacekeeping operations for a long time. At the same time, certain peace processes Norway has facilitated have not been dealt with by the Security Council. This does not, of course, mean that there is not also a need for monitoring and control mechanisms in these cases.

On the contrary, monitoring may be particularly important in conflicts that are not prominently placed on the agenda of the UN. Monitoring mechanisms, based on independent observers, can be important in the essential task of confidence building. Such mechanisms are also essential in ensuring that agreements are respected and that violations have real political cost, including on the international level.

The extent to which the parties at the negotiating table are willing to establish concrete mechanisms related to monitoring can also serve as an indicator of their real political will to a negotiated and fair settlement.

Experience since the cease-fire in Sri Lanka was signed in February 2002 shows that the Sri Lanka Monitoring Mission (SLMM) has been absolutely essential. On previous occasions when peace efforts broke down, third parties have cited the lack of a comparable mechanism as a contributing factor. The SLMM is continually following the situation on the ground with a view to dealing with problems immediately so that they do not lead to a negative spiral with political consequences, as we saw, for example, in the Middle East when the current Intifada began. The SLMM is unarmed and is responsible for ongoing conflict resolution at the micro-level. In the cease-fire agreement between the parties, it is specified that the SLMM is 'the final authority to interpret the agreement'. In practice this mandate means that the SLMM's role goes beyond passively monitoring the cease-fire agreement. The SLMM, through its Head of

Mission, is continually confronted with questions related to compliance with and implementation of the agreement which require its independent consideration. In accordance with the agreement, the parties expect the SLMM to make an independent interpretation in any disputes that may arise in various situations.

Norway played an active role in getting the parties to agree to establish the SLMM and has gained considerable experience from the practical implementation. However, it is important to keep a close watch on the situation with a view to identifying aspects that could be improved. The SLMM is under Norwegian leadership and includes Norwegian personnel. Given the political sensitivity of the process, it is important to maintain a small, manageable team where the leadership has close contact with the rest of the personnel on a regular basis, in order to avoid misunderstandings and ensure that the various incidents that arise are dealt with in a consistent and coordinated manner. For the sake of efficiency, it is important that the team has good mobility and a good communication apparatus.

Norwegian leadership of the SLMM has enabled good communication between the facilitator and the observer forces. At the same time, the team is largely regarded as being 'Norwegian' and as an extension of the facilitator role. Thus, any criticism of the SLMM can easily be generalised to Norway as facilitator and vice versa. By the same token, having the presence represented by the monitoring mission gives a facilitator certain credibility.

Norway also has experience from other monitoring missions outside the auspices of the UN, such as in Nuba Mountains/Sudan, Hebron/Middle East (TIPH) and Aceh/Indonesia. Through these engagements we are gaining practical experience in the planning and operation of such mechanisms. In some cases this has proven to be a time-consuming process. We are becoming increasingly capable of establishing such missions relatively quickly and providing personnel and qualified leaders from Norway. It is important that this capacity is maintained and institutionalised so that the experience gained and routines developed can be transferred from one process to another.

Today Norwegian personnel are recruited to monitoring and control missions through the defence establishment and an emergency roster established by the government (NORSTAFF). Routines are now being established that will make it possible to respond quickly and effectively to any needs as soon as they arise and in cases where there is no time for long-term planning.

Monitoring mechanisms may be relatively costly. Given their demonstrated importance to peace and reconciliation, it is essential that priority be given to funding for such mechanisms.

7. Humanitarian Aid and Development Assistance

When the parties to a conflict fail to take responsibility for the civilian population, the humanitarian challenges are left to the international community. The increase in the number of internal conflicts in the past ten years has led to a great increase in the need for humanitarian aid. Norway is a major actor in international humanitarian efforts, which has led in turn to it becoming involved in new conflict areas. There are also a number of cases where conflicts have arisen in areas where Norway was already involved in long-term development cooperation.

When conflicts become protracted, this raises the question of whether the assistance effort should just passively save lives, or whether it should be directed also towards solving the conflict itself. Another reason why this question is relevant is that in some cases, providing humanitarian aid or development assistance may contribute to prolonging a conflict in the sense that it enables one or more parties to continue using violence and military force (while being bailed out by international actors on humanitarian issues). In this way, assistance risks consolidating a situation, if and when there is reduced incentive for the parties to seek new and prudent solutions.

Norway's involvement in peace efforts has generally come about in connection with humanitarian efforts and other cooperation where Norwegian non-governmental actors have been involved, such as in Guatemala. In many ways, peace and reconciliation efforts are a natural extension of the humanitarian commitment. In a number of conflict situations it has quickly become apparent that humanitarian efforts in themselves are insufficient, and that the resources are more effectively used if they are combined with a political effort to promote peace and reconciliation.

Financial and technical assistance efforts in the context of a peace and reconciliation process should contribute to real peace dividends that benefit the people. People must experience concretely that peace improves the conditions of their lives, in terms of security, social services, reconstruction and economic development. Real peace dividends can contribute importantly to generate popular support and momentum for a political process.

Norway focuses on bringing the international community together and thereby leveraging peace dividends. Donor conferences are important steps in this regard. Such conferences have recently been held in Oslo concerning the processes in Sri Lanka and Sudan. Dialogue between the parties to create a framework conducive to donor assistance must be taken seriously and can potentially also serve a purpose in facilitating improved understanding for each other's needs.

In order to be an effective partner, it is generally important to maintain flexibility of budgetary means and to be able to deliver targeted assistance quickly. In some situations there may be room for using experience of peace and reconciliation efforts to a greater degree as a basis for planning humanitarian aid and more long-term assistance.

As highlighted throughout this chapter, a political process must go hand in hand with real peace dividends. Norway is committed to remain involved in the important implementation stages after peace negotiations have been completed. Post-conflict peace building efforts, including security sector reforms, are indispensable. Transitional and long-term aid can help the parties consolidate the results achieved around the negotiating table. However, the contributions of donors and impartial facilitators can never substitute for the real political will of the parties themselves.

8. Concluding Remark

In closing, let me leave you with a few concepts to be considered in third party facilitation: impartiality, inclusiveness, financial capacity, long-term focus, realism.

Chapter IX

THE ROLE OF THIRD PARTIES IN THE NEGOTIATION AND IMPLEMENTATION OF INTRASTATE AGREEMENTS: AN EXPERIENCE-BASED APPROACH TO UN INVOLVEMENT IN INTRASTATE CONFLICTS

Francesc Vendrell[*]

1. INTRASTATE CONFLICTS

Of the some 110 conflicts that have arisen since the creation of the United Nations (UN), at most 10 percent have been inter-state conflicts, whereas 90 percent have tended to be intrastate. My thirty-four years experience at the UN resulted in my involvement in a variety of intrastate conflicts. While this says something perhaps about my background and my interest in human rights and self-determination issues, it also says a lot about the increasing UN involvement in intrastate conflicts.

Intrastate conflicts fall into two categories. Firstly, there are conflicts about the distribution of power within the state and the denial of participation to certain sections of that state. The denial by the military and the elite of a participatory role in governance to the majority of the population as well as the widespread and gross human rights violations were the root of the problem in Guatemala and El Salvador. The same was the case in Haiti after President Aristide was overthrown by the military. It is in those conflicts that the UN has been able to play a significant role. In Central America and Africa, the UN has often been involved in power sharing issues and helping to bring about the end of conflicts related to those issues.

A second category of intrastate conflicts, accounting for some 40-50 percent of conflicts, relates to claims to self-determination, autonomy or minority status by a defined group of people within a given area of an existing state. Only on

---

[*] European Union Special Representative in Afghanistan; former UN Assistant Secretary-General Head of the Special Mission to Afghanistan (UNSMA).

M. Boltjes (ed.), Implementing Negotiated Agreements
© 2007, Kreddha International and T·M·C·ASSER PRESS, The Hague, The Netherlands

very rare occasions has the UN been able to intervene in such cases. The opposition of governments to allowing the UN to play a mediating role in such conflicts has been even stronger than opposition to UN intervention in the first type of intrastate conflicts. In this context, when I refer to the UN, I mean not so much the inter-governmental organs such as the General Assembly and the Security Council, but the Secretary-General and his inherent good offices role. Of course it is undeniable that a Security Council or General Assembly resolution calling for the good offices of the Secretary-General can be very helpful in promoting the role of the Secretary-General, but it is not indispensable for him to undertake this role.

2. Conflicting UN Charter Principles Conditioning UN Involvement in Intrastate Conflicts

In the second category of intrastate conflicts two conflicting UN Charter principles are usually at play: the principle of self-determination and the principle of territorial integrity. In this respect it is of fundamental importance to underscore that the UN Charter does not enshrine a *right* to self-determination, but refers to the *principle* of self-determination in Articles 1 and 55. On the other hand, territorial integrity is defined as a *right* in Article 2(4) of the UN Charter. In most cases where the UN has been involved in self-determination issues, it has been in connection with Trust or Non-Self Governing Territories (NSGTs), which were given the right to self-determination and independence in the 1960 Declaration on the Granting of Independence to Colonial Countries and Peoples, contained in GA Resolution 1514(XV). What constitutes a NSGT was defined shortly afterwards in Resolution 1541(XV). However, the decision whether to include a given territory in the list of NSGTs has been, in practice, in the hands of the Special Committee on Decolonisation, frequently referred to as the Committee of Twenty-Four. The membership of this committee, unlike that of most other UN bodies, is not periodically renewed, with member states serving for as long as they so wish. This has resulted in a lop-sided third world membership and in the perpetuation in it of some states with authoritarian governments, or with a particular axe to grind.

It should be noted that when Resolution 1514 was adopted, some governments managed to insert a provision in this declaration that 'any attempt aimed at the partial or total disruption of the national unity and the territorial integrity of a state is incompatible with the purposes and principles of the Charter of the United Nations.'[1] This inclusion, combined with the way in which a non-self

---

[1] Paragraph 6 of Resolution 1514 (XV).

governing territory was defined in Resolution 1541, resulted first of all in the development of the so-called blue water principle. According to this principle, a territory is not considered 'colonial' if it is contiguous to the metropolitan power. Thus, for example, the Asian republics of the USSR were never classified as non-self governing, since they formed a territorial continuum with Russia, whereas Portugal's overseas territories were included in the list, even though, under the then Portuguese constitution, they were regarded as 'provinces' with the same rights as the metropolis.

Increasingly, paragraph 6 of Resolution 1514 was interpreted by the committee and by the General Assembly as denying the right to self-determination to the people of a NSGT if that territory was subject to a historical claim by an adjacent or neighbouring state. The cases of Gibraltar, claimed by Spain, or the Falklands/Malvinas, claimed by Argentina, are classic examples. In these cases the committee, while not necessarily demanding that these territories be returned to the claimant state, have usually called for negotiations between the colonial power and the claimant state to resolve the dispute. But the provision in Article 6 has also been interpreted to refer also to the territorial integrity of the NSGT itself, and to the sanctity of its borders as defined by the colonial power. Thus the committee has always looked askance at petitions from the inhabitants of a part of an NSGT to exercise *their* own right to self-determination. Examples are numerous: Barotseland in relation to Zambia, Buganda *vis-à-vis* Uganda and Anguilla in relation to St Kitts-Nevis (though a local rebellion led to the United Kingdom detaching Anguilla from the other two islands before St Kitts became independent). So, when the Bougainvillians petitioned the Committee of Twenty-Four in 1972 asking for *their* right to self-determination, they were firmly told that they had no such right, since they were part of the Australian Trust Territory of New Guinea. (In fact, Australia administered New Guinea and Papua, which was technically an Australian dependent territory, jointly and both territories became independent together as Papua New Guinea in August 1975). Another curious result of this interpretation has been that, since France had divided West and Central Africa administratively into fourteen separate territories, they each emerged in 1960 as separate independent states with a combined population far smaller than Nigeria's, whereas the latter, in keeping with the British practice of creating federations, emerged as a single independent state.

While colonialism is blamed for many of the conflicts that have broken out since 1945, it is the hasty decolonisation processes that are often their root cause. Israel/Palestine, Kashmir, East Timor, the civil wars in Angola and Mozambique are cases in point.

3. UN Intervention in Inter- or Intrastate Disputes of a Self-Determination Nature

As already stated above, the number of disputes related to the exercise of the right to self-determination in which the UN has been involved is relatively small and even more so in cases of intrastate conflict. Some conflicts, such as those concerning Cyprus, Kashmir, Bosnia or the Middle East have a self-determination component, but they are clearly inter-state disputes as well. The little known case of Bahrain is an interesting example of the successful use of quiet, preventive diplomacy by the Secretary-General. In that case, the Secretary-General persuaded Iran to drop quietly its claim to Bahrain on the eve of its independence from Britain in 1970. Of course the solution was easier to reach in so far as Iran was not in actual possession of Bahrain.

Three of the self-determination cases in which the Secretary-General has been involved relate to territories that were in the list of NSGTs. The first was West Papua, a Dutch colony claimed by Indonesia on the grounds that it had been administered as part of the Dutch East Indies before 1940 and thus, in Indonesia's view, its people had no separate right to self-determination but fell under the exception contained in paragraph 6 of Resolution 1514(XV). Under heavy US pressure, the Netherlands agreed in 1962 to surrender control over West Papua to Indonesia with the proviso that an 'act of free choice' under UN auspices would take place a few years later to determine the wishes of the inhabitants. In what must be one of the least glorious chapters in UN history, the Secretariat acceded to Indonesian pressure to conduct the 'act of free choice' in 1969 not through the hallowed principle of one person one vote, but by soliciting publicly the views of Indonesian-appointed members of district councils, who unsurprisingly declared their support for union with Indonesia. The General Assembly endorsed West Papua's accession to Indonesia in 1971.

The second case (in which the Secretary-General is still involved) is the Western Sahara, a former Spanish colony occupied by Morocco in 1975. The issue is yet to be resolved, despite an agreement signed in 1990 to hold a UN-administered referendum in the territory.

The third case is East Timor, with which I was deeply involved over many years up to the end of 1999. It may be recalled that Indonesia's invasion of East Timor in December 1975 had been condemned by the Security Council. However, unlike what subsequently happened when Argentina invaded the Falkland/Malvinas in 1982 or Iraq occupied Kuwait in 1990, neither the administering power, Portugal, nor the Security Council were in a position or had the political inclination to react as Britain or the Council did in those two situations. Furthermore, as the years passed, opposition in the Security Council and in the General Assembly to continued Indonesian occupation waned. This was the result of a combination of factors including the cold war, Indonesia's importance, its membership of the Non-Aligned Movement and of the Organisation of the Islamic Conference, as well as the geographical isolation and political insignificance of East Timor. Indeed it was generally assumed that support for independence among the territory's seven hundred thousand inhabitants would wane with the passage of time. It was precisely at the point when, in 1982, the General Assembly appeared to be evenly divided on the future of East Timor that the Secretary-General stepped in and offered his good offices to resolve the problem. These were accepted by Indonesia and Portugal in 1983. Owing to Indonesia's firm opposition to the inclusion of the East Timorese as a party, the parties to the negotiations were Indonesia and Portugal, while the pro-independence East Timorese were kept closely informed by the Secretary-General's representatives of the progress (or lack thereof) in the negotiations from 1992 on.

Bearing the case of West Papua in mind, my main effort for most of the time of my involvement in the East Timor case was to prevent a bad settlement, since the conditions were not there to achieve a fair settlement in accordance with the UN Charter. The role of a mediator does not necessarily consist in finding the middle of the road in order to strike a balance between the demands advanced by both sides. It is rather to achieve a just settlement, for only such a settlement will stand the test of time. If a third party or an international organisation becomes involved in mediating a conflict, the golden rule ought to be that *it is better to have no settlement than a bad or unfair settlement*

4. GOVERNMENT ACCEPTANCE OF THIRD PARTY INVOLVEMENT

Governments are often unwilling to accept the involvement of the UN or of intergovernmental organisations to resolve internal disputes. One reason is governments' fear of internationalisation. Governments fear that third party involvement may strengthen the position of the non-governmental side. This does not only apply to territory-related disputes, but to other kinds of intrastate conflicts as well. In addition, other states are often reluctant to apply pressure on a government to accept the UN or another third party to resolve the latter's internal conflict. And the stronger the central government is and the wider its international projection, the more difficult it is for a third party to be accepted as a mediator by that government. Another reason is the fear of the so-called 'domino effect'. This was a factor with Papua New Guinea and to an even larger extent with Indonesia. These governments feared that giving autonomy or independence to a part of 'their' territory would lead to uncontrolled demands by other groups in their state. While this fear is sometimes well founded, in other cases it is not, but it is a useful tool to refuse UN or other third party mediation.

Governments are more inclined to accept third party mediation in conflicts that are at a stage of *mutually hurting stalemate*, meaning when both parties realise that they have reached a stalemate that is unlikely to be broken by military means. Regretfully, the UN has often been too slow in actively proposing its mediation at this key stage of a conflict. That is probably the reason why governments like that of Norway or other international organisations are becoming increasingly involved in the mediation of intrastate disputes rather than the UN.

Pressure exerted at the right time by friendly governments on another to accept third party involvement can be extremely helpful. Thus UN involvement in Bougainville was facilitated by Australia and New Zealand, which encouraged the Papua New Guinea (PNG) government to accept it.

Acceptance of third party involvement is also facilitated if the parties are already familiar with the person likely to be appointed as the mediator or facilitator. In the case of PNG it was relatively easier to involve the UN because of the personal relations I had built previously with the Bougainvillian representatives as well as with senior members of the PNG government, some dating back to the time when I was a lecturer in constitutional law at the University of Papua New Guinea. This personal relationship facilitated my efforts to persuade the PNG government that acceptance of UN involvement would not lead to the dissolution or breakdown of the country.

A very useful way for the UN to eventually become involved in the settlement of a conflict is for the personnel of the UN Department of Political Affairs to travel on a frequent basis to the countries they cover, not so much to pinpoint problems, but simply to talk to and build trust with the governments and non-governmental actors, even before a crisis emerges.

Calls for UN intervention usually occur in the wake of a widely publicised bloody incident or civil war. That is the time when public opinion and governments wake up. The 1991 Santa Cruz cemetery massacre in East Timor awakened, at least temporarily, international public opinion, particularly in Australia and Portugal, where people started exerting pressure on their respective governments to take action. Unfortunately a non-publicised conflict is much harder for the UN to mediate. A conflict about competing territorial claims to the same territory by different states is of course different for the UN, because it has the character of an inter-state conflict, as was the case with East Timor and the Western Sahara.

The change of government, the fall of a regime or the dissolution of a state, as in the case of the Soviet Union and former Yugoslavia also provide a window of opportunity for third party involvement. A change of regime often goes hand in hand with a period of self-doubt or fresh thinking on the part of the new authorities. This was the case for instance with Portugal after the Carnation

Revolution, Spain after the death of Franco and Indonesia after the fall of Suharto. This period of uncertainty is unlikely to last for long. The measure of self-government that the Basques and the Catalans achieved at the time of the drafting of the new constitution in 1978 benefited from the fact that the advocates of democracy and of regional autonomy had worked hand in hand under the dictatorship and in the transition. The UN achieved a breakthrough in East Timor when the overthrow of Suharto led to a period of self-doubt among his successors and within the Indonesian army, and when the advocates of democracy in Indonesia felt a common bond with the East Timorese nationalists. This window of opportunity was unlikely to remain open for long and we at the UN had to move quickly to pin Indonesia down into accepting an act of popular consultation (a referendum by another name) by the East Timorese, a prize that had eluded us for the previous twenty-four years.

5. Mediation, Good Offices, Facilitation and Negotiation

Once third party involvement has been accepted, it is best to be humble in the kind of role one is to play and not to become bogged down with terminology. For instance, 'mediation' is a threatening term for governments and even for the non-governmental side with the implication, felt by some, that the mediator may acquire the right to impose a solution if the parties fail to agree to one in the negotiations. Consultation, good offices, facilitation, or even observation are easier to accept, often with the same result as mediation.

I suppose that in my years of involvement in settling disputes I never mediated. I *negotiated*, but I never felt that I was meant to be equidistant between the parties. In the case of East Timor, for example, being equidistant between Portugal and Indonesia and Indonesia and the Timorese, would have meant allowing Indonesia to get away with the annexation of East Timor irrespective of the wishes of the inhabitants.

Most intrastate negotiations are characterised by asymmetry between the parties. It is therefore impossible to ask the two parties to make the same number or level of concessions. Typically at the beginning of a process most concessions must come from the government side, since the other side has only one or two major concessions to make: usually to end the fighting or the violence and to accept disarmament. These are major concessions for the non-governmental side which, if conceded too early in the process, would leave it with no cards to play at a later stage in the talks. Therefore, concessions by the non-governmental side may need to be postponed towards the final stage of the negotiations. This is not always easy for the governmental side to accept, and it may find itself being criticised by its own supporters for making too many unilateral concessions. One way out of this dilemma is to agree at the beginning of the negotiating process that any agreement arrived at will be kept in the freezer and nothing will be finally agreed or implemented until everything has been agreed. This is the way we proceeded in El Salvador and Guatemala.

It is often the case that there are several competing third parties, e.g., the UN and a regional or sub-regional organisation, offering their good offices to the parties in conflict. I have always been quite firm in telling the parties to choose one mediator and not several. In my experience, too many cooks in the kitchen usually leads to a bad meal. The parties tend to favour one mediator over the other, often leading to conflicts between the mediators themselves. Mediation played by more than two hands rarely plays itself well.

It is essential to ensure the involvement of the real decision makers or at least of their plenipotentiaries during the negotiations. The decision makers at any rate ought to be involved at the time when agreements are arrived at. That is difficult to achieve in situations when the de facto decision makers are the armed forces, since they are rarely present during the negotiations. The negotiations are usually left in the hands of the foreign ministry. Experience shows that it is extremely difficult to bring the military to the table. In Guatemala, thanks to clever guerrilla negotiating tactics, the army participated in the negotiating process, though their involvement did not necessarily guarantee their compliance with the peace agreement signed in 1996.

For the third party, it is important to understand the culture of the parties concerned, even if it is impossible to become fully acquainted with it. During the Cairns Talks on Bougainville in December 1995, one of my colleagues became extremely inpatient about the way the process was being conducted, which was in accordance with the Melanesian way of negotiation, at times with seemingly nothing happening at all and other times with talks involving every single member of the huge delegations. It is important to listen to the parties and their accounts of the history of the conflict. It is also important to do some reading of the history of the conflict on your own and not to rely only on the version of events given by the two sides, which is often subjective and self-serving.

6. Carrots, Sticks and Groups of Friends

It is obvious that carrots and sticks are very useful tools in the hands of a negotiator. These are not often available to a UN negotiator. It is usually extremely difficult within the UN system to bring the UNDP to agree to condition its assistance to a country on progress in UN-mediated negotiations. Since the UNDP follows an independent approach, it may happen that while the special envoy of the Secretary-General is being rebuffed by a government, a UNDP senior official will be having a cosy lunch with the foreign minister in the course of which the inflexibility of the government will go unmentioned. Governments too face similar lack of coordination between their foreign and ODA ministries and departments, though rarely at the level I have seen it happen within the UN.

A good way to strengthen the negotiator's hand is to organise meetings with donors, particularly with the IMF and the World Bank, to discuss packages of assistance if the negotiations succeed.

Another useful instrument is the establishment of a Group of Friends of the Secretary-General. I have found that it helps to have a few governments that support the peace-making efforts of the Secretary-General through such an instrument. The existence of a Group of Friends can also help to strengthen the weaker side in the negotiations or to balance out the unwanted intervention of other countries in the conflict. While the Group of Friends works well in intrastate conflicts not involving territorial claims, the mechanism is less useful in conflicts involving self-determination claims and should be used very carefully. I opposed, for example, the establishment of a Group of Friends in the East Timor talks, because it would have been difficult to find governments not inclined to support Indonesia's stand on the issue. It was only when the process ripened in 1999 that we set-up a Group of Friends, consisting of Australia, Japan, New Zealand, the United Kingdom and the United States, which played an invaluable role in the months preceding and following the popular consultation.

In selecting the Friends, several factors ought to be taken into account, including the policies being pursued by the governments concerned, their willingness to subordinate themselves to the guidelines set by the Secretary-General, the personalities of the ambassadors on the spot and of key foreign ministry officials, etc. One must always remember that behind an institution there are always human beings and that their personalities will play an important part in their membership of a Group of Friends.

Experience has taught me that both governments and negotiators have an innate tendency to lean on the weak and appease the strong. This approach makes it of course easier to achieve quick results, though not necessarily the right results. Instead, what makes an agreement more likely to last is the conviction held by both sides that *the agreement reached represents the best agreement that could be achieved under the current circumstances.*

7. Implementation of Autonomy and Self-Determination Arrangements

The best approach to achieve the implementation of agreements regarding autonomy and self-determination is through constitutional arrangements, such as entrenched clauses and, in particular, double entrenchment. At the same time the existence of democratic structures and the rule of law in the country can contribute greatly to make these agreements durable.

The need to build up institutions, to establish rule of law and, in particular, to build up a sound judicial system – which is usually the most difficult aspect of any institution-building process – is of vital importance. The holding of elections and the drafting of constitutions are important elements in the implementation of agreements, while the creation of a good judicial system is an element for the establishment of the rule of law. After twenty-seven years of democratic rule the judicial system continues to be the weakest part of the new Spanish state. The same phenomenon can be observed in Latin America and is very much the case in Afghanistan at the moment, where reform of the judicial system has proven extremely hard to achieve. Helping the autonomous entity to build a responsible police force, as well democratising and reforming the military throughout the state are essential elements for ensuring lasting results. The lack of thorough reform of the military in Guatemala is a factor in the fact that only partial success was achieved in the implementation of the peace agreement.

The interest of third countries, in particular of neighbours, in the implementation of the settlement is of course another way of encouraging implementation. This is particularly the case when the interest of such a country is motivated by permanent factors, such as geography or ethnic or religious ties.

Observing and monitoring elections in the entity which is achieving self-government is another way of assisting in the settlement implementation, yet in a very punctual and time-limited manner.

The sudden acceptance, in January 1999, by Indonesian President Habibie that East Timor could secede if its people so wished, had been preceded by eight months of intense debate and consultations concerning an autonomy status for East Timor. Many people regretted that Habibie had not waited to see if agreement on such a broad autonomy statute was possible. The broad autonomy arrangement, which UN mediators put forward, failed to be accepted because Indonesia was unwilling to allow for its review after a five year period, a condition regarded as essential by the East Timorese. Present in our minds was the precedent of the Eritrean autonomy agreed in 1952 by the Emperor of Ethiopia, Haile Selassie, and unilaterally revoked by him in 1960, which led to the thirty year war for Eritrean independence. In retrospect, it seems likely that, even if an agreement for a temporary wide ranging autonomy statute had been reached, the Indonesian army would have violated it, as happened with the 4 May 1999 agreement to hold the referendum in East Timor. While governments were committed in the months following the signature of the Indonesian-Portuguese agreement to ensure its implementation, it seems unlikely that this international commitment would still have been there to ensure a review of the autonomy arrangement five years down the line.

8. VERIFICATION AND ARBITRATION

My personal experience has been much more with negotiation than with verification, which is an essential aspect of implementation of an agreement. The question arises whether the UN should verify agreements that it has not negotiated itself. The UN should be cautious in accepting to verify agreements such as those in the Democratic Republic of the Congo or Angola, in 1992, which it did not negotiate, but where the UN is handed the task of ensuring its implementation without the means of carrying it out.

In any verification-activity two things should be borne in mind: firstly the desire for an early-exit strategy on the part of third governments. This is currently the case of Bougainville, where there are pressures on the Security Council to close the UN political mission in Bougainville. Whereas, of course, neither the UN nor any other institution should stay in a place forever, *the* biggest verification-related problem is premature exit. In addition to the difficulty of maintaining the interest of governments on the issue beyond a certain time, another major problem is coping with the diplomatic tendency to wear rose-tinted glasses when verifying the implementation of agreements, especially when money and projects are involved.

Regional involvement can be helpful to ensure the implementation of an agreement as is shown in the cases of Northern Ireland and New Caledonia. By virtue of the Matignon Accords of 1988, a referendum was scheduled to take place fifteen years after their signature. The countries belonging to the Pacific Islands Forum can play an important role in ensuring that France actually carries it out. Recourse to arbitration or to the International Court of Justice, where possible, also offers an interesting avenue to achieve the implementation of agreements.

The success or failure of a peace agreement may not become evident for a considerable period of time. Success is fairly clear in those self-determination conflicts where the people have been able to exercise freely their right to self-determination, as has been the case with East Timor. At the end of the day the peoples of the country or countries involved in the peace settlement are the best placed to evaluate its success.

Chapter X

IMPLEMENTING THE FRAMEWORK AGREEMENT IN MACEDONIA: THE ROLE OF THE INTERNATIONAL COMMUNITY

Niek Biegman[*]

Makedonija – situated in the Southern Balkans: Serbia and Kosovo to the North, Albania West, Greece South, Bulgaria East; size: Netherlands minus 10 percent, two million inhabitants – was a 'republic' of Yugoslavia since the end of World War II and got independence thrust upon her when Yugoslavia fell apart in 1991. It soon developed into a state which was very much monopolised by the (± two-thirds) majority of Christian-orthodox ethnic Macedonians.[1] Minorities, especially the ethnic Albanians[1] (± 23 percent) were tolerated but made to feel non-central. eMacedonians took – and had possessed already – a disproportionate share of the jobs in state and state-run institutions. Both the Macedonian language and the Christian-orthodox religion were preponderant. It was an example of nation-building based on the majority, in this case especially at the expense of the eAlbanians. Before Macedonia's independence and ever since the constitution of 1974, the eAlbanians had had an objectively equal status with the eMacedonians in Yugoslavia. Since 1991, they were second-class citizens in their country.

The eAlbanian political parties – Macedonia always had a coalition government in which an eAlbanian party participated – were unsuccessful in remedying this situation and they hardly tried. This was a system were the eMacedonian and the eAlbanian party elites left one another in peace, to be free to profit from their position in their own region.

There is in the Balkans a curious competition about who has been there the longest. The Greeks, of course, think they descend from the ancient Greeks. There is a measure of plausibility there. The Albanians claim descent from the Illyrians, largely unproven, but this claim gives them some historical prestige as well. Not to be outdone, the Macedonians consider themselves as descen-

---

[*] Former NATO Senior Civilian Representative in Macedonia.
[1] 'Ethnic Macedonians' and 'ethnic Albanians' will henceforth be abbreviated to: 'eMacedonians' and 'eAlbanians'.

M. Boltjes (ed.), Implementing Negotiated Agreements
© 2007, Kreddha International and T·M·C·ASSER PRESS, The Hague, The Netherlands

dants of the ancient Macedonians of Alexander the Great, which gives them a lead of a thousand years over Slavs like the Serbs and the Bulgarians. Only the Turks cannot point at anything more than a proven six hundred years of residence, which makes them newcomers in the eyes of everyone else. I sometimes try to point out the irrelevance of all this, – but my only allies are the Turks. Whatever the historical justification may have been, the eMacedonians upon independence went through a period of nationalistic euphoria, and in that spirit wrote a constitution for their new country, which was passed with the eAlbanian representatives in the parliament voting against it.

So, the Macedonians monopolised the new state, but they had their troubles, too. The Greeks did not recognise their name, the Bulgarians did not recognise their language, which they saw as a Bulgarian dialect, and the Serbs did not recognise their church. Maybe this made the eMacedonians more unsure of themselves and less willing to give the eAlbanians a better deal.

eAlbanian frustration over this situation might not have led to a near civil war if Kosovo and the South-Serbian eAlbanian Presevo area had not revolted in 1998/99 and 2000, respectively. When these conflicts were more or less successfully (for the eAlbanians) resolved, some eAlbanian fighters tried their luck in Macedonia. Local support was tiny in the beginning, but grew exponentially, largely because of the heavy-handed reaction by the Macedonian security forces to the rebellion. After only a few months the country was on the brink of a civil war.

At that stage, an extraordinary international coalition took up the challenge of halting the crisis. It consisted of NATO, the EU, the OSCE and the United States, a formidable combination, determined to prevent at last and at least one war within the former Yugoslavia after failures in Croatia, Bosnia and up to a point in Kosovo. Lord Robertson and Solana visited Macedonia thirteen or fourteen times, often together. The main eMacedonian and eAlbanian parties (two plus two) were made to unite in a grand coalition government and then negotiated among themselves with intensive facilitation on the part of the EU, the United States and the OSCE. With the aim of halting and preventing violence, NATO officials acted as intermediaries between the Macedonian institutions and the international community on the one hand and the rebels on the other. The crisis ended in August 2001, with a Framework Agreement[2] signed by the President of Macedonia, the leaders of the four parties, and the representatives of the EU and the United States. The Agreement dealt with the position of minorities – especially those over 20 percent, i.e., the eAlbanians –, their language, equitable representation in state institutions, and decentralisation. The

---

[2] The text of the Framework Agreement is included in Appendix E.

Agreement had been agreed by the rebel movement, the National Liberation Army (NLA; Albanian abbreviation UCK). The NLA disbanded and disarmed (in principle), and received an amnesty in return.

The Macedonia envisaged by the Framework Agreement is a multi-ethnic, unitary state. Unitary, because a federal solution could have been seen as a first step towards total separation of the eAlbanian areas and their joining with neighbouring Albania and Kosovo into a greater Albania, thereby upsetting all other fragile Balkan borders. There is a strong pledge to decentralise though, and that is going to be the main task for the rest of this year. Besides, decisions by the parliament affecting the non-eMacedonians can according to the Framework Agreement only be taken with a majority of the votes 'within which there must be a majority of the votes of representatives claiming to belong to the communities not in the majority in the population of Macedonia.'

Since August 2001, the Framework Agreement has been in the process of being translated into legislation, the Albanian language has been introduced into the parliament, and decentralisation is in the making. Increasing the percentage of eAlbanians in the institutions is more difficult, since one does not wish to put eMacedonians who are now employed there out into the street; they would not find anything else to do and there is no money to create new jobs in that sector.

The international community is taking an active interest in the implementation of the Framework Agreement, based on the provisions of its Annex C. There, 'the parties invite the international community to facilitate, monitor and assist in the implementation of the provisions of the Framework Agreement ... to be coordinated by the European Union in cooperation with the Stabilisation and Association Council.' Various specific tasks are allotted to the Council of Europe, the European Commission, the World Bank, the UNHCR, the OSCE, the United States and (elsewhere in the text of the Agreement) NATO. A group of 'Principals' emerged, consisting of the representatives of the EU, NATO, the OSCE and the United States, who monitor the implementation of the Agreement in a more general sense.

The role that the international community plays in Macedonia is, of course, infinitely more modest – though I will not right away say less important – than it is in, say, Bosnia or Kosovo. We are not in the business of ruling a country. We are not present on the basis of a resolution of the Security Council. All we do is try to be helpful. But our advice is being taken very seriously, largely because Macedonia wants to be a member of NATO and the EU. That gives us a lot of leverage when we insist on the implementation of the Framework Agreement.

The containment of the crisis, and thereby the prevention of another disastrous civil war, was the result of a collective effort, in which no institution worked at putting itself on the map at the expense of others, but in which all cooperated for peace. Both in the method and in the result, this was a huge success.

The four institutions that helped bring about the Framework Agreement have since then stuck together in watching over its implementation. The way in which we are going about this in Skopje reflects the way in which the Agreement came about: a very high degree of cooperation, mutual respect and transparency, continuous contact, an absence of competition; and, of course, very frequent contact with the Macedonian authorities. The four of us meet at least twice a week; once just the four, and once with other organisations active in the country such as UN bodies, the Hague war crimes tribunal, and the Red Cross. The EU is *primus inter pares*, in that the meetings are held at the EU office, and chaired by the EU Special Representative.

Each of the so-called Principals has his own niche: the EU and the United States are working on the translation of the Framework Agreement into legislation, a huge task requiring an important effort on the part of the government. The OSCE works on the re-introduction of the police into the Former Crisis Areas, the development of more modern methods of policing and the recruitment of new officers, largely from the minorities. NATO is interested in the security situation in a very wide sense, including – but that is of course true for all of us – the relationship between the ethnicities. NATO also takes an interest in the items mentioned in the preamble of the NATO Treaty, like democracy and the rule of law, and the freedom and quality of the press. These items are important in the context of future NATO membership of Macedonia.

Apart from looking after their own tasks, Principals very often operate together, both in exchanging information on the security situation and in approaching our Macedonian counterparts, for instance on the implementation of the amnesty.

NATO has a certain advantage over the others in our contacts with the eAlbanians, especially as regards those belonging to the former NLA. The fact that NATO was the go-between for them in their dealings with the international community and the Macedonian authorities and that they handed their weapons in to NATO was important in this regard. Long after the end of operation Harvest, when the weapons were collected, the NATO ambassador retained a quasi-monopoly on contacts with the NLA leader Ali Ahmeti, even after he had founded his own party and after it had been recognised by the government. Ever since the NATO Council authorised me to see him at the end of April 2002, I visited him on a weekly basis. Both the NATO security presence and my office have kept up contacts with former NLA commanders, who often have a lot of influence in the towns and villages of the Former Crisis Areas.

Until the start of the present mandate, the official task of the NATO security presence, called Task Force Fox until December 2002, which by the way was not run by my office but by the Senior Military Representative, was the protection of foreign observers in the Former Crisis Areas. The real vocation of the Task Force was facilitating the return of the Macedonian police by establishing – both with the villagers and with the police – a certain feeling of security. It made it possible for the villagers to accept the police back without fear of being mistreated and for the police to dare to come back without fear of being taken revenge against. This was a gradual and successful process. Apart from that, especially during the period before the September elections, Task Force Fox and my office cooperated in collecting information on disturbances that could be expected and then in preventing them. Through our many contacts and together with other participants we were instrumental in restraining eAlbanian reactions to some provocations. Often, the mere presence of a few NATO soldiers proved sufficient to defuse a tense situation.

NATO's security presence was mainly a political operation, of only a few hundred soldiers, well integrated in the other efforts of the international community and essentially at the service of the Macedonian government. Maximum transparency between the 'eyes and ears' of the international community – Task Force Fox, the OSCE and the European Monitoring Mission – was required and achieved. Often, we could provide valuable first-hand information to the government, which did not yet have its own forces all over the area.

Concluding Remarks

All in all, I think the NATO security presence has been a very interesting experiment. It was the first of its kind in a way, and has helped to create conditions for our host country to get back on its feet again. The take-over of the operational element by the EU does not mean that NATO's interest as such has decreased. NATO will have an important advisory role to play in the restructuring of the armed forces. The NATO Civilian Liaison Office will stay at least for a while, as will the Ambassador. We will continue to cooperate with the other members of the international community as actively and intensively as before, until the country can do without us, which I hope will happen soon.

Why has the international community been more successful in Macedonia than elsewhere in the Balkans? I think it is due to a combination of factors.

First, lessons were learned in previous conflicts; one of them being that speedy preventative action is essential and that lack of it will result in massive loss of life and property. In Bosnia it took more than three years before some decisive military action halted the genocide. In Kosovo a year went by. In Macedonia the need was felt to prevent the civil war, and it was possible to keep the total number of dead below two hundred. This meant that Macedonia came out of the crisis largely unharmed and unperverted. There is an important residual problem of corruption and criminalisation, and there certainly is a lack of love between the ethnicities, but all this seems to be manageable. We do not aim as high as to require mutual love. We will make do with mutual respect and tolerance.

Second, Macedonia is a small country – two million inhabitants – and the international community can mobilise important leverage; especially NATO and the EU, on account of Macedonia wanting to be a member of both organisations. Of course, we would not want to dictate and there is genuine respect for the government of this sovereign state, but when we think we can give good advice, we will do so and be listened to. The United States, of course, carries its own weight. The explicit reference in the Framework Agreement to facilitation, monitoring and assisting in its implementation on the part of the international community provides an important legal basis for our effort.

Third, we were fortunate in that the leader of the eAlbanian fighters, Ali Ahmeti, developed into a mature and responsible politician at an amazing speed. He founded his own party in June 2002 and obtained a landslide victory in September of the same year with a very moderate platform, which essentially calls for the implementation of the Framework Agreement and nothing more. He is on excellent terms with NATO and with the other members of the international community as well. Still, the eAlbanians have to be reminded from time to time to better consider the position of the smaller minorities (Turks, Roma, etc.). It was already said about the Bengalis, but it is true for the Israeli Jews and many others, including the Macedonian Albanians, that those who have suffered do not thereby obtain a better understanding of the suffering of others.

Also, the party that won the September 2002 election on the eMacedonian side, though by no means historically blameless in inter-ethnic matters, lacks the chauvinist and backward looking rhetoric of those who were in power before. It seems genuinely willing to carry out to the Framework Agreement. Again, we feel they could be more generous towards their eAlbanian coalition parties.

Fourth, and perhaps most important, there is no competition for turf among the members of the international community. We work together as a collective, which enhances our effectiveness immeasurably.

Fifth, the presence of a modest military force has proven to be very useful in calming down and preventing incidents and provocations. It will be important not to withdraw too early, but it will be as important to leave in time, before a dependency syndrome sets in.

Chapter XI

ADJUDICATION OF INTRASTATE DISPUTES: A REVIEW OF POSSIBLE MECHANISMS

Wendy Miles[*]

This chapter introduces the various international dispute resolution bodies that may be able to adjudicate on intrastate disputes[1] and assesses which of those bodies, if any, are best suited for the determination and/or administration of such disputes.

1. DISPUTE RESOLUTION AGREEMENTS

An important element of peace negotiations between population groups and states is the agreement of an enforceable dispute resolution mechanism for resolving existing outstanding disputes and/or any future disputes. Dispute resolution agreements may be either: (i) integral to a relevant international instrument such as a convention or treaty (and therefore effective upon signing and ratification of the convention or treaty); (ii) expressly contained in the peace agreement negotiated between the state and the population group or otherwise provided for in the peace agreement by reference to a separate, future agreement; or, alternatively, (iii) entered into by the state and the population group after a dispute has arisen in respect of a previous agreement or settlement.

---

* Partner at Wilmer Cutler Pickering Hale and Dorr LLP.

[1] The term 'intrastate disputes' in this chapter refers to conflicts between population groups (for example an autonomous region, non-self governing territory, indigenous people or minority) and the governments of the states that exercise jurisdiction over those population groups. Conflicts or potential conflicts may arise, for instance, as a result of struggles for independence or varying degrees of self government, the desire to maintain territorial integrity, confrontation over the ownership and use of natural resources, or issues of cultural identity or minority rights. See Kreddha website at <http://kreddha.org/kreddha.asp?LangId=1> (2 August 2006). Intrastate disputes do not include disputes of an international nature, i.e., disputes with a foreign element.

M. Boltjes (ed.), Implementing Negotiated Agreements
© 2007, Kreddha International and T·M·C·ASSER PRESS, The Hague, The Netherlands

Examples of conventions containing dispute resolution agreements between contracting states include: Article 32 of the Convention for the Protection of the Marine Environment of the North-East Atlantic ('OSPAR Convention') and Section 5 of the United Nations Convention on the Law of the Sea establishing the International Tribunal on the Law of the Sea ('ITLOS'). The relevant articles of these agreements are reproduced in Appendices F and G respectively.

One example of a type (ii) dispute resolution agreement was in the context of the Dayton peace negotiations in Bosnia-Herzegovina. The town of Brcko was one of the final issues considered in the last two days of the negotiations. Dayton left the status of Brcko to be decided by arbitration. Under the terms of the Dayton Accords, the parties agreed to binding arbitration of the disputed portion of the inter-entity boundary line in the Brcko area. The arbitration was governed by the UNCITRAL Rules[2] and the parties to the arbitration were the two entities which make up the Republic of Bosnia-Herzegovina: the Federation of Bosnia and Herzegovina and the Republika Srpska. Article V, relating to the arbitration agreement, is reproduced in Appendix H. Ultimately, there were three awards in which the Arbitral Tribunal, rather than drawing a boundary line in the area under dispute, designed an administrative regime. The final award established a permanent self-governing Brcko District of Bosnia and Herzegovina that is independent of the Federation of Bosnia and Herzegovina and the Republika Srpska. A summary of the final award is included in Appendix I.

Similarly, in the Eritrea-Yemen arbitration, Eritrea and Yemen signed an Agreement on Principles in May 1996, by which they renounced recourse to force against one another and undertook to 'settle their dispute on questions of territorial sovereignty and of delimitation of maritime boundaries peacefully.' To that end, they agreed to establish an agreement instituting an arbitral tribunal and agreed that '… concerning questions of territorial sovereignty, the Tribunal shall decide in accordance with the principles, rules and practices of international law applicable to the matter, and on the basis, in particular, of historic titles.' In October 1996 Eritrea and Yemen entered into a detailed arbitration agreement, in accordance with the terms of their Agreement on Principles. The Eritrea-Yemen arbitration agreement and extracts of the arbitration award are reproduced in Appendices J and K respectively.

A type (iii) dispute resolution agreement was entered into in *Larsen v. The Hawaiian Kingdom By Its Council of Regency*, an arbitration administered by the Permanent Court of Arbitration ('PCA'). In that situation, the parties had not agreed to go to arbitration prior to the claimant initiating its claim at the PCA.

---

[2] See section 2.b on the UNCITRAL Rules.

Nonetheless, in the Terms of Reference (the agreement to the procedural order and scope of a case being brought to arbitration) the parties included an agreement to submit to the PCA tribunal's binding authority. Extracts of the *Larsen* arbitration award are reproduced in Appendix L.

2. INTERNATIONAL DISPUTE RESOLUTION BODIES

A state's national courts are the immediate and obvious choice of forum in which to resolve disputes arising within the state. These usually have established procedures for determining disputes between the state itself and individuals within its territory in accordance with the applicable national law. Nonetheless, a state's national courts may not necessarily provide the most efficient or most effective method of dispute resolution for the parties involved. Furthermore, some national courts are not seen to be impartial or independent decision-makers in disputes involving the state as a party, particularly where highly sensitive political issues are at stake. In view of these concerns, parties to intrastate peace agreements may need to look to alternative forms of dispute resolution outside of the national court system. Fortunately, there are a number of options available.

In the past twenty years, contact between members of the international community has increased markedly as a result of increased trade and investment and the effect of that on diplomatic relations and territorial issues. In response, the international community has created international dispute resolution bodies, both permanent courts and less formal institutions, designed to deal with the multitude of commercial and non-commercial issues that arise as a result of the increase in contact between states. In turn, parties have begun to use international courts and tribunals to resolve disputes of a public and private international law nature, as well as disputes involving matters of national law, in preference to the applicable national courts. In addition, various arbitral institutions to which parties may agree to grant the authority to administer disputes between individuals (and increasingly, between individuals and states), are now being appointed in all manner of international commercial disputes.

2.1 Use of international courts in intrastate disputes

It is the role of international courts and quasi-judicial bodies to apply international law between signatory states, subject to jurisdiction of relevant national courts. The decisions of these international judicial bodies are final and legally binding, although enforcement may be problematic given that the concept of state sovereignty prevails in international law.

2.1.1 International Court of Justice

The main international court is the International Court of Justice ('ICJ'). The ICJ was set-up under the Charter of the United Nations (UN) in 1946 and has a dual role: to adjudicate on disputes between member states of the UN (currently numbering 191 states) and to provide advisory opinions to UN bodies. It has a permanent bench of fifteen judges, elected by the UN General Assembly to serve a term of nine years. In theory, the judges are independent and do not represent the opinions of their respective countries.

The ICJ has jurisdiction to adjudicate disputes between member states of the UN only. Therefore, neither individuals nor groups (or non-UN member states) are entitled to appear before the ICJ. Further, the ICJ's jurisdiction is limited to situations where the state has explicitly accepted jurisdiction, despite all state parties to the UN Convention necessarily being parties to the ICJ's statute. Since 1946 only seventy-six judgments have been handed down by the ICJ. However, the ICJ continues to play an important role in international affairs in the advisory sense.

It is unlikely that the Statute of the ICJ, or indeed the Charter of the UN, will be amended to permit intrastate disputes to be adjudicated by the ICJ. Nonetheless, decisions of the ICJ provide relevant jurisprudence relating to customary international law principles, which may affect the rights of groups of peoples. The ICJ is able to, and has, pronounced on territorial and border disputes between countries. For example the case concerning sovereignty over Pulau Ligitan and Pulau Sipadan required the ICJ to decide whether these two small islands belonged to either Indonesia or Malaysia.[3]

Similarly, the case concerning East Timor dealt with the right of the people of East Timor to self-determine, although the ICJ dispute was between Portugal and Australia. Portugal commenced proceedings against Australia concerning Australia's alleged failure to respect the administrative powers of Portugal in East Timor. Portugal objected to a treaty between Australia and Indonesia on the exploitation of an area of the continental shelf between Australia and East Timor (the Timor Gap). The ICJ declined jurisdiction to entertain the action because to have done so would have meant ruling on whether Indonesia, which had not accepted the jurisdiction of the ICJ, could have lawfully concluded the treaty. However, the ICJ did emphasise that East Timor remained a non-self-governing territory and its people had the right to self-determination.

The ICJ also produced an Advisory Opinion in respect of the Western Sahara dealing with the two questions: was the Western Sahara at the time of colonisation

---

[3] A summary of the case is available at <http://www.icj-cij.org/icjwww/ipresscom/ipress2002/ipresscom2002-39bis_inma_20021217.htm> (2 August 2006).

by Spain a territory belonging to no one; and what were the legal ties of this territory with the Kingdom of Morocco and the Mauritanian Entity? The UN General Assembly had asked the ICJ to give advice on those questions with the intention of deciding whether or not the question of the sovereignty of the territory should be considered by the UN Committee for Decolonisation. The ICJ held that, although some of the region's tribes had historical ties to Morocco, the ties were insufficient to establish 'any tie of territorial sovereignty' between the Western Sahara and Morocco. It further found that there were no 'legal ties' that might preclude the application of the UN General Assembly resolution as to the decolonisation of the territory or the exercise of self-determination.

The ICJ does have jurisdiction to make orders against member states and is prepared to exercise that jurisdiction. In the *Case Concerning the Military and Paramilitary Activities in and against Nicaragua (Nicaragua* v. *United States of America)*, the ICJ found that the United States' activities in Nicaragua were contrary to international law, and awarded significant compensation to Nicaragua. Among other things the ICJ found that the United States, by training, arming, equipping, financing and supplying the contra forces or otherwise encouraging, supporting and aiding military and paramilitary activities in and against Nicaragua, acted against the Republic of Nicaragua in breach of its obligations under customary international law not to intervene in the affairs of another state.

2.1.2 *Regional permanent international courts*

A number of groups of states have also established separate regional courts with the distinct roles of: (a) upholding the laws in an area of economic cooperation; and (b) dealing with human rights disputes relating to common interests between the member states. In the former role, these courts frequently have jurisdiction only in respect of member states. In relation to human rights disputes, these courts usually can hear complaints by nationals against a member state. Selected specialist regional courts in Europe, the Americas and Africa are discussed below.

- Europe

The European Court of Justice ('ECJ') is responsible for determining disputes relating to European Union law. The ECJ is able to confer rights on an individual and the national courts of member states must uphold those rights. Individuals may apply for the annulment of a provision of EU law that directly affects them. The volume of work of the ECJ has been enormous, with 8,600 cases considered by it since 1952.

The European Court of Human Rights ('ECHR') has jurisdiction to determine disputes arising under the European Convention for the Protection of Human Rights and Fundamental Freedoms. It has authority to provide remedies for states (which are party to the European Convention for the Protection of Human Rights and Fundamental Freedoms) or individuals (who are nationals of a state party) who prove that their rights have been violated by a member state. Legal aid funding is available to complainants.

In addition, the European Free Trade Association Court and the Benelux Court of Justice have specific jurisdiction to deal with commercial disputes relating to their specified regions.

- Americas

The international courts in the Americas are similarly structured to the European courts. The Central American Court of Justice ('CACJ') and the Inter-American Court of Human Rights ('IACHR') are the primary bodies and there are several more specialised courts with more limited jurisdiction.

The CACJ, although set-up nearly a century ago, remained ineffective until it was given a new lease of life under the Protocol of Tegucigalpa in 1991. The CACJ has jurisdiction to adjudicate on disputes between individuals and the state, although the individual must first prove that all domestic remedies have been exhausted.

The IACHR has jurisdiction to consider human rights issues in limited circumstances. state parties to the 1969 American Convention on Human Rights first need to give consent to the jurisdiction of the IACHR for either a specific period of time or a specific case. Such consent is not implicit upon ratification of the convention. The judiciary sits only part-time and individuals are required first to file any claims with the Inter-American Commission, thus reducing the practical effect of the body further.

Other courts in the Americas include the Court of Justice of the Andean Community ('TJAC') and the Caribbean Court of Justice ('CCJ'), both of which have limited jurisdiction within smaller regions but extend beyond the relevant national courts.

- Africa

Similarly, there is a pan-African Court of Justice for the economic community ('COMESA') and an anticipated African Court of Human Rights ('ACHPR').

Retaining more flexibility than some other regional courts, the COMESA Court has jurisdiction to hear disputes among member states and disputes referred by the COMESA Market Council for breaches of the Market's rules, and to act as an arbitral institution in respect of disputes arising out of contracts between a COMESA institution and another party. Despite its broad jurisdiction, to date only four disputes have been registered with the COMESA Court. The ACHPR is yet to be established. It is anticipated that the ACHPR will enable citizens of ratifying countries to bring actions under any UN human rights treaty or convention signed and ratified by member state. However, individuals will only be entitled to bring a claim if the relevant state has expressly agreed they may do so at the time of ratification.

The structures of the various regional international courts are based on a model similar to the ICJ. They are formed to deal with inter-state (as opposed to intrastate) disputes within particular regions. As with the ICJ, there may be jurisprudence from these bodies that would assist certain population groups but, as a general proposition, such bodies are probably not the most suitable fora in which to resolve intrastate disputes of the nature dealt with in this publication.

2.2 Use of arbitration in intrastate disputes

Apart from the various international courts and quasi-judicial bodies, there are several international arbitral institutions that have been established to deal with the administration of international disputes, usually of a commercial nature. These are not courts *per se* but, instead, are administrative bodies that are responsible for managing and administering disputes commenced under their authority. Parties who have agreed to resolve their disputes by arbitration may nominate an arbitral institution to support the arbitral process. Under the rules of all of the international arbitral institutions, the parties are free to appoint an arbitrator or arbitral tribunal by consent. If the agreed appointment procedure fails, the institution is usually able to enforce a default appointment procedure in accordance with the parties' agreement and/or the governing rules. Almost all of the international arbitral institutions now administer arbitrations in accordance with the UNCITRAL Rules of Arbitration or their own institutional rules, which are usually based on the UNCITRAL model.

There are distinct advantages to arbitration as a method of dispute resolution. Arbitration is less formal and more flexible than court proceedings. Arbitral decisions are final and binding on the parties and the proceedings and outcome can be kept confidential. Usually, the arbitral tribunal will be constituted on the basis of an uneven number of judges. Each party is able to choose an equal number of tribunal members and the final member is expected to be impartial. The arbitrators selected by the parties usually have specialised knowledge of the issues involved. Before parties submit to arbitration they must agree on what procedures to adopt and they have a wide degree of autonomy to do so.

Among other things, decisions must be taken as to what law will apply, whether the proceedings are to be *ad hoc* or institutional and the location and language of the hearings.

There is an argument, put forward by some international writers, that international public law issues, including issues relating to sovereignty, self-determination and autonomy (as opposed to issues of private national and/or international law) are too unwieldy and political to be addressed by international arbitrators.[4] However, this criticism is not entirely fair. The reality is that arbitration permits parties to choose their arbitrators (ensuring that the appointees are able to deal with the issues that arise), the parties are free to determine the scope of the dispute that is put before those arbitrators and the parties are free to agree the procedural rules that will enable them to mitigate the risk of an aberrant outcome in any arbitral award.

2.2.1 *UNCITRAL Model Arbitration Rules*

In 1976, the UN Commission on International Trade Law ('UNCITRAL') promulgated the UNCITRAL Model Arbitration Rules ('UNCITRAL Rules').[5]

The UN General Assembly expressly recognised the value of arbitration as a method of settling disputes arising in the context of international commercial relations and believed that the establishment of rules for *ad hoc* arbitration – acceptable in countries with different legal, social and economic systems – would significantly contribute to the development of harmonious international economic nations. Most major international arbitral institutions are now able to administer *ad hoc* arbitrations under the UNCITRAL rules. (*Ad hoc* arbitration is conducted without an administering authority and, often, without the aid of institutional procedural rules.)

Although the UNCITRAL rules were initially intended for use in commercial disputes between parties from different states, their flexibility has allowed their use to be greatly extended. As the UNCITRAL website explains:

> The UNCITRAL Arbitration Rules are intended to be used by any public entities or private parties in the conduct of dispute settlement proceedings if they so wish. Nothing in the Rules limits their use to nationals of States which are Member States of the Commission.[6]

---

[4] See J.H Barton and M.C. Greenberg, 'Lessons of the Case Studies' in M.C. Greenberg, J.H. Barton and M.E. McGuinness (eds.), *Words Over War* (Lanham, Md, Rowman and Littlefield 2000), 358.

[5] <http://www.uncitral.org/pdf/english/texts/arbitration/arb-rules/arb-rules.pdf> (2 August 2006).

[6] <http://www.uncitral.org/en-index.htm> (2 August 2006). For example, the case in *Larsen* (above) was brought under the UNCITRAL Rules. It is also possible to bring a dispute against a

The UNCITRAL rules have proved so popular that most international arbitral institutions now base their own rules on them. In 1982, UNCITRAL issued 'Recommendations to Assist Arbitral Institutions and Other Interested Bodies with Regard to Arbitrations under the UNCITRAL Arbitration Rules' in order to help institutions to adopt the UNCITRAL rules, and offered to provide administrative and appointing authority services.

The links between the Permanent Court of Arbitration and the UNCITRAL rules are strong. The Optional Rules for Arbitrating Disputes between Two Parties of Which Only One is a State (discussed in more detail below), which operate under the PCA, are almost exactly the same as the UNCITRAL rules. The UNCITRAL rules specifically designate the Secretary-General of the PCA as the appointing body for the purpose of appointing the arbitral tribunal where parties cannot agree or, alternatively, permit the Secretary-General to designate another appointing body.[7]

2.2.2 Ad hoc arbitration

The UNCITRAL rules are designed specifically for *ad hoc* proceedings. Adoption of a set of pre-existing rules in arbitration enables parties to eliminate the difficulties and tedium of having to draft their own rules, and also minimise the risk that the parties' arbitration is unable to proceed because the parties cannot agree on matters such as: appointment of arbitrators, choice of law, scope of the arbitration, location, procedures for presentation of argument and evidence and the like. The primary advantage of *ad hoc* arbitration lies in its flexibility. It is possible to adapt the rules to the expectations of the parties although cooperation in that (or any) respect may be difficult once a dispute has arisen.

2.2.3 International arbitral institutions

There is a significant number of international arbitral institutions available to administer international arbitrations in accordance with the parties' agreement.

- The Permanent Court of Arbitration

The Permanent Court of Arbitration (PCA) was set-up under the aegis of the 1907 Convention for the Pacific Settlement of International Disputes and its

---

State under the UNCITRAL Rules; see *Himpurna California Energy Ltd.* v. *Republic of Indonesia* (Interim Award of 26 September 1999 and Final Award of 16 December 1999, published in *Mealey's International Arbitration Report* 15 (February 2000) A-1—A-20 and B-1—B-20).

[7] See UNCITRAL Rules Article 7(2)(b).

ancestor, the 1899 Convention, which bore the same name. Although not actually a permanent court in the manner of the ICJ, the PCA is an institution that provides a stable secretariat for the facilitation of arbitrations. The PCA complements the ICJ in offering the international community a range of options for the peaceful resolution of disputes. Arbitration was one of the methods of peaceful settlement listed in Article 33 of the UN Charter. The PCA has broader jurisdiction than the ICJ insofar as it is able to deal with arbitrations involving private parties and international organisations as well as states. The PCA provides flexible instruments of dispute resolution that can be used by a variety of individuals, groups or statutes.

Given its fairly venerated status in the history of international dispute mechanisms, the PCA has dealt with relatively few cases. By 2002 there had been only forty-one cases submitted for resolution before the PCA.[8] In some ways, the ICJ overtook the PCA in prominence as, historically, international disputes have been between states. However, as international disputes have gained complexity in nature, the PCA has been called upon with increasing regularity to assist in the administration of disputes. In 2002 alone, the PCA served as registry for seven arbitrations. The PCA now offers a broad range of services for resolving disputes between states, disputes between states and private parties and disputes in which intergovernmental organisations are involved.

An important development was the introduction in 1993 by the PCA of Optional Rules for Arbitrating Disputes between Two Parties of Which Only One is a State. (Extracts are reproduced in Appendix M. A full copy of the Rules may be found at the PCA website <http://www.pca-cpa.org>) The main difference between these and the UNCITRAL rules is that the Optional Rules require one party to be a state. The Optional Rules require the state party to agree to a waiver of its sovereign immunity (as discussed below). The Optional Rules also permit a three member tribunal to continue to arbitrate if one arbitrator fails to participate in the arbitration. In all other respects, the Optional Rules are the same as the UNCITRAL rules.

Some key features of the Optional Rules, which illustrate their flexibility, include the provision that proceedings may be conducted in any language, if agreed by the parties. In relation to appointment of the arbitral tribunal, the rules are designed to ensure that the arbitral tribunal is properly constituted. Each state party to the 1899 and 1907 Conventions is entitled to nominate four arbitrators to serve on the list of arbitrators kept by the PCA. However, parties are not obliged to choose arbitrators from that list and are free to nominate

---

[8] See Annual Report of PCA 2002, available at <http://www.pca-cpa.org/ENGLISH/AR/annrep02.htm> (2 August 2006).

arbitrators from elsewhere (although the arbitrators on the PCA list include many of the highest ranking figures in dispute resolution from member countries). It is possible for any party to challenge the appointment of an arbitrator (Articles 9-12) and, furthermore, the tribunal may rule on its jurisdiction.[9]

Almost a decade on, the application of the Optional Rules to intrastate disputes has not been fully tested. An exceptional case heard by a PCA tribunal was *Larsen* (discussed above). Initially, the parties in *Larsen* applied for arbitration under the Optional Rules, but by mutual consent changed the arbitration agreement to apply the UNCITRAL rules. The key difference is that the former require that one party is a state. The International Bureau of the PCA had refused to permit *Larsen* to continue unless the claim was brought under the UNCITRAL rules, because there was a question whether the respondent (the Hawaiian Kingdom) was a 'state' within the meaning of the Optional Rules. The case illustrates the value of having the UNCITRAL rules in place as an alternative set of rules to govern PCA administered arbitrations. In any event, *Larsen* was dismissed by the PCA for lack of jurisdiction. The dispute involved the United States which was not a party to the relevant arbitration agreement. In coming to its conclusion, the tribunal set out a detailed discussion on the relevant international law. In that conclusion, the tribunal made it clear that the scope of the UNCITRAL rules (and indeed the authority of PCA tribunals) should not be limited, stating, for example, that:

> [t]here appears no reason why the UNCITRAL Rules cannot be adapted to apply to a non-contractual dispute.[10]

It is also possible to bring a dispute to the PCA under agreed rules that are neither the Optional Rules (or any other PCA rules) nor the UNCITRAL rules, but something else entirely. The *Ireland* v. *United Kingdom (OSPAR)* dispute has as the rules for its arbitration those decided among the parties.[11] The dispute is brought pursuant to the 1992 Convention for the Protection of the Marine Environment of the North-East Atlantic, which provides for the rules applying to arbitration brought under its cover. However the parties were able to amend those rules and were guided, as opposed to bound, by them.

---

[9] 'Arbitral tribunal shall have power to determine the existence or the validity of the contract of which an arbitration clause forms a part' (Article 21(2)).

[10] *Larsen* v. *the Hawaiian Kingdom by its Council of Regency*, PCA award available at <http://www.pca-cpa.org/PDF/LHKAward.PDF> (2 August 2006).

[11] The rules of procedure can be found at <http://pca-cpa.org/PDF/OSPAR%20Rules%20 of%20Procedure%20—%20final.pdf> (2 August 2006).

A fundamental aspect of the optional rules, which makes them particularly attractive for intrastate disputes is that, once a state has agreed to their application, it cannot then claim that it has immunity from prosecution and therefore refuse to be involved in the process or abide by any award. Waiver of sovereign immunity from jurisdiction is provided for by the PCA in Article 1, paragraph 2 of the optional rules. The waiver must be explicitly expressed by the state.

Another positive institutional aspect of the PCA is its Financial Assistance Fund for Settlement of International Disputes for Developing Countries. A party who can claim for funding can include:

> ... any institution or enterprise owned and controlled by such State, which has concluded an agreement for the purpose of submitting one or more disputes, whether existing or future, for settlement under the auspices of the Permanent Court of Arbitration by any of the means administered by the Permanent Court of Arbitration, and which State, at the time of requesting financial assistance from the Fund, is listed on the 'DAC List of Aid Recipients' prepared by the Organisation for Economic Cooperation and Development (OECD).[12]

Historically, there have been four successful applications for funding, two from Asian states and two from African states. Unfortunately, only '... a State that is a party to the Convention of 1899 or 1907, or any institution or enterprise owned and controlled by such State, ... listed on the DAC List of Aid Recipients prepared by the ... OECD[13] can qualify for the purposes of funding. That definition does not include individuals, groups of individuals, or peoples, which are likely to be involved in arbitrations against states arising pursuant to intrastate peace agreements.

The main benefit of the PCA is its flexible approach to rules of procedure and the ability of non-state parties to bring disputes. There is no clear political (or economic) reason why state parties, individuals or peoples should not consent to arbitration under the auspices of the PCA, provided that appropriate procedural rules could be agreed to deal with the particular nature of the disputes between the parties. As with all alternative dispute resolution procedures, the most important step is for the parties to consent to the dispute resolution procedure.

---

[12] Permanent Court of Arbitration Financial Assistance Fund for Settlement of International Disputes, Article 5.
[13] Ibid.

- The International Court of Arbitration of the International Chamber of Commerce

The International Chamber of Commerce International Court of Arbitration (the ICC Court of Arbitration) can be seen as representative of a wider type of arbitral institution, which caters mainly for international commercial disputes but which may be adapted to accommodate any form of business dispute, providing the parties consent. The ICC Court of Arbitration describes itself as an independent system of arbitration offering flexibility and neutrality to parties. The main facets to these claims are the ability to choose the language, the place of the arbitration, the rules of law, the nationality of the arbitrators and the legal representation of the parties. Like the PCA, the ICC does not have a permanent seat of judges for the determination of substantive disputes, but instead acts as a secretariat or registry to oversee arbitrations run under its auspices. The ICC Court of Arbitration itself is comprised of representatives appointed by each member state. The role of the ICC Court of Arbitration is to make administrative decisions in respect of ICC arbitrations. The substantive decision-making power is vested in the arbitral tribunal, which is usually appointed by the parties by consent.

The ICC arbitration rules contain many of the same essential elements that are present in the UNCITRAL rules (including appointment of and challenge to arbitrators, conduct of proceedings and awards) but also contain additional procedural features (such as terms of reference) that are specific to the ICC. A copy of the ICC Rules of Arbitration may be found at the ICC International Court of Arbitration website at <http://www.iccwbo.org/court/eEnglish/rules/rules.asp>. Although the ICC Court of Arbitration rules have developed independently of UNCITRAL rules, it is fair to say that each has influenced the other.[14] The amendments to the ICC rules in 1998 included some harmonisation with the UNCITRAL rules (i.e., to allow for partial or interlocutory awards by the arbitrators) but in other ways the ICC remains independent (e.g., a request for arbitration must be filed rather than a simpler notice for arbitration under UNCITRAL).[15]

The ICC Court of Arbitration allows for the arbitration of disputes involving two or more parties. Article ten states that there may be multiple parties, either as claimant or respondent, so long as they are parties to the arbitration agreement. There is also no limit as to whom the parties can be; either a state, a state

---

[14] P. Sanders (ed.), *Yearbook, Commercial Arbitration* (Deventer, Netherlands, Kluwer Law International) Vol. II (1977), 172-224.

[15] Y. Derains and E. Schwartz, *A Guide to the New ICC Rules of Arbitration 1998* (The Hague, Kluwer Law International 1998).

entity, a population group or an individual may be a party to ICC Court of Arbitration proceedings. It is true that:

> The Rules are therefore commonly said to have as one of their fundamental characteristics a 'universal' character, meaning that they are intended for use in any country, under any law and in accordance with any system of legal procedure.[16]

Unfortunately, the ICC Secretariat has recently indicated that, given that its purpose is to deal with business disputes, it is currently unable to administer intrastate disputes that are of a non-business nature. Therefore, unless there is a commercial aspect to a particular intrastate dispute (which is feasible if, for example, ownership of valuable natural resources is at stake) the ICC Court of Arbitration is not, until or unless its current rules are amended, a suitable institution for the administration of such disputes.

The ICC Court of Arbitration has an obvious commercial focus, which could be both positive and negative for intrastate disputes that do contain a business aspect. The secretariat is set-up to deal with a large number of complex cases and will therefore not be overwhelmed by a large intrastate arbitration. The confidentiality of parties can be assured as awards do not have to be published. The arbitrators are required to be independent of the parties, and must sign a declaration to this effect (Article 7). Article 15 does provide that the sole arbitrator or the chairman is to be of a nationality different to that of the parties.

As the ICC Court of Arbitration has this commercial focus, advances as to cost which are calculated on a percentage as to the amount in issue must be paid by the time of delivery of the terms of reference. This may be prohibitive to minority groups that do not have access to sufficient funds. With the expense however comes a secretariat that is a very efficient machine with a global customer base. In 2002, 593 requests for arbitration were filed with the ICC Court of Arbitration. Those requests involved 1,622 parties from 126 different countries and independent territories. The seats of the arbitrations were based in forty-three different countries throughout the world. Arbitrators of sixty-two different nationalities were appointed or confirmed under the ICC Rules with the amount in dispute exceeded one million US dollars in 54 percent of new cases. In 9.4 percent of cases, at least one of the parties was a state or a state entity.

A unique feature of ICC arbitration, the terms of reference, serve the useful purpose of bringing the arbitrators and parties together at an early stage in order to identify the issues they will be required to deal with (and procedural details).

---

[16] Derains and Schwartz, *Guide to the New ICC Rules*.

A significant proportion of ICC arbitration cases are amicably settled at the stage of the terms of reference.

The President of the ICC, Mr Robert Briner has said:

> Of the total number of cases submitted to ICC for arbitration, many do not go as far as a binding award but are resolved through the parties coming to a mutual understanding. This may be evidenced in awards by consent, which make up around 12 percent of all awards rendered each year [average over the last ten years]. In addition it may be assumed that the cause of many case withdrawals at an earlier stage of the proceedings is the fact that the parties have settled their difference between themselves.[17]

- Other international arbitration institutions

In addition to the PCA and ICC Court of Arbitration, there are numerous other international arbitral institutions based in different countries, which administer international arbitrations in a similar manner to the ICC, usually under UNCITRAL rules or their own rules based on the UNCITRAL model. These include the London Court of International Arbitration ('LCIA') in England, the American Arbitration Association ('AAA') in the US, the China International Economic and Trade Arbitration Commission ('CIETAC') in China , the Stockholm Chamber of Commerce Arbitration Institute ('SCCA') in Sweden, the Singapore International Arbitration Centre ('SIAC') in Singapore and the Hong Kong International Arbitration Centre ('HKIAC') in Hong Kong, to name a few. Despite the proliferation of international arbitral institutions throughout the world, it is fair to say that in the international commercial arbitration community the ICC remains the most widely known and accepted international arbitral institution. Almost all of the above named institutions, as with the ICC, focus on business disputes. However, some may be more willing and able to deal with non-business disputes (e.g., the LCIA rules do not limit its application to business disputes).

- Specialised international tribunals

Several specialised arbitral tribunals have been established to deal with specific issues arising between states, between states and individuals within those states, and between states and nationals of other states. Examples include the Iran-United States Claims Tribunal,[18] the United Nations Compensation Commis-

---

[17] *ADR – International Applications, A Special Supplement to the ICC International Court of Arbitration Bulletin 2001* (Paris, ICC Publishing S.A.), Introduction.

[18] After the detention of fifty-two United States nationals at the US embassy in Tehran, and the subsequent freeze of Iran's assets by the United States., the Iran-United States Tribunal was

sion, and the Claims Resolution Tribunal for Dormant Accounts in Switzerland. The use of specialised international tribunals in disputes between states and individual nationals is relatively new. Many of these were established following World War II, but have only recently risen to prominence. The jurisdiction of these bodies is often limited by the convention that established them.

The Iran-United States Claims Tribunal is a useful model because of the large number of claims considered by it (in excess of 4,000) and because the Tribunal adopted the UNCITRAL Model Arbitration Rules. The Tribunal's jurisdiction was defined primarily to include claims arising out of contracts between two state parties or one state and a national of the other. Although most of its work was commercial, it also dealt with treaty interpretation and other public international law issues, including nationalisation and state responsibility. The Tribunal was constituted to ensure that its members were of different nationalities.

In the context of intrastate disputes, a situation may arise where a number of separate but related disputes require resolution (for example, individuals or smaller groups of individuals within the broader population group have separate grievances and/or rights to compensation). In such a situation a single arbitral body, along the lines of the Iran-United States Claims Tribunal, could be established to deal with all related complaints.

3. The Enforceability of Arbitration Agreements and Awards

A critical aspect of the use of arbitration to resolve intrastate disputes is the relevant state's approach to enforcement of the arbitration agreement and any ultimate award. The Convention on the Recognition and Enforcement of Foreign Arbitral Awards of 1958 (the 'New York Convention') provides that all signatories agree to enforce foreign arbitral awards made in the territory of any member state. Only states may be signatories to the New York Convention and at present, 122 states have signed. One of the goals of the New York Convention was to encourage maximum acceptance of arbitration as a means of dispute resolution. In order to do so across a large number of very diverse states and

---

established to resolve the outlying dispute between the two countries. Algeria was appointed as the neutral mediator. The Tribunal has dealt with a massive six hundred claims up to 2002 and was well-equipped to deal with large and complex claims. However, the Tribunal was only permitted to deal with the claims of US nationals against Iran, and vice versa. The rules relating to the establishment of the Iran-United States Tribunal can be found at <http://www.iusct.org/tribunal-rules.pdf> (2 August 2006).

cultures, it has been necessary to introduce a qualification to the obligation to enforce agreements and awards. Article V(2)(b) of the New York Convention provides that enforcement of arbitral awards will not conflict with the basic morals and legal principles of the place of enforcement. Therefore, an arbitral award may be unenforceable if a 'competent authority' in the state where enforcement is sought finds that recognition or enforcement of that award could be contrary to the state's public policy.[19]

The main public policy grounds for a national court to refuse to enforce an award are: (a) illegality of subject-matter; (b) lack of due process; and (c) lack of reasons in the award. It is not actually clear whether Article V(2)(b) relates to matters of public policy based on national law (i.e., internal public policy adopted to recognise national laws, regulations and customary provisions within the state in accordance with that state's beliefs and the moral standards it considers necessary to govern people within that state) as well as matters of public policy based on international customs and law (a narrower category of transnational standards such as human rights). Most national courts that have been required to rule on the issue have determined that the New York Convention is referring to the narrower category of international public policy.[20] However, this remains a matter for interpretation by the relevant national courts in individual states and the outcome in certain states remains uncertain.

4. Conclusion

The need for alternative dispute resolution mechanisms to resolve intrastate disputes and disputes arising out of the implementation (or non-implementation) of intrastate peace agreements exists because non-state parties often do not perceive national courts to be independent or neutral decision-making bodies.

A broad range of international dispute resolution bodies exists. Arguably, the international courts, including regional courts, will not provide a suitable forum for the determination of disputes of an intrastate nature. Intrastate disputes necessarily involve at least one non-state party and only states have standing before the international courts. Having said that, both states and certain UN bodies are permitted to seek advisory opinions from the International Court of Justice, which may indirectly assist non-state parties to resolve certain intrastate dis-

---

[19] Hakeem Seriki, 'Enforcement of Foreign Arbitral Awards and Public Policy – A Note of Caution', *Alternative Dispute Resolution Law Journal* (2000) 192 at 195.

[20] A.J. Van den Berg, *The New York Arbitration Convention of 1958: Towards a Uniform Judicial Interpretation* (The Hague, TMC Asser Institute, 1981), 359-368.

pute issues. The Western Sahara and East Timor cases illustrate how this process works in practice. Alternatively, individuals are entitled to commence claims before international and/or regional human rights courts and such claims may provide another indirect route by which parties may enable international courts to consider issues arising from intrastate disputes.

There are strong arguments in favour of the international arbitration model of dispute resolution providing the most flexible, independent and reliable model for the resolution of intrastate disputes. The consensual nature of the arbitral process enables parties to agree to submit their dispute to an arbitral tribunal of their choice, as well as choose arbitrators in whom they have confidence. Parties may determine whether the proceedings are to be public or private and may design the conduct and procedure to best meet the requirements of their case. Parties are able to establish *ad hoc* arbitral tribunals or, alternatively, use existing arbitral institutions. A number of international arbitral institutions are available to administer proceedings, most notably the Permanent Court of Arbitration and, in disputes of a commercial nature, the International Court of Arbitration of the International Chamber of Commerce. The Permanent Court of Arbitration is particularly well-suited for dealing with intrastate disputes and already has rules of procedure in place designed for cases between state and non-state parties.

To date, neither the Permanent Court of Arbitration nor any other international arbitral institution has been appointed as administering authority in respect of an intrastate dispute (i.e., a conflict between a population group (for example an autonomous region, non-self governing territory, indigenous people or minority) and the government of the state that exercises jurisdiction over that population group). Public policy issues affecting the enforceability of any arbitration agreement or award relating to an intrastate dispute need to be carefully considered. It may be that the political nature of intrastate disputes calls for a political process of dispute resolution rather than a more formalised legal process.

Nonetheless, arbitration is internationally recognised as an effective and equitable means of settling disputes where diplomacy has failed. The potential for utilising arbitration mechanisms exists and there are sound arguments in favour of doing so. Questions as to how these mechanisms can best be used to help resolve intrastate disputes, the types of disputes that they are best suited for and the procedures that may be most appropriate for states and non-state parties, should be the subject of further study.

Chapter XII

THE SETTLEMENT OF TREATY OF WAITANGI CLAIMS OF MAORI GROUPS IN AOTEAROA/NEW ZEALAND

Morris Te Whiti Love[*]

This chapter looks at the process for the settlement of Maori claims based on the Treaty of Waitangi, signed in 1840 by the British Crown[1] and Maori tribes from all parts of Aotearoa/New Zealand.[2] The claims concern the alienation and appropriation of Maori land by the British Crown and private individuals in violation of the treaty over a period of one hundred and sixty years.

In Aotearoa/New Zealand the disputes that have arisen out of the failure of the Crown to implement and honour the Treaty of Waitangi with respect to land rights and control over natural resources of the Maori people are now being resolved through a process of negotiation between the government and the claimants with the help of an independent tribunal which investigates the claims. Thus, some 160 years after the treaty was concluded, a serious effort is being made to implement its key provisions, to rectify past violations, and to compensate for what can no longer be implemented.

---

[*] Former Director of the Waitangi Tribunal.

[1] The 'Crown' in its simplest form was the sovereign – in this case Queen Victoria. Aotearoa/New Zealand still maintains the British Sovereign, with a representative, the Governor General resident in Aotearoa/New Zealand. Even today Maori see the Crown as an abstraction represented by the British Sovereign. However in practical terms for this publication, the Crown today is effectual through the New Zealand Government and its statute making powers.

[2] *Te Tiriti o Waitangi* (The Treaty of Waitangi*)* was signed first at Waitangi in the Bay of Islands in New Zealand on 6 February 1840. This original version in Maori is held at the National Archives in Wellington. There were several versions signed around the country by some 550 Chiefs through 1840, one being in English. Three versions are now used for official reference and are included as Appendix 1 of the Treaty of Waitangi Act 1975. Both Maori and English texts are reproduced in Appendix N.

M. Boltjes (ed.), *Implementing Negotiated Agreements*
© 2007, Kreddha International and T·M·C·ASSER PRESS, The Hague, The Netherlands

1. ORIGINS OF THE MAORI CLAIMS

1.1 **Events leading up to the Treaty of Waitangi**

The formal and acknowledged start of the British colonisation of Aotearoa/New Zealand was 6 February 1840,[3] the day the Treaty of Waitangi was signed. Up to the early 1830's, the British, who had established themselves in New South Wales, Australia, had no great desire to establish a formal relationship with Aotearoa/New Zealand. It was the arrival of the first batch of British colonists in Wellington in early 1840, brought there by the British New Zealand Company, a private colonisation venture, that forced the hands of the British administration in New South Wales. They sent a young naval officer, Captain William Hobson, to be Lieutenant Governor of New Zealand and to enter into a treaty with the Maori people.

In the first days of February 1840, the chiefs of many of the northern *hapu* (sub-tribes) gathered at Waitangi to discuss the treaty to be proffered by the British. Waitangi was just across the water from a town called Kororareka (now called Russell). This town was known as the 'hell hole of the Pacific' where traders, whalers, sealers, and others, including some Maori, plied drink. Maori provided women in exchange for goods and liquor. However, many of the chiefs had converted to their own form of Christianity. For them and other Maori, law and order had become a major issue and the treaty promised to bring European law and order to this unruly town. The treaty also held the promise of prosperity for Maori through trade in markets such as Australia and further afield.

On 5 February 1840 most of the chiefs still rejected the notion of a treaty and were preparing to go home. Hobson persuaded the chiefs to stay until 6 February, however, and hastily completed the drafting of the treaty that same night. When it was presented to the Maori in the morning,[4] the chiefs, lead by one of its most vigorous opponents, decided to sign it. Hobson quickly set-up the ceremony for the signing and when the principal chiefs started to come forward to sign, others were not to be outdone, until most of those chiefs present had signed.

The Treaty was a simple and pithy document, consisting of a single page of text. It begins with a preamble stating the desire of the Queen of the United

---

[3] Claudia Orange, *The Treaty of Waitangi* (Wellington: Allen & Unwin in association with Port Nicholson Press, 1987), 6-11.

[4] Orange, *The Treaty of Waitangi*, 51-53: 'By Thursday morning, 6 February, the chiefs had come to the decision that the treaty business should be concluded immediately so they could return home. .... There was confusion on the Thursday morning as Hobson had set the public meeting for Friday 7. In the end he consented that only signatures would be accepted; no discussion would be allowed.'

Kingdom to 'protect [the] just Rights and Property [of Maori] and to secure to them the enjoyment of Peace and Good Order.' It further states the need, 'in consequence of the great number of Her Majesty's Subjects who have already settled in New Zealand and the rapid extension of Emigration ... which is still in progress', to treat with the Maori 'for the recognition of Her Majesty's sovereign authority over the whole or any part of those islands.'[5] The preamble is followed by three articles written in both English and Maori, summarised as follows:

(a) the first article of the Treaty cedes sovereignty (or 'governance',[6] or 'complete government'[7] in the Maori version) to the British Crown;
(b) the second article guarantees to the chiefs full exclusive and undisturbed possession of their lands, estates, forests, fisheries and other properties they wish to retain. It also states that Maori land can only be sold to the Crown;
(c) the third article extends to Maori all the rights and privileges of British subjects.

The Treaty was taken around the country for signature by those tribes not present at the initial signing. Although some tribes did not sign the Treaty, it was gradually seen to have general application throughout the whole country. It signalled the introduction of British law and the introduction of a British form of government. The formalisation of this process through legislation came a little later in 1852.

1.2 Alienation of Maori land

The Treaty of Waitangi was soon regarded by the British as a Treaty of cession and not as a means to protect the rights of Maori. Agents of the British Crown actively set about purchasing much of the South Island (152,232 km^2) although they did so with the intent of providing extensive reserves for Maori. However, reserves were not provided as promised. In some cases they were much reduced in size, while some reserves were not established at all.[8] Just after the turn of

---

[5] The Treaty of Waitangi (English text signed at Waikato Heads in March or April 1840. This text became the 'official' version.).

[6] In explanation of the Treaty to Maori familiar with the Bible, the term 'kawanatanga' was explained as being equivalent to the Roman Governor of Judea, Pontious Pilate at the time of Jesus. Hence 'governorship'.

[7] Sir Hugh Kawharu, Translation of the Maori text, reproduced in Appendix N.

[8] Waitangi Tribunal, Ngai Tahu Report, (Wai 27) (Wellington, Brooker and Friend Ltd, 1991).

the century the situation for a number of Maori had become so bad that an Act of Parliament was passed to make provision for landless natives in the South Island.[9] The need for this legislation is indicative of the fact that the Maori did not get a good deal and that the main beneficiary of the land provisions under the Treaty was the Crown.[10]

The period from 1840 to 1865 saw significant Crown purchasing of Maori land, but for various reasons, especially the stolid resistance from Maori, the land sales slowed considerably after that. As the demand for land from settlers increased, the government was pressured to find new mechanisms to acquire land. As land rights throughout the country could only be obtained by means of a Crown grant and the Maori no longer retained aboriginal title to the lands they held, Maori lands were brought into a system of land transfer managed by a Native Land Court. The ostensible purpose of this court was to ensure that Maori maintained sufficient land for their subsistence, but the unstated purpose was to find new and innovative ways to separate Maori from their land. One of the principal tools was the process of 'individualisation of title'.[11] That process saw the division of land and the transfer of it from *hapu* or collective ownership to a group of owners each with individual rights to alienate. Initially, no matter how many individuals had rights to the land, only ten owners were featured on the title. Any owner could enter into a process for the alienation of land. This mechanism proved to be very effective in facilitating the alienation of Maori land and the settlement of European farmers and landlords.

As Maori resistance to alienation became stronger, the government adopted more forceful means. In Taranaki, Waikato and the Bay of Plenty British troops were brought in. Although ostensibly there to protect the European population, the troops attacked Maori, which precipitated a war. Surprisingly, the British found Maori more than a match for the well-trained British regiments fresh from campaigns in India, South Africa and Europe. Finally, it was not military might but legislative power that conquered Maori. The government copied the Irish rebellion laws of the United Kingdom and applied them to declare Maori to be in rebellion. This allowed the government to enact the New Zealand Settlements Act of 1863, designed to promote peaceful settlement through confiscation of land from natives deemed to be in rebellion.[12]

---

[9] South Island Landless Natives Act 1906

[10] The 1852 Constitution saw a significant shift towards self-government away from the Colonial Office in Great Britain to the colonial parliament in New Zealand.

[11] D.V. Williams, *'Te Kooti tango whenua': The Native Land Court 1864-1909* (Wellington, Huia Publishers, 1999), 64.

[12] New Zealand Settlements Act 1863, Preamble: 'And whereas a large number of the Inhabitants of several districts of the Colony have entered into combinations and taken up arms with the object of attempting the extermination or expulsion of the European settlers and are now engaged in open rebellion against Her Majesty's authority ...'

To add insult to injury, land was given to so-called 'loyal' natives, who had little or no traditional rights to the land. The effect of this legislation was that a second level of grievances between various parts of the Maori community was created.[13] These 'micro-disputes' still influence the resolution of Maori claims today.

2. THE TREATY OF WAITANGI ACT AND THE ESTABLISHMENT OF THE WAITANGI TRIBUNAL

As the events described above indicate, there are many historical bases for Maori grievances and for the disputes between Maori and the Crown. Maori have consistently articulated grievances and protests relating to the failure of the Crown to implement and honour the Treaty of Waitangi. In particular, the grievances have related to the loss of Maori land and resources, and the desire for *tino rangatiratanga*, or authority and control over resources. Up to the 1970's, these grievances remained largely unresolved. The anger of the Maori found new political expression around that time, which coincided with such movements as the Black Power movement in the United States and the rise of indigenous consciousness globally. The annual commemorations of the signing of the Treaty at Waitangi on 6 February had become a seat of protest action, particularly from the people of the north (Te Tai Tokerau – Northland). The protest actions were highlighted by the Maori occupation of significant pieces of disputed land such as Bastion Point overlooking Auckland harbour and adjacent to some of the most expensive real estate in Aotearoa/New Zealand. This occupation persisted for over a year and was finally ended by police intervention and with the arrest of the leaders of the occupation.[14] Nationally, the objective of raising public awareness of Maori grievances was achieved.

The rising tide of Maori protest over the loss of land and the fact that the Treaty of Waitangi received little or no official recognition resulted in the passage of the Treaty of Waitangi Act in 1975. A young Labour Party, Maori politician, Matiu Rata was responsible for the passage of the Act, which provided for the establishment of the Waitangi Tribunal. However it had little effect until over five years later with the appointment of Chief Judge Eddie Durie as the chairperson of the Tribunal (he was also made Chief Judge of the Maori Land Court in 1980).

---

[13] See New Zealand Settlements Act 1863, ss 5, 6.
[14] This matter was later to be settled through the Waitangi Tribunal after it reported on the matter in its Orakei Claim Report.

The main function of the Waitangi Tribunal is to inquire into, report findings and make recommendations to ministers of the Crown, on claims submitted by Maori on matters relating to the Treaty of Waitangi. Although the Tribunal is a standing commission of inquiry and as such is independent, it is nonetheless an important component in the government's strategic policy of making significant progress towards the negotiation of fair and affordable settlements based on well founded grievances under the Treaty of Waitangi.

The first ten years of the Tribunal's operations were restricted to contemporary claims directed at legislation and actions of the Crown which were seen to be contrary to the principles of the Treaty of Waitangi. In 1985, the Treaty of Waitangi Amendment Act gave the Tribunal powers to look at historical claims dating back to 1840.[15] Moreover, with the rapid growth of the historical claims in the late 1980s, a structure was developed to provide for a process for negotiating settlements directly with the government. Gradually, in the 1980's, process replaced protest as the work of the Waitangi Tribunal slowly became effective and as the process for the negotiated settlement of Treaty of Waitangi claims was put in place. The Tribunal has now registered over one thousand claims and over one hundred and eighty have been reported on and/or settled in negotiation with the government.[16]

Although not a court, the Tribunal is often viewed by Maori as a court. It is perceived by many Maori as engaged in the delivery of substantive justice in areas where Maori claims are not otherwise justiciable and have not been so throughout history. The Tribunal is also seen to give effect to the Treaty of Waitangi which, though generally not part of domestic law, is seen by Maori as the foundation of it.

3. Social and Political Context of Tribunal Operations

Tribunal claims are heard within the social context of Maori over-representation in negative statistics such as those relating to health problems, social welfare, imprisonment and mortality. There is also a widening gap between Maori and non-Maori in terms of educational achievement, economic advancement, and employment.[17] Many Maori have made appeals to the Government to increase their ability to develop themselves through more equitable access to land

---

[15] The Treaty of Waitangi Amendment Act 1985, to amend section 6 of The Treaty of Waitangi Act 1975.

[16] Annual Report of the Department for Courts, 2001, 103.

[17] Ministry of Maori Development, Te Puni Kokiri, 'Progress Towards Closing Social and Economic Gaps Between Maori and Non-Maori', A Report to the Minister of Maori Affairs, 1998.

and other natural resources. The effects of the loss of land, with its allied loss of viable economic bases for Maori tribes over the last century, are exacerbated by the loss in employment in the last thirty years. This has all contributed to the impoverishment of Maori. However, balancing against these negative statistics are increased recognition of the importance of *te reo Maori* (Maori language), higher levels of Maori cultural awareness and pride, and the blossoming of Maori theatre and arts. The number of young Maori becoming fluent speakers and well versed in the culture is growing in a way not matched previously in the twentieth century. The recognition of Maori language, culture, and history by non-Maori is also increasing, especially amongst school children. Moreover, Maori business has seen growth that is unprecedented in modern times.

Maori grievances generally originate from the attitudes and actions of past generations. They are passed down to current generations, both through stories and histories and through the social, cultural, and economic conditions in which many Maori live today. The focus on past grievances is diverting the energies of many Maori away from pressing current social and economic needs and prevents Maori from taking control of their own futures. It is difficult to move beyond the historical grievance if that grievance is not acknowledged and resolved. In this respect, the Waitangi Tribunal provides an important forum in which grievances can be acknowledged and recommendations for resolution can be made.

While the present focus of the Tribunal is on historical claims, there are an increasing number of claims arising from contemporary government actions as well as claims relating to ownership and development of natural resources. In the course of an inquiry, and especially when conducting remedies hearings, the contemporary situation often becomes the focus. Contemporary grievances are more keenly felt as they affect people's everyday lives in a very direct sense. At present, however, contemporary claims are only heard if there is an urgent need that arises from an irreversible action that would prejudice a claimant. Priority is given, in the Tribunal, to investigation of historical grievances based on the Treaty.

The settlement of Treaty claims not only recognises the validity of historical claims, but also provides the certainty necessary for the development of New Zealand's economy. The Tribunal process of investigation and reporting provides the society with a clear basis for settlement of grievances, allowing the settlement negotiation process to move ahead progressively. In the longer term, the land and resources used in Treaty settlements can also help form an economic base for the Maori and address some of the social problems affecting their communities. In this way, the successful settlement of historical claims benefits both the claimant group and, indirectly, the non-Maori community in that area. The Tribunal influences the wider community significantly and non-

Maori New Zealanders are becoming more aware of the Treaty and the benefits of resolving claims for New Zealand society as a whole.

The Waitangi Tribunal has also attracted international interest as a mechanism for the development of human rights law relating to indigenous people. It is a forum in which issues such as land and cultural rights can be addressed and information made widely available. Conversely, the international arena has been an important influence in the development of thinking about the Treaty of Waitangi. Developments such as the adoption of the Draft Declaration of the Rights of Indigenous Peoples of 1993 and the overturning of the doctrine of *terra nullius* in the Mabo decision in Australia reflect significant ideological shifts in other countries.[18] Such developments generate a need for us to continuously review New Zealand's approach to the rights of indigenous peoples and Treaty issues. Even international trade agreements such as the GATT[19] are the subject of Treaty of Waitangi considerations and may well generate associated 'side-agreements' to deal with these issues.

4. COMPOSITION OF THE WAITANGI TRIBUNAL

The Waitangi Tribunal is a specialist body whose members are appointed for their knowledge and experience. The total membership reflects the partnership in the Treaty of Waitangi through an approximately equal representation of senior Maori and of Pakeha (non-Maori) of equivalent standing. Unlike court judges, Tribunal members are expected to bring a range of skills and previous knowledge of the matters likely to come before them. For example, in a hearing on historical claims there is at least one professional historian. Maori members of the Tribunal bring not only knowledge of Maori history and traditions, but often contribute to procedural decisions concerning processes appropriate to the Maori. Members are appointed for three-year terms. Appointments are made by the governor general on the recommendation of the minister of Maori affairs in consultation with the minister of justice.[20]

Members constitute a pool from which between three and seven are drawn for any one inquiry. As most members work for the Tribunal on a part-time

---

[18] United Nations, Draft Declaration on the Rights of Indigenous Peoples, 1993. The Draft Declaration was agreed upon by the members of the Working Group on Indigenous Populations (WGIP) established in 1982. The Working Group is a subsidiary organ of the Sub-Commission on the Prevention of Discrimination and Protection of Minorities, which itself is a subsidiary of the UN Commission on Human Rights. *Mabo* v. *Queensland (No 2)* (1992) 107 ALR 1.

[19] General Agreement on Tariffs and Trade.

[20] See s 4(2)(b) of the Treaty of Waitangi Act 1975

basis only, many have limited availability to hear a number of claims per year. The acting chairperson, Chief Judge Joe Williams, is also the chief judge of the Maori Land Court. Other judges of the Maori Land Court, while not members of the Tribunal, may preside at any Tribunal inquiry. Any member of the Tribunal with at least seven years standing as a barrister and solicitor of the High Court may also preside at an inquiry.

The Tribunal members receive administrative support from the Department for Courts (of which the Waitangi Tribunal administration is a part) and are also supported by approximately fifty staff from a variety of disciplines.

5. THE PARTIES

5.1 Representation of the Crown

As claims are against the Crown, it is necessary for the Crown to present its position before the Tribunal and it does that generally through the Crown Law Office (CLO). The CLO staff draw on the expertise of contracted historical researchers and specialists of government departments. CLO lawyers present the Crown case.

For claims under negotiation, the Office of Treaty Settlements coordinates the Crown side and prepares the Crown case, with advice from the CLO.

5.2 Maori representation: customary representation, modern representation, and level of representation

Establishing mandated representatives for tribal groups to negotiate settlements has been very difficult and a major impediment to the resolution of claims. Three inter-related aspects of this issue are: customary representation, modern representation and level of representation. The issue of customary representation raises the further issue of which *hapu* (sub-tribe) or *iwi* (tribe) has customary rights to a particular area of land or resources. The question of modern representation raises the issue of what modern bodies or associations should represent Maori and non-Maori groups. The level of representation raises the question of what matters are appropriately settled at the *hapu, iwi* and national level.

Two statutory mechanisms currently assist the Tribunal in its consideration of the issue of Maori representation. These are section 6A of the Treaty of Waitangi Act of 1975, which enables the Tribunal to refer a case on the question of customary representation to the Maori Appellate Court, and section 30 of the

Ture Whenua Maori Act of 1993,[21] that enables questions of modern day representation to be referred to the Maori Land Court at the request of any court, commission or tribunal, or the chief executive, or the judge of the Maori Land Court. The current Tribunal feels that it would be more helpful if customary issues were referred to the Maori Land Court in the first instance and to the Maori Appellate Court only on appeal. The Tribunal also believes, as with references under section 30, that the court should sit with additional members with expertise in Maori custom when hearing customary issues.

The question of customary representation is a most vexed issue that is spawned by the claims resolution process itself. Representation issues would be simplified if it were clear to claimants that all groups with proven claims are entitled to some compensation, and that compensation need not depend upon the definition of boundaries. Issues concerning the level of representation could be resolved by assuring adequate protection for, and recognition of, sub-groups in the settlement structure. The question of customary representation might also be alleviated by the staged restoration of tribal endowments within economically sustainable limits.

6. THE MANDATE AND POWERS OF THE WAITANGI TRIBUNAL

The principal function of the Waitangi Tribunal is to inquire into and report on claims by Maori[22] that 'any statute or regulation, or any past or present Crown policy, practice, act or omission is, or was, inconsistent with the principles of the Treaty of Waitangi and is prejudicial to an individual Maori or group of Maori' (section 6).[23] Where a claim is well founded, the Tribunal may recommend appropriate relief or the action required to prevent similar prejudice arising in the future (section 6(3)(4)).

The Tribunal also has the power to refer claims to mediation. A tribunal member, the director of the Tribunal or some other person can be appointed as mediator. Claimants can request that a mediator be appointed if they believe that the whole or major parts of their claim can be settled by mediation. Claims referred to mediation that cannot be settled in this way can still come back to the Tribunal for a full hearing. Filing a claim with the Waitangi Tribunal does not

---

[21] s30(1)(b) Te Ture Whenua Maori Act 1993 or The Maori Land Act 1993 is 'An Act to reform the laws relating to Maori land in accordance with the principles set out in the Preamble to this Act.'

[22] s5(1)(a) of the Treaty of Waitangi Act 1975.

[23] The references in brackets in this and the following paragraphs are to sections of the Treaty of Waitangi Act 1975.

prevent claimants from opening or continuing negotiations with the Crown over any matter in the claim.

The Tribunal's recommendations are not usually binding on the Crown. However, since 1988, the Tribunal has been able to make binding recommendations for the transfer to Maori of certain state lands assets (principally state enterprise and education assets, forest lands and certain railway lands) including those sold to third parties (ss.8B and 8HC). These recommendations effectively mature as orders (see also section X on the implementation of Tribunal recommendations). In addition, parliament may refer bills to the Tribunal to report on their possible inconsistency with the Treaty, although this has yet to happen (section 8). The Tribunal also has exclusive authority to determine the 'meaning and effect' of the Treaty of Waitangi (s.5).

7. Claims, Claims Management and Research

The claims received by the Tribunal can be classified as: historical (arising from past Government actions); contemporary (arising from current government actions); and conceptual (generic claims mostly relating to 'ownership' of natural resources). *Historical claims* include: confirmations of pre-Treaty purchases; Crown (and some private) purchases till 1865 under Crown-Maori negotiations; Crown and private purchases under the Native Land Court system; land confiscations and expropriations (including public works); title arrangements and land development under the Native Land Court system; and tribal autonomy. One tribal claim may encompass all or many of these issues. *Current claims* include destruction of traditional fisheries, significant or sacred site protection, foreshore and seabed, island rocks and underwater sites, geothermal resources[24] and a variety of water resources such as lakes, rivers, springs along with forests and even mountain peaks. *Conceptual claims* may deal with the Maori language, access to justice, social welfare funding, broadcasting (both television and radio as a means to disseminate language), and many of the elements of government policy including the claims settlement policies themselves.

Given the large number of claims before the Tribunal at any one time, it is essential that priorities are set. Large historical claims currently take precedence over contemporary claims.[25] The Tribunal is continuously developing

---

[24] Geothermal resources include superheated water and steam from underground, heated pools, heated mud and geothermal minerals carried with the heated water.

[25] The Tribunal is aware that it influences the order in which claims are heard through its allocation of research funding, and that the seriatim hearing of claims has created inequities, advantaging those claims that are first heard and reported on.

more efficient ways to manage and research the large number of historical claims now registered with it. It has developed several initiatives over the last ten years to assist in the efficient management of claims.[26] These initiatives have resulted in a complex inquiry process in which the various Maori districts pursue

---

[26] The first was the Rangahaua Whanui (to research broadly) research program, set-up in 1993 and completed in 1997. The purpose of this programme was to establish a broader context for considering issues arising from claims. The focus of the programme was on loss of Maori land. For the purposes of the programme, the country was divided into fifteen geographical districts, and the research needs for each district were determined. In addition to research on these districts, eighteen national themes were also identified and researched. The national themes include: inland waterways; the trust administration of Maori reserves; goldfields and other mining policy and legislation; foreshores; public works takings; and Tino Rangatiratanga: Maori in the political and administrative system. The objectives of this program were to provide equal research time to all historical claims, to explore issues germane to several claims, to avoid research duplication, and to obtain a national overview of the claims position.

A second initiative, the 'casebook method' aimed at improving the efficiency of the claims process by ensuring that all claims are adequately researched in advance of the commencement of hearings. Further, to comply with the rules of natural justice and for reasons of efficiency and economy, the Tribunal grouped for concurrent inquiry all claims which affect or relate to the assets of a particular area. For example, historical claims involving tribal resources are heard with all claims relating to those resources. Under the casebook approach, research for claims with a common set of interests and issues in an area is completed prior to the first hearing.

In 2000, the Tribunal developed a faster and more effective inquiry process, with an emphasis on adding value to the settlement of claims via direct Crown-claimant negotiations. The new approach introduced interlocutory conferences to clarify the factual basis of the case and the issues in agreement in an early stage, to isolate and define the contested issues, and then have a fast, efficient hearing on the matters in dispute. It also provided ways assess claimant representation and to stop the proliferation of small, identical claims, both of which were slowing the standard district inquiries.

The new approach sought to address issues of mandate and representation, which have been a significant obstacle to settlements, as early as possible in the process. The issues of representation are dealt with by the Tribunal in an open and transparent manner. The people (claimant community) can see their leaders perform and endorse (or not) their leadership. Representation continues to be addressed through the process in a way that reinforces the tribal leadership but gives the claimant community a chance to challenge that before the people.

The new approach is aimed at not only making the Tribunal process more compact, but also to reduce the time in the settlement process carried out by the Office of Treaty Settlements. The Tribunal's new approach and its later developments are expected to reduce the overall costs associated with the hearing and settlement negotiation processes by reducing the indirect costs of duplication and delay and the direct costs of disputes to claimants and the Crown.

In 2001-2002, some parties approached the Tribunal with requests for further tailoring of the Tribunal's process in their districts. After careful consideration, the Tribunal has proposed a modification of its new approach in the Central North Island districts. The possible tailoring of the Tribunal's inquiry to the needs of parties in a district may be extended to others on request.

The result is a complex inquiry process in which some districts are still going through the original district casebook process, some are following the path of the new approach, and others are or may pursue quicker, tailored versions of the new approach.

inquiry processes that are tailored to their particular needs. At the same time, these inquiry processes have in common that they are: fair to all parties, public and transparent, and carried out with an appropriate evidential base. They also provide a report to parties on the claims and add significant value to the negotiation and settlement of claims.

The Tribunal has many requests for urgent contemporary hearings. In these cases claimants and the Crown may be heard on whether urgency should be granted. The Tribunal endeavours to hear cases where the contemporary government action complained of may have some irreversible consequence. Requests for urgency are submitted on a regular basis and a determination is made on each to see if it gets heard. Some have been declined. The Tribunal does not grant urgency to accommodate illegal occupations and will not generally intervene on matters that are, or could be, the subject of court proceedings.

Historical research is a vital part of the Treaty claims settlement process. The inquiry into claims involves considerable historical interpretation. It is therefore important that the Tribunal has the benefit of well-prepared and documented arguments. The maintenance of the Tribunal's own research capacity and a strong research unit within the Crown Law Office are seen as essential, as is the maintenance of the Crown Forestry Rental Trust's large research capacity. The Tribunal also funds claimants to conduct their own research. This has produced some work of uneven quality that has generated extra auditing costs. On the other hand, the engagement of professionals, while more cost efficient, has left claimants rightly complaining of the capture of their claims by academics.

Research to date suggests there is not one tribal group without a valid claim of one sort or another. This was apparent to the Tribunal as early as 1987 and led the Tribunal to believe that the most practical course was to concentrate on positive programmes for the restoration of the economic base of the tribes according to appropriate tribal groupings. There is nothing in subsequent research to cause the Tribunal to resile from that opinion.

8. The Two-Phase Claims Settlement Process

Claims generally proceed through two stages. The first is an inquiry on the facts and a full report of the results of the inquiry by the Tribunal. Nearly all well-founded claims proceed to the second stage and are negotiated directly with the Crown, through the Office of Treaty Settlements, usually after the completion of the Tribunal process. Exceptions are claims settled in mediation and claims in which the Tribunal exercises its powers to hold a hearing on remedies and to make recommendations that in time bind the Crown. In case negotiations are not preferred or if they fail, parties are heard on remedies and the Tribunal reports its recommendations.

Both stages of the Treaty of Waitangi Act claims settlement process: a) the Waitangi Tribunal inquiry and reporting process and, b) the process of bilateral negotiations between Maori representatives and the Crown through the Office of Treaty Settlements are described below.

8.1 The Waitangi Tribunal inquiry and reporting process

Any Maori may lodge a claim, either as an individual or on behalf of a group of claimants. Once a written claim is lodged, the registrar assesses whether the requirements of the Treaty of Waitangi Act have been satisfied. These requirements include that the applicant be a Maori[27] and that the act(s) or omission(s) of the Crown on which his or her claim will rely be specified. If these requirements have not been met, the claim is referred back to the claimant for further information. Otherwise, the Tribunal issues a direction that the matter be registered as a claim by allocating a number to it and placing it on the Tribunal's register of claims.

8.1.1 *Preparations for the hearing*

The Tribunal both researches the claims itself and provides funding for claimants to research their claims.[28] Once all issues arising in all related claims have been researched, compiled into a casebook, filed with the Tribunal and made available to all parties, the claim is ready for hearing.[29] This process usually takes a number of years. Both the claimants and the Crown then have the opportunity to select the venue for the hearing of their respective submissions. The presiding officer of the panel hearing the claim and the legal counsel also hold conferences before and during the hearing to determine procedural matters such as the order in which submissions will be heard.

8.1.2 *The hearing*

The hearing normally proceeds as follows: the claimant group(s) state(s) their claim; claimant and/or Tribunal researchers speak to the main themes of their reports; the Tribunal receives submissions from other interested parties who

---

[27] For the purposes of the Treaty of Waitangi Act 1975 a Maori is defined as being the descendant of a Maori.

[28] Another potential source for claimant funding is the Crown Forestry Rental Trust, established under the Crown Forest Assets Act in 1989. Civil legal aid may be obtained through the Legal Services Board.

[29] If necessary, the claim can be amended once this research has been completed.

have requested to be heard; the Crown responds to the submissions and claimant evidence; the claimants reply. The Tribunal may commission further research, make further inquiries, or commission an opinion on the evidence heard to that point, as it sees fit. Then the Crown and claimants counsel present their closing arguments. Throughout the hearing there is an opportunity for the Tribunal and other parties to question the evidence given and submissions made.

Although bound by the rules of natural justice and subject to High Court review, the Tribunal is not limited to the evidence and argument of the parties. It may receive material that would not be accepted as evidence by the courts. Cross-examination is permitted and is usual, although it is not encouraged for those giving traditional evidence, usually elders. It is usually the case that the evidence of *kaumatua* (elders) is in the nature of contextual evidence, which should not be subject to legal argument. If in fact the evidence does go to the particular issues of a claim it may be subject to cross-examination as would the expert evidence of historians.

Claims must fit the broad parameters of the Tribunal's jurisdiction, but need not have the specificity of court pleadings, nor is the Crown obliged to file a statement of defence. Issues generally emerge during the inquiry and are collated prior to final legal submissions. However, a practice is developing where issues are identified earlier in the process. Because the Tribunal is a commission of inquiry, it may hear anyone who has an interest greater than the public at large. Public notices are given and members of the public regularly make submissions at hearings. Those with special interests may be treated as third parties.

The Tribunal is able to set its own special procedures. It may adopt Maori hearing protocols and hearings are generally held on the *marae* (traditional community centres).[30] In practice, the Tribunal tries to balance the legal domain and the Maori domain. Although Maori protocol precedes the start of each week of hearings and concludes them, much of the hearing process itself is like a court with presentation and examination addressed through counsel representing the parties. The Tribunal often hears evidence given in Maori and accompanied by *waiata*, a song usually written for the occasion to compliment the evidence. The Tribunal may also refer cases on a question of law to the general courts and cases on questions of custom to the Maori Appellate Court.

---

[30] *Marae* refers to the collective of buildings and land that have formed the centre of each Maori community from pre-European times. They generally include a large meeting house (Wharenui) where hearings are conducted and a forecourt (*marae atea*) where ritual greetings are performed prior to the hearings.

8.1.3 *The Tribunal report with findings and recommendations*

When the hearing is complete, the Tribunal considers whether the claim is well founded. Sometimes it issues an interim report on its findings, and it may recommend that the Crown and claimants negotiate a settlement of the claim. The Tribunal can also offer to assist the negotiation by holding further hearings on remedies. Where the Tribunal issues a final report including detailed recommendations on remedies, the Crown decides whether to put recommendations into effect, and if so, how. There is no further Tribunal involvement in the claims settlement process following the final report.

8.2 The bilateral negotiation process

Once the Tribunal has reported to the government and the claimants on an inquiry of a claim, the claimants will move from the judicially driven Tribunal process into the politically driven negotiated settlement process run by the Office of Treaty Settlements. Aspects of this process include: Crown assessment of the claims, mandating, formulating the deed of mandate, funding, reaching agreement on the terms of negotiation, reaching an 'agreement in principle' or signing a 'heads of agreement', agreeing on the deed of settlement, settlement legislation, statutory acknowledgements, deeds of recognition, and protocols, all of which are described below.

8.2.1 *Crown assessment of claims*

The Crown assesses the claimant's research to establish whether it clearly sets out the breaches of the Treaty, the proof thereof and whether it covers the issues over which the claimants seek to negotiate. The Tribunal's report is the usual starting point for this and is often sufficient to move to the next step. The Crown agrees the claims are well-founded and confirms claimants are large natural groups.

8.2.2 *Mandating*

Mandating is the process by which the claimant group chooses representatives and gives them the authority to enter into discussions and agreements with the Crown on their behalf. Sometimes the claimant group may confirm the mandate of an existing representative organisation. The mandate gives the representatives authority to appoint negotiators.[31] The Crown has developed a procedure

---

[31] Office of Treaty Settlements, 'Healing the past, building a future', 2003, 41-53.

to verify that it is dealing with the right claimant group representatives, that the representatives are properly mandated to negotiate a settlement, that they have a process to ensure accountability and a process to identify as many members of the claimant group as possible.

8.2.3 *Deed of mandate*

This is a formal statement prepared by the claimant group, which describes what the mandate covers and how it was approved. It furthermore defines the claimant group, states the claims that are intended to be settled, identifies the area to which the claim relates and states who has the authority to represent the claimant group in negotiations.

8.2.4 *The Crown negotiation team*

The Crown negotiating team is made up of officials from the Office of Treaty Settlements, the Treasury and the Department of Conservation in the main, and negotiates on behalf of the minister in charge of Treaty of Waitangi negotiations and other ministers.

8.2.5 *Funding*

The Crown contributes towards certain expenses for mandated groups, including costs related to the processes of establishing the mandate, agreeing on the terms of negotiation and starting formal negotiations. Costs related to reaching a draft deed of settlement and the development of a post-settlement governance entity are also covered, as well as the cost of ratification to confirm a deed of settlement. This funding is over and above any settlement.

8.2.6 *Terms of negotiation*

A set of terms of negotiation needs to be agreed on prior to the start of the negotiations, featuring the objectives of both the Crown and the claimant. The terms also state that after reaching a settlement of all the historical claims of the claimant group, neither the courts nor the Waitangi Tribunal will be able to consider the issues in the settlement. A settlement is full and final.[32]

---

[32] The findings of the Waitangi Tribunal cannot generally be appealed to higher courts except on judicial review. Negotiated settlements all contain terms precluding the ability to take any part of the deed of settlement or the settlement legislation into the courts.

Both Crown and claimants will develop negotiating briefs. Objectives of the Crown include that settlements be comprehensive and settle all the claimant group's historical claims, that they remove the sense of grievance, be fair and durable and provide a foundation for an improved relationship between the Crown and the claimant group. While the claimants' objectives will vary considerably from one claimant group to another, most will be looking to establish a sufficient economic base to sustain income to support all of the *marae* and to support objectives such as education, health and the welfare of the tribe.

A claimant's brief usually clarifies what breaches and prejudice claimants consider should be included. It describes the affected land area and culturally important sites as well as the commercial asset interests and resolves issues regarding other claimant group interests in a site. This may be very detailed for larger claimant groups and include a detailed approach to negotiating relationships with both government departments and local government bodies. The negotiating brief sets out the tribe's aspirations in the negotiation process particularly with respect to specific pieces of land the tribe wishes to own, have control over, or have an influence over. These areas often include conservation land held by the government.

8.2.7   'Agreement in principle' and 'heads of agreement'

Once the broad outline of a settlement is agreed on there can be an exchange of letters to achieve an agreement in principle. A more formal and time-consuming approach is for the parties to sign a heads of agreement. Either of these documents becomes public.

8.2.8   Deed of settlement

A deed of settlement is the comprehensive and final agreement between the Crown and the claimant group. It sets out in detail the redress the Crown will give to the claimant group in order to settle their claims. The redress may include the Crown's acknowledgement and apology, payment of cash, the transfer of lands within the claims area, and mechanisms for recognising other important interests that the claimant group may have. The deed can also include the parties' intentions regarding the ongoing treaty relationship between the Crown and the claimant group. The cabinet approves the content of a deed of settlement, before it is initialled by mandated representatives, and prior to ratification by the wider claimant group.

8.2.9 *Settlement legislation*

Usually, legislation is required for the deed to become unconditional. Prior to the introduction of legislation the claimant group will have ratified and established a governance entity to hold and manage the settlement assets. Settlement legislation follows faithfully the deed of settlement agreed by the claimant group and the cabinet for the government. The legislation is an act that binds the government, however it is not entrenched legislation. The settlement legislation will often amend other legislation to have effect.

8.2.10 *Statutory acknowledgements and deeds of recognition*

The Crown may agree in a settlement to acknowledge in legislation a statement by the claimant group of their special association with an area or feature. Because of the Crown's recognition of the association of the claimant group with the site or feature, the statutory acknowledgement strengthens the notification provisions of the Resource Management Act of 1991, which regulates the management of many natural and physical resources such as fresh water, land and air and controls environmental effects.[33]

If a statutory acknowledgement has been made, the minister of the Crown responsible for managing the area may also enter into a deed of recognition over the land under management. A deed of recognition will provide that the claimant group must be consulted on specific matters and that the relevant minister must have regard to their views.

8.2.11 *Protocols*

A protocol is a statement issued by a minister of the Crown or other statutory authority, that sets out how a particular government agency intends to interact with a claimant group so that the latter can have input into the decision-making process of that government agency, and exercise its functions, powers and duties in relation to specified matters within its control.

9. SUBSTANCE OF SETTLEMENTS

Settlements may involve an acknowledgement and apology from the government stating the past wrongs they are compensating for; compensation in the

---

[33] Many aspects of a claim and the settlement of those claims involve natural resources. This does not include fish (fresh and sea species) or Crown minerals which are regulated in other legislation.

form of money and the transfer of lands and a variety of water resources including important sites within the claims area; mechanisms for recognising other important interests that the claimant group may have, like language issues and access to justice and social welfare funding; agreements on the parties' intentions regarding ongoing relationships between Crown entities and Maori claimant groups; and the establishment of tribal governance entities with a certain degree of autonomy and self-management.

An example of a relationship protocol was established in the deed of settlement for Ngati Ruanui with the ministry of fisheries. The protocol is issued by a minister of the Crown setting out how the particular agency intends to:

- exercise its functions, powers and duties in relation to specific matters within its control in the claimant group's area;
- interact with the claimant group on a continuing basis and enable that group to have input into its decision-making process.

To illustrate the latter point, prior to the settlement of an other claim, the large Ngai Tahu claim, and as a part of the settlement process, Ngai Tahu negotiated to get an enabling piece of legislation called the Te Runanga o Ngai Tahu Act which established a senate-like governance structure called a Runanganui with representatives from their 'sub-states' called papatipu runanga. This was a very significant move to provide Ngai Tahu with a high degree of tribal autonomy.

10. IMPLEMENTATION OF TRIBUNAL RECOMMENDATIONS AND SETTLEMENTS RESULTING FROM BILATERAL NEGOTIATIONS

The minister of Maori affairs receives the Tribunal's reports and the Ministry of Maori Development monitors and reports annually on the implementation of the Tribunal's recommendations. These annual reports – though not issued for a number of years now – are addressed to the parliament and become public when tabled. In general the government has no obligation to implement Waitangi Tribunal recommendations. However, as discussed earlier in section 6 above, since 1988, the Tribunal has been able to make binding recommendations for the transfer to Maori of certain state lands assets (principally state enterprise and education assets, forest lands and certain railway lands), including those sold to third parties These recommendations effectively mature as orders. Furthermore, successive governments have agreed to deal with most historical claims through the direct bilateral negotiation process provided for.

Mechanisms to monitor the implementation of the settlements are still being developed. Within the settlement legislation[34] some provisions are made concerning the fiduciary responsibilities of the government with regard to the settlements. The government has a duty to ensure that tribes do not, through their own mismanagement, put the economic base acquired in a settlement at risk. By and large tribes are able to utilise their settlement assets freely with a minimum of restriction.

The durability of settlements, which means that they are full and final, is considered of great importance by the government and probably by the settling tribes as well. Durability comes from the settlement negotiations and from the way the assets are used after the settlement. Durability from the negotiation process can be ensured by careful inclusion in the settlement of assets and of mechanisms which address the key grievances. The Waitangi Tribunal reports often provide guidance on these issues. The selection and training of suitable people for leadership roles in the governance entity to be established to manage the settlement assets (and other aspects of the settlement) is all important for the durability of any settlement. It is also essential that the tribes have sufficient economic base to draw their own people out of both the public and private sector to work for the tribe.

11. PRIVY COUNCIL

The Privy Council in Britain has been the highest court of appeal in Aotearoa/ New Zealand since the establishment of the colonial government in the nineteenth century. The Privy Council is made up of the Law Lords, who are members of the British House of Lords. Maori, rightly or wrongly, have seen the Privy Council as one of the embodiments of the Crown. Maori often likened an appeal to the Privy Council as an appeal directly to 'The Crown', that is, to the British monarch. A limited number of appeals are granted leave to go to the Privy Council from New Zealand courts. In the entire history of appeals to the Privy Council (established in 1833) there have only been sixteen cases taken on specific Maori or Treaty issues and of these only six have been successful. In recent times the Maori cases have largely been sent back to the New Zealand Court of Appeal. These can include appeals from cases in the New Zealand Court of Appeal and in the Maori Appellate Court. Cases from the Waitangi Tribunal cannot go directly to the Privy Council but must go through either of these courts. Twelve New Zealand judges have sat on the Privy Council over the years, and some of them sat on New Zealand cases.

---

[34] See also subsection 8.2.9 (Settlement Legislation) above.

In a very recent development, the New Zealand government has voted to do away with appeals to the Privy Council in London in favour of a Supreme Court based in New Zealand and made up only of local judges.

12. Conclusions

The Treaty of Waitangi has been used and abused in its 163 years of existence. The Treaty was abused by the British colonisers to impose their rule on the Maori and to alienate and appropriate Maori land. It was put aside as 'a simple nullity' by Chief Judge Prendergast in 1877, when adjudicating a land claim between a Maori chief and the Church of England.[35] In practice, the Treaty did remain a simple nullity, legally and politically, until the enactment of the Treaty of Waitangi Act in 1975. With the establishment of the Waitangi Tribunal, which conducts its inquiries on the basis of the Treaty, and the negotiation process that leads to settlements between Maori groups and the Crown, the implementation of the Treaty has become the basis of an important process of dispute resolution between the Crown and the Maori people today.

The Treaty of Waitangi Settlement Act process for the settlement of Maori claims through the Waitangi Tribunal inquiry and reporting process and through bilateral negotiations between the Crown and Maori groups has developed extensively over the last twenty-five years. Although settlements still take a considerable amount of time to conclude there is now a much greater certainty that a reasonable outcome will result from the process. Settlements do not just involve compensation in the form of money and land, but include significant agreements on ongoing relationships between Crown entities and Maori claimant groups.

Settlements negotiated between the government (Crown) and Maori tribes also involve the establishment of tribal governance entities which may be said to be tribal governments. These tribal entities are not truly sovereign as they are subject to the state; however they do have a degree of autonomy and self-management. Although they relate to a territory (*takiwa*), within such a territory there is usually a large non-Maori community, often including cities and towns.

The settlement deeds and the associated legislation are agreements between tribal groups and the government that compensate for past wrongs and usually

---

[35] 1877 3 NZ Jur R (NS) SC 72. This case was between Wi Parata (a Legislative Councillor) and the Bishop of Wellington. For some time, efforts had been made to have a land grant revert to its former Maori owners because the terms of the original grant (that was to be used for educational purposes) were not being fulfilled. In giving his decision, Chief Justice James Prendergast declared that the treaty was a legal 'nullity' because it had not been incorporated in domestic law.

include a specific apology from the government stating the past wrongs they are compensating for. The settlements often establish a sustainable economic base for a tribe. They do not usually compensate individuals, but they may well provide for smaller groupings within any particular settlement if that is appropriate and is negotiated.

The Tribunal has heard and reported on claims covering ninety percent of the South Island of New Zealand which, by area, accounts for nearly half of the landmass of Aotearoa/New Zealand. In terms of the Maori population, just over twenty percent has completed the Tribunal process. Eight percent of these have received a settlement.[36] In the next ten to fifteen years we are likely to see the conclusion of settlements of most of the historical Treaty claims in Aotearoa/New Zealand. What that process will have achieved will be the establishment of strong Maori entities (tribal governments) with significant asset bases and clear relationships with the government and their communities to ensure that settlements will endure. This will allow Maori as tribes to move on from historical grievance and develop a high degree of economic and political independence within the overall state.

The process seems long and complex, just as the nature of the historical grievances it is set-up to redress. Although it is a work in progress, there is considerable optimism from those involved in the process. Casual observers from the outside may be critical or even claim the process is racist, elitist and just plain wrong. Driven by a strong sense of social justice, however, successive governments of different political persuasions in Aotearoa/New Zealand have committed to completing the process within a reasonable timeframe, so as to settle much of the anger generated in the colonial period.

---

[36] Ministry of Justice, 'Annual Report', 2001.

Appendices

A   Northern Ireland Peace Agreement: The Agreement reached in the multi-party negotiations, 10 April 1998
B   Agreement of the Central People's Government and the Local Government of Tibet on Measures for the Peaceful Liberation of Tibet, 23 May 1951
C   Chittagong Hill Tracts Accord, 2 December 1997
D   De Gasperi-Gruber Agreement (Paris Treaty), 5 September 1946
E   Macedonia Framework Agreement, 13 August 2001
F   Convention for the Protection of the Marine Environment of the North-East Atlantic, 22 September 1992
G   United Nations Convention on the Law of the Sea, 10 December 1982
H   General Framework Agreement for Peace in Bosnia and Herzegovina, 14 December 1995
I   Introductory Note – Arbitral Tribunal for the Dispute over Inter-entity Boundary in Brcko Area: the Federation of Bosnia and Herzegovina v. the Republika Srpska – Final Award (5 March 1999)
J   Eritrea-Yemen Arbitration Agreement, 3 October 1996
K   Government of the State of Eritrea v. Government of the Republic of Yemen, Award of the Arbitral Tribunal in the First Stage (Territorial Sovereignty and Scope of the Dispute), 9 October 1998
L   Larsen v. the Hawaiian Kingdom, Arbitration Award, 5 February 2001
M   Permanent Court of Arbitration Optional Rules for Arbitrating Disputes between Two Parties of Which Only One Is a State (effective 6 July 1993)
N   Treaty of Waitangi, 6 February 1840 (English and Maori texts)

Appendix A
The Northern Ireland Peace Agreement:
The Agreement reached in the multi-party negotiations, 10 April 1998[*]

Extracts

DECLARATION OF SUPPORT
  1. We, the participants in the multi-party negotiations, believe that the agreement we have negotiated offers a truly historic opportunity for a new beginning.
  2. The tragedies of the past have left a deep and profoundly regrettable legacy of suffering. We must never forget those who have died or been injured, and their families. But we can best honour them through a fresh start, in which we firmly dedicate ourselves to the achievement of reconciliation, tolerance, and mutual trust, and to the protection and vindication of the human rights of all.
  3. We are committed to partnership, equality and mutual respect as the basis of relationships within Northern Ireland, between North and South, and between these islands.
  4. We reaffirm our total and absolute commitment to exclusively democratic and peaceful means of resolving differences on political issues, and our opposition to any use or threat of force by others for any political purpose, whether in regard to this agreement or otherwise.
  5. We acknowledge the substantial differences between our continuing, and equally legitimate, political aspirations. However, we will endeavour to strive in every practical way towards reconciliation and rapprochement within the framework of democratic and agreed arrangements. We pledge that we will, in good faith, work to ensure the success of each and every one of the arrangements to be established under this agreement. It is accepted that all of the institutional and constitutional arrangements – an Assembly in Northern Ireland, a North/South Ministerial Council, implementation bodies, a British-Irish Council and a British-Irish Intergovernmental Conference and any amendments to British Acts of Parliament and the Constitution of Ireland – are interlocking and interdependent and that in particular the functioning of the Assembly and the North/South Council are so closely inter-related that the success of each depends on that of the other.
  6. Accordingly, in a spirit of concord, we strongly commend this agreement to the people, North and South, for their approval.
  […]

STRAND ONE
DEMOCRATIC INSTITUTIONS IN NORTHERN IRELAND
  1. This agreement provides for a democratically elected Assembly in Northern Ireland which is inclusive in its membership, capable of exercising executive and legislative authority, and subject to safeguards to protect the rights and interests of all sides of the community.
  […]
  Transitional Arrangements
  35. The Assembly will meet first for the purpose of organisation, without legislative or executive powers, to resolve its standing orders and working practices and make preparations

---

[*] Source: United States Institute of Peace, <http://www.usip.org/library/pa/ni/nitoc.html> (2 Aug. 2006).

for the effective functioning of the Assembly, the British-Irish Council and the North/South Ministerial Council and associated implementation bodies. In this transitional period, those members of the Assembly serving as shadow ministers shall affirm their commitment to non-violence and exclusively peaceful and democratic means and their opposition to any use or threat of force by others for any political purpose; to work in good faith to bring the new arrangements into being; and to observe the spirit of the Pledge of Office applying to appointed ministers.

Review

36. After a specified period there will be a review of these arrangements, including the details of electoral arrangements and of the Assembly's procedures, with a view to agreeing any adjustments necessary in the interests of efficiency and fairness.

[...]

STRAND TWO
NORTH/SOUTH MINISTERIAL COUNCIL

1. Under a new British/Irish Agreement dealing with the totality of relationships, and related legislation at Westminster and in the Oireachtas, a North/South Ministerial Council to be established to bring together those with executive responsibilities in Northern Ireland and the Irish Government, to develop consultation, co-operation and action within the island of Ireland – including through implementation on an all-island and cross-border basis – on matters of mutual interest within the competence of the Administrations, North and South.

2. All Council decisions to be by agreement between the two sides. Northern Ireland to be represented by the First Minister, Deputy First Minister and any relevant Ministers, the Irish Government by the Taoiseach and relevant Ministers, all operating in accordance with the rules for democratic authority and accountability in force in the Northern Ireland Assembly and the Oireachtas respectively. Participation in the Council to be one of the essential responsibilities attaching to relevant posts in the two Administrations. If a holder of a relevant post will not participate normally in the Council, the Taoiseach in the case of the Irish Government and the First and Deputy First Minister in the case of the Northern Ireland Administration to be able to make alternative arrangements.

3. The Council to meet in different formats:

(i) in plenary format twice a year, with Northern Ireland representation led by the First Minister and Deputy First Minister and the Irish Government led by the Taoiseach;

(ii) in specific sectoral formats on a regular and frequent basis with each side represented by the appropriate Minister;

(iii) in an appropriate format to consider institutional or cross-sectoral matters (including in relation to the EU) and to resolve disagreement.

4. Agendas for all meetings to be settled by prior agreement between the two sides, but it will be open to either to propose any matter for consideration or action.

5. The Council:

(i) to exchange information, discuss and consult with a view to co-operating on matters of mutual interest within the competence of both Administrations, North and South;

(ii) to use best endeavours to reach agreement on the adoption of common policies, in areas where there is a mutual cross-border and all-island benefit, and which are within the competence of both Administrations, North and South, making determined efforts to overcome any disagreements;

(iii) to take decisions by agreement on policies for implementation separately in each jurisdiction, in relevant meaningful areas within the competence of both Administrations, North and South;

APPENDIX A 257

(iv) to take decisions by agreement on policies and action at an all-island and cross-border level to be implemented by the bodies to be established as set out in paragraphs 8 and 9 below.

6. Each side to be in a position to take decisions in the Council within the defined authority of those attending, through the arrangements in place for co-ordination of executive functions within each jurisdiction. Each side to remain accountable to the Assembly and Oireachtas respectively, whose approval, through the arrangements in place on either side, would be required for decisions beyond the defined authority of those attending.

7. As soon as practically possible after elections to the Northern Ireland Assembly, inaugural meetings will take place of the Assembly, the British/Irish Council and the North/South Ministerial Council in their transitional forms. All three institutions will meet regularly and frequently on this basis during the period between the elections to the Assembly, and the transfer of powers to the Assembly, in order to establish their modus operandi.

8. During the transitional period between the elections to the Northern Ireland Assembly and the transfer of power to it, representatives of the Northern Ireland transitional Administration and the Irish Government operating in the North/South Ministerial Council will undertake a work programme, in consultation with the British Government, covering at least 12 subject areas, with a view to identifying and agreeing by 31 October 1998 areas where co-operation and implementation for mutual benefit will take place. Such areas may include matters in the list set out in the Annex.

9. As part of the work programme, the Council will identify and agree at least 6 matters for co-operation and implementation in each of the following categories:
(i) Matters where existing bodies will be the appropriate mechanisms for co-operation in each separate jurisdiction;
(ii) Matters where the co-operation will take place through agreed implementation bodies on a cross-border or all-island level.

10. The two Governments will make necessary legislative and other enabling preparations to ensure, as an absolute commitment, that these bodies, which have been agreed as a result of the work programme, function at the time of the inception of the British-Irish Agreement and the transfer of powers, with legislative authority for these bodies transferred to the Assembly as soon as possible thereafter. Other arrangements for the agreed co-operation will also commence contemporaneously with the transfer of powers to the Assembly.

11. The implementation bodies will have a clear operational remit. They will implement on an all-island and cross-border basis policies agreed in the Council.

12. Any further development of these arrangements to be by agreement in the Council and with the specific endorsement of the Northern Ireland Assembly and Oireachtas, subject to the extent of the competences and responsibility of the two Administrations.

13. It is understood that the North/South Ministerial Council and the Northern Ireland Assembly are mutually inter-dependent, and that one cannot successfully function without the other.

14. Disagreements within the Council to be addressed in the format described at paragraph 3(iii) above or in the plenary format. By agreement between the two sides, experts could be appointed to consider a particular matter and report.

15. Funding to be provided by the two Administrations on the basis that the Council and the implementation bodies constitute a necessary public function.

16. The Council to be supported by a standing joint Secretariat, staffed by members of the Northern Ireland Civil Service and the Irish Civil Service.

17. The Council to consider the European Union dimension of relevant matters, including the implementation of EU policies and programmes and proposals under consideration in the

EU framework. Arrangements to be made to ensure that the views of the Council are taken into account and represented appropriately at relevant EU meetings.

18. The Northern Ireland Assembly and the Oireachtas to consider developing a joint parliamentary forum, bringing together equal numbers from both institutions for discussion of matters of mutual interest and concern.

19. Consideration to be given to the establishment of an independent consultative forum appointed by the two Administrations, representative of civil society, comprising the social partners and other members with expertise in social, cultural, economic and other issues.

ANNEX

Areas for North-South co-operation and implementation may include the following:
1. Agriculture – animal and plant health.
2. Education – teacher qualifications and exchanges.
3. Transport – strategic transport planning.
4. Environment – environmental protection, pollution, water quality, and waste management.
5. Waterways – inland waterways.
6. Social Security/Social Welfare – entitlements of cross-border workers and fraud control.
7. Tourism – promotion, marketing, research, and product development.
8. Relevant EU Programmes such as SPPR, INTERREG, Leader II and their successors.
9. Inland Fisheries.
10. Aquaculture and marine matters
11. Health: accident and emergency services and other related cross-border issues.
12. Urban and rural development.
Others to be considered by the shadow North/ South Council.

STRAND THREE
BRITISH-IRISH COUNCIL

1. A British-Irish Council (BIC) will be established under a new British-Irish Agreement to promote the harmonious and mutually beneficial development of the totality of relationships among the peoples of these islands.

2. Membership of the BIC will comprise representatives of the British and Irish Governments, devolved institutions in Northern Ireland, Scotland and Wales, when established, and, if appropriate, elsewhere in the United Kingdom, together with representatives of the Isle of Man and the Channel Islands.

3. The BIC will meet in different formats: at summit level, twice per year; in specific sectoral formats on a regular basis, with each side represented by the appropriate Minister; in an appropriate format to consider cross-sectoral matters.

4. Representatives of members will operate in accordance with whatever procedures for democratic authority and accountability are in force in their respective elected institutions.

5. The BIC will exchange information, discuss, consult and use best endeavours to reach agreement on co-operation on matters of mutual interest within the competence of the relevant Administrations. Suitable issues for early discussion in the BIC could include transport links, agricultural issues, environmental issues, cultural issues, health issues, education issues and approaches to EU issues. Suitable arrangements to be made for practical co-operation on agreed policies.

6. It will be open to the BIC to agree common policies or common actions. Individual members may opt not to participate in such common policies and common action.

7. The BIC normally will operate by consensus. In relation to decisions on common policies or common actions, including their means of implementation, it will operate by agreement of all members participating in such policies or actions.

8. The members of the BIC, on a basis to be agreed between them, will provide such financial support as it may require.

9. A secretariat for the BIC will be provided by the British and Irish Governments in co-ordination with officials of each of the other members.

10. In addition to the structures provided for under this agreement, it will be open to two or more members to develop bilateral or multilateral arrangements between them. Such arrangements could include, subject to the agreement of the members concerned, mechanisms to enable consultation, co-operation and joint decision-making on matters of mutual interest; and mechanisms to implement any joint decisions they may reach. These arrangements will not require the prior approval of the BIC as a whole and will operate independently of it.

11. The elected institutions of the members will be encouraged to develop interparliamentary links, perhaps building on the British-Irish Interparliamentary Body.

12. The full membership of the BIC will keep under review the workings of the Council, including a formal published review at an appropriate time after the Agreement comes into effect, and will contribute as appropriate to any review of the overall political agreement arising from the multi-party negotiations.

BRITISH-IRISH INTERGOVERNMENTAL CONFERENCE

1. There will be a new British-Irish Agreement dealing with the totality of relationships. It will establish a standing British-Irish Intergovernmental Conference, which will subsume both the Anglo-Irish Intergovernmental Council and the Intergovernmental Conference established under the 1985 Agreement.

2. The Conference will bring together the British and Irish Governments to promote bilateral co-operation at all levels on all matters of mutual interest within the competence of both Governments.

3. The Conference will meet as required at Summit level (Prime Minister and Taoiseach). Otherwise, Governments will be represented by appropriate Ministers. Advisers, including police and security advisers, will attend as appropriate.

4. All decisions will be by agreement between both Governments. The Governments will make determined efforts to resolve disagreements between them. There will be no derogation from the sovereignty of either Government.

5. In recognition of the Irish Government's special interest in Northern Ireland and of the extent to which issues of mutual concern arise in relation to Northern Ireland, there will be regular and frequent meetings of the Conference concerned with non-devolved Northern Ireland matters, on which the Irish Government may put forward views and proposals. These meetings, to be co-chaired by the Minister for Foreign Affairs and the Secretary of State for Northern Ireland, would also deal with all-island and cross-border co-operation on non-devolved issues.

6. Co-operation within the framework of the Conference will include facilitation of co-operation in security matters. The Conference also will address, in particular, the areas of rights, justice, prisons and policing in Northern Ireland (unless and until responsibility is devolved to a Northern Ireland administration) and will intensify co-operation between the two Governments on the all-island or cross-border aspects of these matters.

7. Relevant executive members of the Northern Ireland Administration will be involved in meetings of the Conference, and in the reviews referred to in paragraph 9 below to discuss non-devolved Northern Ireland matters.

8. The Conference will be supported by officials of the British and Irish Governments, including by a standing joint Secretariat of officials dealing with non-devolved Northern Ireland matters.

9. The Conference will keep under review the workings of the new British-Irish Agreement and the machinery and institutions established under it, including a formal published review

three years after the Agreement comes into effect. Representatives of the Northern Ireland Administration will be invited to express views to the Conference in this context. The Conference will contribute as appropriate to any review of the overall political agreement arising from the multi-party negotiations but will have no power to override the democratic arrangements set up by this Agreement.

RIGHTS, SAFEGUARDS AND EQUALITY OF OPPORTUNITY
[...]

New Institutions in Northern Ireland

5. A new Northern Ireland Human Rights Commission, with membership from Northern Ireland reflecting the community balance, will be established by Westminster legislation, independent of Government, with an extended and enhanced role beyond that currently exercised by the Standing Advisory Commission on Human Rights, to include keeping under review the adequacy and effectiveness of laws and practices, making recommendations to Government as necessary; providing information and promoting awareness of human rights; considering draft legislation referred to them by the new Assembly; and, in appropriate cases, bringing court proceedings or providing assistance to individuals doing so.

6. Subject to the outcome of public consultation currently underway, the British Government intends a new statutory Equality Commission to replace the Fair Employment Commission, the Equal Opportunities Commission (NI), the Commission for Racial Equality (NI) and the Disability Council. Such a unified Commission will advise on, validate and monitor the statutory obligation and will investigate complaints of default.

7. It would be open to a new Northern Ireland Assembly to consider bringing together its responsibilities for these matters into a dedicated Department of Equality.

8. These improvements will build on existing protections in Westminster legislation in respect of the judiciary, the system of justice and policing.

Comparable Steps by the Irish Government

9. The Irish Government will also take steps to further strengthen the protection of human rights in its jurisdiction. The Government will, taking account of the work of the All-Party Oireachtas Committee on the Constitution and the Report of the Constitution Review Group, bring forward measures to strengthen and underpin the constitutional protection of human rights. These proposals will draw on the European Convention on Human Rights and other international legal instruments in the field of human rights and the question of the incorporation of the ECHR will be further examined in this context. The measures brought forward would ensure at least an equivalent level of protection of human rights as will pertain in Northern Ireland. In addition, the Irish Government will:

- establish a Human Rights Commission with a mandate and remit equivalent to that within Northern Ireland;
- proceed with arrangements as quickly as possible to ratify the Council of Europe Framework Convention on National Minorities (already ratified by the UK);
- implement enhanced employment equality legislation;
- introduce equal status legislation; and
- continue to take further active steps to demonstrate its respect for the different traditions in the island of Ireland.

A Joint Committee

10. It is envisaged that there would be a joint committee of representatives of the two Human Rights Commissions, North and South, as a forum for consideration of human rights issues in the island of Ireland. The joint committee will consider, among other matters, the possibility of

establishing a charter, open to signature by all democratic political parties, reflecting and endorsing agreed measures for the protection of the fundamental rights of everyone living in the island of Ireland.

[…]

DECOMMISSIONING

1. Participants recall their agreement in the Procedural Motion adopted on 24 September 1997 'that the resolution of the decommissioning issue is an indispensable part of the process of negotiation', and also recall the provisions of paragraph 25 of Strand 1 above.

2. They note the progress made by the Independent International Commission on Decommissioning and the Governments in developing schemes which can represent a workable basis for achieving the decommissioning of illegally-held arms in the possession of paramilitary groups.

3. All participants accordingly reaffirm their commitment to the total disarmament of all paramilitary organisations. They also confirm their intention to continue to work constructively and in good faith with the Independent Commission, and to use any influence they may have, to achieve the decommissioning of all paramilitary arms within two years following endorsement in referendums North and South of the agreement and in the context of the implementation of the overall settlement.

4. The Independent Commission will monitor, review and verify progress on decommissioning of illegal arms, and will report to both Governments at regular intervals.

[*sic*]

6. Both Governments will take all necessary steps to facilitate the decommissioning process to include bringing the relevant schemes into force by the end of June.

[…]

POLICING AND JUSTICE

1. The participants recognise that policing is a central issue in any society. They equally recognise that Northern Ireland's history of deep divisions has made it highly emotive, with great hurt suffered and sacrifices made by many individuals and their families, including those in the RUC and other public servants. They believe that the agreement provides the opportunity for a new beginning to policing in Northern Ireland with a police service capable of attracting and sustaining support from the community as a whole. They also believe that this agreement offers a unique opportunity to bring about a new political dispensation which will recognise the full and equal legitimacy and worth of the identities, senses of allegiance and ethos of all sections of the community in Northern Ireland. They consider that this opportunity should inform and underpin the development of a police service representative in terms of the make-up of the community as a whole and which, in a peaceful environment, should be routinely unarmed.

2. The participants believe it essential that policing structures and arrangements are such that the police service is professional, effective and efficient, fair and impartial, free from partisan political control; accountable, both under the law for its actions and to the community it serves; representative of the society it polices, and operates within a coherent and co-operative criminal justice system, which conforms with human rights norms. The participants also believe that those structures and arrangements must be capable of maintaining law and order including responding effectively to crime and to any terrorist threat and to public order problems. A police service which cannot do so will fail to win public confidence and acceptance. They believe that any such structures and arrangements should be capable of delivering a policing service, in constructive and inclusive partnerships with the community at all levels, and with the maximum delegation of authority and responsibility, consistent with the foregoing principles.

These arrangements should be based on principles of protection of human rights and professional integrity and should be unambiguously accepted and actively supported by the entire community.

3. An independent Commission will be established to make recommendations for future policing arrangements in Northern Ireland including means of encouraging widespread community support for these arrangements within the agreed framework of principles reflected in the paragraphs above and in accordance with the terms of reference at Annex A. The Commission will be broadly representative with expert and international representation among its membership and will be asked to consult widely and to report no later than Summer 1999.

4. The participants believe that the aims of the criminal justice system are to:
- deliver a fair and impartial system of justice to the community;
- be responsive to the community's concerns, and encouraging community involvement where appropriate;
- have the confidence of all parts of the community; and
- deliver justice efficiently and effectively.

5. There will be a parallel wide-ranging review of criminal justice (other than policing and those aspects of the system relating to the emergency legislation) to be carried out by the British Government through a mechanism with an independent element, in consultation with the political parties and others. The review will commence as soon as possible, will include wide consultation, and a report will be made to the Secretary of State no later than Autumn 1999. Terms of Reference are attached at Annex B.

6. Implementation of the recommendations arising from both reviews will be discussed with the political parties and with the Irish Government.

7. The participants also note that the British Government remains ready in principle, with the broad support of the political parties, and after consultation, as appropriate, with the Irish Government, in the context of ongoing implementation of the relevant recommendations, to devolve responsibility for policing and justice issues.

[...]

[...]

VALIDATION, IMPLEMENTATION AND REVIEW
Validation and Implementation

1. The two Governments will as soon as possible sign a new British-Irish Agreement replacing the 1985 Anglo-Irish Agreement, embodying understandings on constitutional issues and affirming their solemn commitment to support and, where appropriate, implement the agreement reached by the participants in the negotiations which shall be annexed to the British-Irish Agreement.

2. Each Government will organise a referendum on 22 May 1998. Subject to Parliamentary approval, a consultative referendum in Northern Ireland, organised under the terms of the Northern Ireland (Entry to Negotiations, etc.) Act 1996, will address the question: 'Do you support the agreement reached in the multi-party talks on Northern Ireland and set out in Command Paper 3883?'. The Irish Government will introduce and support in the Oireachtas a Bill to amend the Constitution as described in paragraph 2 of the section 'Constitutional Issues' and in Annex B, as follows:

(a) to amend Articles 2 and 3 as described in paragraph 8.1 in Annex B above and

(b) to amend Article 29 to permit the Government to ratify the new British-Irish Agreement.

On passage by the Oireachtas, the Bill will be put to referendum.

3. If majorities of those voting in each of the referendums support this agreement, the Governments will then introduce and support, in their respective Parliaments, such legislation as may be necessary to give effect to all aspects of this agreement, and will take whatever

ancillary steps as may be required including the holding of elections on 25 June, subject to parliamentary approval, to the Assembly, which would meet initially in a 'shadow' mode. The establishment of the North-South Ministerial Council, implementation bodies, the British-Irish Council and the British-Irish Intergovernmental Conference and the assumption by the Assembly of its legislative and executive powers will take place at the same time on the entry into force of the British-Irish Agreement.

4. In the interim, aspects of the implementation of the multi-party agreement will be reviewed at meetings of those parties relevant in the particular case (taking into account, once Assembly elections have been held, the results of those elections), under the chairmanship of the British Government or the two Governments, as may be appropriate; and representatives of the two Governments and all relevant parties may meet under independent chairmanship to review implementation of the agreement as a whole.

Review procedures following implementation

5. Each institution may, at any time, review any problems that may arise in its operation and, where no other institution is affected, take remedial action in consultation as necessary with the relevant Government or Governments. It will be for each institution to determine its own procedures for review.

6. If there are difficulties in the operation of a particular institution, which have implications for another institution, they may review their operations separately and jointly and agree on remedial action to be taken under their respective authorities.

7. If difficulties arise which require remedial action across the range of institutions, or otherwise require amendment of the British-Irish Agreement or relevant legislation, the process of review will fall to the two Governments in consultation with the parties in the Assembly. Each Government will be responsible for action in its own jurisdiction.

8. Notwithstanding the above, each institution will publish an annual report on its operations. In addition, the two Governments and the parties in the Assembly will convene a conference 4 years after the agreement comes into effect, to review and report on its operation.

ANNEX: AGREEMENT BETWEEN THE GOVERNMENT OF THE UNITED KINGDOM OF GREAT BRITAIN AND NORTHERN IRELAND AND THE GOVERNMENT OF IRELAND

The British and Irish Governments:

Welcoming the strong commitment to the Agreement reached on 10th April 1998 by themselves and other participants in the multi-party talks and set out in Annex 1 to this Agreement (hereinafter 'the Multi-Party Agreement');

Considering that the Multi-Party Agreement offers an opportunity for a new beginning in relationships within Northern Ireland, within the island of Ireland and between the peoples of these islands;

Wishing to develop still further the unique relationship between their peoples and the close co-operation between their countries as friendly neighbours and as partners in the European Union;

Reaffirming their total commitment to the principles of democracy and non-violence which have been fundamental to the multi-party talks;

Reaffirming their commitment to the principles of partnership, equality and mutual respect and to the protection of civil, political, social, economic and cultural rights in their respective jurisdictions;

Have agreed as follows:

ARTICLE 1

The two Governments:

(i) recognise the legitimacy of whatever choice is freely exercised by a majority of the people of Northern Ireland with regard to its status, whether they prefer to continue to support the Union with Great Britain or a sovereign united Ireland;

(ii) recognise that it is for the people of the island of Ireland alone, by agreement between the two parts respectively and without external impediment, to exercise their right of self-determination on the basis of consent, freely and concurrently given, North and South, to bring about a united Ireland, if that is their wish, accepting that this right must be achieved and exercised with and subject to the agreement and consent of a majority of the people of Northern Ireland;

(iii) acknowledge that while a substantial section of the people in Northern Ireland share the legitimate wish of a majority of the people of the island of Ireland for a united Ireland, the present wish of a majority of the people of Northern Ireland, freely exercised and legitimate, is to maintain the Union and accordingly, that Northern Ireland's status as part of the United Kingdom reflects and relies upon that wish; and that it would be wrong to make any change in the status of Northern Ireland save with the consent of a majority of its people;

(iv) affirm that, if in the future, the people of the island of Ireland exercise their right of self-determination on the basis set out in sections (i) and (ii) above to bring about a united Ireland, it will be a binding obligation on both Governments to introduce and support in their respective Parliaments legislation to give effect to that wish;

(v) affirm that whatever choice is freely exercised by a majority of the people of Northern Ireland, the power of the sovereign government with jurisdiction there shall be exercised with rigorous impartiality on behalf of all the people in the diversity of their identities and traditions and shall be founded on the principles of full respect for, and equality of, civil, political, social and cultural rights, of freedom from discrimination for all citizens, and of parity of esteem and of just and equal treatment for the identity, ethos and aspirations of both communities;

(vi) recognise the birthright of all the people of Northern Ireland to identify themselves and be accepted as Irish or British, or both, as they may so choose, and accordingly confirm that their right to hold both British and Irish citizenship is accepted by both Governments and would not be affected by any future change in the status of Northern Ireland.

ARTICLE 2

The two Governments affirm their solemn commitment to support, and where appropriate implement, the provisions of the Multi-Party Agreement. In particular there shall be established in accordance with the provisions of the Multi-Party Agreement immediately on the entry into force of this Agreement, the following institutions:

(i) a North/South Ministerial Council;

(ii) the implementation bodies referred to in paragraph 9 (ii) of the section entitled 'Strand Two' of the Multi-Party Agreement;

(iii) a British-Irish Council;

(iv) a British-Irish Intergovernmental Conference.

ARTICLE 3

(1) This Agreement shall replace the Agreement between the British and Irish Governments done at Hillsborough on 15th November 1985 which shall cease to have effect on entry into force of this Agreement.

(2) The Intergovernmental Conference established by Article 2 of the aforementioned Agreement done on 15th November 1985 shall cease to exist on entry into force of this Agreement.

ARTICLE 4

(1) It shall be a requirement for entry into force of this Agreement that:

(a) British legislation shall have been enacted for the purpose of implementing the provisions of Annex A to the section entitled 'Constitutional Issues' of the Multi-Party Agreement;

(b) the amendments to the Constitution of Ireland set out in Annex B to the section entitled 'Constitutional Issues' of the Multi-Party Agreement shall have been approved by Referendum;

(c) such legislation shall have been enacted as may be required to establish the institutions referred to in Article 2 of this Agreement.

(2) Each Government shall notify the other in writing of the completion, so far as it is concerned, of the requirements for entry into force of this Agreement. This Agreement shall enter into force on the date of the receipt of the later of the two notifications.

(3) Immediately on entry into force of this Agreement, the Irish Government shall ensure that the amendments to the Constitution of Ireland set out in Annex B to the section entitled 'Constitutional Issues' of the Multi-Party Agreement take effect.

In witness thereof the undersigned, being duly authorised thereto by the respective Governments, have signed this Agreement.

Done in two originals at Belfast on the 10th day of April 1998.

ANNEX 1

The Agreement Reached in the Multi-Party Talks

ANNEX 2

Declaration on the Provisions of Paragraph (vi) of Article 1 In Relationship to Citizenship

The British and Irish Governments declare that it is their joint understanding that the term 'the people of Northern Ireland' in paragraph (vi) of Article 1 of this Agreement means, for the purposes of giving effect to this provision, all persons born in Northern Ireland and having, at the time of their birth, at least one parent who is a British citizen, an Irish citizen or is otherwise entitled to reside in Northern Ireland without any restriction on their period of residence.

Appendix B
The Agreement of the Central People's Government and the Local Government of Tibet on Measures for the Peaceful Liberation of Tibet, 23 May 1951*

The Tibetan nationality is one of the nationalities with a long history within the boundaries of China and, like many other nationalities, it has done its glorious duty in the course of the creation and development of the great motherland. But over the last hundred years and more, imperialist forces penetrated into China, and in consequence, also penetrated into the Tibetan region and carried out all kinds of deceptions and provocations. Like previous reactionary Governments, the KMT [Guomindang] reactionary government continued to carry out a policy of oppression and sowing dissension among the nationalities, causing division and disunity among the Tibetan people. The Local Government of Tibet did not oppose imperialist deception and provocations, but adopted an unpatriotic attitude towards the great motherland. Under such conditions, the Tibetan nationality and people were plunged into the depths of enslavement and suffering. In 1949, basic victory was achieved on a nation-wide scale in the Chinese people's war of liberation; the common domestic enemy of all nationalities – the KMT reactionary government – was overthrown; and the common foreign enemy of all nationalities – the aggressive imperialist forces – was driven out. On this basis, the founding of the People's Republic of China and of the Central People's Government was announced. In accordance with the Common Programme passed by the Chinese People's Political Consultative Conference, the Central People's Government declared that all nationalities within the boundaries of the People's Republic of China are equal, and that they shall establish unity and mutual aid and oppose imperialism and their own public enemies, so that the People's Republic of China may become one big family of fraternity and cooperation, composed of all its nationalities. Within this big family of nationalities of the People's Republic of China, national regional autonomy is to be exercised in areas where national minorities are concentrated, and all national minorities are to have freedom to develop their spoken and written languages and to preserve or reform their customs, habits, and religious beliefs, and the Central People's Government will assist all national minorities to develop their political, economic, cultural, and educational construction work. Since then, all nationalities within the country, with the exception of those in the areas of Tibet and Taiwan, have gained liberation. Under the unified leadership of the Central People's Government and the direct leadership of the higher levels of People's Government, all national minorities have fully enjoyed the right of national equality and have exercised, or are exercising, national regional autonomy. In order that the influences of aggressive imperialist forces in Tibet may be successfully eliminated, the unification of the territory and sovereignty of the People's Republic of China accomplished, and national defence safeguarded; in order that the Tibetan nationality and people may be freed and return to the big family of the People's Republic of China to enjoy the same rights of national equality as all other nationalities in the country and develop their political, economic, cultural, and educational work, the Central People's Government, when it ordered the People's Liberation Army to march into Tibet, notified the local government of Tibet to send delegates to the Central Authorities to hold talks for the conclusion of an agreement on measures for the peaceful liberation of Tibet. At the latter part of

---

* Source: M.C. van Walt van Praag, *The Status of Tibet: History, Rights and Prospects in International Law* (Boulder, CO: Westview Press, 1987), 337-340.

April, 1951, the delegates with full powers from the Local Government of Tibet arrived in Peking. The Central People's Government appointed representatives with full powers to conduct talks on a friendly basis with the delegates of the Local Government of Tibet. The result of the talks is that both parties have agreed to establish this agreement and ensure that it be carried into effect.

1. The Tibetan people shall be united and drive out the imperialist aggressive forces from Tibet; that the Tibetan people shall return to the big family of the motherland – the People's Republic of China.

2. The Local Government of Tibet shall actively assist the People's Liberation Army to enter Tibet and consolidate the national defences.

3. In accordance with the policy towards nationalities laid down in the Common Programme of the Chinese People's Political Consultative Conference, the Tibetan people have the right of exercising national regional autonomy under the unified leadership of the Central People's Government.

4. The Central Authorities will not alter the existing political system in Tibet. The Central Authorities also will not alter the established status, functions and powers of the Dalai Lama. Officials of various ranks shall hold office as usual.

5. The established status, functions, and powers of the Panchen Ngoerhtehni shall be maintained.

6. By the established status, functions, and powers of the Dalai Lama and of the Panchen Ngoerhtehni is meant the status, functions and powers of the 13th Dalai Lama and of the 9th Panchen Ngoerhtehni when they were in friendly and amicable relations with each other.

7. The policy of freedom of religious belief laid down in the Common Programme of the Chinese People's Political Consultative Conference will be protected. The Central authorities will not effect any change in the income of the monasteries.

8. The Tibetan troops will be reorganised step by step into the People's Liberation Army, and become a part of the national defence forces of the Central People's Government.

9. The spoken and written language and school education of the Tibetan nationality will be developed step by step in accordance with the actual conditions in Tibet.

10. Tibetan agriculture, livestock raising, industry and commerce will be developed step by step, and the people's livelihood shall be improved step by step in accordance with the actual conditions in Tibet.

11. In matters related to various reforms in Tibet, there will be no compulsion on the part of the Central Authorities. The Local Government of Tibet should carry out reforms of its own accord, and when the people raise demands for reform, they must be settled through consultation with the leading personnel of Tibet.

12. In so far as former pro-imperialist and pro-KMT officials resolutely sever relations with imperialism and the KMT and do not engage in sabotage or resistance, they may continue to hold office irrespective of their past.

13. The People's Liberation Army entering Tibet will abide by the above-mentioned policies and will also be fair in all buying and selling and will not arbitrarily take even a needle or a thread from the people.

14. The Central People's Government will handle all external affairs of the area of Tibet; and there will be peaceful co-existence with neighbouring countries and the establishment and development of fair commercial and trading relations with them on the basis of equality, mutual benefit and mutual respect for territory and sovereignty.

15. In order to ensure the implementation of this agreement, the Central People's Government will set up a military and administrative committee and a military area headquarters in Tibet, and apart from the personnel sent there by the Central People's Government it will absorb as many local Tibetan personnel as possible to take part in the work. Local Tibetan personnel

taking part in the military and administrative committee may include patriotic elements from the Local Government of Tibet, various district and various principal monasteries; the namelist is to be prepared after consultation between the representatives designated by the Central People's Government and various quarters concerned, and is to be submitted to the Central People's Government for approval.

16. Funds needed by the military and administrative committee, the military area headquarters and the People's Liberation Army in the purchases and transportation of food, fodder, and other daily necessities.

17. This agreement shall come into force immediately after signatures and seals are affixed to it.

Signed and sealed by delegates of the Central people's Government with full powers:

Chief Delegate: Li Wei-han (Chairman of the Commission of Nationalities Affairs);

Delegates: Chang Ching-wu, Chang Kuo-hua, Sun Chih-yuan

Delegates with full powers of the Local Government of Tibet:

Chief Delegate: Kaloon Ngabou Ngawang Jigme (Ngabo Shape)

Delegates: Dzasak Khemey Sonam Wangdi, Khentrung Thuptan, Tenthar, Khenchung Thupten Lekmunn Rimshi, Samposey Tenzin Thundup

Appendix C
Chittagong Hill Tracts Accord,
2 December 1997*

Under the framework of the constitution of Bangladesh and having fullest and firm confidence in the sovereignty and integrity of Bangladesh the national Committee on CHT Affairs, on behalf of the government of the People's Republic of Bangladesh and the Parbattya Chattagram Jana Samhati Samiti, on behalf of the inhabitants of the Chittagong Hill Tracts, with an objective to elevate political, social, cultural, educational and financial rights and to expedite socio-economic development process of all citizens in CHT, arrive at an agreement described in four parts as below:

A) GENERAL

1. Both sides, considering CHT as Tribal Populated Region, recognised the necessity for protection of the character of this region and for overall development of it.

2. Both sides, in accordance with the decisions and responsibilities state in these paragraphs under this agreement, determined to make, change, amend and add concerned rules and procedures as per laws/rules.

3. With an aim to observe the implementation process of this agreement an Implementation Committee shall be formed with the persons stated below
   a. A member to be nominated by the Prime Minister – Convenor
   b. Chairman of the Task Force formed under this agreement – Member
   c. President of the Parbattya Chattagram Jana Samhati Samiti – Member

4. This agreement shall be in force from the date of signing the agreement. This agreement shall remain in force until all steps and measures according to this agreement are completed by both sides.

B) HILL DISTRICT LOCAL GOVT. COUNCIL/HILL DISTRICT COUNCILS

Both sides agreed to change, amend, add and repeal the Hill District Local Government Council Acts, 1989. (Rangamati Hill District Local Government Council Act, 1989, Bandarban Hill District, Local Government Council Act, 1989 and Khagrachari Hill District Local Government Council Act, 1989) and its various sections described as below :

1. The term 'Upajati' shall be in force.

2. The name of the Hill District Local Government Council shall be Hill District Council.

3. Who is not a tribal and possesses land legally in the Hill District and generally lives at a certain address in the Hill District he shall be meant 'non-tribal permanent resident'.

4. a. There shall be 3 (three) seats for women in every Hill District Council. There shall be one-third of the said seat for non-tribal women.

   b. Sub-section (1), (2), (3) and (4) of section 4 of the original rule shall exist.

   c. The words 'Deputy Commissioner' and 'of the Deputy Commissioner' placed in the second line of sub-section (5) of the section 4 shall be replaced with the words 'Circle Chief' and 'of the Circle Chief' respectively.

   d. Following sub-section shall be added in the section 4:
   Whether a person is a non-tribal shall be determined, along with the identity of non-tribal to which he belongs, by the concerned Circle Chief on the provision of submission of certificate

---

* Source: Chittagong Hill Tracts Commission, 'Chittagong Hill Tracts: Text of the Peace Agreement and Comments', *Indigenous Affairs* 1 (1998), 50.

from concerned Headman/Pourasabha Chairman/Union Parishad Chairman and no person can be a candidate for the office of the non-tribal member without a certificate from the concerned Circle Chief in this behalf.

5. It is narrated in the section 7 that a person elected chairman and member shall make an oath or announce confirmation before Divisional Commissioner of Chittagong. By amendment of it there shall be added the portion that the members shall make oath or announce confirmation before 'Justice of High Court Division' in lieu of 'Divisional Commissioner of Chittagong'.

6. In lieu of the words 'Divisional Commissioner of Chittagong' shall be placed the words 'as per election procedure' in the fourth line of section 8.

7. The words 'three years' placed in the second line of section 10 shall be replaced with the words 'five years'.

8. There shall be a provision in the section 14 that – If the office of the Chairman falls vacant and in absence of the Chairman a tribal member elected by other members of the Council shall preside and perform other responsibilities.

9. The existing section 17 shall be replaced with the sentences mentioned as below:
A person shall, under the Act, be eligible to be enrolled in the electoral roll, if
(1) he is a citizen of Bangladesh;
(2) his age is not less than 18 years;
(3) he is not declared mentally unsound by any competent court;
(4) he is a permanent resident of Hill District.

10. The words 'determination of electoral constituency' shall be added in the sub-section (2) of section 20.

11. There shall be a provision in the sub-section (2) of section 25: The chairman and in absence of him a tribal member elected by other members shall preside over all the meeting of the Council.

12. As all the area of Khagrachari District is not included in the Mong Circle, so the words 'Mong Circle Chief and Chakma Circle Chief' shall be placed in lieu of the words 'Mong Chief of Khagrachari' in the section 26 of the Khagrachari Hill District Council Act. Similarly facility of attending the meetings of the Rangamati Hill District Council by Bohmong Circle Chief also shall be maintained. In the same way there shall be a provision of attending the meetings of the Bandarban Hill District Council by Bohmong Circle Chief.

13. There shall be provision in the sub-sections (1) and (2) of section 31 that –
There shall be a Chief Executive Officer as secretary in the Council. Tribal Officers shall be given priority in this post.

14. a. There shall be a provision in the sub-section (1) of section 32 that-
For the proper conduct of its affairs the Council may with the approval of the government, create posts of various categories of officers and employees.
b. The sub-section (2) of section 32 shall, by amendment, be made as follows:
The Council may, in accordance with regulations, appoint, transfer, suspend, dismiss, remove class three and class four employees and inflict any other punishment on them.
Provided that, priority to the tribals is maintained in the matter of the said appointment.
c. There shall be provision in the sub-section (3) of section 32 that – The government in consultation with the Council may, as per regulation, appoint, transfer, suspend, dismiss, remove or inflict any other punishment on other officers of the Council.

15. In the sub-section (3) of section 33 shall be mentioned 'as per regulation'.

16. The words 'or any other way determined by the government' placed in the third line of sub-section (1) of section 36 shall be omitted.

17. The original rule shall be in force in the fourth of sub-section (1) of section 37.

18. Sub-section (3) of section 38 shall be repealed and by amendment, the sub-section (4) shall be framed as follows:

At any time before the expiry of the financial year, if deemed necessary, budget may be framed and sanctioned.

19. In the section 42 the following sub-section shall be added –

The Council with the fund received from the government shall formulate initiate and implement development projects on the subjects transferred and all the development works initiated at the national level shall be implemented by the concerned ministry/department through the Council.

20. The word 'government' placed in the second line of sub-section (2) of section 45 shall be replaced with the word 'Council'.

21. By amendment of rules of sections 50, 51 and 52 the following section shall be made –

'The government, if deemed necessary may advice or order the Council, in order to ensure conformity with the purpose of the Act. If the govt. is satisfied that anything done or intended to be done by the Council or on behalf of the Council is not conformity with law or contrary to public interest the government may seek information and clarification and give advice or instruction to the Council on concerned matters in writing'.

22. The words 'if the period of supersession is completed' shall be repealed and in lieu of them shall be added 'within ninety days of supersession' before the words 'this Act'.

23. The words 'of the government' in the third and fourth lines of section 61 shall be replaced with the words 'of the ministry'.

24. a. By amendment of sub-section (1) of section 62 – this section shall be made as follows:

'Notwithstanding anything contained in any Act for the time-being in force, all members of the rank of Sub-Inspector and below of Hill District Police shall be appointed by the Council in manner laid down by regulations and the Council may transfer and take disciplinary action against them as per procedure laid down by regulation: provided that in the matter of such appointment tribals shall be given priority'.

b. By repealment of the words 'on the provision of all other laws for the time-being in force' placed in the second line of sub-section (3) of section 62 shall be placed the words 'as per rule and regulation'.

25. The words 'giving assistance' placed in the third line of the section 63 shall be in force.

26. By amendment of the section 64 the following sub-sections shall be made –

1. Notwithstanding anything contained in any law for the time-being in force, no land within the boundaries of Hill District shall be given in settlement, purchased, sold and transferred including giving lease without prior approval of the Council:

provided that this provision shall not be applicable in case of areas within the reserved forests, Kaptai Hydro-electricity Project, Betbunia Earth Satellite Station, State-owned industries and factories and lands recorded in the name of government.

2. Notwithstanding anything contained in any law for the time-being in force, no lands, hills and forests within the boundaries of the Hill District shall be acquired and transferred by the government without consultation and consent of the Hill District Council.

3. The Council may supervise and control functions of Headman, Chairman Amin, Surveyor, Kanungo and Assistant Commissioner (land).

4. Fringe land in Kaptai Lake shall be given in settlement on priority basis to original owners.

27. By amendment of section 65 this section shall be framed as follows:

Notwithstanding anything contained in any other law for the time-being in force, responsibility of collecting land development tax shall be entrusted in the Council and the said tax collected in the District shall be credited to the Council Fund.

28. By amendment of section 67 it shall be made as follows – 'If deemed necessary for co-ordination of activities between the Council and govt. authorities, government or the Council shall put proposal on certain matter(s)'.

29. By amendment of sub-section (1) it shall be made as follows – 'The government having discussion with the Council may, by notification in the official gazette, make rules for carrying out the purposes of this Act and even after having rules made the Council shall have special right to file petition for reconsideration of the said rules'.

30. By omission of the words 'with the prior approval of the government' placed in the first and second line of the sub-section (1) of section 69 and to add the following portion after the words 'may' –

'provided that if the government differs with any part of the regulation made by the Hill District Council then the government shall give advice or instruction for amendment of the said regulation'.

a. The words mentioned in the (h) of sub-section (2) of section 69 'transfer of power of Chairman to any officer' shall be omitted.

31. Section 70 shall be omitted.

32. By amendment of section 79 it shall be made as follows—'If any law by the Jatiyo Sangsad or any other authority, applicable to Hill District, is found to be hurtful to the District or objectionable to the tribal people in the opinion of the Council, it may file a petition in writing to the government stating the reasons of its being hurtful or objectionable for the purpose of amending or relaxing its application and the govt. shall, in the light of the petition, adopt necessary measures'.

33. The word 'supervision' shall be added after the word 'order' in the No.1 of the function of the Council of the first schedule.

a. The following subjects shall be added in the No. 3 of the function of the Council-
  (1) Vocational training;
  (2) Primary education in mother tongue;
  (3) Secondary education.

b. The words 'or protected' placed in sub-section 6(b) of the function of the Council in the first schedule shall be omitted.

34. The following subjects shall be added in the functions and responsibilities of the Hill District Council:
Land and land management
a. Police (local)
b. Tribal law and social justice
c. Youth welfare
d. Environment preservation and development
e. Local tourism
f. Improvement trust and other local govt organisations except Pourasabha and Union Councils
g. Licencing for local trade and business
h. Proper utilisation of water resources of rivulets, canals, ponds except Kaptai lake and irrigation
i. Preservation of death, birth and other statistics
j. Money lending and trade
k. Jhum cultivation.

35. The following sectors and sources shall be included in the taxes, rates, tolls and fees to be imposed by the Council as stated in the second schedule:
Registration fee from non-mechanical transports
a. Tax on sale and purchase of goods
b. Holding tax from land and buildings
c. Tax from sale of domestic animals

d. Fees from cases of social justice
e. Holding tax on government and non-government industries
f. Part of royalty from forest resources
g. Supplementary tax from cinema, theatre and circus etc.
h. Part of royalty from licence or lease for exploration and extraction of mineral resources given by the government
i. Tax from business
j. Tax from lottery
k. Tax from fishing.

C) CHITTAGONG HILL TRACTS REGIONAL COUNCIL

1. A Regional Council shall be formed in co-ordination with the 3 Hill District Local Government Council provided that various sections of the Hill District Local Government Council Act, 1989 (Act No. 19, 20 and 21 of 1989) shall be amended with an aim to make the 3 Hill District Local Government Councils more powerful and effective.

2. Chairman bf this Council shall be elected indirectly by the elected members of the Hill District Councils where status shall be equivalent to a State Minister and he must be a Jumma.

3. The Council shall be formed with 22 (twenty two) members including the Chairman. Two-third of the members shall be elected from among the tribals. The Council shall determine its procedure of functioning.

Composition of the Council shall be as follows :-
- Chairman – 1
- Members tribal (men) – 12
- Members tribal (women) – 2
- Members non-tribal (men) – 6
- Members non tribal (women) – 1

Among the tribal men members 5 persons shall be elected from among the Chakma tribe, 3 persons from the Marma tribe, 2 persons from the Tripura tribe, 1 person from the Murung and Tanchongya tribes and 1 person from the Lusai, Bawm, Pankho, Khumi, Chak and Khiyang tribes.

Among the non-tribal men members 2 persons shall be elected from each district. Among the tribal women members 1 woman shall be elected from the Chakma tribe and 1 woman from other tribes.

4. 3 (three) seats shall be reserved for women in the Council. One-third shall be non-tribals.

5. The members of the Council shall be elected indirectly by the elected members of the Hill District Councils. Chairman of three Hill District Councils shall be ex-officio members of the Council and they shall have voting rights.

Eligibility and non-eligibility of the members of the Council shall be similar to that of the Hill District Council.

6. The term of the Council shall be 5 (five) years.

7. There shall be a chief executive officer in the Council equivalent to a Joint Secretary and priority to a tribal candidate shall be given in appointment to this post.

8. a. If the office of the Chairman of the Council falls vacant then a Chairman shall be elected from among the tribal members for an interim period by the members of Hill District Councils.

b. If any office of a member of the Council falls vacant on any reason then that shall be filled through by-election.

9. a. The Council shall supervise and co-ordinate the subjects vested under the Hill District Councils including co-ordination of all development activities conducted under the three Hill District Councils. Besides these, if there is found any lack of co-ordination and

inconsistency among the three Hill District Councils in discharging their responsibilities the decision of the Regional Council shall be taken as final.
 b. The Council shall supervise and co-ordinate local councils including the municipalities.
 c. Regional Council may co-ordinate and supervise in the matters of general administration, law and order and development of the three Hill Districts.
 d. The Council may co-ordinate the activities of the NGOs along with conducting of management of calamities and relief works.
 e. Tribal laws and social justice shall be under the control of the Council.
 f. The Council may issue licence for heavy industry.
 10. The CHT Development Board shall discharge its responsibilities under general and overall supervision of the Council. In case of appointment of Chairman of the Development Board competent tribal candidate shall be given priority.
 11. If the Regional Council finds any rule of the 1900 CHT Regulation and other related laws, rules and ordinances contradictory to the 1989 Hill District Council Acts then the govt shall remove that inconsistency by law according to recommendation of and in consultation with the Regional Council.
 12. Until and unless Regional Council is constituted through direct and indirect election, the government may by constituting an interim Regional Council, entrust the responsibilities of the Council.
 13. If the govt makes any law on CHT it shall be in having discussion and in consultation with the Regional Council. If there arises the necessity to amend any such law or to make any new law which may be harmful for development of the 3 Hill District or the welfare of the tribals, the Council may file a petition or put recommendation to the govt.
 14. The fund of the Council shall be created from the following sources:
 a. fund received from the Hill District Councils' fund
 b. money or profits from all properties vested in and managed by the Regional Council
 c. grant and loan from the govt or any other authority
 d. grant from any institution or individual
 e. profit accruing from investment by the Regional Council
 f. any other moneys received by the Regional Council
 g. money received from such sources of incomes as the govt may direct to be placed at the disposal of the Regional Council.

D) REHABILITATION, GENERAL AMNESTY AND OTHER MATTERS
 1. An agreement has been signed between the govt and the refugee leaders on March 9, 1997 with an aim to take back the tribal refugees from India's Tripura State based on the 20-Point Facilities Package. In accordance with the said agreement repatriation of the refugees started since March 28, 1997. This process shall continue and with this in view, the JSS shall provide all kinds of possible co-operation. The internal tribal evacuees of 3 districts shall, after determination, be rehabilitated by the Task Force.
 2. After signing agreement between the govt and the JSS and implementation of it as well as after rehabilitation of the tribal refugees and internal tribal evacuees the govt shall start survey of land in CHT as soon as possible and after proper inquires ownership of land shall be recorded and ensured.
 3. The govt shall ensure providing two acres of lands to each landless family and the family who possesses less than 2 acres of lands, provided lands were available in the local areas. If requisite lands are not available then grove land shall be provided.
 4. A commission (land commission) headed by a retired justice shall be formed for settling land disputes. This commission, in addition to settle disputes of lands of the rehabilitated tribal refugees, shall have fullest power for cancellation of ownership of those lands and hills which

have been so far illegally settled and occupied. No appeal can be made against the judgement of this commission and decision of this commission shall be final. This (arrangement) shall be applicable in case of fringe land also.

5. This commission shall be set up with the following members:
a. Retired justice
b. Circle Chief (concerned)
c. Chairman of the Regional Council/representative
d. Divisional Commissioner/Additional Commissioner
e. Hill District Council Chairman (concerned).

6. a. The term of the commission shall be three years. But the term of it can be extended in consultation with the Regional Council.
b. Commission shall settle disputes according to the existing rules, customs and usages of Chittagong Hill Tracts.

7. The tribal refugees who received loan from the govt but could not use them properly due to conflicting situation shall be exempted with the interests.

8. Allotment of lands for rubber plantation and other purposes: All the non tribals and non locals who were given in settlement of lands for rubber plantation and other purposes but had not implemented any projects within the past 10 years or had not utilised their lands properly, settlement of these lands shall be cancelled.

9. The govt shall allot additional fund, on priority basis, with an aim to implement more number of projects in CHT. New projects formulated with an aim of making necessary superstructures for development in the area, shall be implemented on priority basis and the govt shall provide fund for these purposes. The govt shall, having consideration about the environment in the region, encourage to develop tourism for tourists from the country and abroad.

10. Quota reservation and scholarships: – Until development equal to other region of the country the govt shall continue reservation of quota system in govt services and educational institutions for the tribals. With an aim to this purpose, the govt shall grant more scholarships for the tribal students in the educational institution. The govt shall provide necessary scholarships for research works and receiving higher education in abroad.

11. The govt and elected representative shall make efforts to maintain separate culture and tradition of the tribals. The govt in order to develop the tribal cultural activities at the national level it shall provide necessary patronisation and assistance.

12. The Jana Samhati Samiti shall submit to the govt the lists of its all members including the armed ones and the arms and ammunition under its possession and control within 45 days of signing this agreement.

13. The government and the Jana Samhati Samiti jointly shall determine the date and place for depositing arms within the 45 days of signing this agreement. After determination of date and place for depositing arms by the members included in the list of the Jana Samhati Samiti the govt shall ensure security for return of JSS members and their family members to normal life.

14. The govt shall declare amnesty for the members who shall deposit their arms and ammunition on the scheduled date. The govt shall withdraw the cases against whom cases have been lodged.

15. If anyone fails to deposit arms on the scheduled date the govt shall take lawful measures against him.

16. After the return of all JSS members to normal life general amnesty shall be given to them and the permanent residents who were involved in the activities of the JSS.
a. In order to providing rehabilitation to all returnee JSS members a lump sum of Taka 50,000/- shall be given to each family.

b. All the JSS members including the armed ones against whom cases have been lodged, warrant of arrest and police circular for apprehension issued and punishment has been sentenced/inflicted in the absence, after surrendering of arms and return to normal life all the cases, warrants of arrest, police circulars and punishment sentenced in the absence against them shall be exempted as soon as possible. If JSS members are detained in the jails they also shall be released.

c. Similarly after surrendering of arms and return to normal life no cases can be lodged, warrant issued and punishment inflicted against anyone only for the reason that he was a JSS member.

d. All the members of the JSS who took loans from various banks and organisations of the govt but could not utilise them properly those loans including the interests shall be exempted.

e. The JSS members who were posted in the services of the govt or govt institutions they shall be reinstated in their own posts and services and the JSS members and their family members shall be given appointment in accordance with their competence. In this case, the rule of the govt for relaxation of age shall be followed.

f. The JSS members shall be provided bank loans on easier terms and conditions to give assistance for cottage industry, horticulture etc. self-employment activities.

g. The children of JSS members shall be provided educational facilities and their certificates received from foreign educational Boards and institutions shall be taken as valid.

17. After signing the agreement between the government and the Jana Samhati Samiti and immediately after the return of the JSS members to normal life all the temporary camps of military, Ansar and Village Defence Party shall be taken back to permanent installations except the Border Security Force (BDR) and permanent cantonments (3 at the 3 District Hqs. and Alikadam, Ruma and Dighinala) by phases and with this in view, time limit shall be determined. In case of deterioration of law and order situation, natural calamity and such other works the army can be deployed under the civil administration like all other parts in the country as per necessary laws and rules. In this case, Regional Council may, according to necessity or time, request the proper authority for the purpose of getting assistance.

18. Permanent residents of CHT, on priority basis to the tribals, shall be appointed to all posts of officers and employees at all levels of govt, semi-govt, council offices and autonomous bodies in CHT.

Provided that in case of non-availability of qualified candidate among the permanent residents of CHT for a particular post, appointment in that post may be made on deputation from the govt for a term of certain period.

19. A ministry on Chittagong Hill Tracts Affairs shall be established by appointing a Minister from among the tribals. An Advisory Council shall be formed to assist this ministry with the persons stated below –

1. Minister on CHT Affairs
2. Chairman/representative, Regional Council
3. Chairman/representative, Rangamati Hill District Council
4. Chairman/representative, Bandarban Hill District Council
5. Chairman/representative, Khagrachari Hill District Council
6. Member of Parliament, Rangamati
7. Member of Parliament, Khagrachari
8. Member of Parliament, Bandarban
9. Chakma Raja
10. Bohmong Rnja
11. Mong Raja
12. Three members from non-tribal permanent residents of Hilly areas nominated by the government from three Hill Districts.

This agreement is framed as above in Bengali language and is done and signed in Dhaka on the date of 02 December, 1997 as per 18 Agrahayan 1404 Bengali year.
   On behalf of the inhabitants of Chittagong Hill Tracts
SD/-
(Jyotirindra Bodhipriya Larma)
President
Parbattya Chattagram Jana
Samhati Samiti
On behalf of the government of the Peoples Republic of Bangladesh
SD/-
(Abul Hasanat Abdullah)
Convenor
Hill Tracts Affairs, government of Bangladesh

Appendix D
The De Gasperi-Gruber Agreement
(Paris Treaty),
5 September 1946*

1- German speaking inhabitants of the Bolzano province and of the neighbouring bilingual townships of the Trento Province will be assured a complete equality of rights with the Italian-speaking inhabitants, within the framework of special provisions to safeguard the ethnical character and the cultural and economic development of the German-speaking element.

In accordance with legislation already enacted or awaiting enactment the said German-speaking citizens will be granted in particular:

(a) elementary and secondary teaching in the mother-tongue;

(b) parification [sic] of the German and Italian languages in public offices and official documents, as well as in bilingual topographic naming;

(c) the right to re-establish German family names which were italianized in recent years;

(d) equality of rights as regards the entering upon public offices, with a view to reaching a more appropriate proportion of employment between the two ethnical groups.

2- The populations of the above mentioned zones will be granted the exercise of an autonomous legislative and executive regional power. The frame within the said provisions of autonomy will apply, will be drafted in consultation also with local representative German-speaking elements.

3- The Italian Government, with the aim of establishing good neighbourhood relations between Austria and Italy, pledges itself, in consultation with the Austrian Government and within one year from the signing of the present Treaty:

(a) to revise in a spirit of equity and broad-mindedness the question of the options for citizenship resulting from the 1939 Hitler-Mussolini agreements;

(b) to find an agreement for the mutual recognition of the validity of certain degrees and University diplomas;

(c) to draw up a convention for the free passengers and goods transit between Northern and Eastern Tyrol both by rail and, to the greatest possible extent, by road;

(d) to reach special agreements aimed at facilitating enlarged frontier traffic and local exchanges of certain quantities of characteristic products and goods between Austria and Italy.

Gruber
De Gasperi

5 September 1946

* Source: M. Gehler and K. Gruber, *Reden und Dokumente 1945-1953: Eine Auswahl* (Wien/Köln/Weimar, Arbeitskreis Europäische Integration, Historische Forschungen, Veröffenlichungen 2, 1994), 146.

Appendix E
Macedonia Framework Agreement,
13 August 2001*

Extracts

The following points comprise an agreed framework for securing the future of Macedonia's democracy and permitting the development of closer and more integrated relations between the Republic of Macedonia and the Euro-Atlantic community. This Framework will promote the peaceful and harmonious development of civil society while respecting the ethnic identity and the interests of all Macedonian citizens.

1. Basic Principles

1.1. The use of violence in pursuit of political aims is rejected completely and unconditionally. Only peaceful political solutions can assure a stable and democratic future for Macedonia.

1.2. Macedonia's sovereignty and territorial integrity, and the unitary character of the State are inviolable and must be preserved. There are no territorial solutions to ethnic issues.

1.3. The multi-ethnic character of Macedonia's society must be preserved and reflected in public life.

1.4. A modern democratic state in its natural course of development and maturation must continually ensure that its Constitution fully meets the needs of all its citizens and comports with the highest international standards, which themselves continue to evolve.

1.5. The development of local self-government is essential for encouraging the participation of citizens in democratic life, and for promoting respect for the identity of communities.

2. Cessation of Hostilities

2.1. The parties underline the importance of the commitments of July 5, 2001. There shall be a complete cessation of hostilities, complete voluntary disarmament of the ethnic Albanian armed groups and their complete voluntary disbandment. They acknowledge that a decision by NATO to assist in this context will require the establishment of a general, unconditional and open-ended cease-fire, agreement on a political solution to the problems of this country, a clear commitment by the armed groups to voluntarily disarm, and acceptance by all the parties of the conditions and limitations under which the NATO forces will operate.

3. Development of Decentralized Government

3.1. A revised Law on Local Self-Government will be adopted that reinforces the powers of elected local officials and enlarges substantially their competencies in conformity with the Constitution (as amended in accordance with Annex A) and the European Charter on Local Self-Government, and reflecting the principle of subsidiarity in effect in the European Union. Enhanced competencies will relate principally to the areas of public services, urban and rural planning, environmental protection, local economic development, culture, local finances, education, social welfare, and health care. A law on financing of local self-government will be adopted to ensure an adequate system of financing to enable local governments to fulfill all of their responsibilities.

3.2. Boundaries of municipalities will be revised within one year of the completion of a new census, which will be conducted under international supervision by the end of 2001. The revision

---

* Source: United States Institute of Peace, <http://www.usip.org/library/pa/macedonia/pa_mac_08132001.html> (2 August 2006).

of the municipal boundaries will be effectuated by the local and national authorities with international participation.

3.3. In order to ensure that police are aware of and responsive to the needs and interests of the local population, local heads of police will be selected by municipal councils from lists of candidates proposed by the Ministry of Interior, and will communicate regularly with the councils. The Ministry of Interior will retain the authority to remove local heads of police in accordance with the law.

4. Non-Discrimination and Equitable Representation

4.1. The principle of non-discrimination and equal treatment of all under the law will be respected completely. This principle will be applied in particular with respect to employment in public administration and public enterprises, and access to public financing for business development.

4.2. Laws regulating employment in public administration will include measures to assure equitable representation of communities in all central and local public bodies and at all levels of employment within such bodies, while respecting the rules concerning competence and integrity that govern public administration. The authorities will take action to correct present imbalances in the composition of the public administration, in particular through the recruitment of members of under-represented communities. Particular attention will be given to ensuring as rapidly as possible that the police services will generally reflect the composition and distribution of the population of Macedonia, as specified in Annex C.

4.3. For the Constitutional Court, one-third of the judges will be chosen by the Assembly by a majority of the total number of Representatives that includes a majority of the total number of Representatives claiming to belong to the communities not in the majority in the population of Macedonia. This procedure also will apply to the election of the Ombudsman (Public Attorney) and the election of three of the members of the Judicial Council.

5. Special Parliamentary Procedures

5.1. On the central level, certain Constitutional amendments in accordance with Annex A and the Law on Local Self-Government cannot be approved without a qualified majority of two-thirds of votes, within which there must be a majority of the votes of Representatives claiming to belong to the communities not in the majority in the population of Macedonia.

5.2. Laws that directly affect culture, use of language, education, personal documentation, and use of symbols, as well as laws on local finances, local elections, the city of Skopje, and boundaries of municipalities must receive a majority of votes, within which there must be a majority of the votes of the Representatives claiming to belong to the communities not in the majority in the population of Macedonia.

6. Education and Use of Languages

6.1. With respect to primary and secondary education, instruction will be provided in the students' native languages, while at the same time uniform standards for academic programs will be applied throughout Macedonia.

6.2. State funding will be provided for university level education in languages spoken by at least 20 percent of the population of Macedonia, on the basis of specific agreements.

6.3. The principle of positive discrimination will be applied in the enrolment in State universities of candidates belonging to communities not in the majority in the population of Macedonia until the enrolment reflects equitably the composition of the population of Macedonia.

6.4. The official language throughout Macedonia and in the international relations of Macedonia is the Macedonian language.

6.5. Any other language spoken by at least 20 percent of the population is also an official language, as set forth herein. In the organs of the Republic of Macedonia, any official language other than Macedonian may be used in accordance with the law, as further elaborated in Annex B. Any person living in a unit of local self-government in which at least 20 percent of the population speaks an official language other than Macedonian may use any official language to communicate with the regional office of the central government with responsibility for that municipality; such an office will reply in that language in addition to Macedonian. Any person may use any official language to communicate with a main office of the central government, which will reply in that language in addition to Macedonian.

6.6. With respect to local self-government, in municipalities where a community comprises at least 20 percent of the population of the municipality, the language of that community will be used as an official language in addition to Macedonian. With respect to languages spoken by less than 20 percent of the population of the municipality, the local authorities will decide democratically on their use in public bodies.

6.7. In criminal and civil judicial proceedings at any level, an accused person or any party will have the right to translation at State expense of all proceedings as well as documents in accordance with relevant Council of Europe documents.

6.8. Any official personal documents of citizens speaking an official language other than Macedonian will also be issued in that language, in addition to the Macedonian language, in accordance with the law.

7. Expression of Identity

7.1. With respect to emblems, next to the emblem of the Republic of Macedonia, local authorities will be free to place on front of local public buildings emblems marking the identity of the community in the majority in the municipality, respecting international rules and usages.

8. Implementation

8.1. The Constitutional amendments attached at Annex A will be presented to the Assembly immediately. The parties will take all measures to assure adoption of these amendments within 45 days of signature of this Framework Agreement.

8.2. The legislative modifications identified in Annex B will be adopted in accordance with the timetables specified therein.

8.3. The parties invite the international community to convene at the earliest possible time a meeting of international donors that would address in particular macro-financial assistance; support for the financing of measures to be undertaken for the purpose of implementing this Framework Agreement, including measures to strengthen local self-government; and rehabilitation and reconstruction in areas affected by the fighting.

9. Annexes

The following Annexes constitute integral parts of this Framework Agreement:

A. Constitutional Amendments
B. Legislative Modifications
C. Implementation and Confidence-Building Measures

10. Final Provisions

10.1. This Agreement takes effect upon signature.
10.2. The English language version of this Agreement is the only authentic version.
10.3. This Agreement was concluded under the auspices of President Boris Trajkovski.

Done at Skopje, Macedonia on 13 August 2001, in the English language.

Annex A
Constitutional amendments
Preamble

The citizens of the Republic of Macedonia, taking over responsibility for the present and future of their fatherland, aware and grateful to their predecessors for their sacrifice and dedication in their endeavors and struggle to create an independent and sovereign state of Macedonia, and responsible to future generations to preserve and develop everything that is valuable from the rich cultural inheritance and coexistence within Macedonia, equal in rights and obligations towards the common good – the Republic of Macedonia, in accordance with the tradition of the Krushevo Republic and the decisions of the Antifascist Peopleís Liberation Assembly of Macedonia, and the Referendum of September 8, 1991, they have decided to establish the Republic of Macedonia as an independent, sovereign state, with the intention of establishing and consolidating rule of law, guaranteeing human rights and civil liberties, providing peace and coexistence, social justice, economic well-being and prosperity in the life of the individual and the community, and in this regard through their representatives in the Assembly of the Republic of Macedonia, elected in free and democratic elections, they adopt....

[. . .]

Article 7

(1) The Macedonian language, written using its Cyrillic alphabet, is the official language throughout the Republic of Macedonia and in the international relations of the Republic of Macedonia.

(2) Any other language spoken by at least 20 percent of the population is also an official language, written using its alphabet, as specified below.

(3) Any official personal documents of citizens speaking an official language other than Macedonian shall also be issued in that language, in addition to the Macedonian language, in accordance with the law.

(4) Any person living in a unit of local self-government in which at least 20 percent of the population speaks an official language other than Macedonian may use any official language to communicate with the regional office of the central government with responsibility for that municipality; such an office shall reply in that language in addition to Macedonian. Any person may use any official language to communicate with a main office of the central government, which shall reply in that language in addition to Macedonian.

(5) In the organs of the Republic of Macedonia, any official language other than Macedonian may be used in accordance with the law.

(6) In the units of local self-government where at least 20 percent of the population speaks a particular language, that language and its alphabet shall be used as an official language in addition to the Macedonian language and the Cyrillic alphabet. With respect to languages spoken by less than 20 percent of the population of a unit of local self-government, the local authorities shall decide on their use in public bodies.

Article 8

(1) The fundamental values of the constitutional order of the Republic of Macedonia are:
– the basic freedoms and rights of the individual and citizen, recognized in international law and set down in the Constitution;
– equitable representation of persons belonging to all communities in public bodies at all levels and in other areas of public life;

[. . .]

Article 19

(1) The freedom of religious confession is guaranteed.

(2) The right to express one's faith freely and publicly, individually or with others is guaranteed.

(3) The Macedonian Orthodox Church, the Islamic Religious Community in Macedonia, the Catholic Church, and other Religious communities and groups are separate from the state and equal before the law.

(4) The Macedonian Orthodox Church, the Islamic Religious Community in Macedonia, the Catholic Church, and other Religious communities and groups are free to establish schools and other social and charitable institutions, by ways of a procedure regulated by law.

[. . .]

Article 48

(1) Members of communities have a right freely to express, foster and develop their identity and community attributes, and to use their community symbols.

(2) The Republic guarantees the protection of the ethnic, cultural, linguistic and religious identity of all communities.

(3) Members of communities have the right to establish institutions for culture, art, science and education, as well as scholarly and other associations for the expression, fostering and development of their identity.

(4) Members of communities have the right to instruction in their language in primary and secondary education, as determined by law. In schools where education is carried out in another language, the Macedonian language is also studied.

[. . .]

Article 56

[. . .]

(2) The Republic guarantees the protection, promotion and enhancement of the historical and artistic heritage of Macedonia and all communities in Macedonia and the treasures of which it is composed, regardless of their legal status. The law regulates the mode and conditions under which specific items of general interest for the Republic can be ceded for use.

[. . .]

Article 69

[. . .]

(2) For laws that directly affect culture, use of language, education, personal documentation, and use of symbols, the Assembly makes decisions by a majority vote of the Representatives attending, within which there must be a majority of the votes of the Representatives attending who claim to belong to the communities not in the majority in the population of Macedonia. In the event of a dispute within the Assembly regarding the application of this provision, the Committee on Inter-Community Relations shall resolve the dispute.

[. . .]

Article 77

(1) The Assembly elects the Public Attorney by a majority vote of the total number of Representatives, within which there must be a majority of the votes of the total number of

Representatives claiming to belong to the communities not in the majority in the population of Macedonia.

(2) The Public Attorney protects the constitutional rights and legal rights of citizens when violated by bodies of state administration and by other bodies and organisations with public mandates. The Public Attorney shall give particular attention to safeguarding the principles of non-discrimination and equitable representation of communities in public bodies at all levels and in other areas of public life.

[...]

Article 78

(1) The Assembly shall establish a Committee for Inter-Community Relations.

(2) The Committee consists of seven members each from the ranks of the Macedonians and Albanians within the Assembly, and five members from among the Turks, Vlachs, Romanies and two other communities. The five members each shall be from a different community; if fewer than five other communities are represented in the Assembly, the Public Attorney, after consultation with relevant community leaders, shall propose the remaining members from outside the Assembly.

(3) The Assembly elects the members of the Committee.

(4) The Committee considers issues of inter-community relations in the Republic and makes appraisals and proposals for their solution.

(5) The Assembly is obliged to take into consideration the appraisals and proposals of the Committee and to make decisions regarding them.

(6) In the event of a dispute among members of the Assembly regarding the application of the voting procedure specified in Article 69(2), the Committee shall decide by majority vote whether the procedure applies.

[...]

Article 84

The President of the Republic of Macedonia

[...]

– proposes the members of the Council for Inter-Ethnic Relations; (to be deleted) . . . .

[...]

Article 86

(1) The President of the Republic is President of the Security Council of the Republic of Macedonia.

(2) The Security Council of the Republic is composed of the President of the Republic, the President of the Assembly, the Prime Minister, the Ministers heading the bodies of state administration in the fields of security, defence and foreign affairs and three members appointed by the President of the Republic. In appointing the three members, the President shall ensure that the Security Council as a whole equitably reflects the composition of the population of Macedonia.

(3) The Council considers issues relating to the security and defence of the Republic and makes policy proposals to the Assembly and the Government.

[...]

Article 104
(1) The Republican Judicial Council is composed of seven members.
(2) The Assembly elects the members of the Council. Three of the members shall be elected by a majority vote of the total number of Representatives, within which there must be a majority of the votes of the total number of Representatives claiming to belong to the communities not in the majority in the population of Macedonia.

[...]

Article 109
(1) The Constitutional Court of Macedonia is composed of nine judges.
(2) The Assembly elects six of the judges to the Constitutional Court by a majority vote of the total number of Representatives. The Assembly elects three of the judges by a majority vote of the total number of Representatives, within which there must be a majority of the votes of the total number of Representatives claiming to belong to the communities not in the majority in the population of Macedonia.

[...]

Article 114
[...]
(5) Local self-government is regulated by a law adopted by a two-thirds majority vote of the total number of Representatives, within which there must be a majority of the votes of the total number of Representatives claiming to belong to the communities not in the majority in the population of Macedonia. The laws on local finances, local elections, boundaries of municipalities, and the city of Skopje shall be adopted by a majority vote of the Representatives attending, within which there must be a majority of the votes of the Representatives attending who claim to belong to the communities not in the majority in the population of Macedonia.

Article 115
(1) In units of local self-government, citizens directly and through representatives participate in decision-making on issues of local relevance particularly in the fields of public services, urban and rural planning, environmental protection, local economic development, local finances, communal activities, culture, sport, social security and child care, education, health care and other fields determined by law.

[...]

Article 131
(1) The decision to initiate a change in the Constitution is made by the Assembly by a two-thirds majority vote of the total number of Representatives.
(2) The draft amendment to the Constitution is confirmed by the Assembly by a majority vote of the total number of Representatives and then submitted to public debate.
(3) The decision to change the Constitution is made by the Assembly by a two-thirds majority vote of the total number of Representatives.
(4) A decision to amend the Preamble, the articles on local self-government, Article 131, any provision relating to the rights of members of communities, including in particular Articles 7, 8, 9, 19, 48, 56, 69, 77, 78, 86, 104 and 109, as well as a decision to add any new provision relating to the subject matter of such provisions and articles, shall require a two-thirds majority vote of the total number of Representatives, within which there must be a majority of the votes

of the total number of Representatives claiming to belong to the communities not in the majority in the population of Macedonia.

(5) The change in the Constitution is declared by the Assembly.

Annex B
Legislative Modifications

The parties will take all necessary measures to ensure the adoption of the legislative changes set forth hereafter within the time limits specified.

1. Law on Local Self-Government

The Assembly shall adopt within 45 days from the signing of the Framework Agreement a revised Law on Local Self-Government. This revised Law shall in no respect be less favorable to the units of local self-government and their autonomy than the draft Law proposed by the Government of the Republic of Macedonia in March 2001. The Law shall include competencies relating to the subject matters set forth in Section 3.1 of the Framework Agreement as additional independent competencies of the units of local self-government, and shall conform to Section 6.6 of the Framework Agreement. In addition, the Law shall provide that any State standards or procedures established in any laws concerning areas in which municipalities have independent competencies shall be limited to those which cannot be established as effectively at the local level; such laws shall further promote the municipalities' independent exercise of their competencies.

2. Law on Local Finance

The Assembly shall adopt by the end of the term of the present Assembly a law on local self-government finance to ensure that the units of local self-government have sufficient resources to carry out their tasks under the revised Law on Local Self-Government. In particular, the law shall:

– Enable and make responsible units of local self-government for raising a substantial amount of tax revenue;

– Provide for the transfer to the units of local self-government of a part of centrally raised taxes that corresponds to the functions of the units of local self-government and that takes account of the collection of taxes on their territories; and

– Ensure the budgetary autonomy and responsibility of the units of local self-government within their areas of competence.

3. Law on Municipal Boundaries

The Assembly shall adopt by the end of 2002 a revised law on municipal boundaries, taking into account the results of the census and the relevant guidelines set forth in the Law on Local Self-Government.

4. Laws Pertaining to Police Located in the Municipalities

The Assembly shall adopt before the end of the term of the present Assembly provisions ensuring:

– That each local head of the police is selected by the council of the municipality concerned from a list of not fewer than three candidates proposed by the Ministry of the Interior, among whom at least one candidate shall belong to the community in the majority in the municipality. In the event the municipal council fails to select any of the candidates proposed within 15 days, the Ministry of the Interior shall propose a second list of not fewer than three new candidates, among whom at least one candidate shall belong to the community in the majority in the municipality. If the municipal council again fails to select any of the candidates proposed within 15 days, the Minister of the Interior, after consultation with the Government, shall select the local head of police from among the two lists of candidates proposed by the Ministry of the Interior as well as three additional candidates proposed by the municipal council;

– That each local head of the police informs regularly and upon request the council of the municipality concerned;
– That a municipal council may make recommendations to the local head of police in areas including public security and traffic safety; and
– That a municipal council may adopt annually a report regarding matters of public safety, which shall be addressed to the Minister of the Interior and the Public Attorney (Ombudsman).

5. Laws on the Civil Service and Public Administration

The Assembly shall adopt by the end of the term of the present Assembly amendments to the laws on the civil service and public administration to ensure equitable representation of communities in accordance with Section 4.2 of the Framework Agreement.

6. Law on Electoral Districts

The Assembly shall adopt by the end of 2002 a revised Law on Electoral Districts, taking into account the results of the census and the principles set forth in the Law on the Election of Members for the Parliament of the Republic of Macedonia.

7. Rules of the Assembly

The Assembly shall amend by the end of the term of the present Assembly its Rules of Procedure to enable the use of the Albanian language in accordance with Section 6.5 of the Framework Agreement, paragraph 8 below, and the relevant amendments to the Constitution set forth in Annex A.

8. Laws Pertinent to the Use of Languages

The Assembly shall adopt by the end of the term of the present Assembly new legislation regulating the use of languages in the organs of the Republic of Macedonia. This legislation shall provide that:
– Representatives may address plenary sessions and working bodies of the Assembly in languages referred to in Article 7, paragraphs 1 and 2 of the Constitution (as amended in accordance with Annex A);
– Laws shall be published in the languages referred to in Article 7, paragraphs 1 and 2 of the Constitution (as amended in accordance with Annex A); and
– All public officials may write their names in the alphabet of any language referred to in Article 7, paragraphs 1 and 2 of the Constitution (as amended in accordance with Annex A) on any official documents.

The Assembly also shall adopt by the end of the term of the present Assembly new legislation on the issuance of personal documents.

The Assembly shall amend by the end of the term of the present Assembly all relevant laws to make their provisions on the use of languages fully compatible with Section 6 of the Framework Agreement.

9. Law on the Public Attorney

The Assembly shall amend by the end of 2002 the Law on the Public Attorney as well as the other relevant laws to ensure:
– That the Public Attorney shall undertake actions to safeguard the principles of non-discrimination and equitable representation of communities in public bodies at all levels and in other areas of public life, and that there are adequate resources and personnel within his office to enable him to carry out this function;
– That the Public Attorney establishes decentralized offices;
– That the budget of the Public Attorney is voted separately by the Assembly;
– That the Public Attorney shall present an annual report to the Assembly and, where appropriate, may upon request present reports to the councils of municipalities in which decentralized offices are established; and
– That the powers of the Public Attorney are enlarged:

– To grant to him access to and the opportunity to examine all official documents, it being understood that the Public Attorney and his staff will not disclose confidential information;
– To enable the Public Attorney to suspend, pending a decision of the competent court, the execution of an administrative act, if he determines that the act may result in an irreparable prejudice to the rights of the interested person; and
– To give to the Public Attorney the right to contest the conformity of laws with the Constitution before the Constitutional Court.

10. Other Laws

The Assembly shall enact all legislative provisions that may be necessary to give full effect to the Framework Agreement and amend or abrogate all provisions incompatible with the Framework Agreement.

Annex C
Implementation and confidence-building measures

1. International Support

1.1. The parties invite the international community to facilitate, monitor and assist in the implementation of the provisions of the Framework Agreement and its Annexes, and request such efforts to be coordinated by the EU in cooperation with the Stabilization and Association Council.

2. Census and Elections

2.1. The parties confirm the request for international supervision by the Council of Europe and the European Commission of a census to be conducted in October 2001.

2.2. Parliamentary elections will be held by 27 January 2002. International organisations, including the OSCE, will be invited to observe these elections.

3. Refugee Return, Rehabilitation and Reconstruction

3.1. All parties will work to ensure the return of refugees who are citizens or legal residents of Macedonia and displaced persons to their homes within the shortest possible timeframe, and invite the international community and in particular UNHCR to assist in these efforts.

3.2. The Government with the participation of the parties will complete an action plan within 30 days after the signature of the Framework Agreement for rehabilitation of and reconstruction in areas affected by the hostilities. The parties invite the international community to assist in the formulation and implementation of this plan.

3.3. The parties invite the European Commission and the World Bank to rapidly convene a meeting of international donors after adoption in the Assembly of the Constitutional amendments in Annex A and the revised Law on Local Self-Government to support the financing of measures to be undertaken for the purpose of implementing the Framework Agreement and its Annexes, including measures to strengthen local self-government and reform the police services, to address macro-financial assistance to the Republic of Macedonia, and to support the rehabilitation and reconstruction measures identified in the action plan identified in paragraph 3.2.

4. Development of Decentralized Government

4.1. The parties invite the international community to assist in the process of strengthening local self-government. The international community should in particular assist in preparing the necessary legal amendments related to financing mechanisms for strengthening the financial basis of municipalities and building their financial management capabilities, and in amending the law on the boundaries of municipalities.

5. Non-Discrimination and Equitable Representation

5.1. Taking into account i.a. the recommendations of the already established governmental commission, the parties will take concrete action to increase the representation of members of communities not in the majority in Macedonia in public administration, the military, and public enterprises, as well as to improve their access to public financing for business development.

5.2. The parties commit themselves to ensuring that the police services will by 2004 generally reflect the composition and distribution of the population of Macedonia. As initial steps toward this end, the parties commit to ensuring that 500 new police officers from communities not in the majority in the population of Macedonia will be hired and trained by July 2002, and that these officers will be deployed to the areas where such communities live. The parties further commit that 500 additional such officers will be hired and trained by July 2003, and that these officers will be deployed on a priority basis to the areas throughout Macedonia where such communities live. The parties invite the international community to support and assist with the implementation of these commitments, in particular through screening and selection of candidates and their training. The parties invite the OSCE, the European Union, and the United States to send an expert team as quickly as possible in order to assess how best to achieve these objectives.

5.3. The parties also invite the OSCE, the European Union, and the United States to increase training and assistance programs for police, including:
– professional, human rights, and other training;
– technical assistance for police reform, including assistance in screening, selection and promotion processes;
– development of a code of police conduct;
– cooperation with respect to transition planning for hiring and deployment of police officers from communities not in the majority in Macedonia; and
– deployment as soon as possible of international monitors and police advisors in sensitive areas, under appropriate arrangements with relevant authorities.

5.4. The parties invite the international community to assist in the training of lawyers, judges and prosecutors from members of communities not in the majority in Macedonia in order to be able to increase their representation in the judicial system.

6. Culture, Education and Use of Languages

6.1. The parties invite the international community, including the OSCE, to increase its assistance for projects in the area of media in order to further strengthen radio, TV and print media, including Albanian language and multiethnic media. The parties also invite the international community to increase professional media training programs for members of communities not in the majority in Macedonia. The parties also invite the OSCE to continue its efforts on projects designed to improve inter-ethnic relations.

6.2. The parties invite the international community to provide assistance for the implementation of the Framework Agreement in the area of higher education.

Appendix F
Convention for the Protection of the Marine Environment of the North-East Atlantic, 22 September 1992[*]

Selected articles

[...]

ARTICLE 10
COMMISSION
1. A Commission, made up of representatives of each of the Contracting Parties, is hereby established. The Commission shall meet at regular intervals and at any time when, due to special circumstances, it is so decided in accordance with the Rules of Procedure.
2. It shall be the duty of the Commission:
(a) to supervise the implementation of the Convention;
(b) generally to review the condition of the maritime area, the effectiveness of the measures being adopted, the priorities and the need for any additional or different measures;
(c) to draw up, in accordance with the General Obligations of the Convention, programmes and measures for the prevention and elimination of pollution and for the control of activities which may, directly or indirectly, adversely affect the maritime area; such programmes and measure may, when appropriate, include economic instruments;
(d) to establish at regular intervals its programme of work;
(e) to set up such subsidiary bodies as it considers necessary and to define their terms of reference;
(f) to consider and, where appropriate, adopt proposals for the amendment of the Convention in accordance with Articles 15, 16, 17, 18, 19 and 27;
(g) to discharge the functions conferred by Articles 21 and 23 and such other functions as may be appropriate under the terms of the Convention;
3. To these ends the Commission may, inter alia, adopt decisions and recommendations in accordance with Article 13.
4. The Commission shall draw up its Rules of Procedure which shall be adopted by unanimous vote of the Contracting Parties.
5. The Commission shall draw up its Financial Regulations which shall be adopted by unanimous vote of the Contracting Parties.

[...]

ARTICLE 22
REPORTING TO THE COMMISSION
The Contracting Parties shall report to the Commission at regular intervals on:
(a) the legal, regulatory, or other measures taken by them for the implementation of the provisions of the Convention and of decisions and recommendations adopted thereunder,

---

[*] Source: OSPAR Commission for the Protection of the Marine Environment of the North-East Atlantic, <http://www.ospar.org/eng/html/welcome.html> (2 August 2006).

including in particular measures taken to prevent and punish conduct in contravention of those provisions;
(b) the effectiveness of the measures referred to in subparagraph (a) of this Article;
(c) problems encountered in the implementation of the provisions referred to in subparagraph (a) of this Article.

ARTICLE 23
COMPLIANCE
The Commission shall:
(a) on the basis of the periodical reports referred to in Article 22 and any other report submitted by the Contracting Parties, assess their compliance with the Convention and the decisions and recommendations adopted thereunder;
(b) when appropriate, decide upon and call for steps to bring about full compliance with the Convention, and decisions adopted thereunder, and promote the implementation of recommendations, including measures to assist a Contracting Party to carry out its obligations.

[…]

ARTICLE 32
SETTLEMENT OF DISPUTES
1. Any disputes between Contracting Parties relating to the interpretation or application of the Convention, which cannot be settled otherwise by the Contracting Parties concerned, for instance by means of inquiry or conciliation within the Commission, shall at the request of any of those Contracting Parties, be submitted to arbitration under the conditions laid down in this Article.
2. Unless the parties to the dispute decide otherwise, the procedure of the arbitration referred to in paragraph 1 of this Article shall be in accordance with paragraphs 3 to 10 of this Article.
(a) At the request addressed by one Contracting Party to another Contracting Party in accordance with paragraph 1 of this Article, an arbitral tribunal shall be constituted. The request for arbitration shall state the subject matter of the application including in particular the Articles of the Convention, the interpretation or application of which is in dispute.
(b) The applicant party shall inform the Commission that it has requested the setting up of an arbitral tribunal, stating the name of the other party to the dispute and the Articles of the Convention the interpretation or application of which, in its opinion, is in dispute. The Commission shall forward the information thus received to all Contracting Parties to the Convention.
3. The arbitral tribunal shall consist of three members: each of the parties to the dispute shall appoint an arbitrator; the two arbitrators so appointed shall designate by common agreement the third arbitrator who shall be the chairman of the tribunal. The latter shall not be a national of one of the parties to the dispute, nor have his usual place of residence in the territory of one of these parties, nor be employed by any of them, nor have dealt with the case in any other capacity.
4. (a) If the chairman of the arbitral tribunal has not been designated within two months of the appointment of the second arbitrator, the President of the International Court of Justice shall, at the request of either party, designate him within a further two months' period.
(b) If one of the parties to the dispute does not appoint an arbitrator within two months of receipt of the request, the other party may inform the President of the International Court of Justice who shall designate the chairman of the arbitral tribunal within a further two months' period. Upon designation, the chairman of the arbitral tribunal shall request the party which has not appointed an arbitrator to do so within two months. After such period, he shall inform the President of the International Court of Justice who shall make this appointment within a further two months' period.

5. (a) The arbitral tribunal shall decide according to the rules of international law and, in particular, those of the Convention.

(b) Any arbitral tribunal constituted under the provisions of this Article shall draw up its own rules of procedure.

(c) In the event of a dispute as to whether the arbitral tribunal has jurisdiction, the matter shall be decided by the decision of the arbitral tribunal.

6. (a) The decisions of the arbitral tribunal, both on procedure and on substance, shall be taken by majority voting of its members.

(b) The arbitral tribunal may take all appropriate measures in order to establish the facts. It may, at the request of one of the parties, recommend essential interim measures of protection.

(c) If two or more arbitral tribunals constituted under the provisions of this Article are seized of requests with identical or similar subjects, they may inform themselves of the procedures for establishing the facts and take them into account as far as possible.

(d) The parties to the dispute shall provide all facilities necessary for the effective conduct of the proceedings.

(e) The absence or default of a party to the dispute shall not constitute an impediment to the proceedings.

7. Unless the arbitral tribunal determines otherwise because of the particular circumstances of the case, the expenses of the tribunal, including the remuneration of its members, shall be borne by the parties to the dispute in equal shares. The tribunal shall keep a record of all its expenses, and shall furnish a final statement thereof to the parties.

8. Any Contracting Party that has an interest of a legal nature in the subject matter of the dispute which may be affected by the decision in the case, may intervene in the proceedings with the consent of the tribunal.

9. (a) The award of the arbitral tribunal shall be accompanied by a statement of reasons. It shall be final and binding upon the parties to the dispute.

(b) Any dispute which may arise between the parties concerning the interpretation or execution of the award may be submitted by either party to the arbitral tribunal which made the award or, if the latter cannot be seized thereof, to another arbitral tribunal constituted for this purpose in the same manner as the first.

Appendix G
United Nations Convention on the Law of the Sea, 10 December 1982*

Selected articles

[...]

PART XI

SECTION 5. SETTLEMENT OF DISPUTES AND ADVISORY OPINIONS

Article 186
  Seabed Disputes Chamber of the International Tribunal for the Law of the Sea
  The establishment of the Seabed Disputes Chamber and the manner in which it shall exercise its jurisdiction shall be governed by the provisions of this section, of Part XV and of Annex VI.

Article 187
  Jurisdiction of the Seabed Disputes Chamber
  The Seabed Disputes Chamber shall have jurisdiction under this Part and the Annexes relating thereto in disputes with respect to activities in the Area falling within the following categories:
  a. disputes between States Parties concerning the interpretation or application of this Part and the Annexes relating thereto;
  b. disputes between a State Party and the Authority concerning: (i) acts or omissions of the Authority or of a State Party alleged to be in violation of this Part or the Annexes relating thereto or of rules, regulations and procedures of the Authority adopted in accordance therewith; or (ii) acts of the Authority alleged to be in excess of jurisdiction or a misuse of power;
  c. disputes between parties to a contract, being States Parties, the Authority or the Enterprise, state enterprises and natural or juridical persons referred to in article 153, paragraph 2 (b), concerning:
    i. the interpretation or application of a relevant contract or a plan of work; or
    ii. acts or omissions of a party to the contract relating to activities in the Area and directed to the other party or directly affecting its legitimate interests;
  d. disputes between the Authority and a prospective contractor who has been sponsored by a State as provided in article 153, paragraph 2 (b), and has duly fulfilled the conditions referred to in Annex III, article 4, paragraph 6, and article 13, paragraph 2, concerning the refusal of a contract or a legal issue arising in the negotiation of the contract;
  e. disputes between the Authority and a State Party, a state enterprise or a natural or juridical person sponsored by a State Party as provided for in article 153, paragraph 2(b), where it is alleged that the Authority has incurred liability as provided in Annex III, article 22;
  f. any other disputes for which the jurisdiction of the Chamber is specifically provided in this Convention.

---

* Source: UN Division for Oceans and Law of the Sea, <http://www.un.org/Depts/los/convention_agreements/texts/unclos/closindx.htm> (2 August 2006).

Article 188
Submission of disputes to a special chamber of the International Tribunal for the Law of the Sea or an ad hoc chamber of the Seabed Disputes Chamber or to binding commercial arbitration
1. Disputes between States Parties referred to in article 187, subparagraph (a), may be submitted:
a. at the request of the parties to the dispute, to a special chamber of the International Tribunal for the Law of the Sea to be formed in accordance with Annex VI, articles 15 and 17; or at
b. the request of any party to the dispute, to an ad hoc chamber of the Seabed Disputes Chamber to be formed in accordance with Annex VI, article 36.
2. a. Disputes concerning the interpretation or application of a contract referred to in article 187, subparagraph (c) (i), shall be submitted, at the request of any party to the dispute, to binding commercial arbitration, unless the parties otherwise agree. A commercial arbitral tribunal to which the dispute is submitted shall have no jurisdiction to decide any question of interpretation of this Convention. When the dispute also involves a question of the interpretation of Part XI and the Annexes relating thereto, with respect to activities in the Area, that question shall be referred to the Seabed Disputes Chamber for a ruling.
b. If, at the commencement of or in the course of such arbitration, the arbitral tribunal determines, either at the request of any party to the dispute or proprio motu, that its decision depends upon a ruling of the Seabed Disputes Chamber, the arbitral tribunal shall refer such question to the Seabed Disputes Chamber for such ruling. The arbitral tribunal shall then proceed to render its award in conformity with the ruling of the SeaBed Disputes Chamber.
c. In the absence of a provision in the contract on the arbitration procedure to be applied in the dispute, the arbitration shall be conducted in accordance with the UNCITRAL Arbitration Rules or such other arbitration rules as may be prescribed in the rules, regulations and procedures of the Authority, unless the parties to the dispute otherwise agree.

Article 189
Limitation on jurisdiction with regard to decisions of the Authority
The Seabed Disputes Chamber shall have no jurisdiction with regard to the exercise by the Authority of its discretionary powers in accordance with this Part; in no case shall it substitute its discretion for that of the Authority. Without prejudice to article 191, in exercising its jurisdiction pursuant to article 187, the Seabed Disputes Chamber shall not pronounce itself on the question of whether any rules, regulations and procedures of the Authority are in conformity with this Convention, nor declare invalid any such rules, regulations and procedures. Its jurisdiction in this regard shall be confined to deciding claims that the application of any rules, regulations and procedures of the Authority in individual cases would be in conflict with the contractual obligations of the parties to the dispute or their obligations under this Convention, claims concerning excess of jurisdiction or misuse of power, and to claims for damages to be paid or other remedy to be given to the party concerned for the failure of the other party to comply with its contractual obligations or its obligations under this Convention.

Article 190
Participation and appearance of sponsoring States Parties in proceedings
1. If a natural or juridical person is a party to a dispute referred to in article 187, the sponsoring State shall be given notice thereof and shall have the right to participate in the proceedings by submitting written or oral statements.
2. If an action is brought against a State Party by a natural or juridical person sponsored by another State Party in a dispute referred to in article 187, subparagraph (c), the respondent State may request the State sponsoring that person to appear in the proceedings on behalf of that

person. Failing such appearance, the respondent State may arrange to be represented by a juridical person of its nationality.

Article 191
   Advisory opinions
   The Seabed Disputes Chamber shall give advisory opinions at the request of the Assembly or the Council on legal questions arising within the scope of their activities. Such opinions shall be given as a matter of urgency.

Appendix H
The General Framework Agreement for Peace in Bosnia and Herzegovina,
14 December 1995[*]

Selected articles

[...]

ANNEX 2

Agreement on Inter-Entity Boundary Line and Related Issues

Article I: Inter-Entity Boundary Line
The boundary between the Federation of Bosnia and Herzegovina and the Republika Srpska (the 'Inter-Entity Boundary Line') shall be as delineated on the map at the Appendix.

[...]

Article V: Arbitration for the Brcko Area
1. The Parties agree to binding arbitration of the disputed portion of the Inter-Entity Boundary Line in the Brcko area indicated on the map attached at the Appendix.

2. No later than six months after the entry into force of this Agreement, the Federation shall appoint one arbitrator, and the Republika Srpska shall appoint one arbitrator. A third arbitrator shall be selected by agreement of the Parties' appointees within thirty days thereafter. If they do not agree, the third arbitrator shall be appointed by the President of the International Court of Justice. The third arbitrator shall serve as presiding officer of the arbitral tribunal.

3. Unless otherwise agreed by the Parties, the proceedings shall be conducted in accordance with the UNCITRAL rules. The arbitrators shall apply relevant legal and equitable principles.

4. Unless otherwise agreed, the area indicated in paragraph 1 above shall continue to be administered as currently.

5. The arbitrators shall issue their decision no later than one year from the entry into force of this Agreement. The decision shall be final and binding, and the Parties shall implement it without delay.

[...]

Article VIII: Entry into Force
This Agreement shall enter into force upon signature.

For the Republic of Bosnia and Herzegovina

For the Federation of Bosnia and Herzegovina

---

[*] Source: Office of the High Representative in Bosnia and Herzegovina, <http://www.ohr.int/dpa/default.asp?content_id=370> (2 August 2006).

For the Republika Srpska

Endorsed:

For the Republic of Croatia

Endorsed:

For the Federal Republic of Yugoslavia

Appendix I
Introductory Note – Arbitral Tribunal for the Dispute over Inter-entity Boundary in Brcko Area: the Federation of Bosnia and Herzegovina v. the Republika Srpska – Final Award (5 March 1999)*

Introductory Note by Christoph H. Schreuer**

The General Framework Agreement for Peace in Bosnia and Herzegovina (Dayton Accords) of 14 December 1995[1] establishes an Inter-Entity Boundary Line (IEBL) between the Federation of Bosnia and Herzegovina (Federation of BIH), representing the Bosniac and Croat held part of the country, and the Republika Srpska (RS), representing the Serb held part of the country. No agreement was reached over the IEBL in the Brcko area. The dispute over the Brcko area was particularly sensitive and strategically important. Article V(1) of Annex 2 to the Dayton Accords[2] provided for binding arbitration of the IEBL in the Brcko area.

The parties to the arbitration were the two entities within Bosnia and Herzegovina (BIH), the Federation of BIH and the RS. The parties each appointed one arbitrator. As a consequence of the failure of the two party-appointed arbitrators to agree on a third arbitrator, the President of the International Court of Justice appointed Roberts B. Owen as Presiding Arbitrator in accordance with Article V(2) of Annex 2 to the Dayton Accords. Article V(3) instructed the Tribunal to follow the UNCITRAL Arbitration Rules[3] unless otherwise agreed by the parties. On the merits the Tribunal was to apply 'relevant legal and equitable principles.'

A first award was handed down on February 14, 1997.[4] A second award, the Supplemental Award, was handed down on March 15, 1998. The third award of March 5, 1999, reproduced below, is the Final Award.[5] All three awards bear the signature of the Presiding Arbitrator only. The problem of the Tribunal not being able to reach a majority had been anticipated. In order to meet that contingency, the parties agreed that in the absence of a majority, the decision of the presiding arbitrator would be final and binding upon the parties.[6]

The Tribunal adopted an unusually broad interpretation of its terms of reference. Rather than drawing the boundary line in the area under dispute, it designed an administrative regime. The first award of 1997 created an interim international supervisory system. Supervision was to be exercised mainly by a specially appointed Brcko Supervisor with far-reaching legislative and administrative powers. In particular, he is to ensure the return of former residents, freedom of movement and the protection of all citizens of BIH in the area.

The Supplemental Award of 1998 directed that the supervisory regime created by the first award should continue for the time being. It noted the RS's non-compliance with the Dayton Accords and the lack of cooperation with the Supervisor. It held out the prospect of another award by early 1999 and indicated that its outcome would depend on the compliance of the parties, especially the RS.

The Final Award, reproduced below, finds that there was a massive failure of the Serb authorities, especially in Brcko, to meet the standards set out in the previous awards (paras. 14-33). But it also finds that the Federation's performance in facilitating the return of Serb displaced persons was less than satisfactory (para. 56). Therefore, it establishes a permanent self-governing

---

* Source: International Legal Materials, 38 ILM 534 (1999).

** Edward B. Burling Professor of International Law and Organisation, The Paul H. Nitze School of Advanced International Studies, Johns Hopkins University; and Professor of Law, Department of International Law, University of Salzburg, Austria.

Brcko District of Bosnia and Herzegovina that is part of BIH but is independent of the two entities. The newly formed District will form a single administrative unit (para. 9). The District is under the sovereignty of BIH, but the two entities, the Federation of BIH and the RS, will hold it in condominium (paras. 11, 52). There will be a single unitary, multi-ethnic, democratic government throughout the entire area. The new District government will be subject to the powers of the common institutions of BIH in those areas which are the responsibility of the BIH common institutions. In other respects, the District government will operate on a self-governing basis (paras. 10, 34). The District will have its own democratically elected legislature, executive and judiciary (para. 36). There will be a unified police force under a single command that is independent of the two entities (paras. 36, 40). The IEBL will disappear after a transition period (paras. 8, 11, 39). The Supervisor will retain responsibility for overall coordination but may delegate that responsibility to an appropriate BIH institution (paras. 8, 10, 34, 37).

The strategic importance of the Brcko area, which forms a narrow corridor between the two parts of the RS, was one of the main difficulties in this dispute. Under the terms of the Final Award, neither entity shall allow any of its armed forces to be based in the District (para. 41). Military movements by the RS through the District will continue to be subject to SFOR permission and thereafter will take place only in accordance with the law of BIH and of the District (paras. 42, 53).

An Annex attached to the Final Award sets out the structure of the new District in some detail. The parties are given a 60-day opportunity to provide comments on the Annex (but not on the Award itself) with a view to possible modifications (paras. 35, 63).

Despite its title as Final Award, the Tribunal reserves the right to revisit the case if there is a failure to cooperate with the award's implementation. The Tribunal states that it will remain in existence and will retain jurisdiction over this dispute until the Supervisor, with the approval of the High Representative, has notified the Tribunal that the two entities have fully complied with their obligations to facilitate the establishment of the new institutions and that the institutions are functioning effectively and apparently permanently. Until such notification, the Tribunal reserves the authority to modify the Final Award including, in the event of serious non-compliance, the authority to transfer the District entirely out of the territory of the non-complying entity into the exclusive control of the other (paras. 8, 13, 65-68).

The Tribunal clearly assumed a public order function in deciding this case. Traditionally, arbitration is perceived as a mandate narrowly defined by the parties' agreement. Digression beyond this parameter is sometimes threatened by nullity. The Brcko Tribunal took a much broader view of its function. Despite its seemingly narrow task to determine the Inter-Entity Boundary Line, it took it upon itself to find the optimum solution as determined by the object and purpose of the Dayton Accords. It first created an international system of supervision and then a special neutral regime for the disputed area. The Tribunal took its mandate less from the disputing parties' agreement than from its role as an agent of the international community (See paras. 47-49, 57).

Notes
[1] 35 ILM 75 (1996).
[2] See 35 ILM 113 (1996).
[3] See 15 ILM 701 (1976).
[4] See 36 ILM 396 (1997).
[5] For a more detailed description and discussion of the three awards see Christoph Schreuer, 'The Brcko Award of 14 February 1997', 11 *Leiden Journal of International Law* 71 (1998), Christoph Schreuer, 'The Brcko Supplemental Award of 15 March 1998', 11 *Leiden Journal of International Law* 493 (1998), and Christoph Schreuer, 'The Brcko Final Award of 5 March 1999', 12 *Leiden Journal of International Law* (forthcoming, No. 3, 1999).
[6] See 36 ILM 401 (1997).

Appendix J
Eritrea-Yemen Arbitration Agreement,
3 October 1996[*]

The Government of the State of Eritrea and the Government of the Republic of Yemen (hereinafter 'the Parties');

Prompted by the desire to re-establish their peaceful relations in the spirit of the traditional friendship between their two peoples,

Conscious of their responsibilities towards the international community as regards the maintenance of international peace and security as well as the safeguard of the freedom of navigation in a particularly sensitive region of the world,

Considering the 'Agreement on Principles' between Eritrea and Yemen signed at Paris the twenty-first day of May, 1996 (hereinafter 'the Agreement on Principles');

Have agreed as follows:

Article 1

1. On or before 31 December 1996, the Parties will provide the names and addresses of their appointed arbitrators to one another and to France. The four arbitrators thus named shall meet within two weeks to consider the choice of the President of the Tribunal.

2. Within two weeks thereafter the four arbitrators will narrow their consideration to a list of five names which they will then circulate to the Parties.

3. The Parties will have two weeks from the date of circulation of the list during which they may present their views concerning the list.

4. The four arbitrators shall then attempt to reach agreement on the choice of the President. On reaching agreement, they will inform the Parties that the Tribunal has been formed.

5. If no agreement has been reached by 15 March 1997, they shall so inform the President of the International Court of Justice and, pursuant to the Agreement on Principles, they shall request him to choose the President of the Tribunal. In transmitting this request, the four arbitrators shall make known any views that the Parties have expressed on the choice of the President of the Tribunal. The President of the International Court of Justice shall choose within two weeks and after consultation with the Party-appointed arbitrators. By 31 March 1997 at the latest, he shall notify the Parties, the four arbitrators and France that the Tribunal has been formed and of the name of the President of the Tribunal.

6. The Tribunal shall meet on or before 11 April 1997.

7. All the members of the Tribunal commit themselves to exercise their powers impartially and conscientiously.

8. France shall transmit a certified copy of the Agreement on Principles and of this Arbitration Agreement to the members of the Tribunal as soon as they are chosen.

Article 2

1. The Tribunal is requested to provide rulings in accordance with international law, in two stages.

2. The first stage shall result in an award on territorial sovereignty and on the definition of the scope of the dispute between Eritrea and Yemen. The Tribunal shall decide territorial

---

[*] Source: Permanent Court of Arbitration, <http://www.pca-cpa.org/ENGLISH/RPC/EY/arbagree ER-YE.htm> (2 August 2006).

sovereignty in accordance with the principles, rules and practices of international law applicable to the matter, and on the basis, in particular, of historic titles. The Tribunal shall decide on the definition of the scope of the dispute on the basis of the respective positions of the two Parties.

3. The second stage shall result in an award delimiting maritime boundaries. The Tribunal shall decide taking into account the opinion that it will have formed on questions of territorial sovereignty, the United Nations Convention on the Law of the Sea, and any other pertinent factor.

a) The Tribunal shall describe the course of the delimitation in a technically precise manner. To this end, the geometric nature of all elements of the delimitation shall be indicated and the position of all the points mentioned shall be given by reference to their co-ordinates in the World Geodetic System 1984 (W.G.S. 84).

The Tribunal shall also indicate for illustrative purposes only the course of delimitation on an appropriate chart.

b) After consultation with the Parties, the Tribunal shall designate a technical expert to assist it in carrying out the duties specified in letter a) above.

Article 3

1. The participation of all Tribunal members shall be required for the awards. The presence of all members shall also be required for all proceedings and decisions other than the awards except that the President may determine that the absence of not more than a single member from any proceeding or decision other than the awards is justified for good cause.

2. a) If a member of the Tribunal chosen by a Party is unable or unwilling to act and to continue to perform his functions, this Party shall name a replacement within a period of one month from the date on which the Tribunal declares the existence of the vacancy.

b) If the President of the Tribunal is unable or unwilling to act and to continue to perform his functions, a replacement shall be chosen by the Party-appointed members of the Tribunal within a maximum period of two months from the date on which the Tribunal declares the existence of the vacancy. if they cannot agree within this period, the President of the Tribunal shall be chosen by the President of the International Court of Justice.

c) Where a vacancy has been filled after the proceedings have begun, the proceedings shall continue from the point they had reached at the time the vacancy had occurred.

3. All members of the Tribunal shall be deemed to be present for the purposes of the provisions of paragraph 1 of this Article and notwithstanding the existence of vacancies where the only matter for consideration is the declaration of vacancies for the purposes of paragraph 2 of this Article or where either Party has neglected to fill a vacancy as provided by paragraph 2, letter a) of this Article.

Article 4

1. Subject to paragraph 2 of this Article, the decisions of the Tribunal concerning questions of substance or questions of procedure, including questions related to the competence of the Tribunal or the interpretation of this Arbitration Agreement, shall be made by a majority of its members if those decisions cannot be made unanimously.

2. In the case of an even division of the votes in the circumstances referred to in paragraph 3 of Article 3 above, the vote of the President shall be decisive.

Article 5

Subject to the provisions of this Arbitration Agreement, the Tribunal shall decide on its rules of procedure and on all questions relating to the conduct of the arbitration.

Article 6

1. Each Party, within thirty days of the signature of this Arbitration Agreement, shall designate an Agent, who will represent it and act on its behalf for the purposes of the arbitration, and shall communicate the name and address of its Agent to the other Party and, upon its formation, to the Tribunal.

2. Each Agent so designated shall be entitled to name one Co-Agent or more to act for him where necessary. The name and the address of the Co-Agent(s) so named shall be communicated to the other Party and, upon its formation, to the Tribunal.

Article 7

1. The Tribunal shall sit in London.

2. The Tribunal shall appoint a Registrar after consultation with the Agents, as soon as possible and in any event no later than its first meeting.

The Registrar shall perform his functions impartially and conscientiously.

3. After consultations with the Agents the Tribunal may engage such staff and secure such services and equipment as it deems necessary.

4. The Tribunal may consult any experts of its choice after notice to the Parties. Such experts shall perform their functions impartially and conscientiously.

5. a) At any time during the arbitral proceedings the Tribunal may call upon either Party to produce documents or other evidence relevant to the question within such a period of time as the Tribunal shall determine. Any documents or other evidence so produced shall also be provided to the other Party.

b) if either Party fails to respond to a request for the production of documents or evidence under paragraph a), the Tribunal may draw from this failure any appropriate evidentiary inference and may make an award based upon the evidence before it.

c) At any time during the arbitral proceedings the Tribunal may request if necessary that a nonparty to this Arbitration Agreement provide to it documents or other evidence relevant to the question. Any documents or other evidence so provided shall be transmitted simultaneously to both Parties.

Article 8

1. The proceedings before the Tribunal shall be adversarial.

2. Without prejudice to any question relating to the burden of proof, the proceedings before the Tribunal shall include two stages as follows.

3. The first stage concerning questions of territorial sovereignty and the definition of the scope of the dispute mentioned in Article 2, paragraph 2 of this Arbitration Agreement shall include two phases, one written and the other oral.

3.1 The written pleadings shall consist of:

a) A memorial to be submitted by each Party to the Tribunal and to the other Party not later than 31 August 1997;

b) A counter-memorial to be submitted by each Party to the Tribunal and to the other Party not later than three months after submission of the memorials;

c) Any other pleading that the Tribunal deems necessary, such pleading to be submitted not later than two months after submission of the counter-memorials.

3.2 An oral phase shall follow the written phase.

a) It shall be held at the seat of the Tribunal, at the place and on the dates determined by the Tribunal after consultation with the Agents. The oral phase shall start in so far as possible not later than three months after the submission of the last written pleadings of the Parties under Article 8, paragraph 3.1 above.

b) Each Party shall be represented in the oral phase of the proceedings by its Agent or, as appropriate, by its Co-Agent, and by such counsel, advisers and experts as it may designate.

3.3 At the conclusion of the oral phase, the Tribunal shall declare the end of the proceedings in the first stage. Notwithstanding such declaration, the Tribunal may request from the Parties their written views on any issues necessary for the elucidation of any aspect of the matters before the Tribunal until the award on questions of territorial sovereignty and the definition of the scope of the dispute is rendered.

3.4 The Tribunal shall render its award, which shall be binding, on questions of territorial sovereignty and the definition of the scope of the dispute in so far as possible not later than three months from the end of the proceedings as declared under Article 8, paragraph 3.3 above.

3.5 The Tribunal shall communicate this award to the Agents on the day of its rendering. The Tribunal and the Parties may make public this award as of the day of its rendering.

4. The second stage concerning questions of delimitation of maritime boundaries mentioned in Article 2, paragraph 3 of this Arbitration Agreement shall begin immediately upon the rendering of the award which concludes the first stage. It shall include two phases, one written and the other oral

4.1 The written pleadings shall consist of:

a) A memorial to be submitted by each Party to the Tribunal and to the other Party not later than four months after the rendering of the award on questions of territorial sovereignty and the definition of the scope of the dispute;

b) A counter-memorial to be submitted by each Party to the Tribunal and to the other Party not later than two months after submission of the memorials;

c) Any other pleading that the Tribunal deems necessary, such pleading to be submitted not later than two months after submission of the counter-memorials.

4.2 The oral phase shall follow the written phase.

a) It shall be held at the seat of the Tribunal, at the place and on the dates determined by the Tribunal after consultation with the Agents. The oral phase shall start in so far as possible not later than three months as of the submission of the last written pleadings of the Parties under Article 8, paragraph 4.1 above;

b) Each Party shall be represented in the oral phase of the proceedings by its Agent or, as appropriate, by its Co-Agent, and by such counsel, advisers and experts as it may designate.

4.3 At the conclusion of the oral phase, the Tribunal shall declare the end of the proceedings in the second stage. Notwithstanding such declaration, the Tribunal may request from the Parties their written views on any issues necessary for the elucidation of any aspect of the matters before the Tribunal until the award on questions of delimitation of maritime boundaries is rendered.

4.4 The Tribunal shall render its award on questions of delimitation of maritime boundaries in so far as possible not later than three months after the end of the proceedings before it as declared under Article 8, paragraph 4.3 above.

5. The Tribunal shall be empowered for good cause only to extend the time periods established in this Article on its own or at the request of either Party. The total cumulative extension of the time periods granted by the Tribunal at the request of either Party during the proceedings under the provisions of this sub-paragraph cannot exceed two months for each Party for each stage.

6. The Registrar shall provide the Parties with an address for the filing of their written pleadings and of any other document.

The Registrar shall transmit to the Parties simultaneously copies of all written pleadings and documents upon receipt thereof.

7. If, within the period of time fixed by this Arbitration Agreement or by the Tribunal, either Party fails to make a scheduled appearance or file a written pleading, the Tribunal shall continue the proceedings nonetheless and shall make an award based upon the pleadings before it.

Article 9

1. The written and oral pleadings before the Tribunal shall be in English. Decisions of the Tribunal shall be in English.

The Tribunal shall keep a verbatim transcript of all hearings.

Verbatim transcripts of the oral proceedings shall be communicated to the Agents as soon as possible.

2. All documentary evidence shall be filed in their original languages by the Parties. The parties shall arrange for any translation that they deem necessary for their own preparation of the case.

The Tribunal may avail itself of translation services where it deems appropriate. Any translations thus generated shall be provided to the Parties.

3. All written pleadings and verbatim transcripts of the oral proceedings and all the deliberations of the Tribunal shall be confidential.

4. Members of the public shall not be admitted to the oral proceedings.

Article 10

1. The remuneration of the members of the Tribunal and of the Registrar shall be borne equally by the Parties.

2. The general expenses of the arbitration shall be borne equally by the Parties. The Registrar shall keep a record and render a final account of the expenses.

3. Each Party shall bear all the expenses incurred by it in the preparation and conduct of its case.

Article 11

1. Without prejudice to the provisions of the Agreement on Principles, the Tribunal, either on its own or after examining the request of one of the two Parties, may prescribe any provisional measures which it considers appropriate under the circumstances to prevent irreparable harm or damage to the natural resources of the area or to preserve the status quo as of 21 May 1996. The Parties shall apply such measures within the time period prescribed by the Tribunal.

2. In no event will a request for provisional measures or a prescription of provisional measures affect the time periods for the submission of pleadings or rendering of the awards under Article 8 above.

Article 12

1. a) The awards of the Tribunal shall state the reasons upon which they are based.

b) The awards of the Tribunal shall include the time period for their execution.

c) For each award of the Tribunal, each member of the Tribunal shall be entitled to attach an individual or dissenting opinion.

2. The Tribunal shall notify immediately to the Agents or Co-Agents its awards, signed by the President and the Registrar of the Tribunal, and any individual or dissenting opinion.

3. At the end of the second stage, the Tribunal shall make public both awards and any individual or dissenting opinions.

Article 13

1. The awards of the Tribunal shall be final and binding. The Parties commit themselves to abide by those awards, pursuant to Article 1, paragraph 2 of the Agreement on Principles. They shall consequently apply in good faith and immediately the awards of the Tribunal, at any rate within the time periods as provided for by the Tribunal pursuant to Article 12, paragraph 1(b), of this Arbitration Agreement.

2. The Tribunal is empowered to correct within three months of the rendering of its awards any material error relating to those awards such as arithmetical, mathematical, cartographical or typographical errors. Any such corrections shall in no event affect the timetables set out in Article 8 above.

3. Each Party may refer to the Tribunal any dispute with the other Party as to the meaning and the scope of the awards within thirty days of their rendering. The Tribunal shall render a decision regarding any such dispute within sixty days of the day on which the dispute is referred to the Tribunal. Pending this decision, the time periods for the submission of written pleadings set forth in Article 8 above may be suspended by the Tribunal.

Article 14

1. This Arbitration Agreement shall enter into force thirty days after the date of its signature by the two Parties.

2. The Tribunal shall apply the provisions of this Arbitration Agreement.

Article 15

1. Nothing in this Arbitration Agreement can be interpreted as being detrimental to the legal positions or to the rights of each Party with respect to the questions submitted to the Tribunal, nor can affect or prejudice the decisions of the Arbitral Tribunal or the considerations and grounds on which those decisions are based.

2. In the event of any inconsistency between the Agreement on Principles and this Arbitration Agreement implementing the procedural aspects of that Agreement on Principles, this Arbitration Agreement shall control. Except with respect to such inconsistency, the Agreement on Principles shall continue in force.

Article 16

1. France shall deposit a copy of this Arbitration Agreement within thirty days of its entry into force with the Secretary-General of the United Nations, with the Secretary-General of the Organisation of African Unity, and with the Secretary-General of the Arab League.

2. The President of the Tribunal shall deposit a copy of both awards as soon as possible after the rendering of the award on delimitation of maritime boundaries with the Secretary-General of the United Nations, with the Secretary-General of the Organisation of African Unity, and with the Secretary-General of the Arab League.

IN WITNESS WHEREOF, the undersigned, being duly authorized by their respective Governments, have signed this Arbitration Agreement.

DONE AT PARIS, this third day of October, one thousand nine hundred and ninety-six, in three original copies, each one in the Arabic, English and French languages, the English text being authentic.

[signatures]

Appendix K
Government of the State of Eritrea v. Government of the Republic of Yemen,
Award of the Arbitral Tribunal in the First Stage (Territorial Sovereignty and Scope of the Dispute), 9 October 1998*

Extracts

CHAPTER I—The Setting up of the Arbitration and the Arguments of the Parties
Introduction

1. This Award is rendered pursuant to an Arbitration Agreement dated 3 October 1996 (the 'Arbitration Agreement'), between the Government of the State of Eritrea ('Eritrea') and the Government of the Republic of Yemen ('Yemen') (hereinafter 'the Parties').

2. The Arbitration Agreement was preceded by an 'Agreement on Principles' done at Paris on 21 May 1996, which was signed by Eritrea and Yemen and witnessed by the Governments of the French Republic, the Federal Democratic Republic of Ethiopia, and the Arab Republic of Egypt. The Parties renounced recourse to force against each other, and undertook to 'settle their dispute on questions of territorial sovereignty and of delimitation of maritime boundaries peacefully'. They agreed, to that end, to establish an agreement instituting an arbitral tribunal. The Agreement on Principles further provided that

 . . . concerning questions of territorial sovereignty, the Tribunal shall decide in accordance with the principles, rules and practices of international law applicable to the matter, and on the basis, in particular, of historic titles.

3. Concurrently with the Agreement on Principles, the Parties issued a brief Joint Statement, emphasizing their desire to settle the dispute, and 'to allow the re-establishment and development of a trustful and lasting cooperation between the two countries', contributing to the stability and peace of the region.

4. In conformity with Article 1.1 of the Arbitration Agreement, Eritrea appointed as arbitrators Judge Stephen M. Schwebel and Judge Rosalyn Higgins, and Yemen appointed Dr. Ahmed Sadek El-Kosheri and Mr. Keith Highet. By an exchange of letters dated 30 and 31 December 1996, the Parties agreed to recommend the appointment of Professor Sir Robert Y. Jennings as President of the Arbitral Tribunal (hereinafter the 'Tribunal'). The four arbitrators met in London on 14 January 1997, and appointed Sir Robert Y. Jennings President of the Tribunal.

5. Having been duly constituted, the Tribunal held its first meeting on 14 January 1997, at Essex Court Chambers, 24 Lincoln's Inn Fields, London WC1, UK. The Tribunal took note of the meeting of the four arbitrators, and ratified and approved the actions authorized and undertaken thereat. Pursuant to Article 7.2 of the Arbitration Agreement, the Tribunal appointed as Registrar Mr. P.J.H. Jonkman, Secretary-General of the Permanent Court of Arbitration (the 'PCA') at The Hague and, as Secretary to the Tribunal, Ms. Bette E. Shifman, First Secretary of the PCA, and fixed the location of the Tribunal's registry at the International Bureau of the PCA.

---

* Source: Permanent Court of Arbitration, <http://pca-cpa.org/PDF/EY%20Phase%20I.PDF> (2 August 2006).

6. The Tribunal then held a meeting with Mr. Gary Born, Co-Agent of Eritrea, and Mr. Rodman Bundy, Co-Agent of Yemen, at which it notified them of the formation of the Tribunal and discussed with them certain practical matters relating to the arbitration proceedings.

7. Article 2 of the Arbitration Agreement provides that:

1. The Tribunal is requested to provide rulings in accordance with international law, in two stages.

2. The first stage shall result in an award on territorial sovereignty and on the definition of the scope of the dispute between Eritrea and Yemen. The Tribunal shall decide territorial sovereignty in accordance with the principles, rules and practices of international law applicable to the matter, and on the basis, in particular, of historic titles. The Tribunal shall decide on the definition of the scope of the dispute on the basis of the respective positions of the two Parties.

3. The second stage shall result in an award delimiting maritime boundaries. The Tribunal shall decide taking into account the opinion that it will have formed on questions of territorial sovereignty, the United Nations Convention on the Law of the Sea, and any other pertinent factor.

8. Pursuant to the time table set forth in the Arbitration Agreement for the various stages of the arbitration, the Parties submitted their written Memorials concerning territorial sovereignty and the scope of the dispute simultaneously on 1 September 1997 and their Counter-Memorials on 1 December 1997. In accordance with the requirement of Article 7.1 of the Arbitration Agreement that 'the Tribunal shall sit in London', the oral proceedings in the first stage of the arbitration were held in London, in the Durbar Conference Room of the Foreign and Commonwealth Office, from 26 January through 6 February 1998, within the time limits for oral proceedings set forth in the Arbitration Agreement. The order of the Parties' presentations was determined by drawing lots, with Eritrea beginning the oral proceedings.

9. At the end of its session of 6 February 1998, the Tribunal, in accordance with Article 8.3 of the Arbitration Agreement, closed the oral phase of the first stage of the arbitration proceedings between Eritrea and Yemen. The closing of the oral proceedings was subject to the undertaking of both Parties to answer in writing, by 23 February 1998, certain questions put to them by the Tribunal at the end of the hearings, including a question concerning the existence of agreements for petroleum exploration and exploitation. It was also subject to the proviso in Article 8.3 of the Arbitration Agreement authorizing the Tribunal to request the Parties' written views on the elucidation of any aspect of the matters before the Tribunal.

[…]

Done at London this 9th day of October, 1998

The President of the Tribunal
/s/ Professor Sir Robert Y. Jennings

The Registrar
/s/ P.J.H. Jonkman

Appendix L
Larsen v. the Hawaiian Kingdom, Arbitration Award, 5 February 2001*

Extracts

1. THE PARTIES
1.1 The Claimant is Lance Paul Larsen, a resident of Hawaii. His address is stated in the Notice of Arbitration of 8 November 1999 to be P.O. Box 87, Mountain View, Hawai'i. The Claimant was represented by Ms. Ninia Parks as counsel and agent.
1.2 In the Notice of Arbitration of 8 November 1999 the Respondent is expressed to be 'the Hawaiian Kingdom by its Council of Regency'. Without prejudice to any questions of substance, the Respondent will be referred to in this award as 'the Hawaiian Kingdom'.
1.3 The Respondent is represented by Mr. David Keanu Sai as agent, by Mr. Peter Umialiloa Sai as first deputy agent and by Mr. Gary Victor Dubin as second deputy agent and counsel. The address of the Respondent is stated as P.O. Box 2194, Honolulu, Hawai'i.

2. AGREEMENT TO ARBITRATE
2.1 In Terms of Agreement expressed to be concluded between the Claimant and the Hawaiian Kingdom by its Council of Regency and executed on 30 October 1999 by Ms. Parks, as attorney for the Claimant, and by Mr. Dubin, as attorney for the Hawaiian Kingdom (the Arbitration Agreement), it was agreed as follows:

I. FUNDAMENTAL PROVISIONS
ARTICLE 1
1.The Parties agree to submit the following dispute alleged in the Complaint for Injunctive Relief filed on August 4, 1999, to final and binding arbitration in accordance with the Permanent Court of Arbitration Optional Rules for Arbitrating Disputes between Two Parties of which Only One Is a State, as in effect on the date of this agreement:
a. Lance Paul Larsen, a Hawaiian subject, alleges that the Government of the Hawaiian Kingdom is in continual violation of its 1849 Treaty of Friendship, Commerce and Navigation with the United States of America, and in violation of the principles of international law laid [down] in the Vienna Convention on the Law of Treaties, 1969, by allowing the unlawful imposition of American municipal laws over claimant's person within the territorial jurisdiction of the Hawaiian Kingdom.
b. Lance Paul Larsen, a Hawaiian subject, alleges that the Government of the Hawaiian Kingdom is also in continual violation of the principles of international comity by allowing the unlawful imposition of American municipal laws over the claimant's person within the territorial jurisdiction of the Hawaiian Kingdom.
2. The Parties commit themselves to abide by the decision of the Arbitral Tribunal.
II.ARBITRATION
ARTICLE 2
1. The Arbitral Tribunal shall sit at the Permanent Court of Arbitration at The Hague, the Netherlands.
2. The Arbitral Tribunal shall consist of one arbitrator to be chosen by Keoni Agard, Esq., a Hawaiian national, who shall select the Arbitral Tribunal in conformity with Article 6, section 3 of the Optional Rules for Arbitrating Disputes between Two Parties of which Only One Is a State.

---

* Source: Permanent Court of Arbitration, <http://www.pca-cpa.org/PDF/LHKAward.PDF> (2 August 2006).

3. The International Bureau of the Permanent Court of Arbitration at The Hague shall act as a channel of communications between the parties and the Arbitral Tribunal, and provide secretariat including, inter alia, arranging for hearing rooms and stenographic or electronic records of hearings.

ARTICLE 3

1. The Arbitral Tribunal is requested to provide rulings in two stages, in accordance with International law and Hawaiian Kingdom law.
2. The first stage shall result in an award on the verification of the dominion of the Hawaiian Kingdom. The Arbitral Tribunal shall decide territorial sovereignty in accordance with the principles, rules and practices of international law applicable to the matter, and on the basis, in particular, of historic titles.
3. The second stage shall result in an award of the dispute specified in section 1(a) and 1(b) of article 1 above. The Arbitral Tribunal shall decide taking into account the opinion that it will have formed on questions of territorial sovereignty, the Vienna Convention on the Law of Treaties, 1969, and any other pertinent factors.
4. The Arbitral Tribunal can consult experts of its choice.

2.2 By a Notice of Arbitration dated 8 November 1999 executed by Ms. Parks, expressed as made pursuant to Article 8 of the Arbitration Agreement and addressed to various persons identified as members of the Council of Regency of the Hawaiian Kingdom, the Claimant requested the initiation of arbitral proceedings at 'the facilities of the Permanent Court of Arbitration in The Hague'. The Notice of Arbitration was expressed to be 'a demand pursuant to Article 3, Section 1 of the Permanent Court of Arbitration Optional Rules For Arbitrating Disputes Between Two Parties Of Which Only One Is a State' (the Optional Rules).

2.3 In the Notice of Arbitration the dispute was expressed in the following terms:

3. This dispute arises out of the 1849 Treaty of Friendship, Commerce and Navigation, (hereinafter referred to as 'the 1849 Treaty') which was signed and ratified by both the United States of America and the Hawaiian Kingdom (A true and correct copy of the 1849 Treaty is attached hereto as 'Exhibit 2'). The Claimant in this case, Mr. Larsen, alleges and submits to arbitration, that the Hawaiian Kingdom is in continual violation of both the 1849 Treaty between the Hawaiian Kingdom and the United States of America, and of international law principles as set forth in the Vienna Convention On The Law Of Treaties (hereinafter referred to as 'the Vienna Convention') which was concluded in Vienna on May 23, 1969 and ratified by the Hawaiian Kingdom on July 15, 1999 (true and correct copies of the Vienna Convention and the Hawaiian Kingdom's Ratification of the Vienna Convention are attached hereto as 'Exhibit 3 ' and 'Exhibit 4' respectively) by allowing the continued unlawful imposition and enforcement of American municipal laws within the territorial jurisdiction of the Hawaiian Kingdom.

4. Mr. Larsen has already served an illegally imposed jail sentence resulting directly from the continued unlawful imposition and enforcement of American municipal laws within the Hawaiian Kingdom. Mr. Larsen is also currently facing more jail time for the same reasons. In order to avoid further jail sentencing, and in order to halt the continual imposition and enforcement of American municipal laws over himself, Mr. Larsen hereby requests, as Claimant in this case, from the Arbitral Tribunal to be hereafter convened at the Permanent Court of Arbitration an award in two stages. In the first stage, Claimant requests an award verifying the territorial dominion of the Hawaiian Kingdom. In this first stage, the Arbitral Tribunal shall decide and determine the territorial dominion of the Hawaiian Kingdom under all applicable international principles, rules and practices.

5. In the second stage, Claimant requests an award verifying that the Hawaiian Kingdom is in continual violation of the 1849 Treaty, principles of international law set forth in the 1969 Vienna Convention and principles of international comity by allowing the unlawful imposition of American municipal laws over Claimant's person within the territorial jurisdiction of the Hawaiian Kingdom. As set forth in the said Arbitration Agreement, the Arbitral Tribunal shall sit at the Permanent Court of Arbitration in The Hague, The Netherlands.

2.4 Clause 6 of the Notice of Arbitration stated that the Arbitral Tribunal should consist of one arbitrator to be chosen by Keoni Agard, Esq., stated to be a Hawaiian national resident in Hawai'i (the Appointing Authority).

2.5 By an Amendment to the Special Agreement dated 28 February 2000 the parties agreed that the Arbitral Tribunal should comprise three arbitrators, one to be chosen by each party through the Appointing Authority with the two arbitrators so appointed choosing the presiding arbitrator.

3. APPLICATION OF THE UNCITRAL RULES

3.1 Following a requisition made by the International Bureau of the Permanent Court of Arbitration to the Appointing Authority on 3 December 1999, a First Amendment to Notice of Arbitration of even date, signed by Ms. Parks on behalf of the Claimant and by Mr. Dubin on behalf of the Hawaiian Kingdom, amended the Notice of Arbitration and the Arbitration Agreement by substituting the 'UNCITRAL Arbitration Rules As At Present In Force' (the UNCITRAL Rules) for the PCA Optional Rules as the governing rules for the arbitration.

3.2 By a further Special Agreement made on 25 January 2000, signed by Ms. Parks on behalf of the Claimant and Mr. Sai as agent for the Hawaiian Kingdom, the parties agreed on several procedural matters for the arbitration, including, under Article IV, confirmation that the UNCITRAL Rules apply.

3.3 Under Article II of the Special Agreement the issue to be determined in the arbitration was defined as follows:

> The Arbitral Tribunal is asked to determine, on the basis of the Hague Conventions IV and V of 18 October 1907, and the rules and principles of international law, whether the rights of the Claimant under international law as a Hawaiian subject are being violated, and if so, does he have any redress against the Respondent Government of the Hawaiian Kingdom?

3.4 Article 6 of the Arbitration Agreement further provided:

> Nothing in this Agreement can be interpreted as being detrimental to the legal positions or the rights of each Party with respect to the questions submitted to the Arbitral Tribunal, nor can affect or prejudice the decision of the Arbitral Tribunal or the considerations or grounds on which that decision is based.

4. CONSTITUTION OF THE TRIBUNAL AND SECRETARIAT SERVICES

4.1 In April 2000 the Appointing Authority appointed each of Dr. Gavan Griffith QC and Professor Christopher J. Greenwood QC as members of the Tribunal. After consultation, those two members of the Tribunal jointly appointed Professor James Crawford SC as the President of the Tribunal.

4.2 The appointment of the Tribunal and the terms of that appointment were advised by the Appointing Authority to the Secretary of the Tribunal by letter of 28 May 2000. The parties acknowledged the constitution of the Tribunal by their letter of 9 June 2000 to the Permanent Bureau of the Permanent Court of Arbitration.

4.3 Pursuant to the agreement of the parties in clause 6 of the Arbitration Agreement, and as finally expressed in the Amendment to the Special Agreement, the International Bureau of the Permanent Court of Arbitration was appointed to provide secretariat services and facilities for the arbitration. Ms. Phyllis Pieper Hamilton, First Secretary of the Permanent Court of Arbitration, has served as secretary of the Tribunal.

[...]

AWARD

For the reasons stated above, the Tribunal determines as a matter of international law, which it is directed to apply by Article 3(1) of the Arbitration Agreement:

(a) that there is no dispute between the parties capable of submission to arbitration, and

(b) that, in any event, the Tribunal is precluded from the consideration of the issues raised by the parties by reason of the fact that the United States of America is not a party to the proceedings and has not consented to them.

Accordingly, the Tribunal finds that these arbitral proceedings are not maintainable.

SIGNED as at the Permanent Court of Arbitration, the Peace Palace, Den Haag.

JAMES CRAWFORD SC
GAVAN GRIFFITH QC
CHRISTOPHER GREENWOOD QC

5 February 2001

Appendix M
Permanent Court of Arbitration Optional Rules for Arbitrating Disputes between Two Parties of Which Only One Is a State
(effective 6 July 1993)[*]

Selected articles

INTRODUCTION

These Rules supersede the '1962 Rules of Arbitration and Conciliation for Settlement of International Disputes between Two Parties of Which Only One Is a State.' The Rules are based on the UNCITRAL Arbitration Rules with changes in order to:

(i) indicate the facilitating role of the Secretary-General of the Permanent Court of Arbitration at The Hague, and the availability of the International Bureau to furnish administrative support;

(ii) provide that agreement to arbitrate under the Rules constitutes a waiver of any sovereign immunity from jurisdiction (parties who choose to do so may also provide for waiver of sovereign immunity from execution by adding language such as shown in the optional provisions to the model clause).

(iii) clarify that if a party-appointed arbitrator on a three-person tribunal fails to participate, the other arbitrators have the discretion to continue the proceedings and to render a binding award.

The Rules are optional and emphasize flexibility and party autonomy. For example:

(i) the Rules, and the services of the Secretary-General and the International Bureau of the Permanent Court of Arbitration, are available for use by all States and their entities and enterprises, and are not restricted to disputes in which the State is a party to either The Hague Convention on the Pacific Settlement of International Disputes of 1899 or that of 1907;

(ii) the choice of arbitrators is not limited to persons who are listed as members of the Permanent Court of Arbitration;

(iii) parties have complete freedom to agree upon any individual or institution to be appointing authority. In order to provide a fail-safe mechanism to prevent frustration of the arbitration, the Rules provide that the Secretary-General will designate an appointing authority if the parties do not agree upon the authority, or if the authority they choose does not act.

These Rules are also appropriate for use in connection with multiparty agreements, provided that appropriate changes are made in the procedures for choosing arbitrators and sharing costs. Guidelines to assist parties in adapting these Rules for use in resolving disputes that may involve more than two parties.

A model clause that parties may consider inserting in contracts to provide for arbitration of future disputes and a model clause for arbitration of existing disputes are set forth in English, French and Spanish.

Explanatory 'Notes to the Text' appear below.

---

[*] Source: Permanent Court of Arbitration, <http://www.pca-cpa.org/ENGLISH/BD/BDEN/1STATENG.pdf> (2 August 2006).

PERMANENT COURT OF ARBITRATION OPTIONAL RULES FOR ARBITRATING
DISPUTES BETWEEN TWO PARTIES OF WHICH ONLY ONE IS A STATE
Effective July 6, 1993

Section I. Introductory Rules

Scope of Application
Article 1
1. Where the parties to a contract have agreed in writing that disputes in relation to that contract shall be referred to arbitration under the Permanent Court of Arbitration Optional Rules for Arbitrating Disputes between Two Parties of Which Only One Is a State, then such disputes shall be referred to arbitration in accordance with these Rules subject to such modification as the parties may agree in writing.

2. Agreement by a party to arbitration under these Rules constitutes a waiver of any right of sovereign immunity from jurisdiction, in respect of the dispute in question, to which such party might otherwise be entitled. A waiver of immunity relating to the execution of an arbitral award must be explicitly expressed.

3. These Rules shall govern the arbitration except that where any of these Rules is in conflict with a provision of the law applicable to the arbitration from which the parties cannot derogate, that provision shall prevail.

4. The International Bureau of the Permanent Court of Arbitration at The Hague (the 'International Bureau') shall have charge of the archives of the arbitration proceeding. In addition, the International Bureau shall, upon written request of all the parties or of the arbitral tribunal, act as a channel of communications between the parties and the arbitral tribunal, and provide secretariat services including, inter alia, arranging for hearing rooms, interpretation, and stenographic or electronic records of hearings.
[…]

Section II. Composition of the Arbitral Tribunal

Number of Arbitrators
Article 5
If the parties have not previously agreed on the number of arbitrators (i.e. one or three), and if within thirty days after the receipt by the respondent of the notice of arbitration the parties have not agreed that there shall be only one arbitrator, three arbitrators shall be appointed.

Appointment of Arbitrators (Articles 6 to 8)
Article 6
1. If a sole arbitrator is to be appointed, either party may propose to the other:
(a) The names of one or more persons, one of whom would serve as the sole arbitrator; and
(b) If no appointing authority has been agreed upon by the parties, the name or names of one or more institutions or persons, one of whom would serve as appointing authority.

2. If within thirty days after receipt by a party of a proposal made in accordance with paragraph 1 the parties have not reached agreement on the choice of a sole arbitrator, the sole arbitrator shall be appointed by the appointing authority agreed upon by the parties. If no appointing authority has been agreed upon by the parties, or if the appointing authority agreed upon refuses to act or fails to appoint the arbitrator within sixty days of the receipt of a party's request therefore, either party may request the Secretary-General of the Permanent Court of Arbitration at The Hague (the 'Secretary-General') to designate an appointing authority.

3. The appointing authority shall, at the request of one of the parties, appoint the sole arbitrator as promptly as possible. In making the appointment the appointing authority shall use the following list-procedure, unless both parties agree that the list-procedure should not be used or unless the appointing authority determines in its discretion that the use of the list-procedure is not appropriate for the case:

(a) At the request of one of the parties the appointing authority shall communicate to both parties an identical list containing at least three names;

(b) Within thirty days after the receipt of this list, each party may return the list to the appointing authority after having deleted the name or names to which he objects and numbered the remaining names on the list in the order of its preference;

(c) After the expiration of the above period of time the appointing authority shall appoint the sole arbitrator from among the names approved on the lists returned to it and in accordance with the order of preference indicated by the parties;

(d) If for any reason the appointment cannot be made according to this procedure, the appointing authority may exercise its discretion in appointing the sole arbitrator.

4. In making the appointment, the appointing authority shall have regard to such considerations as are likely to secure the appointment of an independent and impartial arbitrator and shall take into account as well the advisability of appointing an arbitrator of a nationality other than the nationalities of the parties.

Article 7

1. If three arbitrators are to be appointed, each party shall appoint one arbitrator. The two arbitrators thus appointed shall choose the third arbitrator who will act as the presiding arbitrator of the tribunal.

2. If within thirty days after the receipt of a party's notification of the appointment of an arbitrator the other party has not notified the first party of the arbitrator it has appointed:

(a) The first party may request the appointing authority previously designated by the parties to appoint the second arbitrator; or

(b) If no such authority has been previously designated by the parties, or if the appointing authority previously designated refuses to act or fails to appoint the arbitrator within thirty days after receipt of a party's request therefore, the first party may request the Secretary-General to designate the appointing authority. The first party may then request the appointing authority so designated to appoint the second arbitrator. In either case, the appointing authority may exercise its discretion in appointing the arbitrator.

3. If within thirty days after the appointment of the second arbitrator the two arbitrators have not agreed on the choice of the presiding arbitrator, the presiding arbitrator shall be appointed by an appointing authority in the same way as a sole arbitrator would be appointed under article 6.

Article 8

1. When an appointing authority is requested to appoint an arbitrator pursuant to article 6 or article 7, the party which makes the request shall send to the appointing authority a copy of the notice of arbitration, a copy of the contract out of or in relation to which the dispute has arisen and a copy of the arbitration agreement if it is not contained in the contract. The appointing authority may require from either party such information as it deems necessary to fulfil its function.

2. Where the names of one or more persons are proposed for appointment as arbitrators, their full names, addresses and nationalities shall be indicated, together with a description of their qualifications.

3. In appointing arbitrators pursuant to these Rules, the parties and the appointing authority are free to designate persons who are not Members of the Permanent Court of Arbitration at The Hague.
[...]

Section III. Arbitral Proceedings

General Provisions
Article 15
1. Subject to these Rules, the arbitral tribunal may conduct the arbitration in such manner as it considers appropriate, provided that the parties are treated with equality and that at any stage of the proceedings each party is given a full opportunity of presenting its case.
2. If either party so requests at any appropriate stage of the proceedings, the arbitral tribunal shall hold hearings for the presentation of evidence by witnesses, including expert witnesses, or for oral argument. In the absence of such a request, the arbitral tribunal shall decide whether to hold such hearings or whether the proceedings shall be conducted on the basis of documents and other materials.
3. All documents or information supplied to the arbitral tribunal by one party shall at the same time be communicated by that party to the other party and a copy shall be filed with the International Bureau.

Place of Arbitration
Article 16
1. Unless the parties have agreed upon the place where the arbitration is to be held, such place shall be The Hague, The Netherlands. If the parties agree that the arbitration shall be held at a place other than The Hague, the International Bureau shall inform the parties and the arbitral tribunal whether it is willing to provide the secretariat and registrar services referred to in article 1, paragraph 4, and the services referred to in article 25, paragraph 3.
2. The arbitral tribunal may determine the locale of the arbitration within the country agreed upon by the parties. It may hear witnesses and hold meetings for consultation among its members at any place it deems appropriate, having regard to the circumstances of the arbitration.
3. After inviting the views of the parties, the arbitral tribunal may meet at any place it deems appropriate for the inspection of goods, other property or documents. The parties shall be given sufficient notice to enable them to be present at such inspection.
4. The award shall be made at the place of arbitration.

Language
Article 17
1. Subject to an agreement by the parties, the arbitral tribunal shall, promptly after its appointment, determine the language or languages to be used in the proceedings. This determination shall apply to the statement of claim, the statement of defence, and any further written statements and, if oral hearings take place, to the language or languages to be used in such hearings.
2. The arbitral tribunal may order that any documents annexed to the statement of claim or statement of defence, and any supplementary documents or exhibits submitted in the course of the proceedings, delivered in their original language, shall be accompanied by a translation into the language or languages agreed upon by the parties or determined by the arbitral tribunal.
[...]

Section IV. The Award

Decisions
Article 31
1. When there are three arbitrators, any award or other decision of the arbitral tribunal shall be made by a majority of the arbitrators.

2. In the case of questions of procedure, when there is no majority or when the arbitral tribunal so authorizes, the presiding arbitrator may decide on his/her own, subject to revision, if any, by the arbitral tribunal.

Form and Effect of the Award
Article 32
1. In addition to making a final award, the arbitral tribunal shall be entitled to make interim, interlocutory, or partial awards.

2. The award shall be made in writing and shall be final and binding on the parties. The parties undertake to carry out the award without delay.

3. The arbitral tribunal shall state the reasons upon which the award is based, unless the parties have agreed that no reasons are to be given.

4. An award shall be signed by the arbitrators and it shall contain the date on which and the place where the award was made. Where there are three arbitrators and one of them fails to sign, the award shall state the reason for the absence of the signature.

5. The award may be made public only with the consent of both parties.

6. Copies of the award signed by the arbitrators shall be communicated to the parties by the International Bureau. The International Bureau may withhold communicating the award to the parties until all costs of the arbitration have been paid.

7. If the arbitration law of the country where the award is made requires that the award be filed or registered by the arbitral tribunal, the tribunal shall comply with this requirement within the period of time required by law.

Applicable Law, Amiable Compositeur
Article 33
1. The arbitral tribunal shall apply the law designated by the parties as applicable to the substance of the dispute. Failing such designation by the parties, the arbitral tribunal shall apply the law determined by the conflict of laws rules which it considers applicable.

2. The arbitral tribunal shall decide as amiable compositeur or ex aequo et bono only if the parties have expressly authorized the arbitral tribunal to do so and if the law applicable to the arbitral procedure permits such arbitration.

3. In all cases, the arbitral tribunal shall decide in accordance with the terms of the contract and shall take into account the usages of the trade applicable to the transaction.

Settlement or Other Grounds for Termination
Article 34
1. If, before the award is made, the parties agree on a settlement of the dispute, the arbitral tribunal shall either issue an order for the termination of the arbitral proceedings or, if requested by both parties and accepted by the tribunal, record the settlement in the form of an arbitral award on agreed terms. The arbitral tribunal is not obliged to give reasons for such an award.

2. If, before the award is made, the continuation of the arbitral proceedings becomes unnecessary or impossible for any reason not mentioned in paragraph 1, the arbitral tribunal shall inform the parties of its intention to issue an order for the termination of the proceedings. The arbitral tribunal shall have the power to issue such an order unless a party raises justifiable grounds for objection.

3. Copies of the order for termination of the arbitral proceedings or of the arbitral award on agreed terms, signed by the arbitrators, shall be communicated to the parties by the International Bureau. Where an arbitral award on agreed terms is made, the provisions of article 32, paragraphs 2 and 4 to 7, shall apply.

[...]

NOTES TO THE TEXT

These Rules are based on the UNCITRAL Arbitration Rules, with the following modifications:

(i) Modifications to facilitate effective arbitration between a State or State entity, on the one hand, and a non-State party, on the other hand:

Article 1, para. 1; para. 2 (added); para. 3 (renumbered)
Article 2, para. 1
Article 8, para. 3 (added)
Article 13, paras. 1 and 2; para. 3 (added)
Article 15, para. 2
Article 16, para. 3
Article 23
Article 24, para. 3
Article 25, para. 3
Article 26, para. 1
Article 41, para. 1

Throughout the Rules, all fifteen-day time limits placed upon the parties have been made twice as long, e.g., 'thirty days' substituted for 'fifteen days'. In article 37, paragraph 1, 'sixty days' has been substituted for 'thirty days'.

Throughout the Rules, all references to 'his' have been changed to 'his/hers'. The pronoun 'it' ('its') is used when referring to parties and means any person, natural and juridical.

(ii) Modifications to indicate the functions of the Secretary-General and the International Bureau of the Permanent Court of Arbitration:

Article 1, para. 4 (added)
Article 4
Article 15, para. 3
Article 16, para. 1
Article 25, para. 3
Article 32, para. 6
Article 34, para. 3
Article 38, para. (f)
Article 41, paras. 1 and 5

(iii) Other modifications:

Heading preceding article 28

Appendix N
The Treaty of Waitangi,
6 February 1840
(English and Maori texts)*

The Text in English

Preamble
HER MAJESTY VICTORIA Queen of the United Kingdom of Great Britain and Ireland regarding with Her Royal favour the Native Chiefs and Tribes of New Zealand and anxious to protect their just Rights and Property and to secure to them the enjoyment of Peace and Good Order has deemed it necessary in consequence of the great number of Her Majesty's Subjects who have already settled in New Zealand and the rapid extension of Emigration both from Europe and Australia which is still in progress to constitute and appoint a functionary properly authorised to treat with the Aborigines of New Zealand for the recognition of Her Majesty's Sovereign authority over the whole or any part of those islands – Her Majesty therefore being desirous to establish a settled form of Civil Government with a view to avert the evil consequences which must result from the absence of the necessary Laws and Institutions alike to the native population and to Her subjects has been graciously pleased to empower and to authorise me William Hobson a Captain in Her Majesty's Royal Navy Consul and Lieutenant Governor of such parts of New Zealand as may be or hereafter shall be ceded to her Majesty to invite the confederated and independent Chiefs of New Zealand to concur in the following Articles and Conditions.

Article the First
The Chiefs of the Confederation of the United Tribes of New Zealand and the separate and independent Chiefs who have not become members of the Confederation cede to Her Majesty the Queen of England absolutely and without reservation all the rights and powers of Sovereignty which the said Confederation or Individual Chiefs respectively exercise or possess, or may be supposed to exercise or to possess over their respective Territories as the sole Sovereigns thereof.

Article the Second
Her Majesty the Queen of England confirms and guarantees to the Chiefs and Tribes of New Zealand and to the respective families and individuals thereof the full exclusive and undisturbed possession of their Lands and Estates Forests Fisheries and other properties which they may collectively or individually possess so long as it is their wish and desire to retain the same in their possession; but the Chiefs of the United Tribes and the individual Chiefs yield to Her Majesty the exclusive right of Preemption over such lands as the proprietors thereof may be disposed to alienate at such prices as may be agreed upon between the respective Proprietors and persons appointed by Her Majesty to treat with them in that behalf.

---

* Source: New Zealand Ministry for Culture and Heritage, <http://www.treatyofwaitangi.govt.nz/treaty/> (2 August 2006).

Article the Third
In consideration thereof Her Majesty the Queen of England extends to the Natives of New Zealand Her royal protection and imparts to them all the Rights and Privileges of British Subjects.
W HOBSON Lieutenant Governor.

Now therefore We the Chiefs of the Confederation of the United Tribes of New Zealand being assembled in Congress at Victoria in Waitangi and We the Separate and Independent Chiefs of New Zealand claiming authority over the Tribes and Territories which are specified after our respective names, having been made fully to understand the Provisions of the foregoing Treaty, accept and enter into the same in the full spirit and meaning thereof: in witness of which we have attached our signatures or marks at the places and the dates respectively specified.

Done at Waitangi this Sixth day of February in the year of Our Lord One thousand eight hundred and forty.

[*Here follow signatures, dates, etc.*]

The Text in Māori

Preamble
KO WIKITORIA, te Kuini o Ingarani, i tana mahara atawai ki nga Rangatira me nga Hapu o Nu Tirani i tana hiahia hoki kia tohungia ki a ratou o ratou rangatiratanga, me to ratou wenua, a kia mau tonu hoki te Rongo ki a ratou me te Atanoho hoki kua wakaaro ia he mea tika kia tukua mai tetahi Rangatira hei kai wakarite ki nga Tangata maori o Nu Tirani-kia wakaaetia e nga Rangatira maori te Kawanatanga o te Kuini ki nga wahikatoa o te Wenua nei me nga Motuna te mea hoki he tokomaha ke nga tangata o tona Iwi Kua noho ki tenei wenua, a e haere mai nei. Na ko te Kuini e hiahia ana kia wakaritea te Kawanatanga kia kaua ai nga kino e puta mai ki te tangata Maori ki te Pakeha e noho ture kore ana. Na, kua pai te Kuini kia tukua a hau a Wiremu Hopihona he Kapitana i te Roiara Nawi hei Kawana mo nga wahi katoa o Nu Tirani e tukua aianei, amua atu ki te Kuini e mea atu ana ia ki nga Rangatira o te wakaminenga o nga hapu o Nu Tirani me era Rangatira atu enei ture ka korerotia nei.

Ko te Tuatahi
Ko nga Rangatira o te Wakaminenga me nga Rangatira katoa hoki ki hai i uru ki taua wakaminenga ka tuku rawa atu ki te Kuini o Ingarani ake tonu atu-te Kawanatanga katoa o o ratou wenua.

Ko te Tuarua
Ko te Kuini o Ingarani ka wakarite ka wakaae ki nga Rangitira ki nga hapu-ki nga tangata katoa o Nu Tirani te tino rangtiratanga o o ratou wenua o ratou kainga me o ratou taonga katoa. Otiia ko nga Rangatira o te Wakaminenga me nga Rangatira katoa atu ka tuku ki te Kuini te hokonga o era wahi wenua e pai ai te tangata nona te Wenua-ki te ritenga o te utu e wakaritea ai e ratou ko te kai hoko e meatia nei e te Kuini hei kai hoko mona.

Ko te Tuatoru
Hei wakaritenga mai hoki tenei mo te wakaaetanga ki te Kawanatanga o te Kuini-Ka tiakina e te Kuini o Ingarani nga tangata maori katoa o Nu Tirani ka tukua ki a ratou nga tikanga katoa rite tahi ki ana mea ki nga tangata o Ingarani.
(Signed) WILLIAM HOBSON,
Consul and Lieutenant-Governor.

Na ko matou ko nga Rangatira o te Wakaminenga o nga hapu o Nu Tirani ka huihui nei ki Waitangi ko matou hoki ko nga Rangatira o Nu Tirani ka kite nei i te ritenga o enei kupu, ka tangohia ka wakaaetia katoatia e matou, koia ka tohungia ai o matou ingoa o matou tohu. Ka meatia tenei ki Waiangi i te ono o nga ra o Pepueri i te tau kotahi mano, e waru rau e wa te kau o to tatou Ariki.

Ko nga Rangatira o te wakaminenga.

Translation of the Maori text of the Treaty of Waitangi 1840, by Prof. Sir Hugh Kawharu, used with permission

Victoria, the Queen of England, in her concern to protect the chiefs and the subtribes of New Zealand and in her desire to preserve their chieftainship (1) and their lands to them and to maintain peace (2) and good order considers it just to appoint an administrator (3) one who will negotiate with the people of New Zealand to the end that their chiefs will agree to the Queen's Government being established over all parts of this land and (adjoining) islands (4) and also because there are many of her subjects already living on this land and others yet to come. So the Queen desires to establish a government so that no evil will come to Maori and European living in a state of lawlessness. So the Queen has appointed 'me, William Hobson a Captain' in the Royal Navy to be Governor for all parts of New Zealand (both those) shortly to be received by the Queen and (those) to be received hereafter and presents (5) to the chiefs of the Confederation chiefs of the subtribes of New Zealand and other chiefs these laws set out here.

The first

The Chiefs of the Confederation and all the Chiefs who have not joined that Confederation give absolutely to the Queen of England for ever the complete government (6) over their land.

The second

The Queen of England agrees to protect the chiefs, the subtribes and all the people of New Zealand in the unqualified exercise (7) of their chieftainship over their lands, villages and all their treasures (8). But on the other hand the Chiefs of the Confederation and all the Chiefs will sell (9) land to the Queen at a price agreed to by the person owning it and by the person buying it (the latter being) appointed by the Queen as her purchase agent.

The third

For this agreed arrangement therefore concerning the Government of the Queen, the Queen of England will protect all the ordinary people of New Zealand and will give them the same rights and duties (10) of citizenship as the people of England (11).

[signed] William Hobson Consul & Lieut. Governor

So we, the Chiefs of the Confederation of the subtribes of New Zealand meeting here at Waitangi having seen the shape of these words which we accept and agree to record our names and our marks thus.

Was done at Waitangi on the sixth of February in the year of our Lord 1840.

Notes

(1) 'Chieftainship': this concept has to be understood in the context of Maori social and political organisation as at 1840. The accepted approximation today is 'trusteeship'.

(2) 'Peace': Maori 'Rongo', seemingly a missionary usage (rongo – to hear i.e. hear the 'Word'– the 'message' of peace and goodwill, etc).

(3) Literally 'Chief' ('Rangatira') here is of course ambiguous. Clearly a European could not be a Maori, but the word could well have implied a trustee-like role rather than that of a mere 'functionary'. Maori speeches at Waitangi in 1840 refer to Hobson being or becoming a 'father' for the Maori people. Certainly this attitude has been held towards the person of the Crown down to the present day – hence the continued expectations and commitments entailed in the Treaty.

(4) 'Islands' i.e. coastal, not of the Pacific.

(5) Literally 'making' i.e. 'offering' or 'saying' – but not 'inviting to concur'.

(6) 'Government': 'kawanatanga'. There could be no possibility of the Maori signatories having any understanding of government in the sense of 'sovereignty' i.e. any understanding on the basis of experience or cultural precedent.

(7) 'Unqualified exercise' of the chieftainship – would emphasise to a chief the Queen's intention to give them complete control according to their customs. 'Tino' has the connotation of 'quintessential'.

(8) 'Treasures': 'taonga'. As submissions to the Waitangi Tribunal concerning the Maori language have made clear, 'taonga' refers to all dimensions of a tribal group's estate, material and non-material heirlooms and wahi tapu (sacred places), ancestral lore and whakapapa (genealogies), etc.

(9) Maori 'hokonga', literally 'sale and purchase'. Hoko means to buy or sell.

(10) 'Rights and duties': Maori 'at Waitangi in 1840 refer to Hobson being or becoming a 'father' for the Maori people. Certainly this attitude has been held towards the person of the Crown down to the present day – hence the continued expectations and commitments entailed in the Treaty.

(11) There is, however, a more profound problem about 'tikanga'. There is a real sense here of the Queen 'protecting' (i.e. allowing the preservation of) the Maori people's tikanga (i.e. customs) since no Maori could have had any understanding whatever of British tikanga (i.e. rights and duties of British subjects.) This, then, reinforces the guarantees in Article 2.

About the Authors and Other Contributors

The Authors

Niek Biegman
Former NATO Senior Civilian Representative in Macedonia.

Dr. Nicolaas (Niek) Biegman, born in 1936, studied Arabic, Turkish and international law at the University of Leiden, the Netherlands. He wrote his doctoral thesis on the relationship between the Ottoman Empire and the Republic of Dubrovnik. Apart from briefly teaching Turkish and Persian at the university, he spent his active life in the Netherlands Foreign Service, where he held the positions of director general for international cooperation, ambassador to Egypt, Permanent Representative to the United Nations in New York (1992-1997) and to NATO in Brussels (1998-2001). Between 2002 and 2004 he was NATO's senior civilian representative in Skopje. The work in Macedonia centred on the implementation of the Ohrid Agreement (2001), which put an end to a budding civil war between the ethnic Albanian National Liberation Army and the ethnic Macedonian majority. NATO played an active part in facilitating the conclusion of the Agreement, together with the EU, the Organisation for Security and Cooperation in Europe (OSCE), and the United States. During the Orange Revolution in Ukraine in 2004 he represented the presidency of the EU in Kiev.

Miek Boltjes
Director of Dialogue Facilitation, Kreddha.

Drs. Miek Boltjes is Kreddha's director of dialogue facilitation and has shared responsibility for the institutionalisation and management of the organisation since 1999. She holds advanced degrees in international relations as well as communication sciences from the University of Groningen and is a mediator, trainer and advisor on negotiation and conflict resolution processes. At Kreddha Ms. Boltjes co-facilitates three intrastate peace processes. She advises on all procedural and process aspects of the negotiations and has a facilitative role in the substantive talks. Ms. Boltjes was special assistant to the foreign minister of East Timor during that country's transition to independence in 2002. Her responsibilities included liaison with the East Timorese truth and reconciliation commission. Previously she was the executive director of an alternative dispute resolution institute (1998) and responsible for the negotiation and mediation unit of a management training centre (1996-8), both in the Netherlands. The latter involved designing and facilitating training programs and teaching the subject to managers. Prior to that, she worked for the Conflict Management Group in Cambridge, United States, the Foundation on Inter-Ethnic Relations (linked to the Office of the OSCE High Commissioner on National Minorities) and the Unrepresented Nations and Peoples Organisation (UNPO).

Lodi G. Gyari
Special Envoy of His Holiness the Dalai Lama; Chairman of the Council of Kreddha International.

Lodi G. Gyari was born in Nyarong, Eastern Tibet in 1949 where he received a traditional monastic education. Mr. Gyari and his family fled from Tibet to India in 1959. He was editor of the Tibetan Freedom Press and founded the Tibetan Review, the first English language journal published by Tibetans in-exile. He was one of the founding members of the Tibetan Youth Congress and served as its president in 1975. He was elected to the Assembly of Tibetan People's Deputies, the Tibetan parliament in exile, and subsequently became its chairman. He then served as deputy cabinet minister with responsibilities for religious affairs and health. In 1988 he became senior cabinet minister with responsibility for the Department of Information and International Relations (the foreign ministry.) Currently he lives in Washington DC, and is a cabinet advisor and special envoy of His Holiness the Dalai Lama, responsible for establishing a dialogue with the Chinese government. Mr. Gyari is also the executive chairman of the board of the International Campaign for Tibet, an independent Washington based human rights advocacy group.

Denis Haughey
Former Member of the Northern Ireland Assembly; former Minister of the Northern Ireland Executive.

Denis Haughey, born in Coalisland, County Tyrone, holds degrees in politics and history. He was a teacher before his appointment as full-time assistant to John Hume on European affairs from 1980 to 1998. He ran for election against Ian Paisley in 1975 before being elected for Mid-Ulster to the previous Northern Ireland Assembly in 1982, although the Social Democratic and Labour Party (SDLP) refused to take its seats. Inspired and encouraged by the political movements in the United States and elsewhere, he entered politics while at university in the 1960s. He became involved in the civil rights movement and was one of the founder members of the SDLP in 1970, becoming party chairman for five of the most formative years of the party's history (1972-1977). A senior member of the SDLP negotiating team in the talks leading to the Good Friday Agreement, he was a member of the drafting team that wrote all of the basic SDLP documents laying the basis for the Agreement. He was elected Assembly member for Mid-Ulster in 1998. He was also a member of the New Ireland Forum (1983-4) and the Forum for Peace and Reconciliation (1995). He has been a local councillor for the Cookstown District since 1989. He served as international secretary of the SDLP for many years and was the party spokesperson on agriculture prior to devolution. He was appointed junior minister to the Office of the First Minister and Deputy First Minister on 15 December 1999 following devolution from the United Kingdom to Northern Ireland.

Wendy Miles
Partner at Wilmer Cutler Pickering Hale and Dorr LLP.

Wendy Miles is a London-based partner at Wilmer Cutler Pickering Hale and Dorr and a member of that law firm's international arbitration and international litigation practices. She holds degrees in law and arts (history and English literature), including a Master of Laws (with first class honours) from Canterbury University, New Zealand. She is admitted as a barrister and solicitor in New Zealand and as a solicitor in England and Wales, where she also has higher rights of audience. After working for a New Zealand law firm following graduation, she travelled to India where she worked as a research associate at the Tibetan Centre for Human Rights and Democracy in Dharamsala in 1998 and 1999. Her current focus is on international dispute resolution dealing with both private and public international law issues. She has acted as advisor and advocate for a number of international companies and states or state parties in proceedings conducted in various jurisdictions, governed by various substantive and procedural laws and rules. She acts as counsel in international arbitration proceedings administered under several international arbitral institutions (primarily the International Chamber of Commerce (ICC) International Court of Arbitration and the London Court of International Arbitration), as well as in ad hoc proceedings. In 2003 she was appointed alternate New Zealand representative to the ICC Commission on International Arbitration. She is a member of the ICC New Zealand International Arbitration Committee, the International Bar Association, the British Institute of International and Comparative Law and the Chartered Institute of Arbitrators. She is a contributing editor to the *International Comparative Legal Guide to International Arbitration 2004* and *2005* (Global Legal Group).

John Packer
Independent Consultant; Principal Investigator and Project Coordinator, Initiative on Conflict Prevention through Quiet Diplomacy, Human Rights Internet.

John Packer was the director of the Office of the High Commissioner on National Minorities (HCNM) of the Organisation for Security and Cooperation in Europe (OSCE), located in The Hague, until March 2004. In 2003-2004, he was a visiting assistant professor of international law at the Fletcher School of Law and Diplomacy at Tufts University and a fellow at the Carr Center for Human Rights Policy at the John F. Kennedy School of Government at Harvard University. From September 1995 to March 2000, he was senior legal adviser to the HCNM. He was previously a human rights officer at the Office of the United Nations High Commissioner for Human Rights in Geneva where, attached to the then Special Procedures Branch, he held responsibilities for the Commission on Human Rights investigative mandates on, *inter alia*, Iraq, Myanmar (Burma) and the Independence of the Judiciary. Prior to his employment with the UN, he was a consultant for the International Labour Organisation and the UN High Commissioner for Refugees. He holds degrees in political studies and law, including a Master of Laws specialised in international human rights law, was a visiting research fellow at the Lauterpacht Research Centre for International Law at Cambridge University, and has lectured at a number of universities and professional institutions around the world. Both in professional and personal capacities, he has contributed to several conferences and publications, has been since 1991 the associate editor of the *Human Rights Law Journal* and is a member of the editorial board of the *International Journal on Minority and Group Rights*.

Devasish Roy
The Chakma Raja, Chittagong Hill Tracts, Bangladesh; Bangladesh Representative of Commonwealth Association of Indigenous Peoples (CAIP).

Devasish Roy practises law as a barrister in Bangladesh. He graduated from the University of Chittagong, and has a Diploma in Legal Studies from La Trobe University, Australia, and a BA (Honours) degree in law from the University of Kent at Canterbury, United Kingdom. He also holds a Barrister-at-Law degree from the Inns Court School of Law in London. He has been practising law in the Dhaka District Court since 1988 and in the Supreme Court of Bangladesh (High Court Division) since 1991. He is the traditional chief or raja of the Chakma People of the Chittagong Hill Tracts (CHT) and the chief of the Chakma Administrative and Revenue Circle in the CHT. He acted as a facilitator during the final days of peace talks on the CHT, which resulted in the signing of an accord between the Parbatya Chattagram Jana Samhati Samiti and the Government of Bangladesh on 2 December 1997. As part of his advisory responsibilities, he advised the CHT Regional Council regarding the CHT Land Commission law in 2000-2001. He also advised the Ministry of Law and Parliamentary Affairs regarding legislation for the CHT on the justice system and land laws in 2000. As an ex-officio adviser to the Rangamati Hill District Council, CHT, he has advised the council on legal issues, including the proposed transfer of authority of various government departments to the council in September 2000. He has written reports for the ILO (on occupational patterns of indigenous peoples), the European Commission (on Development and Indigenous Peoples of Southeast Asia), the Danish Ministry of Foreign Affairs (for reviewing its policy on indigenous peoples), and Minority Rights Group International (on indigenous peoples and forestry issues and customary laws). He is currently engaged in research work for the UNDP Regional Centre, Bangkok, the ILO and Zurich University. He is also involved with several voluntary organisations working on indigenous issues and is currently the chairperson of a local research and advocacy organisation TAUNGYA and the chairperson of the Hill Tracts NGO Forum, the main representative body of local NGOs of the CHT. He is also the convenor of the National Adivasi Coordination Committee, a national network of indigenous peoples' organisations of different parts of Bangladesh and is a member of several national and international organisations and networks on land rights, human rights and indigenous peoples' rights. He was elected as one of the two co-chairpersons of the Indigenous Peoples' Caucus at the UN Commission of Human Rights' Intersessional Working Group on the Draft Declaration on the Rights of Indigenous Peoples at its 11th session (December 2005 and January-February 2006).

Geir Sjøberg
Adviser, Section for Peace and Reconciliation, Norwegian Ministry of Foreign Affairs.

Geir Sjøberg holds a BS in economics from Vanderbilt University in Nashville, Tennessee. From 1994 to 1997 he was executive officer at the Ministry of Foreign Affairs in Oslo and was a member of Norway's delegations to the climate change and other multilateral negotiations on sustainable development. From 1998 till 2000 he represented the headquarters of the UN Development Programme and did field work in Bulgaria, Peru, the Philippines, and South Africa. During Norway's term on the Security Council, 2001-2002, he was assigned to the Permanent Mission of Norway to the United Nations, where he followed the conflicts of Central and East Africa. In 2003 he became adviser at the Ministry of Foreign Affairs in Oslo, dealing with peace and reconciliation work at the department for human rights, democracy and humanitarian assistance.

Fernand de Varennes
Associate Professor, Murdoch University School of Law, Australia.

Fernand de Varennes is a former director of the Asia-Pacific Centre for Human Rights and the Prevention of Ethnic Conflict and the founding editor-in-chief of the *Asia-Pacific Journal on Human Rights and the Law*. He is an expert on language rights and has done research on international law, human rights, minorities and ethnic conflicts. He has taught on minority rights and ethnic conflicts in numerous institutions around the world, including at the European Academy in Bolzano, Italy, the University of Deusto in Bilbao, Spain, the South Asian Human Rights and Peace Studies Orientation Course in Kathmandu, Nepal, Sam Ratulangi University in Manado, Indonesia, the University of Pécs in Hungary, the Cornell University – Université Paris I Panthéon Sorbonne Summer School in Paris, France, the European Politics Programme at the University of Pécs, Hungary, Turku Law School and Åbo Akademi Institute for Human Rights in Finland, and Seikei University in Tokyo. He has also worked with the United Nations' Working Group on the Rights of Minorities, UNESCO and the OSCE's High Commissioner on National Minorities on these issues. He is senior (nonresident) research associate at the European Centre for Minority Issues in Flensburg, Germany. He recently held the Tip O'Neill Peace Fellowship at INCORE (Initiative on Conflict Resolution and Ethnicity) in Derry, Northern Ireland. He is currently working on a three-volume book on ethnic and internal conflicts worldwide.

Francesc Vendrell
European Union Special Representative in Afghanistan; former UN Assistant Secretary-General Head of the Special Mission to Afghanistan (UNSMA).

Francesc Vendrell holds a law degree from the University of Barcelona, an LL.B. from King's College, University of London, and an MA in modern history from Cambridge University. He joined the United Nations in 1968 and has held a variety of posts at the UN related to political affairs and international law. He was deputy personal representative of the secretary-general for the Central American peace process (El Salvador and Nicaragua) from 1989 to 1991. He also represented the secretary-general during the first phase of the Guatemala peace negotiations between March 1990 and May 1992. In 1993, he served as senior political adviser to the secretary-general's special envoy for Haiti. In his capacity as director for special political assignments in 1992, he was responsible for issues relating to the Caucasus. In addition, between 1987 and 1992, he was also chief and subsequently director for Europe and the Americas in the Office of Research and the Collection of Information in the Office of the Secretary-General. From August 1993 to December 1997, he served as director of the East Asia and Pacific division of the Department of Political Affairs and, between January 1998 and October 1999, as director of the combined Asia and the Pacific division. Since November 1999 he was officer-in-charge of the Office of the Assistant Secretary-General for Political Affairs with responsibility for Asia and the Pacific, the Americas and Europe. He also served as deputy personal representative of the secretary-general for East Timor since June 1999. In

January 2000 he was appointed head of the Special Mission to Afghanistan (UNSMA) with the rank of assistant secretary-general.

Morris Te Whiti Love
Former Director of the Waitangi Tribunal.

Morris Te Whiti Love became director of the Waitangi Tribunal in June 1996. The Waitangi Tribunal plays a key role in the overall process for the settlement of Treaty of Waitangi claims. He was previously involved in Maori resource management. He managed Maruwhenua, the Maori Secretariat in the Ministry for the Environment from 1993 to 1996. Previous to that, he ran a consultancy in resource management with a particular focus on *tangata whenua* issues and the Treaty of Waitangi. Mr. Te Whiti Love's university training was in agricultural engineering where he specialised in water and soil matters. Following this training, he was involved in regional government water management and tertiary teaching in engineering particularly in Lae, Papua New Guinea. He has written articles in New Zealand engineering and other publications on Maori values in relation to water and geothermal resources and contributed to regional policy statements and district plans under the Resource Management Act. Morris Te Whiti Love is very involved in his own tribe and is a trustee of the Te Atiawa/Taranaki *whanui* organisation – the Wellington Tenths Trust. His *marae* is Te Tatau o te Po in Petone.

Jens Woelk
Researcher and Lecturer in Comparative Constitutional Law, University of Trento; Senior Researcher, Institute for Studies on Federalism and Regionalism, European Academy of Bozen/Bolzano (South Tyrol).

Jens Woelk, born in Germany, holds a Ph.D. in comparative constitutional law (thesis on constitutional principles of cooperation in federal and regional systems), University of Regensburg, Bavaria, where he also graduated in legal sciences. From 1994 to 2000 he was a senior researcher at the European Academy Bozen/Bolzano at the Minorities and Autonomies Department. His main fields of interest are comparative constitutional law, especially federalism/regionalism, minority-issues and South-Eastern Europe. He is coordinator for the law area in the masters programme 'Comparative Local Development for the Balkans and Other Areas in Transformation'.

Other Contributors

Robert Atsir
Chief Executive, CDA Finance and Investment Services, Bougainville; former Economic Advisor to the Governor of Bougainville.

Robert Atsir was involved in the peace process in Bougainville and in the Bougainville constitution-making process.

Mustafa Jemiloglu
President of the Mejlis Crimean Tatar National Assembly.

Mustafa Jemiloglu, born in the Crimea, finished secondary school in 1959. After being refused admission to the Central Asian University in Tashkent, he worked at Mirchasul mechanical factory. He was one of the founders of the underground youth-student organisation Crimean Tatar Youth Union in 1961. The organisation was outlawed and its leaders arrested for 'anti-soviet activity'. He was dismissed from the factory and put under the KGB surveillance. In 1962 he entered the Irrigation Institute in Tashkent but once again was dismissed for anti-Soviet views. In May 1966 Mr. Jemiloglu was imprisoned for refusal to serve in the Soviet army. He was arrested six times between 1966 and 1983. In 1974 he went on a 303 day hunger strike, and mustered international support. In April 1987 he was elected to the board of the Central Initiative Group of the Crimean Tatar national movement. Two years later he was elected president of the Central Council of the Crimean Tatar National Movement Organisation (CTNMO). He moved to the Crimea with his family and settled in Bakcchisaray. In June 1991 he was elected president of the Mejlis of the Crimean Tatar people which is the representative body of the Crimean Tatar people. The advocacy and political activity of Mustafa Jemiloglu has been honoured by many awards and honourable titles including international ones, such as the UNHCR award.

Kuupik Kleist
Member of the Parliaments of Greenland and Denmark.

Kuupik Kleist was born in Qullissat and graduated as a social worker from Roskilde University Centre in 1983. He was a member of the Regional Government for Public Works and Traffic from 1991 until 1995, and a member of the Landsting in 1995-1996. From 1996-1999 he was director of the Greenland home rule government's Foreign Affairs Office. He was the owner and director of the consulting firm NIKISI Aps., a member of the governing body of the Inuit Circumpolar Conference (ICC) 1995-1997, and of the board of directors of Nunatta Naqiterivia (South Greenland Printing House). He was chairman of the board of directors of Tele Greenland A/S from 1999 and of the record company, ULO. He was secretary of the Home Rule Commission from 2000-2001. He has been the Inuit Ataqatigiit's candidate in Greenland from 2001.

Gert Van Maanen
Chairman of the Board of Directors, Kreddha Europe.

Gert van Maanen holds a law degree from Leiden University, the Netherlands. He started his career as a lawyer with Nauta Dutil c.s in Rotterdam. In 1973 he worked for the Royal Nedlloyd Group (in-house legal counsel, Personnel Director, Director Fleet Services). From 1989 until 1993 he was a member of the executive board of the ING Bank. In 1994 he became chief executive officer of Oikocredit, the Development Bank of the Churches for Unbankables in the Third World. In 2002 he became a member of the Corporate Chamber of the Amsterdam High Court. During 1996 until 2002 he was chair of RAWOO (Netherlands Development Assistance Research Council). Since 2001 he has been a member of the Netherlands Advisory Council for International Affairs, as well as a board member of Cordaid (a Dutch Catholic donor organisation). He is also a council member of the Wilgespruit Fellowship Centre, South Africa.

John Momis
Visiting Fellow, Pacific Institute of Advanced Studies in Development and Governance, University of the South Pacific; Former Provincial Governor of Bougainville.

John Momis was born in 1942 in Salamaua, Morobe Province. He became governor of Bougainville, Papua New Guinea (PNG) in 1999. He was educated at the Colomban Seminary in Sydney, Australia, and also at the Alexishafen, Madang, Holy Spirit Seminary. He was the elected regional member for Bougainville in the National Parliament of PNG for many years. In 1976 he was appointed by the people of Bougainville to lead negotiations with the national government to establish a Bougainville provincial government. In 1977 he was appointed minister of decentralisation in the PNG government. In 1985 he became minister for public service and deputy prime minister of PNG. He became deputy opposition leader after the government was toppled in a parliamentary vote of no confidence. He stayed in this position until he was appointed minister for provincial affairs in 1988. In 1989 he established a commission to study greater autonomy for provincial governments. In 1992 he was appointed shadow minister for Bougainville affairs. A year later he became deputy opposition leader and in 1994 he was appointed shadow minister for communication, education and culture. As chairperson of the ACP Council of Ministers he successfully negotiated the Lome IV Convention in Brussels in 1995. From 1990 until August 2001 he played a major role in the Bougainville peace negotiations which led to the Bougainville peace agreement.

Pau Puig i Scotoni
Advisor on the Baltic Sea Region for the Secretariat for International Relations, Government of Catalonia.

Pau Puig i Scotoni was born in France and holds a Doctor of Philosophy degree from the University of Lund (1981). In 1982 he presented the lecture 'Surviving without the City Wall – the Catalan case yesterday, today and tomorrow', at the VIIth World Conference on Future Studies in Stockholm. He wrote the book "Baskien och Katalonien: Den långa vägen till självstyre" (The Basque Country and Catalonia: The long road to self-government) in 1986. In 1991 he started working with the Unit for International Relations (later Secretariat of Foreign Affairs) of the Catalan government. In 1998 he published 'Pensar els camins a la sobirania' (Thinking the roads to sovereignty).

Onno Seroo
Director of International Relations, Centre UNESCO de Catalunya.

Onno Seroo holds degrees in both French and Spanish literature, with respective specialisations in Mediterranean and Latin American studies. From 1993 he worked as international relations officer of the UNESCO Centre of Catalonia. He has held positions as general secretary of the Catalan Federation for Human Rights NGOs and the Catalan Federation of UNESCO Associations and as acting executive secretary of Cultures of the World, an international NGO focusing on intercultural cooperation in the globalisation age and its impact on small cultures.

He is a member of the Ad Hoc Committee on Internationally Recognised UNESCO Centres, an independent international expert body that monitors the adequate use of the denomination 'UNESCO Centre'. He is also a member of the International Center for Geopolitical Studies, Geneva. Since August 2002 he has been secretary of the board of Kreddha Europe. Together with Kreddha's executive president Michael van Walt he published the proceedings of the expert conference that UNESCO and the UNESCO Centre of Catalonia hosted on The Implementation of the Right to Self-Determination as a Contribution to Conflict Prevention (Barcelona, 1998). He continues to coordinate the UNESCO Centre of Catalonia's project on self-determination and conflict transformation which seeks to develop international procedures and mechanisms that permit the peaceful resolution of self-determination claims.

Marian Staszewski
Senior Political Advisor, UN Observer Mission to Abkhazia, Georgia.

Marian Staszewski was a member of the Polish Foreign Service from 1971 until 1989, dealing with international security issues. This work included his assignments as Polish delegate to the OSCE Follow-up Meeting in Vienna in

1997-1998, and his appointment as first secretary of the Polish Permanent Mission to the United Nations in New York in 1988-1989. Since 1989 he has worked for the United Nations. He has served in various UN peacekeeping and peacemaking operations, and was deputy head of the Office of the Secretary-General in Iran. Since December 1994 he has been the senior political adviser at the UN Observer Mission in Georgia.

Michael van Walt van Praag
Executive President, Kreddha International.

Dr. van Walt van Praag is Kreddha's executive president and co-founder. He currently facilitates three intrastate peace processes for the organisation and teaches international law at Golden Gate University in San Francisco. Dr. van Walt holds a masters and a doctorate in law from the University of Utrecht, and an LL.M. from Wayne State University in Detroit. He practised law in Washington DC, London and San Francisco with the law firms of Wilmer Cutler and Pickering, and of Pettit and Martin, where he worked on matters involving public international law, commercial law and international arbitration. He served as UN senior legal advisor to the minister of foreign affairs of the East Timor transitional government (UNTAET) in 2002. From 1991 to 1998 he was the general secretary of the Unrepresented Nations and Peoples Organisation (UNPO). During that period he served as UNDP consultant on indigenous peoples in the Sakha Republic of the Russian Federation (1994); legal advisor to the All-Bougainville Leaders Peace Talks in Cairns, Australia (1994); advisor to the Chechen government delegation on their negotiations with the Russian Federation (1994-97); and advisor to the Abkhazian government delegation in peace talks between Georgia and Abkhazia (1993-95). Since 1985 Michael van Walt has been legal advisor to the Office of His Holiness the Dalai Lama and the Tibetan government in exile. He is a member of the Netherlands Development Assistance Research Council (RAWOO), an advisory body of the Netherlands foreign ministry.

Index

A

Abkhazia-Georgia conflict 8, 25, 40
   United Nations' role in
      Friends of Georgia 42-43
      Observer Mission (UNOMIG) 36-37
Aceh conflict (Indonesia) 54
ad hoc arbitration 219
adjudication of disputes 31-34
   arbitral tribunals 32, 46, 203, 212
   in Good Friday Agreement (Northern Ireland, 1998) 98
African Court of Human Rights (ACHPR) 216, 217
'Agenda for Peace' (Annan, 1992) 67
Agreement on Principles (Eritrea-Yemen, 1996) 212, 300-305
agreements on dispute resolution 211-213, 226-227
   see also cease-fire agreements; peace agreements
Ahmeti, Ali 208, 210
Ahtisaari, Martti 103 n17
Albanian conflict (Macedonia) 56, 205-206
alienation of land, from Maori population 231-233
Anglo-Irish Agreement (1985) 93
Anglo-Irish Treaty (1921) 89
Annan, Kofi (secretary-general of UN) 67
Aotearoa/New Zealand
   British colonisation of 230-233
   Treaty of Waitangi (1840) 32-33, 229-231, 250, 318-321
      Act (1975) 237, 238, 242, 250
      Office of Treaty Settlements 241, 244
      Tribunal of 127, 233-249, 250, 251
   tribal autonomy in 248, 250
arbitral tribunals
   adjudication of disputes on peace agreements 32, 46, 203, 212
   appointment of 217, 219
   international 219-226
arbitration 212
   agreements, enforcement of 226-227
   commercial 224-255
   rules of 217, 218-219, 221, 222, 223, 224, 312-317
   settlement of disputes by 217-226, 228, 298-311

arbitrators, appointment and selection of 217, 219, 220-221
arms see weapons
asymmetry
   in government 70
   of power 5, 20-22, 184-187, 199
   in regionalism 171
Atsir, Robert 19, 330
Augustine, St. 49
Australia, and East Timor conflict 214
Austria, and South Tyrol autonomy 8, 34-35, 158, 160, 161, 162-163, 174-175
autonomous entities 24
autonomy 4, 24-25, 70-71, 83, 84
   of Bougainville 28-29, 195
   of Chittagong Hill Tracts 117 n5, 120
   of Crimea 73-76
   cultural 165
   of East Timor 202-203
   of Eritrea 202
   ethnicity as basis for 78
   of Gagauzia (Gagauz Yeri, Moldova) 77-78
   in international law 72-73
   of Kurds 15, 71 n6, 82
   of Macedonia 76-77
   non-territorial 75
   OSCE's views on 4, 81-82
   regional 73, 171, 199
   of South Tyrol 20, 24, 26, 132 n52, 157-158, 172-174
      Austrian role in 8, 34-35, 158, 160, 161, 162-163, 174-175
      De Gasperi-Gruber agreement (Paris Treaty, 1947) 34-35, 159-160, 174, 278
      'The Package of Measures in Favour of the Population of South Tyrol' (1969) 28, 162-163, 175
      Second Autonomy Statute (1971) 23, 164-171, 175-176
   and territorial integrity 4, 70, 194-195
   of Tibet 13, 148-149, 152, 153
   tribal, in New Zealand 248, 250
   of Zanzibar 15
   see also self-determination; self-rule

autonomy arrangements 3-6, 50, 62, 67
   and democracy 14-16, 82-83
   demographic changes and 83
   entrenchment of 164
   erosion of 58
   governmental resistance to 64
   implementation of 70, 85, 157, 201-203
      in South Tyrol 166-171, 175-176
   territorial aspects of 4, 153, 160
   time limits on 28-29
Awami League (Bangladesh) 123 n19

B
Bahrain 196
Bangladesh
   Chittagong Hill Tracts (CHT) Peace
      Accord (1997) 10, 13-14, 115-117, 122-123, 269-277
      deficiencies of 21, 117
      dispute resolution provisions 31
      entrenchment of 130-132
      expectations of 133-134
      implementation of 27, 28, 29, 117-118, 125-126, 129-130, 134-137, 144-146
      land issue in 122, 127
      negotiations 137-139
      opposition to 116
      reception of 123-125
      reconstruction and development phase 41, 139-141
      third party involvement 39, 135-136, 145
      violations of 126, 128
   development aid to 41, 134, 145
   elections in 126 n31
   human rights in 130, 145-146
   Moderate Leaders' Agreement (1988) 138, 139
   National Poverty Reduction Strategy Paper (PRSP, 2005) 129
   Pahari refugees repatriated to 134-135
   Priti Group Accord (1985) 138
Banyamulenge conflict (Congo) 54
Basque autonomy 199
Bastion Point (New Zealand), occupation of 233
Benelux Court of Justice 216
Bengali settlers in Chittagong Hill Tracts (CHT) 120-121, 123-125
   conflict with indigenous population 121-122, 143-144
   rehabilitation of 127, 135
Biegman, Niek 7, 37, 42, 323
blacklisting of terrorist organisations 186-187
Bloody Sunday (Northern Ireland, 1972) 60, 91-92

'blue water principle' 195
BNP (Bangladesh Nationalist Party) 125, 129
Boltjes, Miek 323-324
Bosnia-Herzegovina, Dayton Accords (1995) 212, 296-297
Bougainville
   autonomy of 195
   cease-fire agreement (Papua New Guinea, 1997) 37
   Peace Agreement (Papua New Guinea, 1976) 11
   Peace Agreement (Papua New Guinea, 2001) 18-19
      autonomy arrangements in 28-29
      double entrenchment of 22-23
      women's role in 19-20
Brcko (Bosnia-Herzegovina) 212, 298-299
Briner, Robert 225
British New Zealand Company 230
British-Irish Council (Good Friday Agreement, 1998) 26, 100, 258-259
British-Irish Intergovernmental Conference (Good Friday Agreement, 1998) 26, 100, 259-260
Bush, George W. (president of United States) 108
Bux Khan, Jan (Chakma Raja) 119

C
Canada, Québec Province in 73, 83-84
Caribbean Court of Justice (CCJ) 216
Carter, Jimmy (president of United States) 152
Case concerning the Military and Paramilitary Activities in and against Nicaragua (Nicaragua v. United States) 215
Catalan autonomy 199
cease-fire agreements 139
   humanitarian 182
   in Sri Lanka 182, 188
Central American Court of Justice (CACJ) 216
Central Asia, and China-Tibet conflict 154
Chad, north-south conflict in 54
Chakma (Bangladesh) 142
Chastelain, John de 36, 102
China-Tibet conflict 147-148
   1959 uprising 150
   Dalai Lama's role in 155-156
   negotiations 21, 40, 149-150, 152
   Seventeen Point Agreement (1951) 10, 13, 147-148, 150-151, 153, 266-268
   Strasbourg Proposal (Dalai Lama) 152
   third party involvement 39, 151, 154

Chittagong Hill Tracts (CHT)
  Bengali settlers in 120-121, 123-125
    conflict with the indigenous population 121-122, 143-144
    rehabilitation of 127, 135
  British colonisation of 119-120, 121
  cease-fire agreement in 139
  indigenous population of 116 n3, 117, 118-119
  Moderate Leaders' Agreement (1988) 138, 139
  Pakistani rule of 120, 121
  Peace Accord (Bangladesh, 1997) 10, 13-14, 115-117, 122-123, 269-277
    deficiencies of 21, 117
    dispute resolution provisions 31
    entrenchment of 130-132
    expectations of 133-134
    implementation of 27, 28, 29, 117-118, 125-126, 129-130, 134-137, 144-146
    indigenous culture in 122-123
    land issue in 122, 127
    negotiations 137-139
    peace dividends in 41
    reception of 116, 123-125
    third party involvement 39, 135-136, 145
    and United People's Democratic Front 10-11
    violations of 126, 128
  Priti Group Accord (1985) 138
  reconstruction and development in 41, 139-141
  Regulation (Amendment) Act (2003) 129
  violence in 116, 138 n66, 142-143
CHT *see* Chittagong Hill Tracts
civil organisations 185
civil rights movement, in Northern Ireland 61, 91
civil society, and implementation of peace agreements 182
claims, by Maori 233-236, 238-249, 250-251
coalition roles, of facilitators 180
collective ownership, of land 232
collective representation, in federalism 171
colonisation
  of Chittagong Hill Tracts (CHT) 119-120, 121
  of Ireland 88
  of New Zealand 230-233
COMESA (pan-African Court of Justice) 216-217
Coming out of Violence (Darby, MacGinty et al) 141

Commission on Policing for Northern Ireland (Good Friday Agreement, 1998) 101
Commission of Six (Second Autonomy Statute, South Tyrol, 1971) 167-169, 174
Commission of Twelve (Second Autonomy Statute, South Tyrol, 1971) 167
commissions, for adjudication of disputes 32
Committee of Twenty-Four (Special Committee on Decolonisation, United Nations) 194, 195
competition, among third parties 179, 200, 210
conceptual claims, by Maori 239
conflicts
  economic interests in 11
  ethnic 143-144
  see also intrastate conflicts
Congo (Democratic Republic), Banyamulenge conflict 54
Considine, Tom 101
consociational democracy 165
constitution
  amendment of 23-24
  of autonomous entities 24
  of Bangladesh 131
  of Bougainville 19
  of Denmark 24
  entrenchment in
    of autonomy arrangements 164
    of peace agreements 15, 22, 130, 185
  of Italy 172
  of Macedonia 206
  of Moldova 77
  of New Zealand 232 n10
  of Papua New Guinea 22
  of Spain 199
  of Sri Lanka 59
  of Ukraine 73-74, 75
constitutional court (Italy) 168, 169, 170, 172
Convention 169 (ILO) 45
Convention on the Law of the Sea (United Nations, 1982) 293-295
Convention for the Pacific Settlement of International Disputes (1899 & 1907) 219-220
Convention for the Protection of the Marine Environment of the North-East Atlantic (1992) 221, 290-292
Convention on the Recognition and Enforcement of Foreign Arbitral Awards (New York Convention, 1958) 226-227
conventions, dispute resolution agreements in 212
coordination, among fourth parties 42

Court of Appeal (New Zealand) 249
Court of Justice of the Andean Community (TJAC) 216
courts
   adjudication of disputes in 32, 213
   international human rights 228
   regional international 215-217
Crimea
   autonomy of 73-76
   conflicts in 72
   demographic changes in 83
Crimean Tatars 74-76, 82
Crown Law Office (CLO, New Zealand) 237
cultural autonomy 165
culture
   indigenous, in Chittagong Hill Tracts Peace Accord (Bangladesh, 1997) 122-123
   Maori, recognition of 235
   Melanesian 18
   of parties in intrastate conflicts 200
current claims, by Maori 239
customary representation 237, 238
Cyprus, Greek-Turkish conflict in 54

D

Dalai Lama 147, 148, 151, 152, 155-156
Darby, John 135, 136, 141
Dayton Accords (Bosnia-Herzegovina, 1995) 212, 296-297
decolonisation, and intrastate conflicts 195
decommissioning of weapons
   in Bougainville 19
   by JSS in Bangladesh 115
   in Northern Ireland 36, 97, 98, 101-103, 104-105, 112, 261
deficiencies of peace agreements 12-14, 16, 183
   Chittagong Hill Tracts Peace Accord (Bangladesh, 1997) 21, 117
Delors, Jacques 109
democracy
   and autonomy arrangements 14-16, 82-83
   consociational 165
demographic changes
   in Northern Ireland 83
   in Québec Province 83-84
   in Tibet 154-155
Denmark, constitution of 24
development aid
   in conflict areas 190
   and implementation of peace agreements 40-41
   projects in Chittagong Hill Tracts 41, 139-140

development aid (cont.)
   to Bangladesh 41, 134, 145
   see also peace dividends
devolution of power 74, 79
diplomacy, peace 179
direct rule, of Northern Ireland 92, 93, 105, 110
discrimination 54 n9, 62
   cause of intrastate conflicts 57-58, 66
dispute settlement 31, 293-295
   agreements 211-213, 226-227
   by arbitration 217-226, 228, 298-311
   bodies for 213-217, 227
   and implementation of peace agreements 31-34, 46-47, 135
   in Second Autonomy Statute (South Tyrol) 170
disputes
   adjudication of 31-34
   by arbitral tribunals 32, 46, 203, 212
   in Good Friday Agreement (Northern Ireland, 1998) 98
donor conferences 42, 187, 190
double entrenchment of peace agreements 22-23, 24
   Mizoram Accord (India, 1986) 132 n52
double minority problem, of Northern Ireland 90-91
Downing Street Declaration (Northern Ireland conflict, 1993) 94
Draft Declaration on the Rights of Indigenous Peoples (UN) 146, 236 n18
DUP (Democratic Unionist Party) 96, 98, 113
Durie, Eddie 233

E

East India Company (British) 119, 120
East Timor
   autonomy of 202-203
   conflict with Indonesia 8, 55, 196-197, 199
   International Court of Justice
      jurisprudence on 214
   peace process
      Portugal's role in 8, 36 n62, 214
      United Nations' role in 30 n52, 38, 197, 199
   Santa Cruz cemetery massacre (1991) 198
Easter insurrection (1916, Ireland) 89
economic development and peace 141
   see also peace dividends
economic interests, in conflicts 11
elections
   in Bangladesh 126 n31
   in Bougainville 19

elections (cont.)
    in Macedonia 210
    in Northern Ireland 61, 96-97, 98
    observation and monitoring of 202
    in United Kingdom 88, 89
enactment decrees, of Second Autonomy Statute (South Tyrol, 1971) 169-170, 173
entrenchment
    of autonomy arrangements 164
    of peace agreements 22-25, 185
        Chittagong Hill Tracts Peace Accord (Bangladesh, 1997) 130-132
        constitutional 15, 22, 130, 185
        Mizoram Accord (1986, India) 132 n50
Equality Commission (Northern Ireland) 98, 99
equality of parties 47, 171
Eritrea
    autonomy of 202
    conflict with Ethiopia 54
    dispute with Yemen
        Agreement on Principles (1996) 212, 300-305
        Award of the Arbitral Tribunal in the First Stage (1998) 306-307
Ethiopia, Eritrean conflict in 54
ethnic conflicts, in Chittagong Hill Tracts 143-144
ethnicity, as basis for autonomy 78
EU
    membership
        of Ireland and United Kingdom 106-107
        sought by Macedonia 40, 210
    third party involvement
        in Macedonia conflict 208
        in Northern Ireland conflict 108-109
European Court of Human Rights (ECHR) 216
European Court of Justice (ECJ) 215
European Free Trade Association Court 216
exit strategies, of third parties 203
exploratory roles, of facilitators 180

F
facilitators
    and asymmetry between parties 184-187
    contribution of 180-183, 191
    monitoring mechanisms of 188-189
    Norway 7, 38, 177-179, 180, 183, 186-187, 188, 189-191
    roles of 178-180
    see also mediators
federalism 157
    collective representation in 171

Financial Assistance Fund for Settlement of International Disputes (PCA) 222
financial interests, of Provisional IRA 111, 112
first parties 6, 34
    disputes on implementation of agreements 31-34
    third parties turning into 39
    see also parties
food support, for Bengali settlers in Chittagong Hill Tracts 128
fourth parties 6, 7-8
    mobilisation of 84
    roles of 40-42
Framework Agreement (Macedonia, 2001) 7, 76, 77, 206-207, 279-289
    role of international community 30, 37, 42, 206, 207-210
France, New Caledonia conflict 29, 54
'friends of the peace process', roles of 42-43, 201

G
Gagauzia (Gagauz Yeri, Moldova), autonomy of 77-78
De Gasperi-Gruber agreement (South Tyrol, Paris Treaty, 1947) 34-35, 159-160, 174, 278
General Framework Agreement for Peace in Bosnia and Herzegovina see Dayton Accords (1995)
Georgia-Abkhazia conflict 8, 25, 40
    United Nations' role in
        Friends of Georgia 42-43
        Observer Mission (UNOMIG) 36-37
gerrymandering 90
godfather role, of second parties 8
Good Friday Agreement (Northern Ireland, 1998) 13 n17, 14, 94-96, 255-265
    implementation of 98-105
    institutional arrangements of 25-26, 79-80, 99-101
    reform of 111-112
governments
    asymmetry in 70
    concessions by 199-200
    and implementation of peace agreements
        political will 9-10, 136-137
        resistance 49, 63-66, 67
            in Bangladesh 129-130, 132, 134
    and third party involvement 39, 197-199
Greenland Home Rule Act 24
Groups of Friends of the Secretary-General (United Nations) 42-43, 201

guarantees
  as form of entrenchment 25
  for implementation of peace agreements 38
guarantors, third parties acting as 38
Guatemala, peace process in 183
Gyari, Lodi G. 13, 21, 324

H
Haas, Richard 108
Habibie, Bacharuddin Jusuf (president of Indonesia) 202
Haile Selassie (emperor of Ethiopia) 202
Hasina, Sheikh (prime minister of Bangladesh) 123
Haughey, Denis 8, 13 n17, 14, 36, 324
hearings, of Waitangi Tribunal 242-243
Heath, Edward (prime minister of United Kingdom) 92 n3
Herzegovina
  Brcko area dispute with Serbia 298-299
  Dayton Accords (1995) 212, 296-297
historical claims, by Maori 239-240, 251
historical research, of Maori claims 240 n26, 241, 242
Hobson, William 230
holistic approach, to peace processes 181-182
Hu Jintao (president of China) 150
human rights
  courts 228
  and protection of minority rights 51 n6, 66 n25
    in Bangladesh 145-146
  UN High Commissioner for 30 n52, 44
  violations
    in Bangladesh 130
    and intrastate conflicts 44, 61, 66, 184, 187-188
Human Rights Commission (Northern Ireland) 98, 99
humanitarian aid 190
humanitarian cease-fire agreements 182
Hume, John 94
Hutchinson, Al 101 n14

I
ICC (International Chamber of Commerce) Court of Arbitration 223-225
ILO, Convention 169 45
implementation
  of autonomy arrangements 70, 85, 157, 201-203
    Second Autonomy Statute (South Tyrol, 1971) 166-174, 175-176

implementation (cont.)
  of peace agreements 1, 2, 8-34, 40-41, 43-47
    Chittagong Hill Tracts (Bangladesh, 1997) 117-118, 125-126, 144-146
    civil society participation in 182
    and development aid *see* peace dividends
    and dispute settlement 31-34, 46-47, 135
    Framework Agreement (Macedonia, 2001) 30, 206, 207-210
    Good Friday Agreement (Northern Ireland, 1998) 98-105
    governmental resistance to 49, 63-66, 67
        in Bangladesh 129-130, 132, 134
    incentives 29, 40, 136
    mechanisms for 69-70, 134-137
    mechanisms for 69-70, 136-137
    and negotiations 17, 178
    political will 9-10, 136-137
    Seventeen Point Agreement (China-Tibet, 1951) 150-151, 153
    and trust 11, 17, 64, 80
    verification of 27-28, 203
  of settlements of Waitangi Tribunal 248-249
incentives for implementing peace agreements 29, 40, 136
  see also peace dividends
inclusiveness, of peace processes 181
independence
  of Ireland 88, 89-90
  myths about 84
Independent International Commission on Decommissioning (de Chastelain, Northern Ireland, 1997) 36, 102, 105, 112, 261
Independent Monitoring Commission (Northern Ireland, 2003) 104
India
  and China-Tibet conflict 151, 154
  Mizoram Accord (1986) 131-132
  Nagaland conflict 54
    cease-fire agreement with NSCN (1997) 27
  positive discrimination in 131
indigenous population
  of Chittagong Hill Tracts 116 n3, 117, 118-119
    autonomy of 120
    conflict with Bengali settlers 121-122, 143-144
    and Peace Accord (1997) 122-123

indigenous population (cont.)
  in Indian legislation 131
  of New Caledonia, agreements with France 29
  protection of rights of 146, 236
individual relationships 38
individual rights, to land 232
Indonesia
  Aceh conflict in 54
  East Timor conflict 8, 55, 196-197, 199
  Kalimantan conflict 55
  transmigration policies in 54-55 n10
  West Papua conflict 55, 196
inequality of parties 47
  see also asymmetry of power
institutional arrangements
  in Chittagong Hill Tracts Peace Accord (1997) 13-14, 127
  in Good Friday Agreement (Northern Ireland, 1998) 25-26, 79-80, 99-101
  in Second Autonomy Statute (South Tyrol, 1971) 166-171
  see also mechanisms for implementation
Inter-American Court of Human Rights (IACHR) 216
interdependence 84
intermediaries, local 183
international arbitral tribunals 217, 219-226
international community
  dispute resolution bodies of 213, 227
  and Macedonia Framework Agreement (2001) 30, 37, 42, 206, 207-210
  role in implementing peace agreements 30, 44-45
International Court of Justice (ICJ) 214-215, 227
International Fund for Ireland 109
international guarantees
  as form of entrenchment 25
  for implementation of peace agreements 38
international law
  autonomy concept in 72-73
  and Italy-South Tyrol agreement 163
international mechanisms, for monitoring and verification 27-28
international relations, definition of states in 72
intra-indigenous violence, in Chittagong Hill Tracts 142-143
intrastate conflicts 2-3, 52-53
  causes of 49, 53-59, 66, 67
  and decolonisation 195
  and human rights violations 44, 61, 66, 184, 187-188

intrastate conflicts (cont.)
  and minority rights 3, 51-52, 53, 66
  in mutually hurting stalemate 198
  and separatism 50, 58
  settlement of 3-4, 50, 62, 64, 66, 175
  United Nations involvement in 193-197
  violence in 11, 52-53, 58, 59-61, 65, 91-92, 103, 116, 138 n66, 142-143
intrastate peace agreements see peace agreements
IRA (Irish Republican Army) 60
  Provisional 91, 92, 102
    decommissioning of arms by 97, 98, 101-103, 104-105, 110-111, 112
    financial interests of 111, 112
    violence ceased by 94
  Sinn Fein 94, 96, 98, 102
  truce with British forces 89
Iran-United States Claims Tribunal 225, 226
Iraq
  autonomy of Kurds in 15, 71 n6, 82
  Kurdish conflict in 55
Ireland
  British colonisation of 88
  Easter insurrection (1916) 89
  EU membership of 106-107
  independence of 88, 89-90
  and Northern Ireland conflict 8, 35, 92, 93, 106
  partition of 89
Ireland v. United Kingdom (OSPAR) 221
Irish Home Rule Act (1914) 88
Irish National Party 88
Irish nationalists (Northern Ireland) 26
Israeli-Palestinian conflict 55, 185
Italy-South Tyrol conflict 20, 24, 26, 55, 132 n52, 157-158, 158-161, 172-174, 175
  Austrian role in 8, 34-35, 158, 160, 161, 162-163, 174-175
  'The Package of Measures in Favour of the Population of South Tyrol' (1969) 28, 162-163, 175
  Second Autonomy Statute (1971, South Tyrol) 23, 164-171, 175-176

J
Jamaat-e-Islami Bangladesh 125
Jemiloglu, Mustafa 330
JSS (Jana Samhati Samiti, Bangladesh) 10, 115
  and Chittagong Hill Tracts Peace Accord 117, 123, 125 n24, 126-127, 133, 144-145
  and UPDF 11

judicial systems 202
Jumma people (Chittagong Hill Tracts, Bangladesh) 14

K
Kalimantan conflict (Indonesia) 55
Kleist, Kuupik 24, 45, 330-331
Kosovo, conflicts in 59-60, 206
Kurds
 in Iraq 55
  autonomy of 15, 71 n6, 82
 in Turkey 57

L
land
 alienated by the British from Maori population 231-233
 claims of Maori 127, 229, 233-236, 238-248, 250, 251
 issue in Chittagong Hill Tracts Peace Accord (Bangladesh, 1997) 122, 127
 return of, to Crimean Tartars 75 n14
language policies
 in South Tyrol 165-166
 in Sri Lanka 59
Larma, J.B. 117-118
Larsen v. The Hawaiian Kingdom by its Council of Regency 212-213, 218 n6, 221, 308-311
lead roles, of facilitators 179-180
Lebanon, Muslim-Christian conflict 56
legitimacy, of parties 184-185
Little, David 61
local intermediaries 183
LTTE (Liberation Tigers of Tamil Eelam) 186, 187
Lund Recommendations on the effective Participation of national Minorities in public Life (OSCE) 81, 85

M
Maanen, Gert van 31 n54, 331
Macedonia 205
 Albanian conflict in 56, 205-206
 autonomy of 76-77
 elections in 210
 EU and NATO membership sought by 40, 210
 Framework Agreement (2001) 7, 76, 77, 206-207, 279-289
  role of international community 30, 37, 42, 206, 207-210
 NATO presence in 208-209, 210
MacGinty, Roger 135, 136, 141

Major, John (prime minister of United Kingdom) 94 n4
majority, exclusion of 51 n6, 56
Mallon, Seamus 96
Maori
 land alienated by the British from 231-233
 land claims 233, 250 n35
 and Waitangi Tribunal 127, 229, 233-236, 238-249, 250, 251
 representation of 237-238, 240 n26, 244-245
 rights of, in Treaty of Waitangi (1840) 32-33, 230-231
Maori Appellate Court 237
Maori Land Court 238
marae (traditional Maori community centres) 243 n30
Matignon Accords (New Caledonia, 1988) 29, 203
McWilliam, Monica 99
mechanisms
 for dispute settlement 31
 for implementation
  of autonomy arrangements 166-171, 175
  of peace agreements 69-70, 134-137
  see also institutional arrangements
 for monitoring and verification 27-28, 188-189
media, relations with 182-183
mediation, Waitangi Tribunal claims referred to 238
mediators in intrastate conflicts 6, 7
 United Nations as 197, 198-203
 see also facilitators
Melanesian culture 18
Mexico, Chiapas conflict 56
micro-credit schemes, in Chittagong Hill Tracts 140
Miles, Wendy 32, 46, 47, 325
minorities
 and dominant population groups 5
 in Macedonia 205
 rights of
  and intrastate conflicts 3, 51-52, 53, 66
  protected in peace agreements 62, 63, 67, 145-146
 role in Northern Ireland conflict 90-91
 use of violence by 11, 52-53
Minorities at Risk Project 51
Mitchell, George 104, 105, 107-108
Mizoram Accord (India, 1986) 131-132
Model Arbitration Rules (UNCITRAL) 217, 218-219, 221

Moderate Leaders' Agreement (Bangladesh, 1988) 138, 139
modern representation 237
Mohsin, A. 117
Moldova
  and autonomy of Gagauzia (Gagauz Yeri) 77-78
  constitution of 77
  Transniestr/nistria conflict 56, 78-79
Momis, John 11, 18, 29, 331
monitoring of peace agreements 27-28
  by facilitators 188-189
  United Nations' role in 44, 188
Montenegro 72-73
Montevideo Convention on the Rights and Duties of States (1933) 72 n8
Morocco, and Western Saharan self-determination 56, 196, 215
mutually hurting stalemate situations 137-138, 162, 198
Myanmar, minorities conflict in 56

N
Nagaland conflict (India) 27, 54
National Poverty Reduction Strategy Paper (PRSP, Bangladesh, 2005) 129
Native Land Courts (New Zealand) 232
NATO, presence in Macedonia 208-209, 210
negotiations
  armed forces' involvement 200
  asymmetry of power between parties 20-22, 184
  cease-fire agreements prior to 182
  between China and Tibet 21, 149-150, 152
  on Chittagong Hill Tracts Peace Accord (Bangladesh, 1997) 137-139
  and implementation of peace agreements 17, 178
  inclusiveness of 181
  participation in 18
    of women 19-20, 183
  in settlement of Maori claims 245-246
  in South Tyrol conflict 161
Nehru, Jawaharlal (prime minister of India) 151
New Caledonia conflict 54
  agreements between indigenous population and France 29
  Matignon Accords (1988) 203
New York Convention (Convention on the Recognition and Enforcement of Foreign Arbitral Awards, 1958) 226-227
New Zealand
  British colonisation of 230-233

New Zealand (cont.)
  Treaty of Waitangi (1840) 32-33, 229-231, 250, 318-321
    Act (1975) 237, 238, 242, 250
    Office of Treaty Settlements 241, 244
    Tribunal 127, 233-249, 250, 251
  tribal autonomy in 248, 250
New Zealand Settlement Act (1863) 232
Ngai Tahu (New Zealand) claim 248
Ngati Ruanui (New Zealand) claim 248
NGOs
  in Chittagong Hill Tracts 140
  Norwegian 178
Nicaragua, case against United States at International Court of Justice 215
Niger, Tuareg conflict in 56
NLA (National Liberation Army, Macedonia) 208
non-compliance with peace agreements, sanctions for 29, 135-136
non-self governing territories (NSGTs) 194-195, 196, 214
non-state parties
  concessions by 199
  and dispute resolution 227-228
  representation of 184, 185
non-territorial autonomy 75
non-violence, Dalai Lama's commitment to 148-149, 156
North/South Ministerial Council (Good Friday Agreement) 26, 99-100, 256-258
Northern Bank (Belfast), robbery of 111-112
Northern Ireland 87, 89, 90
  demographic changes 83
  direct rule of 92, 93, 105, 110
  elections in 61, 96-97, 98
  Irish national minority in 90, 91
  Unionist majority in 26, 90, 93, 109-110
Northern Ireland Act (UK) 99
Northern Ireland conflict 57, 60-61, 87-89, 93, 112-113
  Bloody Sunday (1972) 60, 91-92
  double minority problem 90-91
  and EU membership of Ireland and United Kingdom 106-107
  paramilitary groups in 103-104, 110-111, 113
  parties unwilling to settle 109-111
  public opinion on, in Ireland 105-106, 107
  third parties in 107-109
Northern Ireland peace process 113
  decommissioning of arms 36, 97, 98, 101-103, 104-105, 112, 261
  Downing Street Declaration (1993) 94

Northern Ireland peace process (cont.)
  Good Friday Agreement (1998) 13 n17, 14, 94-96, 255-265
    implementation of 98-105
    institutional arrangements of 25-26, 79-80, 99-101
    reform of 111-112
  Ireland's role in 8, 35, 92, 93, 106
  Sunningdale Agreement (1973) 92
  United States as third party in 39 n70
Norway, involvement in peace processes 7, 38, 177-179, 180, 183, 186-187, 188, 189-191
Noumea Accord (New Caledonia, 1998) 29
NSCN (National Socialist Council of Nagaland), cease-fire agreement with India (1997) 27
NSGTs (Non-Self Governing Territories) 194-195, 196, 214

O
O'Neill, Thomas (Tip) P. 109
Optional Rules for Arbitration Disputes between two Parties of which only one is a State (PCA, 1993) 219, 220, 221, 222, 312-317
Orange, Claudia 230 n4
OSCE (Organisation of Security and Cooperation in Europe)
  on autonomy 4, 81-82
  High Commissioner on National Minorities 45-46, 70-71, 80
  involvement in Macedonia 208
  monitoring and democracy building mechanisms 45
ownership
  of intrastate peace agreements 17-19
  of land, in New Zealand 232
  of peace processes 182

P
Pacific Islands Forum 203
'The Package of Measures in Favour of the Population of South Tyrol' (1969) 28, 162-163, 175
Packer, John 5, 15, 24, 38-39 n70, 325-326
Pahari refugees, repatriation to Bangladesh 134-135
Pakistan
  discrimination conflicts in 56
  rule of Chittagong Hill Tracts (CHT) 120, 121
pan-Crimean Tatar Council (*Kurulthai*) 75

Papua New Guinea
  Bougainville conflict
    peace agreements 11, 18-19, 19-20, 22-23, 28-29
    UN role in 198
  constitution of 22
paramilitary groups, in Northern Ireland conflict 103-104, 110-111, 113
participation
  and autonomy 81-82
  of women in peace processes 19-20, 183
parties to intrastate conflicts 6-8
  agreements imposed on other parties 12-13
  asymmetry of power between 5, 20-22, 184-187, 199
  culture of 200
  equality of 47, 171
  see also first parties; second parties; third parties; fourth parties
Patten, Chris 101
PCA *see* Permanent Court of Arbitration
peace
  desire for, in Chittagong Hill Tracts 142
  and economic development 141
peace agreements 157, 200
  deficiencies of 12-14, 16, 183
    Chittagong Hill Tracts Peace Accord (Bangladesh, 1997) 21, 117
  entrenchment of 22-25, 185
    Chittagong Hill Tracts Peace Accord (1997, Bangladesh) 130-132
    constitutional 15, 22, 130, 185
    Mizoram Accord (1986, India) 132 n50
  implementation of 1, 2, 8-34, 40-41, 43-47
    Chittagong Hill Tracts (Bangladesh, 1997) 117-118, 125-126, 144-146
    civil society participation in 182
    and development aid *see* peace dividends
    and dispute settlement 31-34, 46-47, 135
    Framework Agreement (Macedonia, 2001) 30, 206, 207-210
    Good Friday Agreement (Northern Ireland, 1998) 98-105
    governmental resistance to 49, 63-66, 67
    in Bangladesh 129-130, 132, 134
    incentives 29, 40, 136
    and negotiations 17, 178
    political will 9-10, 136-137
    Seventeen Point Agreement (China-Tibet, 1951) 150-151, 153
    and trust 11, 17, 64, 80
    verification of 27-28, 203

peace agreements (cont.)
    institutional arrangements of 13-14, 25-26, 79-80, 99-101, 127, 166-171
    monitoring and verification of 27-28
    non-compliance with, sanctions for 29, 135-136
    ownership of 17-19
    protection of minority rights in 62, 63, 67, 145-146
    and respect for human rights 187-188
    successful 66, 67, 203
peace diplomacy 179
peace dividends 40, 41, 42, 185-186, 190-191
Peace Monitoring Group (Bougainville cease-fire agreement, 1997) 37
peace negotiations *see* negotiations
peace processes
    contribution of facilitators 180-183
    participation of women in 19-20, 183
Permanent Court of Arbitration (PCA, The Hague) 46-47, 212-213, 219-222, 228
    rules of arbitration 219, 220, 221, 222, 312-317
Permanent Forum for Indigenous Issues (UN) 45
political will
    to commit to peace processes 180
    to implement peace agreements 9-10, 136-137
Portugal, role in East Timor peace process 8, 36 n62, 214
positive inducements, for implementation of peace agreements *see* incentives for implementation of peace agreements
power
    asymmetry of 5, 20-22, 184-187, 199
    devolution of 74, 79
    sharing/division of 5, 193
    in Northern Ireland 92, 93
Prendergast, James 250
Priti Group Accord (Bangladesh, 1985) 138
Privy Council (United Kingdom) 33, 249-250
protection
    of marine environment 221, 290-292
    of rights
        of indigenous population 146, 236
        of minorities 51 n6, 62, 63, 67, 145-146
Provisional IRA 91, 92, 102
    decommissioning of arms by 97, 98, 101-103, 104-105, 110-111, 112
    financial interests of 111, 112
    violence ceased by 94
public opinion, on Northern Ireland conflict 105-106, 107

public policy grounds, for unenforceability of arbitration awards 227, 228
Puig i Scotoni, Pau 332

Q
Québec Province
    autonomy of 73
    demographic changes in 83-84

R
Ramaphosa, Cyril 103 n17
Rangahaua Whanui research program (New Zealand) 240 n26
Rata, Matiu 233
Recommendations to assist Arbitral Institutions and other interested Bodies with regard to Arbitrations under the UNCITRAL Arbitration Rules (UNCITRAL) 219
reconciliation processes 182, 183
reconstruction and development, in Chittagong Hill Tracts (CHT) 41, 139-141
regime change 198-199
regional autonomy 73, 171, 199
regional international courts 215-217
regional organisations, and implementation of peace agreements 45-46
regionalism, asymmetry in 171
representation
    collective, in federalism 171
    of Maori 237-238, 240 n26, 244-245
    of non-state parties 184, 185
research, of Maori claims 240 n26, 241, 242
Resolution 1514 (United Nations) 194-195, 196
Resource Management Act (1991, New Zealand) 247
review, of the Good Friday Agreement 104
Rhodesia, exclusion of majority conflict 56
Richardson, John M. 142
Robertson, Lord George 206
Roy, Devasish 9 n11, 10, 14, 16 n22, 18, 28, 29, 41, 326-327
rules for arbitration 217, 218-219, 221, 222, 223, 224, 312-317
Russia, role in Georgia-Abkhazia conflict 8

S
SAARC (South Asian Association for Regional Cooperation) 135 n58
sanctions
    international 186
    for non-compliance with peace agreements 29, 135-136

Santa Cruz cemetery massacre (East Timor, 1991) 198
SDLP (Social Democratic and Labour Party, Northern Ireland) 92, 93, 96
Second Autonomy Statute (1971, South Tyrol) 23, 164-166
   implementation of 166-174, 175-176
second parties 6, 8
   roles of 34-35
self-determination 50-51 n4, 194
   movements for 4, 6, 10-11
      see also non-state parties
   of West Papua 55, 196
   of Western Sahara 56, 196, 214-215
   see also autonomy; non-self governing territories
self-rule 5, 71
   see also autonomy
separatism 50, 58
Seroo, Onno 332
settlement
   of disputes 31, 293-295
      agreements 211-213, 226-227
      by arbitration 217-226, 228, 298-311
      bodies for 213-217, 227
   and implementation of peace agreements 31-34, 46-47, 135
   in Second Autonomy Statute (South Tyrol) 170
   of intrastate conflicts 3-4, 50, 62, 64, 66, 175
   of Maori claims 241-242, 245-249, 250-251
Seventeen Point Agreement (China-Tibet, 195) 10, 13, 147-148, 150-151, 153, 266-268
Sheikh Hasina (prime minister of Bangladesh) 123
Sinn Fein (IRA) 94, 96, 98, 102, 110
Sitges meeting (Kreddha & Centre UNESCO de Catalunya) 2, 137
Sjøberg, Geir 11, 17, 18, 19, 21, 36, 41, 42, 327
SLMM (Sri Lanka Monitoring Mission) 27-28, 31, 188-189
Solana, Javier 206
South Africa, exclusion of majority in 51 n6, 56
South Tyrol-Italy conflict 20, 24, 26, 55, 132 n52, 157-158, 158-161, 172-174, 175
   Austrian role in 8, 34-35, 158, 161, 162-163, 174-175
   De Gasperi-Gruber agreement (Paris Treaty, 1947) 34-35, 159-160, 174, 278

South Tyrol-Italy conflict (cont.)
   'The Package of Measures in Favour of the Population of South Tyrol' 28, 162-163, 175
   Second Autonomy Statute (1971) 23, 164-171, 175-176
sovereign immunity, waiver of 222
Spain
   Basque conflict 57
   judicial system in 202
   regional autonomy in 199
Sri Lanka-Tamil conflict 57, 58-59
   cease-fire agreements 182, 188
   donor conferences 42, 187
   monitoring mission (SLMM) 27-28, 31, 188-189
Staszewski, Marian 25, 38, 43, 332-333
state authorities see governments
states 72
   bilateral relations with regions 171
   dominant groups reflected in 53
   in transition 82
   waiver of sovereign immunity by 222
Stoel, Max van der 71-72
Strasbourg Proposal of Dalai Lama 152
substantial minorities, and use of violence 52-53
Sudan
   discrimination of southern minorities conflict 57
   humanitarian cease-fire agreement in 182
Sunningdale Agreement (Northern Ireland, 1973) 92
supporting roles, of facilitators 180
Supreme Court (Bangladesh) 131
Supreme Court (New Zealand) 33 n57, 250
Suski, Markku 70-71
SVP (*Südtiroler Volkspartei*, South Tyrolean People's Party) 159, 161, 162
Switzerland, regional autonomy in 73
symmetry
   in autonomy arrangements 4-5
   see also asymmetry

T

Tamil conflict (Sri Lanka) 57, 58-59
   cease-fire agreements 182, 188
   donor conferences 42, 187
   monitoring mission (SLMM) 27-28, 31, 188-189
Tanzania, autonomy granted to Zanzibar 15
Tatars, Crimean 74-76, 82
territorial aspects, of autonomy arrangements 4, 153, 160

territorial identification, of substantial minorities 52, 53
territorial integrity, and autonomy 4, 70, 194-195
territories, controlled by non-state parties 185-186
terrorist organisations, blacklisting of 186-187
third parties 6, 7
  in China-Tibet conflict 39, 151, 154
  in Chittagong Hill Tracts conflict 39, 135-136, 145
  competition among 179, 200, 210
  EU 108-109, 208
  exit strategies of 203
  governments resisting involvement of 39, 197-199
  in Northern Ireland conflict 107-109
  roles of 36-40, 84, 85
    facilitation 21-22
    monitoring and verification 27
    resolution of implementation disputes 31, 135
  United Nations 19, 30 n52, 38, 151, 193-197, 198-203
  United States 39 n70, 107-108, 208
Tibet
  autonomy of 13, 148-149, 152, 153
  demographic changes in 154-155
  conflict with China 147-148
    1959 uprising 150
    Dalai Lama's role in 155-156
    negotiations 21, 40, 149-150, 152
    Seventeen Point Agreement (China-Tibet, 1951) 10, 13, 147-148, 150-151, 153, 266-268
    Strasbourg Proposal (Dalai Lama) 152
    third party involvement 39, 151, 154
time limits, of autonomy arrangements 28-29
timing, of autonomy arrangements 83
transition, states in 82
transmigration policies 62
  in Indonesia 54-55 n10
Transnistria conflict (Moldova) 56, 78-79
transparency, need for 173-174
Treaty of Waitangi *see* Waitangi (New Zealand), Treaty of
Treaty of Waitangi Act (1975, New Zealand) 237, 238
Trentino-South Tyrol (Italy), autonomous region 158-159, 160, 164, 172
tribal autonomy, in New Zealand 248, 250
Trimble, David (first minister of Northern Ireland) 96, 98, 102, 104-105
trust
  and implementation of peace agreements 11, 17, 64, 80
  of third parties 38
truth commissions 182
Tuareg conflict (Niger) 56
TU(L)F (Tamil United (Liberation) Front) 58
Ture Whenua Maori Act (Maori Land Act, 1993, New Zealand) 238
Turkey, Kurdish conflict 57

U

UDA (Ulster Defence Association) 91
Ukraine-Crimea conflict 72, 73-76
Ulan Fu 149-150
UNHCR *see* United Nations, High Commissioner for Human Rights
Unionists (Northern Ireland) 26, 90, 93, 109-110
United Kingdom
  colonies of
    Aotearoa/New Zealand 230-233
    Chittagong Hill Tracts (Bangladesh) 119-120, 121
    Ireland 88
  EU membership of 106-107
  and Irish independence 88-89
  and Northern Ireland conflict
    direct rule of 92, 93, 105, 110
    public opinion 105-106
  settlers from, in Northern Ireland 88
  Treaty of Waitangi (New Zealand, 1840) 32-33, 229-231
United Nations
  Commission for International Trade Law (UNCITRAL), Model Arbitration Rules 217, 218-219, 221
  Convention on the Law of the Sea (1982) 293-295
  Development Program (UNDP) 200-201
  Draft Declaration on the Rights of Indigenous Peoples 146, 236 n18
  High Commissioner for Human Rights (UNHCR) 30 n52, 44
  Interim Administration Mission in Kosovo (UNMIK) 60
  International Court of Justice (ICJ) 214-215
  monitoring of peace agreements 44, 188
  Observer Mission in Abkhazia (UNOMIG) 36-37
  Permanent Forum for Indigenous Issues 45
  Secretary-General 45, 67
    Groups of Friends of 42-43, 201

United Nations (cont.)
  Security Council, blacklisting of terrorist organisations 186
  third party role of 193-197, 198-203
    China-Tibet conflict 151
    decommissioning of weapons in Bougainville 19
    East Timor peace process 30 n52, 38, 197, 199
    Italy-South Tyrol conflict 161
    World Conference on Human Rights (1993) 184
United States
  case by Nicaragua at International Court of Justice 215
  third party role of 39 n70, 107-108
    in Macedonia conflict 208
    Northern Ireland conflict 39 n70, 107
UPDF (United People's Democratic Front), and Chittagong Hill Tracts (CHT) Peace Accord (Bangladesh, 1997) 10-11, 116, 123, 125 n24, 134
UUP (Ulster Unionist Party) 92, 93, 96, 97
UVF (Ulster Volunteer Force) 88, 91

V

Varennes, Fernand de 3, 9, 11, 44, 327-328
Vendrell, Francesc 2-3, 7, 12, 18, 21, 36 n62, 38, 43, 328-329
verification, of implementation of peace agreements 27-28, 203
violence in intrastate conflicts 11, 52-53, 58, 59-61, 65
  Chittagong Hill Tracts 116, 138 n66, 142-143
  Northern Ireland 91-92, 103
  see also non-violence

W

Waitangi (New Zealand)
  Treaty of (1840) 32-33, 229-231, 250, 318-321
    Act (1975) 237, 238, 242, 250
    Office of Treaty Settlements 241, 244
    Tribunal 127, 234-249, 250, 251

waiver of sovereign immunity 222
Walt van Praag, Michael van 42, 333
Wang, Jianxin 142
weapons, decommissioning of
  in Bougainville 19
  by JSS in Bangladesh 115
  in Northern Ireland 36, 97, 98, 101-103, 104-105, 112, 261
West Papua conflict (Indonesia) 55, 196
Western Saharan self-determination 56, 196
  International Court of Justice on 214-215
Whiti Love, Morris Te 33, 329
Williams, Joe 237
Woelk, Jens 8, 20, 26, 28, 329
women, participation in peace processes 19-20, 183
World Conference on Human Rights (1993, United Nations) 184

Y

Yemen-Eritrea dispute
  Agreement on Principles (1996) 212, 300-305
  Award of the Arbitral Tribunal in the First Stage (1998) 306-307
Young, Crawford 53
Yugoslavia
  federal structure of 15
  Kosovo conflict 57

Z

Zanzibar, autonomy of 15
Zia, Khaleda (prime minister of Bangladesh) 125 n26